Emerging German-Language Novelists of the Twenty-First Century

Studies in German Literature, Linguistics, and Culture

Emerging German-Language Novelists of the Twenty-First Century

Edited by
Lyn Marven and Stuart Taberner

CAMDEN HOUSE
Rochester, New York

First published 2011 by Camden House
Transferred to digital printing 2012

Camden House is an imprint of Boydell & Brewer Inc.
668 Mt. Hope Avenue, Rochester, NY 14620, USA
www.camden-house.com
and of Boydell & Brewer Limited
PO Box 9, Woodbridge, Suffolk IP12 3DF, UK
www.boydellandbrewer.com

ISBN-13: 978-1-57113-421-9
ISBN-10: 1-57113-421-2

Library of Congress Cataloging-in-Publication Data

Emerging German-language novelists of the twenty-first century / edited
by Lyn Marven and Stuart Taberner.
    p. cm. — (Studies in German literature, linguistics, and culture)
Includes bibliographical references and index.
ISBN-13: 978-1-57113-421-9 (hardcover : alk. paper)
ISBN-10: 1-57113-421-2 (hardcover : alk. paper)
    1. German fiction — 21st century — History and criticism.
I. Marven, Lyn. II. Taberner, Stuart.

PT774.E64 2011
833'.92—dc22

                                                              2011007914

Appendix A, from: Vladimir Vertlib, Chapter 16 of
Das besondere Gedächtnis der Rosa Masur © Deuticke im
Paul Zsolnay Verlag Wien 2001.

Appendix B, "Little Racer," from: Clemens Meyer,
Als wir träumten © S. Fischer Verlag GmbH, Frankfurt am
Main, 2006. Translation © Katy Derbyshire.

This publication is printed on acid-free paper.
Printed in the United States of America.

Contents

Acknowledgments

T HE EDITORS ARE GRATEFUL to the British Academy for a Small Research Grant that funded the workshop that instigated this project, and for funding the translations of the extracts included in the volume. Thanks are also due to the Leeds Humanities Research Institute and the Modern Humanities Research Association for further support.

Introduction: New German-Language Writing since the Turn of the Millennium

Lyn Marven

Emerging Writing

TWENTY YEARS AFTER GERMAN REUNIFICATION, much German-language literary fiction, and particularly that written by a younger generation of authors, is distinctly globalized and transnational in outlook: from subject matter to setting, from the style and language of texts to their swift translation into other languages, a larger number of novels from the German-speaking countries than ever before participate in the worldwide circulation of literary fiction. With three German-language writers awarded the Nobel Prize for Literature in just over a decade — Günter Grass in 1999, Elfriede Jelinek in 2004, and Herta Müller in 2009 — a variety of international bestsellers including Bernhard Schlink's *Der Vorleser* (1995; *The Reader*, 1999), Thomas Brussig's *Helden wie wir* (1995; *Heroes Like Us*, 1997), W. G. Sebald's *Austerlitz* (2001), Daniel Kehlmann's *Die Vermessung der Welt* (2005; *Measuring the World*, 2006), and (as always) books by Günter Grass, not to mention high-profile film adaptations such as Stephen Daldry's *The Reader* (2008), the beginning of the twenty-first century has seen a greater degree of attention focused on contemporary German-language literature than at any time in the last two hundred years.

The present volume concentrates on "emerging" writers — a term intended to describe a rise to prominence on a number of levels and in a range of arenas. Several chapters feature authors whose names have become increasingly familiar to international audiences in the last few years, including Ilija Trojanow, Karen Duve, Julia Franck, and Kehlmann, as well as one or two who have been established longer but are less well-known outside of Germany, such as Sibylle Berg and Sven Regener. Some chapters offer new, more reflective readings of an author's bestseller than are typically generated in the immediate aftermath of its international success, such as Rebecca Braun's chapter on Kehlmann's *Die Vermessung der Welt*; others examine newer or less familiar works, or publications that have followed initial success, such as Valerie Heffernan's chapter on Julia Franck's *Die Mittagsfrau* (Lady Midday, the noonday witch, 2007; published in English as *The Blind Side of the Heart*, 2009) or Heike Bartel's chapter on Karen Duve's *Taxi* (2008), and Kate Roy and Andrew Plowman's chapters on sequels to acclaimed first novels by Yadé Kara and Sven Regener respectively. More pressingly, however, this volume also seeks to introduce a larger number of lesser-known authors and texts to an international audience whose access to German-language writing is often determined by the vagaries of the market and current fashions in publishing and translation.

Indeed, this endeavor is entirely appropriate — the novels analyzed here are for the most part globalized hypertexts, reaching beyond their local context through what Barbara Mennel, writing in this volume, calls "transnational and intermedial intertextuality." The globalization of the novel as a literary form — indeed, the imbrication of literature and globalization — is further reflected in the cosmopolitan plots and content of the novels here, as well as their language.[1] The texts situate themselves within the international (albeit largely English-language) cultural discourses that they reference: music, including rap, reggae, and Russian goth; Spencer Tunick's globally situated photographic art along with the visual language of cinema; the international field of science and the universal sport of soccer; literature from *The Arabian Nights* through Dostoevsky to that bible of the globetrotter, the Lonely Planet guides. Although they are bounded by the specific language in which the texts are written, this too is porous, incorporating other languages, dialects, and even imagery, both as a matter of realism and as textual device.

Contemporary Currents

Yet at the same time, these novels nonetheless relate to the literary historiography of German-language literature and engage with local concerns;[2] they are in that sense also "glocal."[3] The 1990s clamor to find the ultimate *Wenderoman* (novel dealing with the radical changes in Germany around the time of the opening of the Berlin Wall in 1989) or "Berlin novel" may have died down, but we might argue that it is only in the last decade that such texts have emerged.[4] A continuing engagement with reunification and the after-effects of the demise of both East and West Germany marks Clemens Meyer's Leipzig lads in *Als wir träumten* (When we were dreaming, 2006), who come of age around the *Wende* and who look back on the former East with something beyond nostalgia, and also Sven Regener's knowing and sympathetic recreation of 1980s West Berlin in *Der kleine Bruder* (The younger brother, 2008), itself a text that rewrites the author's previous version of the night of 9 November 1989. Similarly, the old/new capital Berlin retains its literary cachet. Terézia

Mora's *Alle Tage* (2004; *Day In Day Out*, 2007), set in the global cross-roads of an archetypal metropolis called "B.," redefines the Berlin novel, while the third installment of Regener's trilogy responds both to his earlier depiction of 1980s Kreuzberg in *Herr Lehmann* (Mr. Lehmann, 2001; published in English as *Berlin Blues*, 2007) — set chronologically later than the subsequent prequels — and to twenty-first-century spatial discourse of the city.

Of the many literary trends in the 1990s, one lasting development seems to be the *Neue Lesbarkeit* (new readability). Readability — largely meaning accessible, immediate writing — is a double-edged sword, as Braun shows in relation to Daniel Kehlmann's bestselling *Die Vermessung der Welt*: its readable style garnered public attention while also leading critics to overlook its complex strategies of identification and familiarity and to dismiss it as merely populist. Readability is not simply a commercial decision, however — it is a distinct literary strategy and narrative technique, often just one among many in an author's palette that is selected for particular effect. Sibylle Berg's narrative style, for example, varies from the readable to postmodern polyphony and playfulness, both across and within texts. These different strategies are not mutually incompatible: in this volume Emily Jeremiah demonstrates that Berg's novel *Die Fahrt* (The journey, 2007) returns to the "palatable and commercial qualities" of her earlier work without sacrificing depth. What is clear in both Kehlmann's and Berg's work is that style or form thus do not necessarily follow from content — difficult subject matter in no way entails a difficult narrative strategy — and indeed, the disjunction of these two elements can be a productive further dimension to a novel's style.

One legacy of readability might be seen in the preponderance of first-person narratives represented here: memorable voices that address the reader directly. Characters that verge on the picaresque are a notable feature of post-reunification novels in the 1990s, particularly from the former East Germany.[5] Here they serve less for satire than for establishing the fictionality of the character, on the one hand, and the immediacy of the narrative, on the other. The strength of Yadé Kara's two novels, *Selam Berlin* (2003) and its 2008 sequel *Cafe Cyprus*, examined here, is the "Hasan sound": the chatty, irreverent, frank tone of her protagonist, Hasan Kazan. Saša Stanišić's young Bosnian boy in *Wie der Soldat das Grammofon repariert* (2006; *How the Soldier Repairs the Gramophone*, 2008) is a deceptively naïve narrator, while the spun-out narrative of Vladimir Vertlib's eponymous Rosa Masur in *Das besondere Gedächtnis der Rosa Masur* (The remarkable memory of Rosa Masur, 2003) is as engrossing as it is unreliable. Sven Regener's trilogy about the laconic drop-out Herr Lehmann, who became a cult character, was initially aligned with the phenomenon of "pop literature," in part due to the author's own star status. His affable protagonist remains too much in focus, however, to fit with the ironic pop textual aesthetics — precisely what gives his novels their appeal. Berg's *Die Fahrt* also displays pop tendencies, from the text's narrative distance from her characters to their disaffection. In *Taxi*, Karen Duve litters the text with facts, names, and historical dates. Neither author fully upholds the political disengagement associated with pop literature, however, espousing nomadic ethics or feminist concerns through the form and content of their novels.

Conversely, many of the novels here wear their learning on their sleeves, from historical research and reenactment (on display in Kehlmann and Trojanow's texts) to intertextual references and engagement with critical theories. Ulrike Draesner's *Mitgift* (literally: Dowry, 2002) draws its plot from the thriller genre, but the theoretically informed text is dense and nonchronological; Juli Zeh references Nietzsche and game theory in *Spieltrieb* (The drive to play, 2004); Berg cites the controversial, and linguistically challenging, French writer and poet Michel Houellebecq. Citationality is in fact a — perhaps paradoxical — aspect of some pop literature, although by no means a defining feature, and the texts in this volume are similarly hybrid in their style.

The end of the 1990s also saw the rise of the so-called literary "Fräuleinwunder" (wonder girls). Volker Hage's oft-cited phrase was a media construct that drew much criticism for trivializing new literary voices that happened to belong to women.[6] Three authors in this volume, Karen Duve, Julia Franck, and Kathrin Schmidt, have been cited among the young women writers so designated. "I was never a girl wonder," Franck protested as late as 2007 when her *Die Mittagsfrau* won the German Book Prize.[7] Their subsequent development, including the novels included here, proves — if proof were needed — that their acclaim is based on literary merit rather than looks, and the fact that this volume features a small majority of women writers should underline that tokenism and separatism are not warranted, if they ever were.[8]

While a number of the women writers in this volume choose to adopt male voices (for example Kara and Mora), others — like Franck — choose to engage with feminist history and theory, although as Valerie Heffernan's chapter on the women's history in *Die Mittagsfrau* shows, one might equally label this novel's focus as "history from below" — that is, a history of the disempowered. Duve depicts the effects of masculinist literature and philosophy on her vulnerable, taxi-driving female protagonist — although her own text references authors from Grass to Kafka — as well as the brutality of the sex industry. Sonja Klocke reads Kathrin Schmidt's *Du stirbst nicht* (You are not going to die, 2009) as a search for feminine agency. These shifting concerns may well presage a generational change. Far from highlighting the author as girl, by contrast, Barbara Mennel argues that Alina Bronsky's *Scherbenpark* (2008; *Broken Glass Park*, 2010) portrays in its protagonist Sascha the globalized figure of the "ghetto girl," who functions in a postfeminist arena; where Franck portrays mothers, Bronsky's interest lies in the daughter.

Franck's novel can also be seen as extending the memory discourses and revisions that have marked representations of German twentieth-century history since reunification and the turn of the century. Her "mother literature" — as opposed to the 1970s and 1980s West German phenomenon of "Väterliteratur" (literature of fathers) — engages only obliquely with the Nazi past, while the striking image of parental abandonment of a child further complicates notions of perpetrators and victims. Set in the present day, Ulrike Draesner's *Mitgift* traces the family narratives of conforming — which have physical consequences for her two sisters — back to wartime experiences of displacement and expulsion. More daringly, Vertlib's Rosa Masur's encounter with a twentieth-century dictator is depicted as fascinating to her German audience: the fact that the dictator in question is Stalin only legitimizes their interest. It is notable, however, that many of the novels here focus on more recent conflicts, particularly the conflicts in the Balkans in the 1990s during the dissolution of the former Yugoslavia. Stanišić depicts the sheer violence of a war that turned friends against each other along ethnic lines, while the trauma of Abel Nema, in Mora's *Alle Tage*, arises from that same conflict, which renders him stateless.

Perhaps indicative of the media age, the novels here share a kind of self-consciousness or self-awareness as literary texts, which is expressed in a number of different ways: Draesner and Duve embed intertextual references to their own oeuvre; Kara and Kehlmann write in a subtly anachronistic mode, where the issues of their novels' ostensible time and place are overlaid with contemporary concerns. Other texts perform their literariness by employing genre features (Berg, Duve), situating their narratives within frameworks that draw attention to the narrating instance (Vertlib), employing alienation effects such as ironic or cryptic chapter titles (Stanišić), or by playing with realism as a mode (Duve). The ironic, cautious, happy endings of *Scherbenpark* or *Mitgift* reinstate a form of family, albeit almost unrecognizable as the biological, nuclear family unit. The premise of Duve's *Taxi* offers an iterative as well as linear narrative; Franck frames the narrative of *Mittagsfrau* with a prologue and an epilogue that offer a counter-perspective and a challenge to both reader and protagonist.

While the novels advertise their status as fictional constructs, the authors seem only too aware of their role or position in the wider cultural field, and in many cases write this into the novels: Kate Roy argues that Kara's Hasan ventriloquizes the author's own responses to interview questions, while Clemens Meyer was called upon to authenticate his characters' physical bodies by displaying his own in the dust-jacket author photo for *Als wir träumten*. Berg subverts her marketing with knowing, sarcastic cover images and author biographies for her novels: *Die Fahrt* features Flickr-style photos that evoke her travels to do research for the novel — the form of the publication thus reinscribes the author within the text. Duve includes a photo of herself as a taxi driver on the cover of *Taxi*, tempting an autobiographical reading that the text's postmodern gestures undermine. Kehlmann's examination of celebrity in *Die Vermessung der Welt* led to his own "celebrification," as Braun demonstrates, and in turn begat his more recent novel with the telling title *Ruhm* (2009; *Fame*, 2010). Sven Regener meanwhile, as Andrew Plowman explains, has had to battle against his own celebrity as a rock musician to convince critics that his literature stands alone and that he cannot be conflated with his protagonist Frank Lehmann; *Der kleine Bruder* responds to the reception of the first two novels of the Herr Lehmann trilogy by stressing the difference between character and author. Conversely, Julian Preece suggests that Ilija Trojanow's success with *Der Weltensammler* (2006; *The Collector of Worlds*, 2008) was aided by the fact that both the author's biography and the novel's themes struck a chord with wider discourses on migration and identity; the author himself has since published further texts where he puts himself into his historical protagonist's shoes. Clearly, the author is an integral part of the narrative: both of the text and of its reception.

Newest Literature

Our line-up includes a number of "minority" voices, reflecting the "Turkish turn" (Leslie Adelson) and "Eastern turn" (Brigid Haines) in contemporary writing.[9] These include winners of the Adelbert-von-Chamisso-Preis, instituted in 1985 and awarded yearly by the Robert Bosch Stiftung to authors writing in German as a second language or to authors from non-German backgrounds; an additional Förderpreis ("Promotional Prize") is given for up-and-coming authors. Vertlib won the Förderpreis in 2001, Kara the Förderpreis in 2004, Stanišić was the main prizewinner in 2008, and Mora was prizewinner in 2010 as well as winning the Förderpreis in 2000.[10] While this development and increasing visibility is entirely welcome, we should be wary of according this literature any special influence just because of the mere fact of the authors' biographies: Stanišić, in Brigid Haines's chapter, objects to the view that so-called minority literature functions to enrich the majority culture, while Kate Roy makes the point, in relation to Yadé Kara's reception, that moving from the margins to the center — or merely reversing the polarity of these categories — does not per se constitute subversion of the mainstream. In the final analysis, these texts are included here as the "newest German literature," the provocative subtitle of Jamal Tuschick's compilation *MorgenLand* (OrientLand) from 2000, and not as representative of a particular background or minority group.

These texts thus demonstratively rewrite and challenge earlier categories of minority writing: it is hard to designate them as "migrant literature" — although a number of the texts' transnational figures move from one country to another, whether unwillingly, through war, like Mora's multilingual, stateless everyman Abel Nema, or by choice, like Vertlib's Masur — as the texts resist such constricting labels. In *Café Cyprus* the nomadic Hasan Kazan migrates from Germany to London, a move that he hopes will sidestep the identity issues of his origins as a West Berlin–born German Turk. Similarly, these novels could not be seen as *Betroffenheitsliteratur* (literature of the afflicted), nor even as authentic accounts. Instead, their writers highlight the fictionality of the voices: they ventriloquize the characters (indeed, Bronsky even writes under a pseudonym). This fictionalization is perhaps most clearly seen where there is a visible disjunction between the author's identity and that of the protagonist, as in Vertlib's and Kara's novels, both of whose narrator-protagonists have a different gender than the authors themselves, or in Stanišić, who uses a child narrator for distance. The act of imaginative creation and empathy resembles Kehlmann's and Trojanow's ventriloquizing of real historical figures. On the other hand, Vertlib shares his character's Jewish background, while Stanišić draws on his own autobiography. These characters illustrate the multiplicity of affiliations and identifications that attend identity: a complex, overlapping set of factors interacting with one another rather than a binary opposition — indeed, at the end of his novel, Vertlib has his Russian-Jewish character Masur, who is a migrant in Germany, encounter French-Arab Muslims, while Turkish-German Hasan associates with expatriate Cypriots and British-Pakistani Londoners. In Mora's *Alle Tage*, almost all the characters are from ethnic or cultural minorities, relating to each other and purporting to be indifferent to the "majority" culture.

In many ways this literature approaches a "postidentity" literature, or what translator Katy Derbyshire memorably calls, in her review of Bronsky's *Scherbenpark*, "the 'fiction about immigrants that isn't about being an immigrant' genre."[10] As Anke Biendarra writes in this volume, these novels are a testament to "a greater variety of German-language literature where classifications based on origin and ethnicity are becoming increasingly moot."

It is the notion of "crossing borders" — as cultural process and identity formation — that is at stake here rather than the economic implications of globalization. The texts engage in complex processes of deterritorialization and reterritorialization, as Roy and Mennel demonstrate, as well as contesting notions of *Heimat* (homeland), as analyzed by Bartel and Jeremiah. Globalization represents the aspirations of Meyer's young men — who never leave Leipzig — and the cultural coordinates for

Bronsky's Sascha, but in Berg's novel it has the effect of engendering root-lessness as much as international connectivity. Travel and movement for its own sake is contrasted with displacement and circulation in Hasan's London, which further displaces Cyprus to London, as the novel's title implies, and overwrites 1990s Britain with contemporary German issues. The legacies of colonialization are also evident, not only in *Cafe Cyprus*'s engagement with British military involvement in Cyprus, but also in Burton's explorations in colonial India. The multiple voices in *Der Weltensammler* allow the colonized to write back, while the "others" encountered by Berg's travelers also puncture the latter's stereotyped expectations; the polyphonic narrative of *Die Fahrt* thus contributes to an aesthetics that displaces the majority view.

Migration is in any case not the sole preserve of those usually designated migrants — as opposed to tourists, travelers, expatriates, or explorers. Berg's globally restless characters as well as Kehlmann's two explorer scientists and Trojanow's Burton set off into the world. As portrayed in the novel, Burton is initially a (perhaps anachronistic, and certainly unexpected) paradigm of openness and willingness to engage with the "Other," while Berg's characters unwittingly reveal prejudices despite their apparently enlightening globetrotting. In Regener's Kreuzberg of the 1980s, the large migrant population (mostly Turks) and the working class or inner-German migrants like Frank Lehmann only rarely interact, and when they do, do so only in the most basic transactions, like buying kebabs.

The City and the Individual

The twenty-first-century location par excellence is the city: according to a recent United Nations report, since 2008, for the first time in history, a majority of the world's population lives in cities and towns.[12] The texts in this volume tend toward city settings: Hamburg, London, Berlin, and beyond. One character's assertion in *Der kleine Bruder* that Berlin is too small and provincial is the same spark that sends Kara's Hasan to London in *Cafe Cyprus* (he makes a similar pronouncement at the end of *Selam Berlin*, Kara's celebrated first novel). For Kara and Duve in particular, the city is an active part of the narrative, constructing the text as their protagonists negotiate the urban geography of London and Hamburg respectively; for Trojanow's Burton, the city is a source of stories. The anonymous cities of Bronsky and Mora's novels highlight the spatial organization of the metropolis and especially the marginalization of migrants in the ghetto. Cities are nodes, transit points within wider networks, but global interconnectedness often collapses within the city: instead, characters experience fragmentation, division, isolation, and disengagement from their surroundings.

The cityscape is marked by violence, or the threat of violence, and unwanted physical proximity. The sensory details — the dirt, smoke, heat, unpleasant smells, and disease — of Trojanow's Bombay or Duve's Hamburg engage the reader corporeally. Burton interacts physically with his populous environment, as a doctor, as a lover, while the fleeting moments of connection for Berg's city-hopping characters come only with physical contact. Schmidt's novel, by contrast, centers on the body, which constitutes the limits of her protagonist's experience; the detailed depiction of the acute illness and painfully slow recovery of Helene Wesendahl draws on Schmidt's own experience of aneurysm; the novel enacts an extreme form of body language. The constrictions of Wesendahl's time in the hospital are, moreover, strangely reminiscent of the experiences of Meyer's imprisoned gang members: all are subject to bodily surveillance and deprivation, to authoritarian power.

While the members of Meyer's criminal fraternity test their masculinity in the confined, all-male environment of the prison, Bronsky's ghetto girl Sascha — whose name, in German, is ambiguously gendered — appropriates signifiers of masculinity that sit uncomfortably on this young woman. At the same time, Bronsky's coming-of-age novel appropriates a conventionally male-centered form, while her protagonist talks back to masculine voices by recycling rapper Eminem's lyrics. Gender remains a contested site of identity: both Draesner and Schmidt highlight the arbitrary gender divide through characters who fall between these categories as transvestite, transsexual, or hermaphrodite; their "crossing-over from one sex to another or a strange, even uncanny, intermingling," as Georgina Paul terms the contravention of gendered nature, has a profound effect on the social categories that seek to uphold division, albeit frequently one that provokes violence.[13] These are by no means new manifestations of gender uncertainty, however: even the Victorian explorer Burton, representative of the patriarchal empire (at the time ruled by a woman), takes on a feminized status as he assimilates into other cultures, illustrating the gendered imagery of colonizer and colonized; he also alters his body to "pass" as a Muslim, but ultimately upholds binary divisions of identity.

How Do You Find It?

One reason for the shape of this volume was to consider the methodological challenge of dealing with "ultracontemporary literature," especially debut novels by new authors who have no established reputation or textual history. Tom Cheesman's study of contemporary Turkish-German novels of settlement[14] begins with a riff on the ambiguously phrased question, "Wie finden Sie sie?" (How do you find them?). Rather than inquiring about Cheesman's critical assessment of such novels, the questioner here, noted critic Irmgard Ackermann, was in fact curious about how Cheesman manages to hear about them in the first place. Both questions are of interest to the current project, however: How do we seek out and discover new novels of worth? And when we do find them, how do we assess their qualities with no consensus or previous reception to fall back on? Critical exchange is invaluable here: the discussions and questions, collective knowledge and collegial atmosphere of the workshop that instigated this volume allowed participants to try out ideas relating to "ultracontemporary" novels. Dealing with often unknown and untested contemporary texts gets to the very heart of our task as academics and literary critics — we are faced with the question that our students so often pose: but how do you know if it is any good?

In selecting the texts, we have tried to cast the net widely. Our sources of new literature are as diverse as the reviews site Perlentaucher.de, the informative websites run by New Books in German and the Goethe-Institut, and the blogs by Katy Derbyshire, among others, which promote, review, and introduce new writing; the many literary prizes that draw attention to new writing, particularly the Bachmann Prize and the Chamisso Prize, as well as more established and mainstream awards such as the German Book Prize; and literary events such as the Lange Leipziger Lesenacht (Leipzig Long Night of Readings), organized to coincide with the Leipziger Buchmesse (Leipzig Book Fair), where up-and-coming authors read en masse for a young and enthusiastic public. Our approach for this volume was to "crowdsource," to draw on the collective knowledge of colleagues in the United Kingdom, Ireland, mainland Europe, and the United States who specialize in contemporary literature. In the first instance, we asked contributors to nominate authors or texts that had impressed them recently and deserved wider attention. In this way we hoped to draw on a collective knowledge that exceeded the editors' own — indeed, one of the pleasures of this project has been discovering new names and voices — and the result was a noticeable enthusiasm, as well as a broader range than we could have put together ourselves.

A number of the names that came up were at the time unfamiliar to us, but have since become much more prominent. Clemens Meyer, for example, is rapidly turning into a literary phenomenon — aided in no small way by his self-assured and carefully staged performances at readings — and Alina Bronsky's debut novel has garnered further attention outside Germany after Tim Mohr's well-received translation, titled *Broken Glass Park*. Our focus here is largely on writers who are "emerging," who have debuted or come to particular prominence during the first decade of the new millennium, and most frequently the novels chosen are the authors' most recent. Many other authors could have had a claim for inclusion: for example, Kevin Vennemann, whose linguistically challenging novels *Nahe Jedenew* (2005; *Close to Jedenew*, 2008) and *Mara Kogoj* (2007) deal with equally challenging histories, or Selim Özdoğan, whose novel *Die Tochter des Schmieds* (The blacksmith's daughter, 2005) features in Fatih Akın's film *Auf der anderen Seite* (On the other side, 2007; released to English-speaking audiences as *The Edge of Heaven*), to name but two.

While we cannot claim to possess the gift of foresight, we have tried to pick texts and writers whose long-term future seems promising and eschew the one-off cause célèbre, such as Charlotte Roche's *Feuchtgebiete* (2008; *Wetlands*, 2009), which attracted much media attention for its scatological and salacious content, both in German and in its English translation by Tim Mohr, and which has divided critics. On the one hand, Roche's provocative debut catapulted her into celebrity — she has well and truly "emerged" — while on the other hand she has not yet published anything further, and it remains to be seen whether this will be the beginning of a long literary career.

Literature does not stand still. As is always the case when dealing with contemporary literature, there is inevitably a time lag between a literary text's publication and the publication of the first critical research on it, which we have tried to minimize as far as possible. When this project was launched (2008–9), many of these texts and even authors were relatively unknown and only recently published: three of the novels in this volume are their authors' debut publications — those of Meyer, Bronsky, and Stanišić; *Alle Tage* is also Mora's first novel after a collection of short stories. By the time this volume appears they will, we hope, have established themselves even further. Equally inevitably, other novels by authors in this volume have appeared that we might have liked to include: Ulrike Draesner's *Vorliebe* (Preference, 2010) would have been as suitable as (and moreover creates links to) her *Mitgift*; Daniel Kehlmann's interlinked short stories *Ruhm*, which draw on the author's experiences with his best-selling *Die Vermessung der Welt*, might also have merited consideration in its own right; Bronsky's second novel, *Die schärfsten Gerichte der tatarischen Küche* (*The Hottest Dishes of the Tartar Cuisine*), was included on the long list of the German Book Prize 2010.

As well, new authors have also appeared on the scene, such as teenager Helene Hegemann, whose vibrant drugs-and-nightclub Berlin novel *Axolotl Roadkill* made waves in late 2009, albeit not always for the right reasons, and is to appear in English (translated by Katy Derbyshire, a contributor to this volume) in January 2012. Finn-Ole Heinrich's stories come recommended by Clemens Meyer; his novel *Räuberhände* (Thief's hands, 2008) is a coming-of-age story with a subtle take on national identities. Larissa Boehning followed up a well-received collection of short stories with the novel *Lichte Stoffe* (Light materials, 2007), a generational novel and a quest to track down a missing painting — and grandfather. Benjamin Stein's *Die Leinwand* (The screen, 2010) plays with the printed form of the book (a provocative decision in these days of electronic readers), starting one story at the front of the book and one at the back: they meet in the middle. These names may well be ones to watch for the coming decade, though no doubt others as yet unknown will also make their mark.

A sign of the vitality of contemporary writing in German is that a substantial number of these novels have already been translated into English, and the chapters refer to published translations whenever available in the interest of bringing these texts to as wide an audience as possible. With that in mind, we are delighted to be able to publish here two translations of excerpts from texts that have not yet appeared in English, both commissioned especially for this volume: one is from Clemens Meyer's *Als wir träumten*, translated by Katy Derbyshire, and the other is from Vladimir Vertlib's *Das besondere Gedächtnis der Rosa Masur*, translated by Jamie Lee Searle. Many thanks are due to the British Academy for funding these translations, to the authors and their German publishers for facilitating the new extracts, to Camden House for recognizing the added value that these translations bring to a volume on contemporary literature, and finally to the translators who have rendered these fascinating and lively voices in English.

The Volume

If the novels here are united by anything, it is their lack of unity: together they highlight the productive variety of writing in the early twenty-first century. This variety extends through literary style, from the densely poetic to the readably colloquial, to the choice of protagonists that spans from young children to older citizens, Germans and non-Germans, and everyone and everything in between. A similar range can be seen in the novels' historical settings, from the painfully contemporary or in some cases, deliberately timeless, to an intentionally anachronistic eighteenth century, and in their geographical locations, from the local specificity of Eastside Leipzig or North London to the global interchangeability of the Western tourist's sightseeing itinerary.

The chapters in this volume focus on one text per author, placing the novel in the context of the author's work as a whole (although three are debut novels), and within wider literary or theoretical trends.[15] Each chapter thus offers a close reading of an individual novel as its main focus while also introducing the writer. The chapters are organized in chronological order to give a snapshot of nearly a decade of literary work.

Lyn Marven examines Ulrike Draesner's *Mitgift* (2002), the author's second novel, which revolves around two sisters, an anorexic and a hermaphrodite. The two sisters' mutable bodies are a function of their family relationships and history; as corporeal fact and literary symbol, they destabilize notions of gender and beauty. Despite its theoretical self-conscious-ness, Draesner's readable narrative ultimately emphasizes the embodiedness of the individual. Stuart Taberner reads Vladimir Vertlib's *Das besondere Gedächtnis der Rosa Masur* (2003) as a performance of Jewish identity in a contemporary Germany where Jewishness still carries a burden of repre-sentation within the cultural field, particularly for authors. The eponymous Rosa Masur, an immigrant from Russia, plays up to these expectations with her lively but unreliable life story.

The story of another pan-European migrant, the multilingual Abel Nema, is related in Terézia Mora's first novel *Alle Tage* (2004). Drawing on diaspora studies and anthropology, Anke Biendarra analyzes the trauma that marks Nema's life and underlies his remarkable linguistic abilities. The text, set in the cosmopolitan, deterritorialized city of "B.," is a labyrinthine narrative: frequent intertextual references enact the decentered, noninte-grated existence of its transnational subjects. As Stephen Brockmann shows, Juli Zeh's second novel *Spieltrieb*, also from 2004, develops the author's interest in contemporary nihilism through its manipulative stu-dent protagonists. Evoking works by Nietzsche, Musil, and Horváth, and acting out modern game theory, the knowledgeable characters are philo-sophical ciphers as much as individuals, but ultimately, so Brockmann sug-gests, the text upholds a realistic morality.

Daniel Kehlmann's fourth novel, *Die Vermessung der Welt* (2005) transformed the author into a household name. Rebecca Braun shows how the two main characters — eighteenth-century scientists Humboldt and Gauß — present opposing approaches to intellectual fame. Kehlmann's self-aware text further enacts the processes of identification and familiarity that constitute modern celebrity. Clemens Meyer also rose rapidly to media attention with his debut novel *Als wir träumten* (2006) despite — or per-haps because of — his self-stylization as an outsider figure. As Frauke Matthes shows, the novel's appeal lies in allowing readers to enter an unknown, closed world of violence and criminality in the former East Germany, where the ghettoized protagonists act out their identity through exaggerated masculinity.

Like Mora's writing, Saša Stanišić's 2006 debut *Wie der Soldat das Grammfon repariert* is part of what Brigid Haines terms the "Eastern turn" in contemporary German-language literature. Depicting the Bosnian conflict of 1992 from a child's perspective, the text employs nonrealist ele-ments and, particularly, the metaphor of sport to investigate nationalism, identity, and violence. Ilija Trojanow's own transnational biography finds an echo in the protagonist of his novel *Der Weltensammler* (2006), Victorian explorer Richard Burton. Julian Preece shows how Burton's intercultural encounters in the novel — predicated on physical proximity, exchange, and imitation — fail to overcome the distance between cultures. Travel is also a theme in Sibylle Berg's fifth novel, *Die Fahrt* (2007), which according to Emily Jeremiah negotiates discourses of *Heimat* and Germanness through its peripatetic characters. Through its aesthetics and its critique of globalization, the novel develops a form of nomadic ethics and affirms the "glocal."

Julia Franck's 2007 novel *Die Mittagsfrau* depicts Germany in the first half of the twentieth century through the story of a woman who eventually abandons her own son. Valerie Heffernan examines the text as a example of matrilineal, woman-centered history. Like Draesner and Schmidt's texts, Franck's novel undermines conventional gendered images, here through a rejection of motherhood. The teenage protagonist of Alina Bronsky's *Scherbenpark* (2008) also defines herself in relation to the memory of her mother, even while adopting masculine behaviors. Barbara Mennel analyzes Russian immigrant Sascha Naimann as a "global ghetto girl," a figure that draws on a transnational discourse of youth and gender. The contemporary girl owes much to cinematic depictions of the ghetto, a marginalized urban space often associated with ethnic minorities.

The protagonist of Karen Duve's intertextual and autobiographical *Taxi* (2008) negotiates the urban space of Hamburg as a taxi driver. Heike Bartel sees the spatial and temporal movement of both taxi and text as representing the postmodern individual; the car both distances driver Alex from the world and forces her into unwelcome intimacy with her passengers. *Café Cyprus* (2008), Yadé Kara's second novel about Berlin-born Hasan Kazan, finds the protagonist exploring London in the 1990s. However, his observations of the city are, as Kate Roy demonstrates, directed toward twenty-first-century Germany. Employing Deleuzian theory, Roy thus elaborates the text's strategies of deterritorialization and reterritorialization. Sven Regener's *Der kleine Bruder* (2008) also revisits a successful character — Herr Lehmann — in the third part of a trilogy, and like Kara's novel, Regener's responds to the way that the author himself and his previous publications were received. As Andrew Plowman shows, the novel maps the mythical West Berlin district of Kreuzberg SO36 in the 1980s, evoking its demise in the coming reunification without nostalgia. The self-conscious narrative is both a memory text and a performance.

Kathrin Schmidt's *Du stirbst nicht* (2009) is a different type of performance, both physical and linguistic: protagonist Helene Wesendahl struggles to regain her memory in the wake of serious illness. Sonja Klocke examines how disability affects Schmidt's protagonist's positionality, forcing her to reconstruct her identity through language and review her previous relationships. The volume concludes with two translations: Katy Derbyshire's rendition of a chapter of Clemens Meyer's *Als wir träumten* shows the author's stylized, colloquial, and studiedly unemotional prose; the episode demonstrates the characters' boyish interest in drinking, gambling, and fast cars. Jamie Lee Searle translates a chapter of Vladimir

Vertlib's *Das besondere Gedächtnis der Rosa Masur*, where Rosa writes a letter to her long-dead friend Mascha, reflecting on death and migrant connections. Rosa's chatty reminiscences are detailed and intimate. These samples are a fitting conclusion to a volume that hopes above all to win new readers for some of the most exciting and innovative voices in German-language literature in the twenty-first century.

Notes

[1] See James Annesley, *Fictions of Globalization* (London: Continuum, 2006) and Suman Gupta, *Globalization and Literature* (Cambridge: Polity, 2009).

[2] Katharina Gerstenberger and Patricia Herminghouse's 2008 volume, *German Literature in a New Century*, which addresses marketing and the literary scene as well as contemporary works of literature, similarly posits continuities in literary trends and traditions as well as transitions and transformations, as the subtitle of their volume suggests. Katharina Gerstenberger and Patricia Herminghouse, eds., *German Literature in a New Century: Trends, Traditions, Transitions, Transformations* (New York: Berghahn, 2008). See also Stuart Taberner, ed., *German Literature in the Age of Globalisation* (Birmingham: Birmingham UP, 2005).

[3] "Glocal," a portmanteau of global and local, suggests the interplay between and simultaneous negotiation of the realms denoted by these terms.

[4] On the "Berlin novel," see especially Katharina Gerstenberger, *Writing the New Berlin: The German Capital in Post-Wall Literature* (Rochester, NY: Camden House, 2008).

[5] See, for example, Jill Twark, *Humor, Satire, and Identity: Eastern German Literature in the 1990s* (Berlin: de Gruyter, 2007), or Tanja Nause, *Inszenierung von Naivität: Tendenzen und Ausprägungen einer Erzählstrategie der Nachwendeliteratur* (Leipzig: Leipziger Universitätsverlag, 2002).

[6] Volker Hage, "Ganz schön abgedreht," *Der Spiegel* 12 (1999): 244–246.

[7] See, for example, Christian Esch, "Ich war nie ein Fräuleinwunder: Buchpreisträgerin Julia Franck hat auf der Messe einiges klarzustellen," *Berliner Zeitung*, 13 October 2007, available online at www.berlinonline.de/berliner-zeitung/archiv/.bin/dump.fcgi/2007/1013/feuilleton/0035/index.html (accessed 1 September 2010).

[8] For further consideration of contemporary writing by women, see Heike Bartel and Elizabeth Boa, eds., *Pushing at Boundaries: Approaches to Contemporary German Women Writers from Karen Duve to Jenny Erpenbeck*, German Monitor 64 (Amsterdam: Rodopi, 2006).

[9] It is perhaps worth pointing out that the multicultural spread of authors in this volume also reflects the interests of the individual contributors and editors, and beyond that, further reflects a difference in UK and US German studies; minority writing has tended to be recognized more swiftly outside Germany than within German academia.

[10] Details of the prize and previous winners can be found on the site www.bosch-stiftung.de/content/language1/html/4595.asp (accessed 1 September 2010).

[11] Katy Derbyshire, "Alina Bronsky: Broken Glass Park," love german books, http://lovegermanbooks.blogspot.com/2010/05/alina-bronsky-broken-glass-park.html (accessed 1 September 2010).

[12] UNFPA State of World Population report 2007, available on www.unfpa.org/swp/2007/english/introduction.html (accessed 1 September 2010).

[13] Georgina Paul, *Perspectives on Gender in Post-1945 German Literature* (Rochester, NY: Camden House, 2009), 9.

[14] Tom Cheesman, *Novels of Turkish German Settlement: Cosmopolite Fictions* (Rochester, NY: Camden House, 2007), vii.

[15] For an introduction to recent trends, see also Stuart Taberner, *German Literature of the 1990s and Beyond* (Rochester: Camden House, 2005) and Stuart Taberner, ed., *Contemporary German Fiction: Writing in the Berlin Republic* (Cambridge: Cambridge UP, 2007).

1: Ulrike Draesner, *Mitgift*: On Bodies and Beauty

Lyn Marven

THE NAKED FIGURE on the paperback edition of Ulrike Draesner's 2002 novel *Mitgift* (literally: Dowry) announces that this is a text dealing with gendered bodies, narratives and images of physicality, and ways of seeing.[1] Turning away from the camera toward an open door, and cropped at the shoulders and knees, the figure is illuminated from behind by a window and is, on second glance at least, relatively androgynous. *Mitgift* explores the embodiedness of individuals and their experience through the central relationship between Aloe, an art historian, and astrophysicist Lukas, who meet while studying at Oxford. The course of their relationship is in turn intertwined with the relationship between Aloe, who develops anorexia, and her sister Anita, born a hermaphrodite. The novel opens with a mystery — why is Aloe now the guardian of Anita's son? But the dramatic revelation, when it finally comes, is underplayed: Anita is killed in a murder-suicide by her husband after she decides to transition (back) to a male body.

This chapter focuses on *Mitgift* rather than more recent publications because, though written after *Lichtpause* (Light break, 1998), it marks her first major novel, one that has only belatedly gained recognition. More importantly, *Mitgift* also sets out and distils the thematic interests that recur in subsequent texts; namely, bodies, relationships, gender, sex, and reproduction. The novel also demonstrates Draesner's continuing exploration of language and competing discourses of understanding, represented most notably by science in the form of astrophysics; the text displays a self-aware interest in critical theory and an informed interrogation of notions of "women's writing."[2]

Draesner wrote a doctorate on Wolfram von Eschenbach's *Parzival* before giving up academic work for writing. Her writing is both playful and intellectual. She published the first of several volumes of poetry in 1995 and to date her poems have met with a wider reception in academic criticism than her prose; her first novel *Lichtpause* is now out of print. She has written short stories, including the collections *Hot Dogs* (2004) and *Richtig liegen* (2011), and a novel about the Munich Olympics hostage crisis and its after-effects, *Spiele* (Games, 2005); she also translates (mostly poetry) from English.[3] In *Vorliebe* (Preference, 2010), astrophysicist Harriet comes back into contact with her first love Peter, a priest, after Harriet's partner Ash accidentally knocks down Peter's wife. The novel details the unraveling of these relationships as Harriet and Peter begin an affair, and, through Harriet, attempts to reconcile scientific and religious modes of understanding the world. *Vorliebe* and *Mitgift* are linked by the theme of astrophysics, and concretely through a minor character, the scientist Erick, who appears in both novels. *Vorliebe* is a love story in the same way that *Mitgift* is a mystery, which is to say it takes the premise but works it into a complex, thoughtful narrative in which not the characters' actions — the plot as such — but the repercussions and reflections take center stage.

Draesner has also published a number of critical essays about literature, which set the parameters for her fictional prose and to some extent anticipate critical analysis of it. In the collection *Schöne Frauen lesen* (which could be translated as either "Reading beautiful women" or "Beautiful women read," 2007), Draesner's choice of authors demonstrates her interest in issues pertinent to *Mitgift*: poetic wordplay (Gertrude Stein, Friederike Mayröcker, the Oulipo poet Michèle Métail), gender images (Virginia Woolf, the cross-gender recommendations for "Further Reading," which direct interested readers from Ingeborg Bachmann to Max Frisch, for example), and scientific discourses (A. S. Byatt, for whom the "Further Reading" lists Charles Darwin). The collection subverts the obviously marketable category of women's writing by also considering Gustave Flaubert among female authors. The essay on Flaubert is called "Madame Bovary, c'est moi" and interrogates the novelist's cross-gender claims, suggesting that his famous phrase should in fact be translated as "she is me," not "I am her," and calling Emma herself "'Madame Charles Bovary,' a strange hybrid of man and woman."[4]

Mitgift: Legacies and Histories

The *Mitgift* of the title is perhaps best translated as legacy, or even inheritance, rather than dowry. In the novel, the term is used in a wider sense — which in fact harks back to the historical etymology of the word[5] — to signal literal or symbolic forms of inheritance: the inescapable chromosomal, psychological, and legal legacies that affect the characters, and that are traced through the multiple narrative levels of the text. The main protagonist Aloe echoes this linguistic shift when she suggests that the old-fashioned notion of the dowry lives on in testamentary endowments: "now the parental donation wasn't when you got married, it came later" (346).

The notion of inheritance links the generations: Aloe's and Lukas's parents are marked by their early experiences during the Second World

War. In a key scene, Anita and Aloe's mother Ingrid describes Anita's condition as "something that defined my life, a role I had waited a long time for. Now she was there. For Holger it was the expulsion, for me it was this" (110). Ingrid believes that she was somehow responsible for Anita's condition (279), although no genetic explanation for Anita's hermaphroditism is given in the text. The effects of these experiences are visited upon their children in turn. Their lives are defined by decisions made according to their parents' determination to fit in rather than stand out: Anita by the decision to operate on her, and Aloe by the secrecy surrounding Anita's body; the sisters' difficult adult relationship is a further legacy of this regulated childhood (104).

In a self-conscious conversation early in the text, Aloe, Lukas, and their friend Patty posit themselves as heirs to their parents, to history, and to their genes: "No one gets away without inheriting something. Maybe what actually matters, Aloe, is that you know where something came from" (46). This phrase is echoed later by Brigitte, Lukas's mother, who comments about her son's precocious mathematical gifts that "you have no idea where something like that comes from" (97).[6] The characters discuss the connotations of *Mitgift*, which contains the German word *Gift* (poison) as well as the English "gift" (which is etymologically linked to *Mitgift*). In the same conversation, Lukas defines it as "the share that you receive from your beloved parents. A gift [*Geschenk*] in fact, or . . .?" and Aloe adds, ". . . a bit of poison [*Gift*]" (46).[7]

Finally, the title also refers to the "dowry" that Anita brings to her marriage; namely, her other male self, which also causes problems for legal bequests: Aloe is first made aware of Anita's decision to transition when she is summoned to her parents' house by a fax that reads "*Inheritance issues.* Their own house on the one hand, and on the other hand Anita, Stefan, and Aloe — they, Ingrid and Holger, wanted to get things in order for their will" (346). Toward the end of the novel, Aloe ponders the word *Mitgift* when she discovers that Anita had left her a sum of money in her will. A legacy in legal terms, this gift also evokes the sense of a dowry, coming shortly after Aloe's fantasy of taking a trip to the seaside with Anita after the latter's operation: "father, mother, and son, the happy trio. She would enjoy it too, no: Axel, he" (361). The fantasy posits Aloe as mother, postoperative Anita as father; the sisters are reconfigured as a male-female couple (prefigured in the details of their parents' will), with "Anita as a man/husband" (361) — significantly, the German term *Mann* can mean husband as well as man. Anita's gift of money to Aloe is a dowry in two senses: it is what she (Anita, writing the will as a legal woman) brings to their parental pairing, and her will also transfers money from the future male partner (Anita as Axel) to the female partner.

It is of course Stefan, Anita's son, who is the most prominent *Mitgift*, and Anita's money will allow Aloe to raise Stefan as a single parent, as dowries are intended to do in the event of a husband's death. The relationship between Aloe and Stefan frames the novel: the text opens with a vivid description of Stefan's seventh birthday party, and each of the five chapters begins on this narrative level. Their initially unclear relationship purports to be the impetus for the retrospective narrative: "Mostly he calls her Aloe, and it will soon be time to tell him the story" (9).[8] The image of nonbiological parenthood is highlighted by an intertextual reference — a literary legacy, one could say — to Kleist's "Das Erdbeben in Chili," where Don Fernando is left with an adopted child after Josefa and Jerónimo are killed: Kleist's texts ends: "when Don Fernando compared Felipe with Juan and the ways in which he had acquired the two of them, it almost seemed to him that he had reason to feel glad."[9] Toward the end of Draesner's text, Aloe experiences a similar emotion: "When Aloe looked at him and thought about the way in which she had acquired him, it almost seemed to her that she had reason to feel glad. Later she felt ashamed of herself for that" (367). Aloe is ashamed for feeling glad to have a child, given her own difficulties in conceiving, but this shame is perhaps also a textual gesture of discomfiture at the self-conscious quotation and an acknowledgement that the "real life" situation exceeds the impact of its literary forebears.

Anita's Story

The third-person narrative of *Mitgift* focuses on the elder sister, Aloe, who develops anorexia as an adult, but the tale of her younger sister Anita's body is the traumatic center of the narrative and has received the most critical attention. "Anita. One story circles the other like a cat round the mouse's escape route; no wonder she can only recall them in conjunction. Lukas and Aloe, Aloe and Anita" (241). Anita's appearance in the text is preceded by the images Aloe has of her external physical form, and particularly by Aloe's feelings toward her: "A life completely devoid of Anita Aphrodita, without having to endure her beauty, having to think about her, without continually seeing her everywhere, without envy. That's what she wanted" (71). As Stephanie Catani shows, Anita's body is thus "doubly constructed," from outside, by Aloe's perspective and her process of remembering, a process reiterated by the novel's associative structure.[10]

Anita, born a female pseudohermaphrodite,[11] undergoes a series of operations as a child to "normalize" her genitalia: "Anita had corrective surgery, she became an unambiguous creature in the realm of men and women, blessed gender binarism" (105). The decision to operate is made by Ingrid, who recounts the horror of giving birth to this monstrous, ambiguously sexed baby — an "it": "The feeling: it came out of your body, Ingrid. Disgusting!" (279). She exhorts the doctors to "make a woman out of her for god's sake" (280). Ingrid's formulation presumes the gender (her) that will be created by surgery (to make a woman) and fixes Anita in the female pronoun. Her imperative enacts explicitly the speech act that produces sex in a newborn child, what Judith Butler refers to as,

> the medical interpellation which . . . shifts an infant from an "it" to a "she" or a "he," and in that naming, the girl is "girled," brought into the domain of language and kinship through the interpellation of gender. But that "girling" of the girl does not end there; on the contrary. . . . The naming is at once the setting of a boundary and the repeated inculcation of a norm.[12]

Anita's condition remains an unspoken family secret, but the process of constructing her femininity is ongoing, as Catani posits: in exclaiming "just look what a beautiful girl she is turning into" (167), Ingrid draws attention both to the exaggerated femininity of her young daughter and to the deliberate construction thereof.[13] Exaggerated femininity is a common physical effect of hermaphroditism, which is further enhanced by the female hormones Anita takes as well as Ingrid's deliberate pursuit of an erotic adult femininity for her.[14] Before deciding to undergo hormone treatment and further surgery to adopt a masculine/male body, Anita lives as a woman: she gets married and bears a child. At Ingrid's suggestion, she even works as a semi-naked model, given her striking, beautiful appearance and the fact that she has no shyness about showing her body after frequent medical examinations.

In puberty, Anita develops a tendency toward pyromania,[15] and nearly burns the family house down; her furious mother yells at her on the street, calling her "Scheißzwitter" (213). This is the first time that Anita's status is acknowledged in public. The term *Zwitter*, which has no real equivalent in English, means hermaphrodite, but here carries the sense of freak (an English term that is also directed at Anita elsewhere in the novel) and is clearly intended as an insult: it enters public discourse and recurs in an encounter with punks, who yell "Hey *Zwitter*" (269) at Anita. The word fascinates Aloe — "Aloe only had a vague idea what *Zwitter* meant; but she immediately understood that it was a particularly hurtful word for Anita" (214) — and much later she looks it up: "*Zwitter*, masculine, was in the dictionary, between *zwitschern* and *zwölf*" (266).

Anita's overdetermined body remains a set of mutable signifiers, inviting interpretation; "you just need to look at her, that's a story in itself" (104), remarks Lukas, inferring from Anita's "little belly" (104) that she is pregnant. The first suggestion that Anita is taking male, rather than female, hormone supplements as a prelude to transitioning is in her changing physical shape, as seen by Aloe:

> I work out every day now.
> A glance, sideways, at Aloe.
> A glance, from Aloe, at Anita's arm muscles. Like Madonna's.
> . . . Anita's voice was deeper than usual, rising when she asked ques-
> tions. A new look on her face, like it belonged to someone who
> wants to get used to giving orders, but doesn't fully trust his own
> authority. (263)

As in many places throughout the novel, the German text here slips
between genders, using the masculine form of "someone" and "who,"
which is customary usage but in this context appears to reveal what Aloe
herself does not yet realize or acknowledge. When Anita explains to Aloe
that she is preparing for the first stage of gender reassignment surgery, this
is preceded by Aloe's vision of Anita's now-masculine features:

> Anita looked completely different.
> Buzz-cut hair. The curls gone. Jeans and T-shirt.
> Hey! she said, in a deep, rich voice.
> The light was falling on her at an angle from behind. So Aloe couldn't
> be sure, but it looked like Anita had a faint beard on the chin and
> around the mouth. She seemed less bony than before, with more
> sinews and firmer muscles. (353–54)

Anita's decision to transition to a male body is an act of regaining control
over the form of her body and, more importantly, its meaning: "My body
has been constantly fiddled around with and I was never asked. Now I
would like to be the one who determines its form" (356). It is only as she
exercises her own agency, in choosing her physical form and gender signification, that Anita comes into focus in the text, conveyed through her
own words in conversations with Aloe.

As befits the focus on her physical appearance, Anita's story is told in
the third person, which allocates her a grammatical gender corresponding to
the external view. By comparison, Jeffrey Eugenides's novel *Middlesex*
(2002), also about a hermaphrodite, uses a first-person narrative to sidestep
Calliope's shifting gender identification.[16] Gender-assigned as a child, Anita
is almost entirely fixed within the feminine pronoun, only taking on the
masculine in Aloe's daydreams of their possible postoperation trip to the sea.
Whereas Eugenides's novel narrates an incestuous family history in order to
explain the genetic inheritance that causes Cal's hermaphroditism, Anita's
condition is medically unexplained, but the bare facts of her condition are
spun into stories by the family: "You always appropriated my body for your
fantasies" (270–71), Anita complains to Aloe, while Lukas comments:

> There was a fact — Anita born with an enlarged clitoris, admittedly
> one that was enlarged like a penis, but all the same: just a bit of flesh,
> a deformity of the vagina — and you all built an incredible story
> around it. (214)

Anita is only described in retrospect: physically, as her body exists only in its postoperative image, and narratively, as the novel works backwards, and through several layers of chronology, to the twin traumas of her body and her death. The narrative gap recalls the characterization of hermaphroditism as the "Geschlecht ohne Ort" (sex/gender with no site) in Joseph Vogl's phrasing,[17] and Anita's penis as Luce Irigaray's "rien à voir" (nothing to be seen).[18]

Aloe's Story

Anita's tale is inseparable from its effects on Aloe and her relationship to her own body. Unraveling the pathology of Aloe's anorexia leads — both structurally in the narrative, and etiologically in medical terms — to her childhood memories that center on Anita: "every (hi)story has a pre-(hi)story" (291).[19] As a psychosomatic condition within a literary text, Aloe's anorexia is both symbolic and physical, and, like Anita's hermaphroditism, it functions throughout the novel as a metaphor as well as medical fact.

Aloe's anorexia is a psychologically plausible response to pressure: she starts dieting as a response to stress and as her relationship with Lukas falters. While her therapist informs Aloe that the nature of her condition is socially and culturally determined — in another age she might have developed other psychosomatic symptoms such as hysteria — food is linked to her need for attention or approval throughout the novel. Aloe takes advantage of the fact that her mother is watching golden girl Anita to take "a slice of toast. Butter. Strawberry jam. Her third slice. She was only allowed two" (167). Anita's hormone tablets are dissolved in cocoa, which Aloe is not allowed to drink: "what's good for Anita is poison for you, Ingrid had said" (168; note the loaded German word for poison: *Gift*). Her relationship with Lukas is also affected by food from the start: she decides to sleep with him based on the way he eats trout, and later feeds him up while she starves herself. The text reflects Aloe's growing obsession: as she starves herself, she sees everything around her in culinary terms: old men are "sticky like baklava, each layer a story about themselves" (84), and the colors of miniatures in the museum where Aloe works, "glowed like saffron, like freshly-cut mango, like melon flesh" (88). The opening scene of the novel, meanwhile, Stefan's seventh birthday party, revolves around an elaborately described *Kalter Hund* (literally, "cold dog," a refrigerator cake). The cake symbolizes Aloe's recovery as well as reconciliation with her history through this family recipe (cf. 287).

Aloe's anorexia is "the body seeking a language" (154). The condition is intertwined with other stories both in its etiology and in its treatment: Aloe's therapy prompts her to remember her family, "a memory rose from her stomach: Holger's story, Ingrid's, Anita's and hers" (152). Retracing

Aloe's memories, the text becomes less a clinical psychological history than a symbolic family history.

> Anita and her. For years Aloe had looked on and believed she was a safe distance from her sister. Believed, like Holger, that she was a "white generation,"[20] living in the innocent spots of history, watching but never affected. It was only after her anorexia that she realized: that's an illusion! and she had begun to remember. (159)

In order to escape the effects of her relationship with Anita, Aloe first has to acknowledge that she is in fact affected by it. Her anorexia is in part an attempt to regain attention for her own sake: "as the sister of the freak, as the shadow of something special, you are nothing. The therapist's words in the anorexic clinic had struck home there. He said Aloe needed to learn to accept that she was normal" (218). Being normal means being "able to live, despite and with Anita" (156).

On Beauty, and Gender

Through Aloe and Anita's clinical conditions, the novel explores discourses of the body within cultural, as well as medical, history. Their respective conditions of anorexia and hermaphroditism are united by notions of gender or androgyny and, perhaps paradoxically, beauty. Aloe wishes to look beautiful (meaning: thin) — "The others grew fat, she grew beautiful" (77) and compares her thinner self to the mythical Helen of Troy. Aloe's aim is to be "identical with the type of woman who waves from the posters, streamlined and beautiful, a dolphin, firm as a phallus" (133).[21] Aloe evokes an image of Anita swimming (one of her modeling jobs), which recurs as a motif in the text. In the German, the ambiguous term *Typ* (type or man) is masculine, so here a male pronoun describes a woman, a form of grammatical hermaphroditism.

The multivalent cultural connotations of beauty are evoked by Draesner's collection of essays, *Schöne Frauen lesen*. It opens with a tongue-in-cheek set of definitions of beauty that pertain to the treatment of the motif in *Mitgift*, from anatomical — "all or nothing" — through biological — "recognized as a handicap, the peacock's tail for example."[22] Under grammar, Draesner notes that the German term *Schöne* is overdetermined, as it can be combined with all three definite articles — that is, it can be masculine, feminine, or neuter.[23] "Anita Aphrodita" (71) is at once exaggeratedly feminine and beautiful beyond gender: "the uncanny glamour, Anita's strangely provocative beauty. . . . Her beauty showed what humans are — man and woman and always a bit of each" (217). Beauty and androgyny are thus two sides of the same coin.

Anita is linked with the goals and effects of anorexia — beauty and androgyny — on a level of narrative symbolism, as well as in the possible psychological motivation for Aloe's disorder. Aloe describes her anorexic body as a form of "body performance, *special thanks to Anita, that* unforeseen gift from the future" (83). Here the sleight of hand in calling Anita a gift (*Geschenk*) links her with that noun's neuter pronouns (*es, das*), which evoke her preoperative gender uncertainty. Dieting ungenders Aloe's body: a common side effect of anorexia is to disturb androgen production. Aloe is informed by her doctor that she might develop male secondary sexual characteristics:

> It may be that you look a bit like a man for a time, but you won't feel like it.
> She immediately thought: it's happening to me! She hadn't known that she could experience this split through anorexia. (153)

Aloe's anorexia is thus not only a psychosomatic response to the effects of Anita's hermaphroditism; on a literary and symbolic level, it allows Aloe to experience the condition that fascinates her. Aloe becomes obsessed with hermaphrodites and the often mythical discourses surrounding their image. At school she researches the Greek and Roman myth that gives the condition its name; ancient representations of hermaphrodites allow her to look from a distance. As an adult, she reads theoretical discourse — "She read Foucault's book about Hercule Barbin, born 1838, a girl first, then a man, read Michel Serres's study *l'Hermaphrodite*, about a story by Balzac" (242) — and later develops an erotic curiosity toward hermaphrodite porn sites, which doubly define the individuals concerned as the object of viewing: "the hermaphrodites were ideal for cameras, practically made for them. They had everything on one body" (234). Hermaphrodites are thus inserted into myth, critical discourse (narratives of thought), art history, and, finally, voyeuristic imagery; all treat the hermaphrodites as overdetermined objects.

However the culmination of Aloe's experiences is an extraordinary sequence toward the end of the novel, shortly before Anita finally reveals her intention to undergo surgery, when Aloe hallucinates that she herself morphs into a man:

> Within seconds, the strange feeling that gripped Aloe became so intense that she had to sit down. Her breasts were shrinking! . . .
> Meanwhile her shoulder muscles were definitely growing, as if her breasts were shifting round there, her hips narrowed, her bum grew smaller, as everything pushed forwards and together — into two balls and a penis. (339)

Not long after this, Aloe imagines addressing her sister: "the glass between us, she would cry: let's tear it down at last!" (351). Evoking a key scene from her childhood where the sisters were separated by a glass door, the empathetic experience enables Aloe to go beyond the objectification of only viewing her sister from afar.

Ways of Seeing

Throughout the novel, the emphasis is on seeing: on the physical differences visible on the sisters' bodies — coded as beauty, or as gender signifiers. Observation is thematized through the scientific gaze of Lukas (and of astrophysicist Harriet in *Vorliebe*), sexual curiosity, and photography. Even the subjective experience of sex is mediated by an external perspective: Aloe sees herself from outside while having sex with Lukas (34), and the couple often watches porn. Aloe's voyeurism gives the lie to the notion of the disinterested gaze: whether through sexual arousal or through the observer-expectancy effect, the novel shows that viewing affects both the viewer and the viewed.

Anita's condition is first broached through the way she presents: Aloe remembers doctors looking at Anita, which prompts the first explicit description of the latter's problematic genitals, "Her enlarged clitoris, her tumescence with a urinary opening, her (some)thing that was nearly a penis, or at least looked damn like one" (105). The narrative structure removes the hermaphroditic body from the textual gaze, instead filtering it through Aloe's memory, and describing it only when it is exposed to the gaze of others:

> the place between Anita's legs, the small protuberance between the lips, around which two bloody crusts curled like tiny snakes. . . . What Aloe saw was worth a clip round the ear. A squashed, coiled worm on a damp, pink, and pale leaf. With threads running through. (171)

This key memory portrays the sight of the uncanny body as taboo; it is indescribable, or unnamable — see the similes and metaphors. Anita, a girl with a penis, counters Freud's view of the female body as a visible absence of male form, or what Luce Irigaray calls the "rien à voir." But Anita doesn't consider her body to have a lack; rather, she refers to her "also-male body" (355), a simultaneity or superimposition of possibilities. It is the (in)visible difference that marks Anita as a hermaphrodite: the punks who harass her simply want "to see what was hermaphrodite about [her]. They said out loud what you could see in everyone else's eyes" (268). Anita drops her trousers — and they flee.

Aloe's punishment for looking at Anita takes the form of exposure to her sister's gaze: she is made to stand naked in the living room behind a glass door, through which Anita stares at her. This chastisement seems to have consequences for Aloe's relationship to her own body: the anorexia is a distortion of her gaze: "Each time her body was still there in the mirror, and each time it was too fat in her eyes" (132). The sisters' eventual reconciliation is symbolized in the same way: Aloe is permitted to look at her sister's now-ambiguous form, when Anita willingly exposes her torso to demonstrate her changing shape:

> Aloe was impressed and touched at having Anita standing bare in front of her, she hadn't seen her like that for years. It was astonishing, you knew of course how a body carries on under a T-shirt, could imagine it at least, but when it was there on view, it always came across as intimate and auratic. Because along with its strength, its vulnerability also appeared. (357)

It is notable that Anita here shows her torso — this time demonstrating her lack of a female physique — while the sight of her ambiguous body evokes traditionally masculine and feminine attributes, strength and vulnerability.

Sex

Against the objective, external, medicalized, and often public views represented by Anita's visualized body and Aloe's changing shape, Draesner's text sets sex, as a subjective, private experience of the body, and as a further facet of the relationship between language and the body. Like Tanja Dückers's *Spielzone* (1999), which also explores gender identities, *Mitgift* is strikingly explicit about sex.[24] It is represented as an extreme experience of the body and its boundaries; frequently, Draesner employs poetic language to convey an emotional and physical sensation that is at the limits of conscious thought and reflection.

Sex is a recurring theme in Draesner's texts: "Gina Regina" in *Hot Dogs* describes the eponymous Gina's no-strings-attached sexual encounters with relish; "Zucken und Zwinkern" (Twitching and winking) in the same volume touches on sibling incest. *Mitgift* explores sexuality in a range of (largely heterosexual) forms, from Ingrid's affair to the zipless sex of Aloe and Lukas's friend Patty. The act of sex recalls the other bodily discourses in the novel: the overcoming of the boundaries of one's own body compares to anorexia, while the image of two bodies briefly becoming one recalls hermaphroditism. Sex is linked to both anorexia and hermaphroditism within the reality of the text, too: Aloe notes that Lukas's sexual interest in her increases as she grows thinner, which further encourages her disorder; and her interest in hermaphrodites (verging on an incestuous desire) leads her to visit specialist porn sites.

Most frequently, sex is the index of the relationship between Aloe and Lukas (and others), the other pair in the triangular configuration of protagonists, "Lukas and Aloe, Aloe and Anita" (241). It is a gauge of their intimacy, charting a course from Lukas's masturbation habits, their first time and contraceptive failure, through to Lukas's repeated visits to a prostitute, and an act that Aloe likens to rape,[25] as well as their later attempts at conception. Sex contributes particularly to Aloe's self-image: when she finds the pornographic postcards that Lukas leaves in her apartment after their first date, she compares herself to the woman pictured on them: "Aloe liked the woman. She too wanted a strong, self-confident body. So she could live an assured life in it, give and take, without exposing herself" (36). The image recalls her admiration of Anita's invulnerable body on the posters.

At same time, sex functions within the novel as an exploration of the possibilities of language. The first time Aloe and Lukas have sex, words are inadequate to the experience: a series of similes and subjunctives attempt to capture the sensations of desire: "As if her bones were expanding, as if Lukas were undressing her skin, stretching her muscles and sinews — as if he were calling her 'by her true likeness'" (31). During sex, the language reflects Aloe's uncertain sense of her body, "under, in, into this silky-quick-torn-laughing-crazy-whatever-it-was that she was, or is, underneath, inside" (32), finally disintegrating into a series of locational prepositions with barely a subject: "above herself — under — in" (32). Immediately afterwards, the language shifts into poetry, abandoning realistic representation altogether: "She entered a leafy, fluorescent world. Lukas slipped from her, a green reflection. He flew, darkened, changed color in a split second, a chameleon, startled in his tree. Aloe listened for something, a wingbeat, an echo of the forest where they had just been. But the green that she saw was just the reflection of the lamp in the hallway" (32).[26]

Conclusion

Mitgift is a novel about bodies and about ways of seeing, about physical experience and the discourses that process, convey, or regulate experience. The text both represents images of the body and reflects upon those images and the mode of representation. Reflection is inextricably linked to its object: as Aloe notes, "interpretation made the world" (271). This understanding is written into the text: the characters themselves contribute to the interpretative framework of the text. Both Aloe and Anita are knowledgeable about the discourses that apply to their own contested bodies:

> Aloe already knew Judith Butler's body theories about *gender* and *sex*, about the body appearing "as a body" only within the prevailing socio-cultural ascriptions, she dutifully pulled out Donna Haraway's "A Manifesto for Cyborgs" once more, and called Patty, who dictated to her: Kristeva, Cixous, Irigaray, but then got caught up in

Chimpanzee Politics: Power and Sex among Apes, cited by Haraway. Modernism versus postmodernism, dialectics, negativism, feminism versus postfeminism versus cyberfeminism. (242)

Draesner imputes to her characters precisely the theoretical discourses that critics have since applied to the novel itself.[27] Despite its self-consciousness though, *Mitgift* nonetheless ultimately upholds a pragmatic, phenomenological viewpoint:

> — But it's an illusion to presume you can go back to something.
> — I know, whispered Anita, I know. For me it isn't about going back. I am aware of all that too, the new conceptions of authenticity and theories of the body, Butler, Foucault, Barthes, the whole postmodern paraphernalia. Let the theory go round in its circles, it's fun for its own sake. But for me, Lollo, it's simply about my everyday life. For me, it's about a possibility that was put in me. I want to make it real. Otherwise I'll just be living out one half of myself, do you understand? (359)

The text thus insists on the embodiedness of the characters' experience, beyond concepts of authenticity and original bodies, and beyond the discourses that theorize these. It shares this focus on corporality with other texts analyzed in this volume, particularly Ilija Trojanow's *Der Weltensammler* and Kathrin Schmidt's *Du stirbst nicht.* Here is confirmation — if it were needed — that the themes of gender and the body are not the preserve of "women's writing." For all its poetic language and postmodern theoretical self-consciousness, Draesner's novel is at heart concerned with the very stuff of our physical experience, with "people, their ties with one another, between each another, reaching right into the body" (304).

Notes

[1] Ulrike Draesner, *Mitgift* (Munich: Luchterhand, 2002); references throughout are to the paperback edition (Munich: btb-Verlag, 2005). All translations are my own.

[2] See also Lyn Marven, "Writing by Women," in *Contemporary German Fiction: Writing in the Berlin Republic,* ed. Stuart Taberner (Cambridge: Cambridge UP, 2007), 159–76.

[3] See Draesner's website, www.draesner.de, for further details.

[4] Ulrike Draesner, *Schöne Frauen lesen* (Munich: Luchterhand, 2007), 66 and 64.

[5] Draesner uses the term as suggested by the Grimms' dictionary, where *Mitgift* is derived from *mitgeben* (to give someone something to take with them, i.e., on his or her way in life); see *Das Deutsche Wörterbuch von Jacob und Wilhelm Grimm*

online at http://germazope.uni-trier.de/Projects/DWB (accessed 1 September 2010).

[6] Tellingly, Aloe and Anita's parents apply this statement to Anita's condition, reacting either by sighing (Ingrid's tacit expression of maternal guilt) or with angry denial (Holger's refusal to accept a genetic cause).

[7] "Die Portion, die du abbekommst von deinen lieben Vorfahren. Eigentlich ein Geschenk, oder . . .? . . . und ein bißchen Gift." Bilingual wordplay is a frequent feature of Draesner's writing: her Bachmann Prize text from 2000, an earlier version of a scene from *Mitgift*, is titled "L Ü C K," playing on *Lücke* (gap), *Glück* (happiness), and the English "luck." See bachmannpreis.orf.at/bp_2000/autoren/draesner_text.htm (accessed 1 September 2010).

[8] In *Vorliebe*, Harriet similarly becomes a stepmother to Ash's son Ben from a former relationship.

[9] Heinrich von Kleist, "Das Erdbeben in Chili," translation by David Luke, "The Earthquake in Chile," in *The Marquise of O— and Other Stories*, trans. David Luke and Nigel Reeves (London: Penguin, 1978), 51–67; here, 67.

[10] Stephanie Catani, "Hybride Körper: Zur Dekonstruktion der Geschlechterbinarität in Ulrike Draesners *Mitgift*," in *Familien, Geschlechter, Macht: Beziehungen im Werk Ulrike Draesners*, ed. Stephanie Catani and Friedhelm Marx (Göttingen: Wallstein, 2008), 75–93; here, 76.

[11] See Armand Marie Leroi, *Mutants* (London: HarperCollins, 2003), chapter 7: female pseudohermaphrodites have female reproductive organs, plus male genitalia (Anita has both a womb and a penis), whereas true hermaphrodites have both sets of organs.

[12] Judith Butler, *Bodies That Matter: On the Discursive Limits of Sex* (New York: Routledge, 1993), 7–8.

[13] Catani, "Hybride Körper," 84–85.

[14] Leroi, *Mutants*, 235.

[15] "A psychologist who deals with these forms of sexual abnormalities told me that the children he works with all have a thing about playing with fire." Ulrike Draesner in interview with Fridtjof Küchemann, originally on faz.net, reproduced on www.draesner.de/de/buecher/mitgift/ (accessed 1 September 2010).

[16] The similarly transsexual Viola (Viktor), in Kathrin Schmidt's *Du stirbst nicht*, analyzed by Sonja Klocke in this volume, also appears first through a first-person perspective in a letter, which leaves her gender unspecified.

[17] Joseph Vogl, cited by Stefan Willer, "Literarischer Hermaphrodismus. Intersexualität im Familienroman, 2002," in *Repräsentationen: Medizin und Ethik in Literatur und Kunst der Moderne*, ed. Bettina von Jagow and Florian Steger (Heidelberg: Universitätsverlag, 2004), 83–97; here, 86.

[18] Luce Irigaray, *Ce sexe qui n'en est pas un* (Paris: Minuit, 1977), 25.

[19] The German term used here, *Geschichte*, can mean both history and story.

[20] The "white generation" refers to the young men who were spared military service due to their birth year.

[21] "Identisch mit dem Typ von Frau, der von Plakaten grüßt, stromlinienförmig schön, ein Delphin, fest wie ein Phallus."

[22] Draesner, *Schöne Frauen lesen*, 7.

[23] Draesner, *Schöne Frauen lesen*, 8.

[24] See Katharina Gerstenberger, *Writing the New Berlin: The German Capital in Post-Wall Literature* (Rochester, NY: Camden House, 2008), especially the chapter "Erotic Sites: Sexual Topographies after the Wall," 24–51.

[25] Similarly in *Vorliebe*, Ash rapes Harriet.

[26] A very similar passage describes Harriet losing consciousness when she unexpectedly spots Peter in *Vorliebe* (Munich: Luchterhand, 2010), 21.

[27] See especially Catani, ""Hybride Körper," Willer, "Literarischer Hermaphrodismus," and my "Writing by Women."

2: Vladimir Vertlib, *Das besondere Gedächtnis der Rosa Masur*: Performing Jewishness in the New Germany

Stuart Taberner

I N CONTEMPORARY GERMAN-LANGUAGE CULTURE, Jews appear with striking frequency in affective elaborations of persecution, flight, extermination, and recovery, against which German remorse in the present can be positively evaluated. In one version, this typically implies a return to a (mythical) German-Jewish symbiosis. Here, we might think of Martin Walser's *Die Verteidigung der Kindheit* (In defense of childhood, 1991), in which the Jewish doctor Halbedel is abused by the Nazis but treated kindly by Alfred's family. Within the narrative economy of the novel, Alfred and his parents are the "true" Germans, the Nazis an aberration.[1] Walser's model for Halbedel, moreover, was almost certainly Victor Klemperer, whose diaries were finally published in 1995; for Walser, who published a eulogy in 1996 for the German-Jewish scholar who endured worsening persecution from 1933 until the Allied bombing of Dresden in February 1945 prevented his imminent deportation to a death camp, Klemperer was an exemplary German patriot.[2] Indeed, by the end of 1996, Hans Reiss reports, Klemperer's recollections of the Nazi period had sold more than 150,000 hardback copies.[3] Subsequently, a selection of his diary entries were reproduced in a paperback for young people;[4] an essay competition was instituted (the Victor Klemperer Youth Prize, to encourage young Germans to chew over worthy subjects); streets were named after him; and a TV serialization, *Victor Klemperer — Ein Leben in Deutschland* (Victor Klemperer — a life in Germany, 1999) firmly established in the popular imagination the notion that he, and assimilated Jews generally, had always embodied a more authentic patriotism than the Nazis' vicious chauvinism. Much was made, then, of his almost comic internalization of the traditionally German valorization of *Bildung* (education), his passion for the "Greats" of German culture, and his insistence that *he* was German and the Nazis no more than barbaric interlopers.

The way Klemperer's diaries resonated with the German public is particularly striking, of course, but a large number of other examples can be cited of a similar desire to reconnect with a German-Jewish past mythologized as harmonious and productive for both sides, certainly before 1933 but also, in many cases, even during Hitler's reign. Thus, we might think of films such as *Comedian Harmonists* (1997), *Aimée und Jaguar* (1999), and *Rosenstraße* (2003),[5] or of Peter Schneider's 2002 book *"Und wenn wir nur eine Stunde gewinnen . . ."* (And if we only gain an hour . . .) documenting the rescue of the musician Konrad Latte by German colleagues and friends, in which the "normality" of the German-Jewish love affair is contrasted with the anomaly of Nazism. Or we might point to Bernhard Schlink's short story "Die Beschneidung" (The circumcision) in his collection *Liebesfluchten* (Flights of love, 2000), which satirizes contemporary German *philo*semitism — a German man has himself circumcised in a desperate attempt to please the family of his American-Jewish girlfriend — while also reaffirming many of its clichés and perhaps even presenting this excess of affection as a form of German suffering.[6] Finally, we might note the many public and private initiatives to rebuild synagogues, rediscover the "lost" Jewish history of German towns, erect memorials, and publish "Jewish memoir-literature."[7] Such has been the surge of interest in Jewish fates, in fact, that German-Jewish journalist Henryk Broder has warned of the "Germanization of the Holocaust" and writer Maxim Biller has inveighed against the "Holocaust trauma as the mother of a long-sought-after German national consciousness."[8]

In a second version of what Jack Zipes has termed the postunification "fascination for things Jewish,"[9] this time related to non-German, Eastern European Jews, the stereotypically exotic Jew is symbolically coded as Other, but similarly fetishized within a celebration of Germany's present-day remorse and newly found tolerance. Here we might point to the marketing of the Scheuenviertel district in central Berlin — associated with immigrant Jews from Eastern European at the turn of the twentieth century — as "Yiddish,"[10] or of klezmer as world music[11] — the latter phenomenon is aptly satirized in Elke Naters's *Lügen* (Lies, 1999), when the narrator listens to a tape cassette "with Jewish songs or some such" that she glibly terms "ethno-stuff."[12] In the renovated complex of buildings in central Berlin known as Hackesche Höfe, for instance, a supposedly Jewish sociability is evoked via romanticized allusions to the immigrant *Ostjuden* (Jews from Eastern Europe) who populated the area from the last quarter of the nineteenth century until they were brutally expelled by the Nazis. The culture of these "East Jews" is thus invoked by the recitals of "Yiddish music in a place of historical resonance" in the Hackesches Hoftheater, or at least it was until the theater closed in 2006.[13] Karen Remmler suggests that such manifestations of nostalgia for the Eastern European Jews who had made themselves at home in Berlin both serve as an "ersatz for German folk culture" and make possible an "imagined cosmopolitanism that would return Germany to a sense of 'normalcy.'"[14] In this regard, we might refer to the confusion that surrounds the representation of the writer Wladimir Kaminer, a post-1990 immigrant from the former Soviet Union who is almost always introduced with an "ethnic tag," sometimes as Jewish, sometimes as Russian, and sometimes as a German writer of Russian descent. These insistent allusions to Kaminer's background may well imply nostalgia for a time from the 1880s when modern, cosmopolitan Berlin attracted talented Jews from across Eastern Europe, but they perhaps also indicate a need to "define" those seen as "non-German" that coexists uncomfortably with the desire to proclaim the inclusiveness of today's "normal" Germany.

Whichever the case, such representations depend, of course, on stereotypes, both positive and negative. The Jew is either virtuous, a victim of history, or ambivalently different, modern yet endearingly anachronistic, more cosmopolitan, shrewder (Jews have to be . . .), or dogged. These old-new clichés do not go entirely unnoticed, it should be noted, and particularly not by those whom they affect most directly. They are mocked, for example, in Rafael Seligmann's *Der Milchmann* (The milkman, 1999), in which the character Weinberg falsely takes credit for an act of altruism in a camp fifty years ago, or in Maxim Biller's novel *Die Tochter* (The daughter, 2000), which opens with the Jewish "hero" masturbating while watching a porn movie starring his daughter.[15]

Performing Jewishness

The examples above demonstrate a startling consistency of contemporary representations of Jews in German-language culture that is well summarized by Oliver Lubrich: "Jews appear primarily in backward-looking narratives . . . usually in the context of historical memory, a theme frequently coupled with the question of German guilt."[16] Indeed, the furious controversies sparked by former chancellor Helmut Kohl's styling of Ignatz Bubis as a "deutscher Patriot" after his death in 1999,[17] by comments by the FDP vice-chairman Jürgen Möllemann and CDU politician Martin Hohmann, in 2002 and 2003, respectively, that Jews might sometimes provoke antisemitism, by Walser's controversial novel *Tod eines Kritikers* (Death of a critic, 2002),[18] or Federal Bank Board member Thilo Sarrazin's remarks on the "Jewish gene" in the summer of 2010,[19] were all characterized by a concern with Germans' self-image rather than whether Jews are able to feel at home in the Federal Republic. Yet it is not only the way Jews are depicted that appears problematic. Individual Jews may also, in addition, be called upon to "perform Jewishness" in order to lend credibility to these representations and to play their prescribed role in defining German identity as rehabilitated, or even as self-confident, democratic, and "normal." Writers such as Broder, Biller, and Seligmann thus seem to be expected to stage stereotypically Jewish attributes for German (and Austrian) audiences. Broder and Biller, in particular, and especially with respect to their essays for the media, are valued for their acerbic — read: Jewish — perspective on German paradoxes that indirectly confirms German tolerance, whereas Seligmann is praised as a sage Jewish voice, gently chiding Germans to consider the feelings of the Jews among them. Similar to the "ethnic performances" of Turkish-German authors such as Feridun Zaimoğlu or Zafer Şenocak,[20] or a more recent, post–cold war wave of arrivals from Eastern Europe or the war-torn ex-Yugoslavia (see, for example, Brigid Haines's chapter on Saša Stanišić in this volume), these self-dramatizations are of course ambiguous: they provide a platform (and a marketing strategy) for the individual but also typecast the group in question. Even Kaminer, whose Jewishness, Sander Gilman notes, "is on the very edges of how he needs to see and sell himself" — he makes only scant reference to his ethnicity — nevertheless finds that "his 'Jewish' perspective in the Federal Republic of Germany remains part of his public persona."[21]

Performing Jewishness is the central theme of Vladimir Vertlib's *Das besondere Gedächtnis der Rosa Masur* (The remarkable memory of Rosa Masur, 2003), the most significant novel to date by this Russian-Jewish author, an emerging writer whose career is becoming firmly established. Vertlib was born in 1966, the son of a refusnik, and is now resident in Austria following his family's failed attempts to settle in Israel and the United States. These trials are described in the first, autobiographically inspired literary endeavors *Abschiebung* (1995) and *Zwischenstationen* (1999), and these texts and his subsequent works may be placed within what Dagmar Lorenz has described as "the new Jewish intellectual culture that emerged during the Waldheim scandal and includes authors such as Robert Schindel, Ruth Beckermann, Anna Mitgutsch, and Doron Rabinovici" and that also alludes to "central European prose writers of the fin-de-siècle and inter-war periods such as Joseph Roth and Elias Canetti" as well as writers searching for "a Jewish identity between tradition and secularization . . . e.g. Isaac Bashevis Singer, Anna Seghers, and Jakov Lind."[22] Focusing here, however, on Vertlib's engagement with a broader *non-Jewish* audience in Germany and Austria, I argue that his character Rosa Masur, who is loosely based on his grandmother, subtly reclaims her story from a well-intentioned but unreflective German culture of Holocaust remembrance, even as she ably performs the required stereotype of the victimized, yet shrewd Jew. The joke, ultimately, is on the German officials who pay for her outlandish fictions, fantasies, and inventions (her many moments of banal but painful reporting go more or less unnoticed) just so long as they can indulge — without guilt — their repressed longing for a voyeuristic, even vicarious, proximity to the horrors of twentieth-century totalitarianism.

Vertlib's work has been aptly described by Brigid Haines as "dialogic."[23] Indeed, his ability to present multiple perspectives in conversation with one another has pleased critics and a range of prominent figures in both Germany and Austria. For example, the president of the Austrian Industrial Organization commended Vertlib upon the award of a literary prize in 2001 as "a personality who teaches us to cross the borders of both state and culture";[24] the scholar Norbert Mecklenburg praises his moving portrayal of his "experience of being a minority and of migration";[25] and Günther Stocker has commended his "multicultural life story" that opens up "entirely new horizons of experience."[26] These, of course, are the stock phrases of the liberal discourse of multiculturalism and cosmopolitanism, and are frequently applied to a range of new writers constituting what Haines has termed the "Eastern turn" in contemporary German literature,[27] including Ilija Trojanow (see Julian Preece's chapter in this volume) and Dimitré Dinev from Bulgaria, Artur Becker and Radek Knapp from Poland, Zsuzsa Bánk and Terézia Mora (see Anke Biendarra's chapter) from Hungary, and Wladimir Kaminer from Russia. At the same time, Vertlib encourages such stylizations, repeating in various outlets, often almost word for word, a heavily biographical understanding of the exile origins of his literary work: "Israel — Austria — Italy — Austria — Netherlands, Israel again — Italy again — Austria again — USA — and finally Austria for good."[28] Similar to Biller and Kaminer, both also journalists as well as writers, Vertlib is a skilled operator in the media and in public debate who knows what is expected of him. Indeed, he is regularly invited by the Austrian newspaper *Die Presse* to comment "from the inside" on the Middle East conflict, Israel, and Jewish writing from around the world.

Almost as soon as its characters have been introduced, *Rosa Masur* offers an unmistakable parody of precisely this unspoken compact between a politically correct, liberal German discourse of openness and of Jews responding to the invitation to offer themselves as representative of both the distresses of displacement and the enrichments of multiculturalism. The ninety-two-year-old Rosa Masur, mother of Kostik and Schelja and wife of Naum (only Kostik is still alive), responds to an advertisement posted by the mayor's office in the (fictional) German town of Gigricht addressed to the region's rather euphemistically named *Zuwanderer* (literally, "those who come to us," a politically correct term for immigrants that frames them as a welcome visitors but not necessarily permanent residents). This advertisement invites recent arrivals to participate in a book project *Fremde Heimat. Heimat in der Fremde* (Home is also foreign. The foreign is also home), to be published to coincide with the municipality's 750th jubilee (which also coincides, conveniently, with the millennium celebrations). The collection is to feature testimonies from each of the town's minorities, including:

> A Turk, a Kurd, a Croatian, a Serb, a Bosnian . . . a Kosovo-Albanian, a North African . . . a Sinti or Roma,[29] a Jew originally from Gigricht (a Holocaust survivor had been so kind as to have declared a willingness to cooperate on the project), a Chinese person, someone else "who is to stand in for all the other left-over smaller minorities" . . . and of course a Russian Jew, since several families from the former Soviet Union had settled in Gigricht.[30]

The irony here is palpable. A politically correct desire to be inclusive, already bordering on the ridiculous, is comically undermined by practical considerations indicative of more profound prejudices. The difference between Turks and Kurds is evident to the German authorities, no doubt on account of well-publicized conflicts between the two immigrant groups. Ex-Yugoslavians, however, are awkward, divided into a bewildering series of subgroups. Africans can all be lumped together (they are the most powerless minority, as a later episode in which an Ethiopian is harassed by the police demonstrates). A "Roma or a Sinti" stands in for "gypsies," a term carefully avoided by the German authorities for its negative connotations even as the implied "either/or" collapses the two groups back into just such an undifferentiated, stereotyped whole. A Chinese person covers Asia, and one more foreigner is required to represent the rest. Finally, Jews are the favored other, permitted two stories: a Holocaust survivor from Gigricht to restore the German-Jewish symbiosis, and a Russian Jew as the truly exotic, and thus all the more precious, eternal victim (of centuries of Eastern European antisemitism and a brief period of Nazi persecution) welcomed into the sanctuary of the new Germany. And the price the Germans are willing to pay for these stories: 50 DM a day and 5,000 DM on the eventual publication of the book (which never happens) — a lucrative fee, then, for the recently arrived Jewish immigrant Rosa Masur to perform her biography. Here, the impression of authenticity is key. Despite the fact that Rosa's German is perfect, as she was a professional translator in the Soviet Union, the town officials thus seem to feel that a rendering into German of her Russian-language narrative is more "true."

This is the framing narrative within which Rosa elaborates her narrative of her childhood in a shtetl in Belarus, marked by pogroms and her — for the time period, and for Eastern European Jewish girls — highly unusual schooling with an itinerant *Melamed* (teacher); of World War One and her family's failed attempt to flee to Canada so that her brother Mojsche might avoid military service; of the revolution and the relatively privileged position of Jews after the Bolshevik seizure of power; of the Second World War and the siege of Leningrad (one of the most significant episodes in the book); and of antisemitism in the postwar Soviet Union and Rosa's immigration to Germany, with Kostik and his wife, after 1990. Her story at first glance thus appears to follow precisely the trajectory desired by her German paymasters, as summarized by Dmitrij Silbermann, her Russian-Jewish translator: "that above all in the Jewish biographies the tragedy, the dislocations and hopes of the twentieth century become visible. The highs and lows of the time, brought to life through the telling of an individual's own experience in which the universal is mirrored in the particular. . . . Or something like that" (37). Rosa begins with a decidedly formulaic opening, invoking trauma (a pogrom in Czarist Russia around 1910 or 1911) as the first childhood memory, the remembering subject's constitution as an "I" in the very moment of distress, and the customary association of Jewish identity with a painful past: "How it all started? The first memory? The scream of a small child. The small child is me. The tinkling of the window panes in the synagogue at the far end of the street" (41). Subsequently, Rosa is thrust into world history, such that her biography becomes properly — or, more likely, implausibly — representative of the way small people became caught up in what Eric Hobsbawm characterized as *The Age of Extremes* (1994): war, revolution, persecution, preferment, flight, new beginnings, and traumatic scarring.

Particularly at the start of her account, Rosa diligently explains Yiddish and Hebrew terms to her German audience, providing a quasi-anthropological introduction to Jewish customs and practices, especially among the Ashkenazi Jews of Eastern Europe, including, for example, references to her father, who studied at a "*yeshiva*, a Talmud academy," to a "*Zaddick*, a leader of the *yeshiva*" and to a "*Ganev* (a scoundrel)" (49), to the "*Schadchen*, the marriage arranger" (52), and to married women wearing wigs, "as is the custom among Orthodox Jews" (74), and so on and so forth. On the one hand, Rosa is obviously aware that it is in her interest that her story be as long as possible, in order to maximize her fee. On the other hand, the lengthy digressions and abundance of ethnic detail are no doubt also part of her performance of Jewishness, that is, her implicit understanding that what her audience requires is an Eastern European–Jewish, *Fiddler on the Roof*–like tale of her gutsy attempt to live a life in the face of unremitting misfortune. Her translator Dmitrij colludes in this stylization of her biography. Initially, he attempts to steer her "narrative flow," but later he simply reworks her narrative in order to maintain suspense and, just as important, does not reveal his suspicions about the truthfulness of a key element of her account to her employers (312–13). What is required of Rosa, it seems, is a hyper-Jewish version of her self, as clichéd as the version of Jewishness performed by the (German) "ethnoband" at the reception held for the town's "foreign fellow citizens" (the German term *ausländische Mitbürger* is the politically correct term here; 413) toward the close of the book: "A Yiddish song, which sounded more Yiddish than all the Yiddish songs that Rosa had heard in her life" (410).

And this is what seems to be offered: a series of lachrymose episodes borne with dogged acceptance and related with enduring pathos, arranged into a composition of finely balanced "chapters" (312). Rosa is thus not only ascribed "a clear-cut identity as a Jew," as Sebastian Wogenstein argues,[31] but also appears to choose to perform this identity.

What Rosa's German paymasters get, therefore, appears to be exactly what they desired — at least if they only read the *summary* version of her voluminous narrative. At the reception mentioned above, the mayor's assistant remarks to Rosa that she has studied the *synopsis* of her conversations with Dmitrij and that "one" can learn a great deal from it, "about life" and about what people "went through" in the twentieth century (408). And the mayor's comments are even more nebulous, insofar as he is able to say only that he finds the *digest* of her life "impressive" (415). Yet Rosa's real story, the one she tells during the more than three hundred and fifty pages given over to it in the book, is manifestly far more complex and certainly not reducible to her Jewishness. At least five major strands feature in her narrative, only two of which directly relate to the fact she is Jewish. First, and of most interest to her German audience, there is the headline story of the discrimination she suffers because of her ethnicity. Second, a major strand throughout her chronicle relates to her experiences as a woman. Third, and related to this, her account contains a never-explicit but nonetheless moving rumination on female friendship, with intimations of a lesbian attraction, and on sex and the strictures of hetero-sexual norms such as marriage and children. Fourth, her narrative alludes — most often in its omissions — to feelings of guilt caused by a family dynamic shaped by her favoring of her brilliant but rather feeble son over her daughter, and by her husband's disconnectedness. Finally, her telling of her life is interlaced with quiet reflections on the repression of memory and on the sudden return of trauma. Her persecution as a Jew is clearly a key element of this dialectic but, in a life as multifaceted as hers, it is emphatically not the only one.

Private concerns — including her life-long attachment to Mascha (even after Mascha's death during the siege of Leningrad, Rosa "talks" to the woman she once dared to kiss [208]); her prolonged battle to get Kostik a place at university during the anti-Jewish hysteria before Stalin's death in 1953, which caused her to neglect her daughter; and her enduring struggle to assert herself as a woman — thus dominate Rosa's narrative. Her Jewish story is interwoven with these experiences. Indeed, it is a nec-essary part of the thick description of her psychological makeup, which dissolves into cliché as soon as it is extracted and made representative, whether of the Holocaust (which she in fact avoided) or, more generally, of other twentieth-century extremes. Just as important, however, is the way Rosa tells her tale. Digression and seemingly extraneous detail no doubt help to boost her fee, yet they also serve to demonstrate her control over her own storylines and her refusal to edit out those elements that have meaning for her. For example, she tells Mascha's story alongside her own, placing greater emphasis on their intimacy than on the fact that Mascha is not Jewish. Similarly, she offers a fulsome account of her son's many illnesses — a stereotypical Jewish mother's trait, of course — even though these will scarcely be of interest to her audience. In addition to digression, however, Rosa also confesses to embellishment — "I find it hard not to embellish the details" (165) — as well as to the omission of painful episodes, such as her relationship with her daughter: "I would prefer not to write about Schelja" (310). Or, she relates horrific events with matter-of-fact precision, refusing to invest them with the teleological significance desired by her German paymasters. Thus her account of the siege of Leningrad cannot be integrated into the wished-for narrative of human misery followed by redemption (presumably in the present-day Federal Republic) but testifies only to the arbitrariness of death and survival: "The men are at the front or already dead. Men are weaker than women. They die first" (265). Above all, within the deviations, gaps, and brutal factuality, Rosa implies a trauma that is hers alone, a complex interaction of injuries, some linked to world history, but some personal. Even as she earns her 50 DM a day, accordingly, her narrative takes on a private significance for her as a form of self-therapy: "Fears that she had often experienced, in the moment itself and then again and again ever since, countless times in her memories and dreams, these fears caught hold of her, dissolved time and space" (402). As Mascha declares, Rosa's telling of her story is never simply a question of making money in order to fulfill Kostik's longing — with which the book opens and closes — to go to Aix-en-Provence: "'don't fool yourself,' the dead woman mocked" (403).

Meeting Stalin . . .

Of all of the strands within Rosa's story, however, there is one that stands out due both to its sheer implausibility and the ease with which it can be extracted out of the rest of her narrative and readily consumed by her German audience, eager as it is for lurid, but quickly digestible, vignettes of twentieth-century horrors. This strand relates to the occasion on which she claims to have met Stalin shortly before his death in 1953, a strand that throws into sharp relief, on account of its facile sensationalism, the painfully banal nature of her daily struggles as a Jew, a woman, and a mother. As the culmination of her efforts to secure Kostik a university place, Rosa states that she wrote to the Soviet dictator, recalling the moment when they had "slept together" in 1922 during a visit to her village. Yet not only does she claim that she wrote to Stalin with the aim of playing on his famed sentimentality — clearly a risky enterprise — she also elaborates a quite astounding account of how he responded to her missive by appearing in her apartment in the middle of the night. Amused by her audacity — Rosa clarifies that they slept together only to the extent that they both fell asleep during a functionary's speech — the Soviet leader, she further claims, then composed a letter requiring the authorities in Leningrad to allow her son to attend university. Following this, he and his entourage left, but not before humiliating some antisemitic neighbors. Dmitrij is surely right to doubt the authenticity of this story, and of the letter from Stalin that Rosa had shown the town officials at the outset of the novel as an inducement to choose her as their "Russian Jew." Indeed, this implausible initiative, which supposedly took place at the very time Jewish doctors were being accused of trying to poison Stalin, is the key vehicle for suspense throughout, with frequent but elusive hints before it is finally related in full toward its conclusion, and has almost certainly been fabricated by Rosa as a means of satisfying her paymasters while leaving her free to tell her real story.

More profoundly, however, Rosa's fictionalization of a clandestine meeting with Soviet leader is most likely inspired by her understanding of the particular manner in which she is expected by the mayor's office to perform her Jewishness as well as by her surprisingly acute insight into the complex psychology of German contrition. If it is to have any credence with her German paymasters, therefore, Rosa's outlandish account of her encounter with Stalin must rely more or less entirely upon its implicit appeal to their *philo*semitic prejudices and stereotypes (which are of course, in part at least, simply reformulated versions of antisemitic commonplaces). Her tall tale thus frames herself as the powerless but wily Jewish woman able to manipulate the Soviet leader, playing the Jewish jester with clever word games and a hazardous tacking back and forth between audacity and deference that flatters the dictator's absolute power. Stalin's backhanded compliment, of course, merely confirms his deep-rooted antisemitic bigotry — "In the course of your centuries of analysis of the Talmud you've learnt to collect words, and game-playing is in your blood in any case" (the German term *spielen,* translated here as "game-playing," may also connote "performance" or "deception," 385) — yet Rosa clearly expects her present-day German audience to share the same underlying prejudice: Jews are adept at extracting themselves from all kinds of precarious situations by resorting to their supposed native wit. (In the philosemitic version, naturally, they are compelled to do so by their persecutors.) This may well be what the mayor actually finds "impressive" about her life; it may also be what his assistant can only hint at in vague circumlocutions about what one may learn from her Jewish story.

What's more, her Stalin fiction may hold a more specific and irresistible attraction for her German hosts. At the close of her conversation with the mayor toward the end of the novel, accordingly, he leans in toward Rosa and asks her, perhaps somewhat shamefaced, what it was like to be in

attendance with Stalin: "What was he like? I mean, face-to-face, in his manner, his aura?" Grasping — once again — what is required of her, she
whispers in his ear the one word he almost certainly most wishes to hear
from the Jewish woman, despite its self-evident redundancy: "Dictatorial"
(416–17). In short, then, Rosa's fictional account of her meeting with the
Soviet leader may offer a safe, suitably "other" yet also vicariously thrilling
focus for a fascination with unbounded and brutal power that is not per-
missible in relation to Germany's own dictatorship. And here the truly
ambivalent nature of the Federal Republic's politically correct contrition
and ostentatious tolerance is perhaps exposed. Whereas Rosa sees little difference between Stalin and his "former buddy Hitler" (385), for her
German admirers it may be a relief to see someone other than themselves
indicted for cruelty, and a relief finally to be among the righteous.

At the very end of *Das besondere Gedächtnis der Rosa Masur*, it transpires that the medieval charter on which the town's 750th-anniversary
celebrations was to be based is a forgery. This may provide a hint that the
oral history that Rosa has undertaken is certainly no less reliable than
document-based, professional history, or it may allude indirectly to the
questionable authenticity of Rosa's letter from Stalin, or both. Whatever
the case, Rosa collects her daily payments — the 5,000 DM is lost since
the book will now not be published — and travels with Kostik and his wife
to Aix-en-Provence. On arriving, they find themselves among Muslim
immigrants, possibly confirming that Leslie Adelson's notion of a "vague
linkage between 'things Jewish' and things 'Turkish' as they negotiate the
German present,"[32] is currently being extended in German-language writing, as Sander Gilman argues, to a recognition of "the parallels between
Jewish and the Muslim experience" with regard to questions of otherness
and assimilation,[33] and now most likely within a wider, transnational, or at
least European space. What Rosa, her son, and daughter-in-law see, therefore, is a North African or Arab presence that cannot be reconciled with
their (and many other Europeans') instinctive understanding of a Europe
in which they might be (almost) accepted as almost white (i.e. as Jews), to
paraphrase Sander Gilman,[34] but Muslims are indisputably foreign. Women
in headscarves and burkas, shops with signs in Arabic script, exotic smells,
and groups of men standing around in excited discussion lead them to
wonder whether they are really in Europe. Somewhat ironically, the
Russian-Jewish immigrants to Germany fail to recognize the wider transformation of the continent of which they are a part and see only an essential otherness rather than a performance, or the reality of hybridization
denoted, for example, in the name of their hotel, Chez Abdul et Ahmed
(426), with its quaint French provincialism and manifestly Arab owners.

Vladimir Vertlib is one of a number of contemporary authors who
address the ambivalent situation of Jews in Germany and Austria in complex, multilayered fictions. To the extent that he frames his exploration of

Jewishness in relation to current debates on integration, multiculturalism, Europeanism, and transnationalism, moreover, Vertlib continues a growing trend among both other Jewish and non-Jewish writers. Indeed, Rafael Seligmann and Maxim Biller are obvious (Jewish) comparisons, as noted above, but one might also cite W. G. Sebald, first and foremost his *Die Ausgewanderten* (The exiles, 1992), with its interweaving of border-crossing Jewish and non-Jewish biographies and complicated relationship to authenticity,[35] or Zafer Şenocak, whose novel *Gefährliche Verwandtschaft* (Perilous kinship, 1998) examines Turkish migration to Germany against the background of biographies shaped by the Holocaust and the Armenian massacre of 1915.[36] At the same time, however, Vertlib's lightness of touch distinguishes him from these established writers. Like other newer writers, he rejects the "rationalizing earnestness and forced profundity" and the "moralizing tone"[37] that he sees as typical of postwar literature and prefers, along with his peers, to emphasize story-telling, readability, and gentle irony. Far from being an outsider — the Russian-Jewish observer of life in Germany and Austria for which he is so often taken — Vertlib is thus very much part of current developments in German-language writing.

Notes

[1] See Stuart Taberner, "'Wie schön wäre Deutschland, wenn man sich noch als Deutscher fühlen und mit Stolz als Deutscher fühlen könnte': Martin Walser's Reception of Victor Klemperer's *Tagebücher 1933–1945* in *Das Prinzip Genauigkeit* and *Die Verteidigung der Kindheit*," *Deutsche Vierteljahrsschrift* 73, no. 4 (1999): 710–32.

[2] Martin Walser, *Das Prinzip Genauigkeit. Laudatio auf Victor Klemperer* (Frankfurt am Main: Suhrkamp, 1996).

[3] Hans Reiss, "Victor Klemperer (1881–1960): Reflections on his 'Third Reich' Diaries," *German Life and Letters* 51, no. 1 (1998): 65–92; here, 66. See also Henry Ashby Turner, "Victor Klemperer's Holocaust," *German Studies Review* 22, no. 3 (1999): 385–96.

[4] Victor Klemperer, *Das Tagebuch 1933–1945. Eine Auswahl für junge Leser,* ed. Harald Roth (Berlin: Aufbau, 1997).

[5] See Stuart Taberner, "Philo-Semitism in Recent German Film: *Aimée und Jaguar, Rosenstrasse* and *Das Wunder von Bern*," *German Life and Letters* 58, no. 3 (2005): 357–72.

[6] See Kathrin Schödel, "'Secondary Suffering' and Victimhood: 'The Other' of German Identity in Bernhard Schlink's 'Die Beschneidung' and Maxim Biller's 'Harlem Holocaust,'" in *Germans as Victims in the Literary Fiction of the Berlin Republic,* ed. Stuart Taberner and Karina Berger (Rochester: Camden House, 2009), 219–32.

[7] Thomas Kraft, Einleitung, in *aufgerissen. Zur Literatur der 90er*, ed. Thomas Kraft (Munich: Piper Verlag, 2000), 11–22; here, 11.

[8] Maxim Biller, "Heiliger Holocaust," in *Deutschbuch* (Munich: Deutscher Taschenbuch Verlag, 2001), 27–29; here, 28.

[9] Jack Zipes, "The Contemporary German Fascination for Things Jewish: Toward a Jewish Minority Culture," in *Reemerging Jewish Culture in Germany. Life and Literature since 1989*, ed. Sander Gilman and Karen Remmler (New York: New York UP, 1994), 15–46.

[10] See, for example, www.info-germany.de/Berlin-Brandenburg/scheunenviertel. html (accessed 1 September 2010).

[11] See Elisabeth Loentz, "Yiddish, Kanak Sprak, Klezmer, and HipHop: Ethnolect, Minority Culture, Multiculturalism, and Stereotype in Germany," *Shofar* 25, no. 1 (2006): 33–62.

[12] Elke Naters, *Lügen* (Cologne: Kiepenheuer & Witsch, 1999), 78.

[13] See www.hackesches-hoftheater.de/index2.htm (accessed 1 September 2010).

[14] Karen Remmler, "Encounters across the Void," in *Unlikely History. The Changing German-Jewish Symbiosis*, ed. Leslie Morris and Jack Zipes (New York: Palgrave, 2002), 3–29; here, 21.

[15] See Stuart Taberner, *German Literature of the 1990s and Beyond* (Rochester: Camden House, 2005), especially the chapter "A German-Jewish Symbiosis?"

[16] Oliver Lubrich, "The Other and the Ordinary: Demystifying and Demusealising the Jew," *European Jewry* 34, no. 2 (2001): 63–79; here, 64.

[17] Kohl used this phrase in a letter written to Bubis's widow. Reported by the Deutsche Presse-Agentur (dpa), 15 August 1999.

[18] See Bill Niven, "Martin Walser's *Tod eines Kritikers* and the Issue of Anti-Semitism," *German Life and Letters* 56, no. 3 (2003): 299–311.

[19] See, for example, www.spiegel.de/politik/deutschland/0,1518,714417,00. html (accessed 1 September 2010).

[20] See Yasemin Yildiz, "Critically 'Kanak': A Reimagination of German Culture," in *Globalization and the Future of German*, ed. Andreas Gardt and Bernd Hüppauf (Berlin: Mouton de Gruyter: 2004), 319–40. See also Tom Cheesman, "Akçam — Zaimoğlu — 'Kanak Attak': Turkish Lives and Letters in German," *German Life and Letters* 55, no. 2 (2002): 180–95.

[21] Sander Gilman, "Becoming a Jew by Becoming a German: The Newest Jewish Writing from the 'East,'" *Shofar* 25, no. 1 (Fall 2006): 16–32.

[22] Dagmar Lorenz, "Vladimir Vertlib, a Global Intellectual: Exile, Migration, and Individualism in the Narratives of a Russian Jewish Author in Austria," in *Beyond Vienna: Contemporary Literature from the Austrian Provinces*, ed. Todd C. Hanlin (Riverside: Ariadne Press, 2008), 230–62. Gilman also discusses Vertlib's work in his "Becoming a Jew by Becoming a German," 28–32.

[23] See Brigid Haines, "Poetics of The 'Gruppenbild': The Fictions of Vladimir Vertlib," *German Life and Letters* 62, no. 2 (2009): 233–44.

[24] Cited in Gilman, "Becoming a Jew by Becoming a German," 28.

[25] Norbert Mecklenburg, "Eingrenzung, Ausgrenzung, Grenzüberschreitung. Grundprobleme deutscher Literatur von Minderheiten," in *Die andere deutsche Literatur*, ed. Manfred Durzak and Nilüfer Kuruyazıcı (Würzburg: Königshausen und Neumann, 2004), 23–30; here, 29.

[26] Günther Stocker, "Aus dem Zeitalter der Extreme," *Literatur und Kritik* 36 (2001): 91–93; here, 93.

[27] Brigid Haines, "The Eastern Turn in Contemporary German, Swiss and Austrian Literature," *Debatte: Journal of Contemporary Central and Eastern Europe* 16, no. 2 (2008): 135–49.

[28] Vladimir Vertlib, "Nichtvorbildliche Lieblingsautoren," in *Helden wie ihr: junge Schriftsteller über ihre literarischen Vorbilder*, ed. Jürgen Jakob Becker and Ulrich Janetzki (Berlin: Quadriga, 2000), 198–204; here, 198. Very similar phrasing occurs in "Und der Schatten dreht sich," *Die Presse*, 15792, *Spektrum* 3 (7 October 2000), and "Schattenbild," *Literatur und Kritik* 34, no. 331/332 (1999): 32–36.

[29] These are the German terms, without equivalents in English, for different subgroups of the Romani people.

[30] Vladimir Vertlib, *Das besondere Gedächtnis der Rosa Masur* (Munich: Deutscher Taschenbuch Verlag, 2007), 35. As an English translation does not exist as yet — an extract from the novel is published in translation for the first time in this volume — all translations are my own. Subsequent page references appear in parentheses in the main body of the text.

[31] Sebastian Wogenstein, "Topographie des Dazwischen: Vladimir Vertlibs *Das besondere Gedächtnis der Rosa Masur*," *Gegenwartsliteratur* 3 (2004): 71–96; here, 75.

[32] Leslie A. Adelson, "Touching Tales of Turks, Germans, and Jews: Cultural Alterity, Historical Narrative, and Literary Riddles for the 1990s," *New German Critique* 80 (2000): 93–124.

[33] Sander Gilman, "Can the Experience of Diaspora Judaism Serve as a Model for Islam in Today's Multicultural Europe?" in *The New German Jewry and the European Context: The Return of the European Jewish Diaspora*, ed. Y. Michal Bodemann (New York: Palgrave Macmillan, 2008), 53–72; here, 65.

[34] See Sander Gilman, *The Jew's Body* (New York: Routledge, 1991).

[35] See Arthur Williams, "W. G. Sebald: A Holistic Approach to Borders, Texts and Perspectives," in *German-Language Literature Today: International and Popular?*, ed. Arthur Williams, Stuart Parkes, and Julian Preece (Oxford: Peter Lang, 2000), 99–118.

[36] See Margaret Littler, "Guilt, Victimhood, and Identity in Zafer Senocak's *Gefährliche Verwandtschaft*," *The German Quarterly* 78, no. 3 (2005): 357–73. See also Katharina Hall, "'Bekanntlich sind Dreiecksbeziehungen am kompliziertesten': Turkish, Jewish and German Identity in Zafer Senocak's *Gefährliche Verwandtschaft*," *German Life and Letters* 56, no. 1 (2003): 72–88.

[37] Vertlib, "Nichtvorbildliche Lieblingsautoren," 198 and 203.

3: Terézia Mora, *Alle Tage*: Transnational Traumas

Anke S. Biendarra

OVER THE LAST TWO DECADES, interest in transnational writing has steadily increased.[1] A growing media coverage and the heightened interest of publishing houses have given authors of non-German or "hyphenated" origin a higher profile in the public sphere and the literary market place. Prestigious literary awards such as the Adelbert von Chamisso Prize — founded in 1985 — have promoted the reception of writers who publish in German although it is not their first language. In January 2010, Terézia Mora, whose highly acclaimed first novel *Alle Tage* (2004; *Day In Day Out*, 2007) is the focus of this chapter, won this important prize for her literary work to date and her manifold activities as a translator and mediator between German and Hungarian culture.[2]

Mora was born in 1971 in Sopron in Hungary, in the border region close to Austria where she grew up as part of the German-speaking minority. Having been brought up "in an Austrian dialect mixed with Hungarian," she learned how to formally write and read German only in high school.[3] When the borders were crumbling in the Eastern Bloc, Mora almost instantly took advantage of her "historical luck"[4] and made her way to Berlin where she has lived since 1990. Having two native languages, she is technically not an "exophonic" writer but a native speaker of a hybrid identity,[5] which made settling in postunification Germany easier and motivated her choice to make German her literary language. Mora first studied Hungarian literature and theater studies at Humboldt University, then script writing at the German Film and Television Academy in Berlin. She is also a well-known literary translator from the Hungarian and has translated works by István Örkény and Peter Esterházy, among others. Since 1998 Mora has worked as a freelance author writing prose, plays for the stage, and scripts for television.

Her literary work to date is characterized by thematic variety, a realistic style of narration that does not psychologize the characters, and an idiosyncratic aesthetic style. The eleven stories in her first book *Seltsame Materie* (Strange matter, 1999) are set in the same border region where Mora grew up. They realistically narrate what life is like in the provincial villages on the Hungarian side of Neusiedler Lake and tell of a crumbling world full of violence, alcoholism, and social marginalization. The stories are linked through their topography, individual characters, and mode of narration. While the themes of borders, violence, and flight are also present in *Alle Tage*, Mora's third book, *Der einzige Mann auf dem Kontinent* (The only man on the continent, 2009), is a surprising departure, dealing with the realities of the contemporary workplace in a rather humorous way. Through its main character, Darius Kopp, a congenial Sancho Panza figure who is lazy, scatterbrained, and hedonistic to a fault, the novel exposes the globalized IT world, its business practices, and the shiny surfaces and commodities of the neoliberal economy. With this very timely text, Mora has landed squarely in the center of the Berlin Republic.

Mora quickly has become a leading writer amidst a number of transnational authors from Eastern and Central Europe who have enjoyed a growing interest in recent years, leading Brigid Haines to speak of an "Eastern turn" in contemporary German-speaking literature.[6] Critics credit especially authors of a younger generation like Terézia Mora, Zsuzsa Bánk, Wladimir Kaminer, Ilija Trojanow (also in this volume), Dimitré Dinev, and others with adding important new voices and aesthetic influences to contemporary German-language literature, and argue that their works should be considered in multiple contexts, such as European literature, literature of trauma, or postcommunist literature.[7] Many critics also find these texts more innovative and interesting than those of native German authors.[8] One could find various reasons for these claims of supposed thematic and aesthetic superiority: most authors with a migratory background functionalize spoken language in a highly reflexive, innovative way, and their aesthetic decisions are often influenced by a tradition of oral narration and multilingualism, which leads to hybrid forms of literature.

The aesthetic practices of intercultural literature are illustrative of a greater variety of German-language literature where classifications based on origin and ethnicity are becoming increasingly moot. While many transnational writers of a younger generation no longer concentrate on the themes of cultural loss and transition that were once common for migrant writers,[9] this thesis is arguable with regards to Eastern and Central European authors. In novels such as *Wie der Soldat das Grammofon repariert* (2006; *How the Soldier Repairs the Gramophone*, 2008) by Saša Stanišić (also in this volume) or Marica Bodrožić's stories in *Tito ist tot* (Tito is dead, 2002), migration and displacement remain central themes. A certain nostalgia for a lost and imagined homeland laces the texts. However, one would indeed find it difficult to assign them a national or cultural specificity due to their literary style, which is equally true for *Alle Tage*. The novel is a compelling example of the way a number of texts create the new aesthetics of a "transnational" literature that seeks to eliminate the "national" in favor of the "global."[10] In this postnational literature, writing and translation are responses to living in a time when the boundaries between and within national cultures are becoming ever more fluid and porous.

War and Displacement

Literary critics met the aesthetic complexity of Terézia Mora's first novel *Alle Tage* and the challenges it poses the reader with an enthusiastic reception. "The one book you must read this fall," instructed Elmar Krekeler;[11] "a wondrous book," gushed Volker Weidermann;[12] "one reads and is intoxicated," wrote an enthusiastic Jörg Magenau.[13] Critics repeatedly commented on Mora's ability to remain in control of her many characters and their narrative digressions[14] and to narrate realistically fundamental topics like the migratory experience and the accompanying human condition.[15] Her realistic, dialogical, and fast-paced writing leads to a distinctly idiosyncratic literary style, as my analysis in this chapter will show.

Alle Tage tells the story of Abel Nema, a migrant from an unnamed Eastern European city "S." who, having just graduated from school, comes to the unspecified Western city "B." Shortly after he flees his homeland to avoid being drafted into the military, a civil war breaks out there; various clues in the novel point to the conflict in former Yugoslavia. To leave the time and setting of the novel deliberately vague is first and foremost a poetological decision, as Mora explains: "One cannot mention the Gestapo, the war in the Balkan region or 9/11 in a casual way. Such words dominate a text, it is about them, no matter what it seems to be about."[16] The nonspecificity of the setting and time of the novel — "let us call the time *now*; let us call the place *here*"[17] — also lends the fate of Abel and other marginalized characters an exemplary quality.

Mora's novel negotiates the topical problem of what it means to be a refugee in times of collapsing nation-states. While the political events remain opaque, Abel Nema and the displaced migrants populating the novel are paradigmatic stand-ins for the problems that ethnic and religious minorities experience when borders are redrawn and governments reconstituted. These problems are directly linked to globalization and its forces. In a globalized world, even civil wars do not remain local conflicts. They generally involve military contributions and financial commitments from various (Western) countries that in turn shape the conflict to some extent and often profit from it.[18] The novel exposes the human consequences that war, as one of the forces of globalization, imposes on the individual: displacement, loss, alienation, and violence are therefore central themes of the text. These forces are not abstract but are interwoven into the fabric of everyday life. Abel thus signifies what war does to us, even if we do not partake in it, and how we carry it with us after peace has been restored: "Abel is: the trauma."[19]

Mora has repeatedly commented on the importance of Ingeborg Bachmann's writing for her own work.[20] *Alle Tage* illustrates an aspect that was also a premise for Bachmann's *Todesarten* project; namely, the question of how violence is a structural principle inherent to our world: "It is a big mistake to believe that one is only murdered in a war . . . — one is murdered amid peace."[21] While Bachmann was primarily concerned with the origins of fascism and the experience of women, *Alle Tage* illustrates the injuries that stem from growing up in the totalitarian systems of communism and socialism, which, according to Mora, bring about an all-encompassing impoverishment of life.[22]

Abel's geographical displacement is another important aspect of his trauma. After his arrival in B., the outbreak of civil war prevents Abel's return to the homeland since the state in which he was born has been split: "And none of these three to five countries felt under any obligation to provide him with citizenship. The same held for his mother, who now belonged to the minority and could not get a passport. He could not leave here; she could not leave there. They phoned" (269). Abel effectively has become stateless and needs to make do in his new country while longing to go back to his homeland "twenty-four hours a day" (394). A victim of an armed conflict, Abel leads an existence in which the outrageous has become the everyday norm, as the novel's title alludes to in its quote of Bachmann's poem.[23] His political displacement, along with the private trauma of being rejected by his father and Ilia Bor, the love of his life, leaves him in a state of existential strangeness, both in his inability to connect and communicate with others as well as in the alienation he causes them.

Trauma and Language

While Abel is a cipher for the immigrant per se,[24] he does possess unusual characteristics that make his experience quite different from that of the average migrant. He speaks the language of the country — it is not clear whether its lingua franca is really German — and it takes him only a week after his arrival to organize "everything a man needs" (97). Much of his success is due to a "miracle that befell him" (73); namely, a gas accident that left him unconscious for three days and almost killed him. Afterwards, Abel realizes that he is now able to learn any language he studies and seeks out his fellow countryman Tibor who is a professor at the local university in B. He instinctively understands that Abel is a linguistic genius and recommends him for a prestigious fellowship that enables him to use the university lab and learn ten languages over the next four years, after which he starts writing a dissertation in comparative linguistics.

Given his talents, Abel Nema would appear to be an ideal *translator* — literally "the person who carries over from one place to another" — to bridge different cultures: he easily adapts to difficult living situations and more than once survives the odds stacked against him. But his wondrous gift comes with serious side effects that foreshadow his failing integration in the new country. He suffers from a form of Post-Traumatic Stress Disorder that leads to tachycardia and is characterized by shortness of breath, dizziness, fear of death, and "depersonalization" (336). Far from being only a medical diagnosis, the feeling of strangeness vis-à-vis the self becomes a metaphor for Abel's psychological state and his migratory existence. He constantly gets lost and has no sense of direction, which causes him to remain completely disoriented in the city he lives in for years. This lack of geographical orientation metaphorically mirrors his displacement in the world. He also has no sense of taste; his numb tongue — *lingua* in Latin — illustrates the merely utilitarian use of his ability. While Abel himself defines language as the order of the world and translation as action (390), his own life is ruled by stasis and the principle of happenstance[25] — which is another indicator that his abilities remain entirely theoretical.

For Abel, learning a language is nothing but a cognitive feat that can be mastered and perfected. It neither translates into intercultural competence and the ability to make true human connections, nor overcomes the social distance from others and his precarious existence as a stateless refugee. Like the lyrical "I" in Bachmann's poem "Exil," another important intertextual reference,[26] Abel drifts through all languages and remains mute, in keeping with his telling name Nema, derived from the Slavic *neme* (mute). Although he has no accent in any language, masking his true origin, he never loses the foreignness his wife Mercedes smells on him on their wedding day (12). Reminiscent of Albert Camus's existentialist novel *L'Étranger* (The stranger, 1942), Mora develops a "poetics of strangeness"[27] that connects many different elements in the novel but is most clearly personified in the main character, who illustrates the failures and the limits of language and communication.

Who Am I and If So How Many?

As the mention of Bachmann and Camus suggests, Terézia Mora alludes to a multitude of literary texts and spins an intricate web of intertextual references. She functionalizes classical and antique narrative patterns such as Dante's *Divine Comedy* and Homer's *Odyssey* and gives a particularly central place to the Bible. The biblical dimension of Abel's name underscores the linkage of language, alienation, and violence that is central to the text. As is immediately apparent, the name references the story of Abel and Cain who kills his brother out of jealousy (Genesis 4:2–16). The intertwinement of love and death is a basic structuring element of Abel's interactions with other people: "That is how it went; that is how it would go from then on: love or kill" (67). Abel's "worldly passion play"[28] is intensified by his direct equation with Jesus — he "looks like a beardless Christ,"[29] is thirty-three years old when he almost dies in a gang attack that occurs on a Friday, he bleeds from a chest wound, and has been hung upside down from a jungle gym. That three women find him, furthermore, adds to the impression of a crucifixion.

His name is also reminiscent of Babel, the cosmopolitan city whose hubristic inhabitants are punished by God with a confusion of their languages and a scattering across the world (Genesis 11:1–9). In addition to his name, the story of Babylon is further alluded to in the description of B. as the "*most pulsating metropolis of their hemisphere*" (96), and the multiplicity of narrative voices that present his story to the reader. By linking Babel and Abel, the novel gestures toward a failure of cultural diversity that is, among other things, represented in Abel's linguistic polyphony.

After taking a near-lethal dose of fly agarics that will leave him unconscious for three days, Abel starts to hallucinate. It is his state of intoxication that makes it possible to "reflect" on his life in this chapter, aptly title "Center" and the only one narrated by him. In his imagined dialogues with both his parents and his father's twelve lovers/disciples, he finally comes to terms with his private traumas. He also finds himself in front of an unnamed tribunal — reminiscent of the trial against Slobodan Milošević in The Hague — that has to decide whether he deserves to live.[30] The chapter culminates in a final conversation with Ilia and Abel's admission of his personal shortcomings, which has a cathartic effect on him: "My decade in hell is over" (398).

Throughout his life in B., Abel had assumed various aliases, which are summarized here in a hallucinatory dialogue with his imagined son:

> Your name is, he says, fading like an old photograph, your name is: Jitoi.
> Abel Nema alias El-Kantarah alias Vargas alias Alegre alias Floer alias des Prados alias I: nods.
> Right, I say. Amen leba. (398)

Two examples might suffice to illustrate the intricacies of Mora's referential system. On the plot level, "Abdellatif El-Kantarah or something like that" (93) refers to an Algerian student under whose name Abel rents a room in Konstantin Tóti's apartment. Yet "El Kantarah" is also the Arabic word for "bridge," which foreshadows Abel's study of languages and his work as a translator. "Celine des Prados," the name given to him at the beginning of his tribunal, is an (incomplete) anagram of "displaced person," and "Amen leba" a palindrome of Abel Nema.[31] Each of these names references a specific period in Abel's life, but the string of aliases indicates that he underwent no personal development. None of the identities he assumed by taking over somebody's room or passport had any real substance: they were all mere signifiers for his lack of a clear identity and his continuous alienation from his own self and others. The one exception is "Alegre" — "the happy one" in Spanish — an alias he assumes by marrying Mercedes. Despite the fact that their union is a fake, it provides Abel for the first time with valid papers and thus a sense of security.

Paranational Communities

Recent studies in sociology and cultural anthropology document that migrant populations in Germany show a high degree of cultural adaptation and integration. Yet they also indicate that many immigrants remain effectively caught between two worlds.[32] Due to limited contact, native Germans do not play a major role in transnational networks; instead, migrants develop individual strategies to carve out a social place in society. They rely on their own networks to facilitate and perform forms of "self integration."[33]

In its narration of Abel and his community, *Alle Tage* implicitly acknowledges this basic premise of the debate on migration; namely, that migrants hardly leave their own transnational microcosms of the immigration society. Most all of the characters Abel encounters seem to be of a different ethnic or national background; at least, there is hardly a "typical German" name to be found in the novel. In his private life, Abel moves exclusively in "paranational communities," which Azade Seyhan defines as groups "that exist within national borders or alongside the citizens of the host country but remain culturally or linguistically distanced from them and, in some instances, are estranged from both the home and the host culture."[34] Abel's only link to "mainstream society" is his later wife, but the names of Mercedes and her biracial son Omar suggest that her family has a migratory background as well.[35]

The novel portrays this dominance of paranational communities as a reality that does not warrant explicit discussion. Abel, his fellow migrants, and their stories simply *constitute* the entire text; their community, albeit labeled a "parallel society" by the mainstream, signifies the very center. Yet the absence of any nonmigratory characters — other than Mercedes and her academic friends to whom Abel never really warms — also suggests that the divide between mainstream and paranational community cannot be overcome. Abel "El Kantarah" remains suspended "in between": he *is* the proverbial bridge that Leslie Adelson has described as a trope used to keep two worlds apart.[36] That many of the characters either become victims (Abel, Konstantin, Kinga, Andre, Ilia) or perpetrators of brutal acts (Kosma, Kontra) leads to the conclusion that the divide between mainstream and paranational community creates displacement, alienation, and violence in the first place.

Narrative Structure and Literary Style

Mora devotes a chapter to each of Abel's companions, all of which provide background information about his upbringing and his attempts at integration. The characters and their own stories are vital since they propel forward a narrative that is characterized by happenstance and stasis on Abel's part. The way these others' stories encircle him provides the discursive structure of the novel — a narrative labyrinth in which Abel and the reader initially are equally lost. They also bring about the specific aesthetic quality of the text.

The chronological complexity that becomes apparent in the macrostructure of chapters and subchapters is matched by the intricacies of the narrative. The perspective constantly switches between the characters and an omniscient narrator. This aesthetic montage of competing voices leads to a simultaneity of information, commentary, and authentic sound bites, and a frequent change between linguistic registers. A passage from the subchapter "A Long Day's Night. Abel" from Chapter V ("Meat") that prefigures the imminent attack on his apartment by Kosma's gang illustrates this complexity:

> What did he (Abel) have in mind? Start a conversation, throw in a few psychiatric-hospital anecdotes picked up somewhere, ask, What's your name? Most likely he had nothing in mind. He has simply had many conversations with children lately, and it worked well.
> I can ask him any question as long as it's in Russian, said Omar to his grandfather in confidence.
> *Any?* Really?
> Any that comes to mind.
> And does he answer?
> As far as I can tell . . .
> Hmm, said Alegria. (I am a little jealous, I must admit.)
> But *this thing* — where was it going? At first you can't account for it; it's almost sociable: the curses, the brutal games. Later it starts moving in an unpleasant direction: they follow you home, write

> Motherfucker in the grime of the butcher's window. He looks so
> normal, said Mercedes years later, that it takes a while before you
> realize he's actually a magnet attracting things strange, absurd, and
> depressing. Once your fate goes off the rails, you bear the sign, said
> Kinga. He just laughed as if he didn't believe her. But this time he did
> notice something in the air and did his best to steer clear of it. (185–
> 86; amended translation[37])

The paragraph begins with a reporting commentary by the extradiegetic
narrator; the perspective then switches abruptly to a dialogue between
Omar and Mercedes's father Alegria who comments in parenthesis on his
mixed feelings regarding his grandson's admiration for Abel. The next
three sentences are arbitrary and could either be an autodiegetic thought
of Abel or an extradiegetic commentary of the narrator. Folded in is a
critical remark by Mercedes about her husband, which together with
Kinga's warning foreshadows Abel's subsequent behavior toward Danko
and his fate of almost being killed by the gang much later.

This technique of montage that Mora employs throughout leads to
vivid, realistic, and frequently filmic descriptions of an accelerated tempo,
not least because a dialogical mode of speech dominates. It is also a form
of storytelling in which both the characters and the omniscient narrator
constantly question the narratives' viability and accuracy:

> From the outside he looks like a perfectly normal man — correction,
> a perfectly normal *person*. Correction: delete the entire sentence,
> because Mercedes realized immediately that even the first part, *from
> the outside*, made no sense when applied to a *person* (man), so there
> was nothing left, nothing that would hold water. *Sometimes I doubt
> whether a single thought . . .* (328)

The reader is left with fragmented, sometimes confusing impressions of
Abel and his actions. The ensuing distance is programmatic because it
highlights Abel's interchangeability as a cipher. The aesthetic form of the
text draws the reader into a hermeneutic labyrinth that signifies Abel's
displacement, his enigmatic qualities, and his mental state toward the end
of the book: "strewn over the earth," "chopped up in chunks," "puzzled"
(355–56).

Spatiality, Mobility, Deterritorialization

The various stories that are related about the other characters mirror and
refract Abel and his attempts at integration by illustrating the negative
sides of the immigrant existence.[38] After his arrival in B., Abel first lives
together with two apartment-mates, an uncommunicative Scandinavian
student called Pal and the hypochondriac Konstantin Tóti. A fellow refu-

gee, the latter's compulsive attempts to help out other migrants turns their apartment into a "transit point" in the "world transit stream" (111), which ultimately leads to the temporary arrest of everyone in the household. Konstantin is Abel's negative projection: he is hardly able to support himself and his meager existence leads to bouts of hysteria and chronic sickliness. Konstantin initially has trouble learning the local language and never really improves (93, 112); the argumentative style that he incessantly broadcasts to his environment ("You are listening to Radio Konstantin. Politics, panorama, weather," 100) causes him to be in trouble often and makes him the victim of violent assaults.

Abel next moves into a chaotic apartment ruled by Kinga, a refugee he first met on the train to B. In obvious reference to their displacement, Kinga declares her apartment its own country, "Anarchia Kingania": "New countries were popping up all over the place; why shouldn't I have one of my own?" (141) Kinga, the "lady warrior" (132), is the most obvious contrast figure to the main character. She acts where Abel remains passive, is unlucky where Abel is blessed, and abused where Abel is loved. Her traumatic upbringing (140) and clinical depression eventually lead to her suicide.

Kinga personifies what sociologist Ulrich Beck has called "an artist of the frontier," a migrant who is highly functional in her own segment of society, functionally multilingual and combining social competence with the willingness to work for low wages. Migrants like Kinga and Konstantin (as well as Janda and Kontra) live a cosmopolitan existence in that they defy the necessity propagated by the nation-state to form a socially and culturally coherent resident population in which "citizens" and "foreigners" are clearly differentiated.[39] Yet the state's need for control ultimately precludes them from succeeding: they cannot receive papers authenticating their existence that would make their integration easier. The fact that none of the immigrants except Janda possess a valid visa is also an implicit criticism of Germany and the European Union's restrictive and ever-tightening immigration policies.[40] *Alle Tage* thus engages, similarly to the novels by Yadé Kara and Saša Stanišić (both discussed in this volume), with contemporary debates about citizenship.

The spatiality of Abel's living arrangements adds important aspects to the narratives of failed integration. The cramped, uncomfortable, and shabby apartments that Abel and his fellow migrants occupy are noticeably removed from the urban realm where the novel takes place. "B.," the *"most pulsating metropolis of their hemisphere"* (94), remains without any local specificity and plays little role for the characters. They move about without ever being anchored in it. Most obviously, this separation stresses again the missing link to mainstream society — Abel and his friends live in dilapidated apartments that not even Mercedes, Abel's sole link to an outside world, ever sets foots in.

Furthermore, it points to the deterritorialization of the migrant existence, i.e., the simultaneous penetration of local worlds by global forces and the dislodging of cultural subjects and objects from particular locations in space and time.[41] The lives of transnational migrants unfold on deterritorialized grounds because they draw on multilocal and imaginary sources and relations. They leave their own cultural realm, yet keep ties to it through transnational networks and communication via electronic media. Closely linked to deterritorialization are concepts of mobility, which are produced in a complicated interplay of political and social ideas, geographic realities, and legal ramifications. Migrants like Abel embody mobility while at the same time highlighting its ambivalent character. Tom Holert and Mark Terkessidis understand mobility not as an operation or an action but as a *state of being*. Immigrants who continue to keep present the imagination of a lost homeland exist perpetually in a "state of present absence": since a future return is impossible, life in the present becomes unfeasible as well.[42] Abel is a concentrated example of this paradox since he has kept alive the link to Ilia and an imaginary life in their hometown all along while in B.: "I could have lived my whole life in the same tree-lined street, a closeted homosexual teacher in the provinces, and been perfectly content" (392). Unable to let go of this connection and overcome his geographical and emotional displacement, Abel is perpetually suspended in a state of in-between. This shapes his life in myriad ways and becomes apparent in the many nights he spends at the Loony Bin bar where time seems neutralized, his disoriented wanderings through the city, and his grand tour, hitchhiking through Europe with Kontra's passport (338–41).

The ambivalence of mobility is also visible in Abel's provisional residences. His first apartment is in a labyrinthine, run-down student residential hall called "The Bastille" (92) that is reminiscent of the courthouse in Kafka's *Prozeß* (The trial, 1925) and provides nothing more than shelter. Kinga's apartment is an enclave whose changing migrant occupants stage a homeland in an attempt to reterritorialize their social space.[43] Different from Abel's other arrangements, living space in Anarchia Kingania provides both sociality and community building. However, since Abel moves out again and Kinga eventually dies, the apartment's function was only transient, confirming that mobility as a state of being plays out within specific, often paradoxical structures: "The living containers of mobility are a permanently temporary solution."[44] Consequently, Abel's room in the back of Carlos's butcher shop is soon ravaged by Kosma's gang; his last apartment that he takes over from someone named Floer without even bothering to change the name tag is derelict, furnished with a few tattered objects, "a broad field of virtually complete neglect" (405). In its utmost shabbiness and solitude, it signifies Abel's physical and mental spiraling downward and almost becomes his final resting place after his near-lethal dose of fly agarics.

Conclusion

Research in anthropology and diaspora studies that focuses on cultural phenomena often assigns transnational mobility and its associated processes a liberatory potential for undermining different structures of oppression. Diasporas and cosmopolitanisms are seen as forces against nationalism, repressive state structures, and exploitative capitalism. Accordingly, the deterritorialized subject becomes vested with agency, originality of vision, and the potential to break down both intellectual boundaries and the territorially bounded nation-state.[45] Such research, however, often does not take into account the continuing and paradoxical effects of nation-states within these globalized developments. In the stories of its migrant characters, *Alle Tage* illustrates how the limitations that the state imposes by refusing them legal status continue to discipline and control them. The novel reinforces this in its rather dystopian ending.

The violent attack by Kosma's gang leaves Abel physically handicapped and suffering from aphasia and amnesia. His previous knowledge of ten languages has been extinguished from his brain: "Contrary to expectations, he has recovered but one language, the local language, though in that language he can only generate simple sentences" (418). His favorite utterance, which brings him great joy, is the sentence he kept repeating after being cut down from the jungle gym: "That's good."

Abel's comment closely alludes to the final words God used when looking at his creation on the sixth day (Genesis 1: 31), which almost seems like a cruel joke, a cynical commentary by an omniscient and ultimately merciless Yahweh. Yet how the individual reader interprets Abel's transformation from destitute migrant to disabled but content family man depends on her own jadedness. While it is unclear how conscious Abel is of his situation, his reunion with Mercedes in a traditional family model that now includes a young daughter in addition to Omar might indicate happiness. Forgetting who he was seems to have settled his formerly ambiguous sexuality; he has finally found the peace that the traumas of his displacement made impossible. He lives completely in the present and only experiences momentary, sensual joys and feelings but no personal emotions or remorse, much like the French clerk Meursault in Camus's *L'Étranger*, who inexplicably shoots an Arab on an Algerian beach.

Yet one cannot overlook that Abel's traumas have been replaced by physical and mental injuries that cause him to be little more than a shell of a man who is still absent from his self and the life of his family. The parable-like ending suggests that existential strangeness will not cease unless people forget their origins and native languages. Transnational subjects such as Abel can achieve emotional closure and integration only at the expense of physical integrity, subjectivity, and agency. Within the narrative cosmos *Alle Tage* presents to the reader, notions of national belonging ultimately cannot be transcended, no matter how many languages one learns or how many borders one crosses. Consequently, the text undermines the notion that transnational mobility and its associated processes can set free any liberatory power. Like Meursault, Abel needs to feel "the gentle indifference of the world"[46] in order to be happy at last, even if the crowd of spectators at his attempted execution consists only of a gang of Roma teenagers.

Notes

Thanks to Leila Lehnen and John H. Smith for their helpful comments on this chapter.

[1] For the purpose of this chapter, I propose that transnational literature includes texts that transcend national boundaries in their awareness of the "processes by which immigrants forge multistranded social relations that link together their societies of origin and settlement," as laid out by Linda Basch, Nina Glick-Schiller, and Cristina Szanton-Blanc in *Nations Unbound: Transnational Projects, Postcolonial Predicaments, and Deterritorialized Nation-States* (London: Routledge, 2006), 7. Furthermore, I rely on Azade Seyhan's definition, which posits that transnational writing addresses issues facing deterritorialized cultures and speaks for "paranational" communities. However, her argument that it operates outside the national canon may not hold true anymore. Azade Seyhan, *Writing outside the Nation* (Princeton: Princeton UP, 2001), 10.

[2] Mora had already won the Chamisso-Förderpreis in 2000 for *Seltsame Materie*, for which she also received the Ingeborg Bachmann Prize. *Alle Tage* won the Förderpreis for Literature, Academy of Arts Berlin 2004; the Prize of the LiteraTour Nord 2004; Mara-Cassens-Prize 2004; and the Prize of the Leipzig Book Fair 2005. In 2009, *Der einzige Mann auf dem Kontinent* made the Long List of the German Book Prize.

[3] "'Don't cry, work.' Interview with Terézia Mora," online magazine *Foreigner.de*, www.foreigner.de/in_terezia_mora.html (accessed 14 January 2010). Unless otherwise noted, all translations from the German are my own.

[4] Anke S. Biendarra, "'Schriftstellerin zu sein und in seinem Leben anwesend zu sein, ist für mich eins.' Ein Gespräch mit Terézia Mora," *Transit* 3, no. 1: 1–9. escholarship.org/uc/item/2c83t7s8 (accessed 18 January 2010).

[5] Exophonic (or, alternatively, exophone) is an emerging term that has been used primarily to describe African literatures written in European languages. Following a suggestion by Yoko Tawada, Chantal Wright uses it as a collective label for non-native speaker writers from various countries. "Writing in the 'Grey Zone': Exophonic Literature in Contemporary Germany," *German as a Foreign Language* 3 (2008): 26–42; here, 39.

[6] Brigid Haines, "The Eastern Turn in Contemporary German, Swiss and Austrian Literature," *Debatte* 16, no. 2 (2008): 135–49.

[7] Brigid Haines, "German-Language Writing from Eastern and Central Europe," in *Contemporary German Fiction. Writing in the Berlin Republic*, ed. Stuart Taberner (Cambridge: Cambridge UP, 2007), 215–29.

[8] Martin Hielscher, for example, assigns transnational authors *Definitionsmacht* (the power to define things) in the literary market place, "Andere Stimmen — andere Räume. Die Funktion der Migrantenliteratur in deutschen Verlagen und Dimitré Dinevs Roman 'Engelszungen,'" *Literatur und Migration* [Sonderband, ed. Heinz Ludwig Arnold] text+kritik 9 (2006): 196–210; here, 207.

[9] David Coury, "Beyond the National: Sarah Khan and the Globalization of German Literature," *German Studies Review* 30, no. 2 (2007): 243–58.

[10] Coury, "Beyond the National,"244.

[11] Elmar Krekeler, "Der Rand der Welt ist ihre Mitte," *Die Welt*, 2 October 2004.

[12] Volker Weidermann, "Aus einer anderen Welt," *Frankfurter Allgemeine Sonntagszeitung*, 8 August 2004, 27.

[13] Jörg Magenau, "Mensch ohne Menschheit," *taz*, 6 October 2004, 9.

[14] Tilman Spreckelsen, "Panik ist der Zustand dieser Welt," *FAZ*, 6 October 2004, L 7.

[15] Meike Fessmann, "Das Gehirn des Gurus," *Der Tagesspiegel*, 19 September 2004, 28.

[16] Mora, "DAS KRETER-SPIEL, oder: Was fängt die Dichterin in ihrer Zeit mit dieser an," *Sprache im technischen Zeitalter* 183 (2007): 333–43; here, 339.

[17] Terézia Mora, *Alle Tage* (Munich: Luchterhand, 2004). Citations are from the translation, *Day In Day Out: A Novel*, trans. by Michael Henry Heim (New York: Harper Perennial, 2007), 5. Subsequent references appear in parentheses in the main body of the text.

[18] See Paul Michael Lützeler, *Bürgerkrieg global: Menschenrechtsethos und deutschsprachiger Gegenwartsroman* (Munich: Wilhelm Fink, 2009), especially chapters 1–4.

[19] Terézia Mora, interview by Tobias Kraft, in Kraft, "Literatur in Zeiten transnationaler Lebensläufe. Identitätsentwürfe und Großstadtbewegungen bei Terézia Mora und Fabio Morábito" (master's thesis, University of Potsdam, 2006), 106. opus.kobv.de/ubp/volltexte/2007/1295 (accessed 21 January 2010).

[20] Terézia Mora, "Die Masken der Autorin. Zum 80. Geburtstag von Ingeborg Bachmann," *Literaturen* 1/2 (2007): 30–35.

[21] Ingeborg Bachmann, *Wir müssen wahre Sätze finden. Gespräche und Interviews*, ed. Christine Koschel and Inge von Weidenbaum (Munich: Piper, 1983), 90.

[22] Mora, "DAS KRETER-SPIEL."

[23] "Der Krieg wird nicht mehr erklärt / sondern fortgesetzt. Das Unerhörte / ist alltäglich geworden" (War is no longer declared, / only continued. The monstrous / has become everyday). Ingeborg Bachmann, "Alle Tage," in *Ingeborg Bachmann, Werke*, ed. Christine Koschel, Inge von Weidenbaum, and Clemens Münster, vol. 1, *Gedichte/Hörspiele/Libretti/Übersetzungen* (Munich: R. Piper & Co, 1978), 46.

English translation from *In the Storm of Roses: Selected Poems,* trans. Mark Anderson (Princeton: Princeton UP, 1986), 53.

[24] Lyn Marven, "Crossing Borders: Migration, Gender, and Language in Novels by Yadé Kara, Jeannette Lander and Terézia Mora," *Gegenwartsliteratur* 8 (2009): 148–64; here, 163.

[25] Andrea Geier, "'Niemand, den ich kenne, hat Träume wie ich': Terézia Moras Poetik der Alterität," in *Zwischen Inszenierung und Botschaft. Zur Literatur deutschsprachiger Autorinnen am Ende des 20. Jahrhunderts,* ed. Ilse Nagelschmidt, Lea Müller-Dannhausen, and Sandy Feldbacher (Berlin: Frank & Timme, 2006), 153–77; here, 169.

[26] "Ich mit der deutschen Sprache / dieser Wolke um mich / die ich halte als Haus / treibe durch alle Sprachen" (I with the German language / this cloud about me / that I keep as a house / drive through all languages). Ingeborg Bachmann, "Exil," in *Ingeborg Bachmann, Werke,* 1:153. English translation from *In the Storm of Roses,* trans. Anderson.

[27] Klaus Siblewski, "Terézia Moras Winterreise. Über den Roman *Alle Tage* und die Poetik der Fremde," *Literatur und Migration* [Sonderband, ed. Heinz Ludwig Arnold], text+kritik 9 (2006): 211–21; here, 213.

[28] Siblewski, "Terézia Moras Winterreise," 218. Abel is attacked by a gang, a persecution that Siblewski attributes to the fact that they simply cannot stand his "foreignness."

[29] Mora, *Day In Day Out,* first page of unnumbered prologue.

[30] The most obvious reference to Milošević's trial is that Abel is seated in a bullet-proof-glass box. He is accused of being a "Balkan substance dealer" who has committed "mass rapes" (375) and other unspeakable crimes. He also conducts his own "defense" as the Serbian leader did.

[31] Kraft undertakes a convincing analysis of all of Abel's aliases in "Literatur in Zeiten transnationaler Lebensläufe," 42–47.

[32] I am referring to the Migranten-Milieu-Studie 2007/2008, which was paid for by the German government and administered by the SINUS-Institute. Analyzed in Carsten Wippermann and Berthold Bodo Flaig, *Lebenswelten von Migrantinnen und Migranten, Aus Politik und Zeitgeschichte* 5 (2009): 3–10; here, 5.

[33] Regina Römhild, "Confronting the Logic of the Nation-State. Transnational Migration and Cultural Globalisation in Germany," *Ethnologia Europaea* 33, no. 1 (2003): 61–72; here, 63.

[34] Seyhan, *Writing outside the Nation,* 10.

[35] What also speaks for this is that Mercedes's mother Miriam has known Tibor since their youth; Tibor is from the same city "S." as Abel.

[36] Leslie Adelson, "Against Between. A Manifesto," in *Unpacking Europe: Towards a Critical Reading,* ed. Salah Hassan and Iftikhar Dadi (Rotterdam: NAi Publishers, 2001), 244–55.

[37] The original translation reads: "It looks so normal . . . that it takes a while before you realize it's actually a magnet attracting things strange, absurd and depressing." This passage refers to Abel, but by using the pronoun "it" instead of "he," the

translation makes the text unnecessarily ambivalent. The German reads "Er sieht so normal aus . . . dass er in Wirklichkeit wie ein Magnet alles Sonderbare, Lächerliche und Traurige anzieht" (*AT*, 188). This is but one example for the challenges of translating Mora. The American translation does not always manage to convey the special character of the aesthetic montage of voices.

[38] Lea Müller-Dannhausen, "'. . . scheiß neue Lust am Erzählen!' Untersuchungen zum Erzählen in Terézia Moras *Alle Tage* und Antje Rávic Strubels *Tupolew 134*," in *Zwischen Inszenierung und Botschaft*, 197–214; here, 198.

[39] Ulrich Beck, *Der kosmopolitische Blick oder Krieg ist Frieden* (Frankfurt: Suhrkamp, 2004), 156–60.

[40] Germany accepted the biggest number of refugees of all the European countries during the Balkan wars of the 1990s (350,000), yet barely 80,000 remain. As an advocate of "temporary protection," Germany expects war refugees to return home as soon as the conflict is over. To prevent their permanent settling, Germany started to repatriate refugees in 1996, regardless of the still-desolate conditions in Bosnia and Kosovo.

[41] John Tomlinson, *Globalization and Culture* (Chicago: U of Chicago P, 1999), 29.

[42] Tom Holert and Mark Terkessidis, "Was bedeutet Mobilität," in *Projekt Migration*, ed. Kölnischer Kunstverein et al. (Cologne: DuMont, 2005), 98–107.

[43] Christian Sieg, "Von Alfred Döblin zu Terézia Mora: Stadt, Roman und Autorschaft im Zeitalter der Globalisierung," in *Globalisierung und Gegenwartsliteratur. Konstellationen — Konzepte — Perspektiven*, ed. Wilhelm Amann, Georg Mein, and Rolf Parr (Heidelberg: Synchron Verlag, 2010), 193–208; here, 205.

[44] Holert and Terkessidis, "Was bedeutet Mobilität," 105.

[45] Aihwa Ong, *Flexible Citizenship. The Cultural Logics of Transnationality* (Durham: Duke UP, 1999), 15.

[46] Albert Camus, *The Stranger*, trans. Matthew Ward (New York: Vintage International, 1989), 122.

4: Juli Zeh, *Spieltrieb*: Contemporary Nihilism

Stephen Brockmann

SINCE THE PUBLICATION OF HER FIRST NOVEL *Adler und Engel* (Eagles and angels) in 2001, Juli Zeh, born in 1974, has developed an impressive reputation in the German literary world as a writer and public intellectual. To date, Zeh has published three other novels: *Spieltrieb* (The drive to play, 2004), *Schilf* (2007; *Dark Matter*, 2010), and, most recently, *Corpus Delicti* (2009), based on a theatrical work by her that premiered in September of 2007.[1] In addition to her novels, Zeh has produced many essays; she frequently engages in political debate in German newspapers and magazines, and in 2005 she publicly supported the Social Democratic Party in the federal election. Zeh is eloquent proof that the younger generation of German writers is not necessarily averse to politics and does not always separate literary from political activity. Indeed, in a 2004 speech Zeh proclaimed that "literature per se has a social and, in the broadest sense of the word, political function," since it "bears the responsibility to close the gaps that are exposed through journalism's attempt to present a supposedly 'objective' — and therefore distorted — picture of the world."[2]

Zeh is also a legal expert. She has studied law and international relations in Germany and Poland, completed two *Staatsexamen*, interned at the United Nations in New York in 2000, and worked in Zagreb and Sarajevo in the aftermath of the conflicts in southeastern Europe in the 1990s.[3] Zeh's interest in the theory and practice of law have had an impact on her novels, in which legal issues play a prominent role. As a fourth area of professional activity, Zeh has also worked as an instructor at the Deutsches Literaturinstitut Leipzig (formerly the Johannes R. Becher Institut), Germany's major professional training program for creative writers, where she was once a student.

Nihilism

In all of her novels, Zeh is concerned with central issues of human existence in Europe in the early twenty-first century. The novels include ample references to current events in Europe and the rest of the world, from the wars in the former Yugoslavia, through the terrorist attack on New York on September 11, 2001, to the US invasion of Iraq in 2003. Zeh is particularly concerned with the problem of nihilism and the possibility — or impossibility — of creating functioning human relationships and social structures in the context of a world perceived by large numbers of its inhabitants as devoid of meaning. Zeh shares a concern with the perceived meaninglessness of contemporary life with other younger German authors, for instance, with Sibylle Berg, who, as Emily Jeremiah notes in chapter 9 of this book, writes about characters with "lives that seem arbitrary and pointless." For Zeh, the perceived lack of meaning in contemporary life extends even to the level of physical description. A typical sentence from *Schilf* describes a piece of interior decoration: "Somewhere a nihilist fountain is bubbling, and in its basin a few goldfish are swimming."[4] At another point in the same novel, the branches and leaves of an artificial plant are described as emitting an intense smell of absurdity (*Schilf*, 79). The physical world around the novel's characters seems to convey to them a message that comes from their own heads: the meaninglessness of existence. A characteristic sentence in *Spieltrieb* describes a moment of silence: "Something was in the air, and it sounded like: you will all die, and it will have no meaning."[5] Sebastian, one of the main characters in *Schilf*, believes that "the human is a hole in nothingness" (*Schilf*, 148). One can compare this to a character in Berg's novel *Ende gut*, who, as Jeremiah points out, proclaims: "we are the generation that is nothing."[6] As will become clear, Zeh also shares Berg's generational concerns. Both authors are centrally concerned with a younger generation that perceives life as fundamentally lacking in intrinsic value.

Even if Zeh's characters do not always articulate such thoughts, Zeh's narrators are likely to. Some characters, however, even — or especially — teenagers, are capable of voicing nihilist thoughts themselves. Some of these characters are avid readers of Friedrich Nietzsche, who, in the second half of the nineteenth century, had predicted that nihilism would dominate the intellectual future of Europe.[7] The eighteen-year-old Alev, one of the main characters in *Spieltrieb*, declares to the fifteen-year-old Ada, another key figure, that "Nietzsche is our great-grandfather, and even today we're squandering his legacy" (277). *Spieltrieb* begins with a question posed by the novel's narrator — characteristically, a judge named Sophie (i.e., wisdom) — about nihilism and nihilism's effect on the relationship between the younger and older generations:

> What if the great-grandchildren of the nihilists have long since moved out of the dusty store for devotional objects that we call our value system? What if they've left the half-emptied warehouses of value and significance . . . in order to return on game paths to the jungle, to a place where we can no longer see, let alone reach them? (7)

Twice during the course of *Spieltrieb*, Ada calls herself and her generation — people born in or after the 1980s — "the great-grandchildren of the
nihilists," both times in conversation with a representative of the older generation of her teachers (309; 492). In the first instance, Ada is in conversation with her respected history teacher Höfling, called Höfi by his students.
In a class discussion, Höfi tells Ada: "One can't talk to you kids . . . you're
terribly old-fashioned. Nihilists!" Alev tries to trump Höfi's criticism by
proclaiming that he and his generation have gone beyond the nihilists
because "at least the nihilists believed that there was something they could
NOT believe in." Höfi's conclusion about the younger generation is:
"There's only one thing left for you: *amor fati*, love for everything that
exists. I wish you the best" (309). Since he says this shortly before jumping
to his death at Ada's feet, Höfi undercuts his own advice. The second time
that Ada proclaims her generation to be the great grandchildren of the
nihilists, she is in conversation with her Polish-born German teacher
Smutek, with whom she is having an affair orchestrated by Alev as a means
of blackmailing and exerting power over the teacher. Smutek asks Ada:

> How then do you come . . . to the belief that nothingness is the
> vanishing point of all human striving?
> I never said that.
> Didn't you call yourselves nihilists?
> As far as I can remember, I once called us the great-grandchil-
> dren of the nihilists.
> So you believe in nothing.
> We no longer have anything to not believe in. The mathematical
> result is that we believe in everything. Everything is equally valid.
> (492)

Readers of *Spieltrieb* know what Smutek does not know: Ada has developed her ideas about her own generation in conjunction with Alev, and her
contention that everything is equally valid comes from Smutek's deceased
colleague Höfi, who had talked about "love for everything that exists."
Whereas a nihilist believes in nothing, Ada and Alev see their generation as
going a step further and believing in everything, with no criteria or hierarchy for declaring certain ideas or concepts more or less valid than others.
In German the words *gleich gültig* (equally valid) also imply the word
gleichgültig (indifferent). Höfi's advice to love the world and everything in
it has been transformed by his pupils into the belief in the meaninglessness
of the world and into an attitude of pure indifference. Ada's and Alev's
philosophy, in turn, has become part of the narrative machinery of the
novel, which starts with the narrator-judge Sophie's positing that Ada and
Alev might be correct in their evaluation of the younger generation, which
may therefore be separated from the generations that came before them.
The novel becomes a test case for whether Ada and Alev are right, as well

as an examination of contemporary life and interpersonal and intergenerational relations in a context devoid of moral structures.

Zeh's Novels

I will return below to *Spieltrieb* for a closer analysis. But first, a brief look at Zeh's other novels — *Adler und Engel*, *Schilf*, and *Corpus Delicti*, whose concerns are closely intertwined with those of *Spieltrieb* — is in order. *Adler und Engel*, the novel that made Zeh a well-known writer, is also about the younger generation, in this case people born in the early 1970s, around the same time as Zeh herself. Max, the first-person narrator and protagonist of the novel, is a once-successful expert in international law who has worked on the legal problems arising from the wars in the former Yugoslavia, and who is addicted to cocaine partly as a result of his relationship with a younger, mentally disturbed girl named Jessie. The novel starts shortly after Jessie has committed suicide, at a moment when Max has descended into depression and separated himself from contact with the outside world. The only exception is a psychology student and radio personality named Clara, who hosts a radio program called "About a Paltry World" that she calls "the program for the depressed, for nihilists, for the left-behind and the lonely, for atomic scientists, dictators, and the simple asshole on the street."[8] It is Max's desperate late-night call to this radio show after Jessie's suicide that sets the novel's plot in motion. Clara has a philosophy that comes close to Nietzschean nihilism and its correlate, the will to power. She declares that with her radio show she wants to teach people "how goddamn inconsequential everything is. That only one thing can bring us a little solace from grand, encompassing boredom: namely, power over other people" (*Adler*, 220). Both Clara and Max are in agreement that the "ultimate question" is: "Where do I come from . . . where am I going, and what in hell is the meaning of all this shit" (*Adler*, 221). Max's view of the law, meanwhile, is free of morality and even of a concept of justice. En route from Leipzig to Vienna, Clara questions him about his values:

> Didn't you ever, she said, have an idea of justice?
> No, I said.
> Of right and wrong?
> No, I said.
> Good and bad?
> No, I said.
> Are all lawyers like that?
> Yes, I said. (*Adler*, 174–75)

The content of this conversation conveys Max's — and by implication the legal profession's — lack of moral values, while the conversation's form suggests his inability to engage in real give-and-take with other people. In *Spieltrieb*, this kind of conversation is referred to as "glib talking at cross-purposes" (309), incapable of producing meaning. Although he is speaking about issues that have been important to the human race for millennia, and about which philosophers have written weighty tomes, some of which he probably had to read in law school, Max restricts himself to simple yes or no answers and does not enter into dialogue with Clara. Max was never an enthusiastic student of the law, to which he came more or less by chance; his experience with European integration and the development of international law in the 1990s has taught him that the enlargement of the European Union in effect meant the expansion of drug and other criminal trafficking throughout Europe. What sounds in public statements by politicians and policymakers like a noble goal — the creation of international law, the enlargement of the EU — winds up in fact to be an expansion of the supply of drugs, weapons, and the profits of criminals. This expansion is accompanied by horrific violence in the former Yugoslavia — violence to which Jessie, the woman Max loves, is a witness. Jessie, the daughter and sister of Viennese drug traffickers who happen to be in league with Max's law firm, kills herself in response to what she has witnessed and been a part of. Max, who had been indifferent to life at the beginning of the novel, tries to save Clara's life at novel's end, even though he has spent much of the last weeks tormenting her. In both its form and content, the novel suggests a younger generation acutely aware of the contemporary crisis of values and of moral hypocrisy. While *Adler und Engel* seems to end on a note of hope, Max's attempt to save Clara comes at the price of cooperating with the drug traffickers whom he had previously opposed. The novel also features a brief appearance by an Austrian artist — strongly resembling the real Günter von Hagens, whose so-called plastinated corpses have been displayed in various "Body Worlds" exhibitions throughout the world — who transforms human bodies into works of art. The corpse of Max's own former friend Shershah has also been recycled in this way, and Max considers himself guilty for Shershah's death. These ghoulish sculptures seem to suggest that human beings have no value beyond their basic materiality, and that whatever is left of them can be bought and sold on the market like any other object.

Schilf, which focuses on an older generation with similar problems, is an absurdist detective novel somewhat in the manner of Friedrich Dürrenmatt's *Der Richter und sein Henker* (The judge and his hangman, 1950) and featuring, like Dürrenmatt's novel, a high-ranking police officer, Commissar Schilf, who has only a short time left to live. Also like Dürrenmatt's novel, *Schilf* features a rivalry between two old acquaintances about the meaning of life and the universe — in this case, two physicists, one of whom believes in the theory of multiple universes, and the other of whom does not. The ethical implications of the theory of multiple universes turn out to be similar to the ethical approach of the young people in *Spieltrieb*: if there is no limit to the number of universes, then there is no meaning or responsibility for any decision or action, even murder. "According to your theory it's not just that the Creator doesn't have to make decisions; nobody does," proclaims one of the physicists (*Schilf*, 300). An action can happen in one world while remaining nothing but a hypothetical possibility in other worlds. The many-worlds theory is thus "a comfortable attempt to get around God" (*Schilf*, 298). The rivalry between the two physicists ultimately turns out to be a struggle between commitment to one's profession and to the world of the intellect (represented by the physicist Oskar) and commitment to one's family (represented by the physicist Sebastian); it also turns out to be a story of homosexual longing and of an absurd, random mistake: a murder committed because of a simple failure to understand a particular word. The misanthrope physicist Oskar, like Alev in *Spieltrieb*, conceives of "life as a game that one has to win" (*Schilf*, 60) and, when confronted with the fact of murder, reacts like the character Raskolnikov in Fyodor Dostoevsky's novel *Crime and Punishment* (1866): "Morality is the duty of stupid people" (*Schilf*, 124). *Schilf* bears a strong resemblance to *Spieltrieb* in its philosophical concerns and in its plot, which features a main character maneuvered by someone else into committing a crime. In *Spieltrieb* the teacher Smutek is induced by blackmail to have sex with his underage student Ada; in *Schilf* the physicist Sebastian is induced by the kidnapping of his son to commit a murder. Both novels suggest a world in which it is relatively easy to manipulate people, but in which even highly intelligent manipulators fail to account for the law of unintended consequences.

In the science fiction novel *Corpus Delicti*, Zeh envisions a political system, approximately in the middle of the twenty-first century, that has solved the problems of the present by instituting an ecologically sustainable dictatorship of health. Smoking and any other harmful activities are forbidden, and the state interferes massively in the private lives of its citizens, even going so far as to organize their mating activities. There are no more cars and highways, and ordinary people live in communities that are strictly separated from nature. Although the political unpleasantness of the late twentieth and early twenty-first centuries is a distant memory, various aspects of political life in *Corpus Delicti* recall the contemporary struggle between Western states and terrorists. In *Corpus Delicti*, the problem of terrorism is a fantasy created by the state in order to keep citizens in line; the novel's protagonist, a woman named Mia Holl, is accused and ultimately condemned for being the leader of a terrorist group that readers know she never had anything to do with, and which probably does not even exist. Mia's real crime is her public refusal to acquiesce in the state's total interference with her own and other people's lives. She is ultimately condemned to a fate that resembles "plastination": her body is to be frozen indefinitely. The novel ends with an ironic happy ending when Mia is "saved" by a pardon: instead of being disposed of and made into a martyr, she will be subjected to even stricter control by the state.

As in her other novels, Zeh paints a grim picture of contemporary European life in *Corpus Delicti*, and the novel is a warning to its readers about where this life may lead in the future. Heinrich Kramer, the journalist and television personality who is Mia's primary antagonist, describes European life in the late twentieth and early twenty-first century:

> After the great wars of the twentieth century a push toward enlightenment had led to the widespread de-ideologization of society. Concepts like nation, religion, and family rapidly lost their meaning. A great era of debunking began. To the surprise of everyone concerned, however, human beings at the turn of the millennium did not feel themselves to be at a higher level of civilization but rather alone and without orientation, i.e., close to a state of nature. Everyone was constantly talking about the decline of values. People had lost all sense of certainty and began to be afraid of each other again. Fear governed the lives of individuals, fear governed politics. People had neglected to consider that every act of destruction must be followed by an act of creation. What were the concrete results? A decline in the birth rate, an increase in diseases caused by stress, people running amok, terrorism. In addition, the overemphasis on private egotism, the disappearance of loyalty, and finally the collapse of social welfare systems. Chaos. Disease. Insecurity.[9]

This description comes close to Nietzsche's concept of an "Umwertung aller Werte" (revaluation of all values) and to the idea that nihilism is not a sustainable way of life. When old values are done away with, new values have to be introduced as a replacement. In *Corpus Delicti*, what comes to replace older values like *Nation, Religion, und Familie* is the value of health, both physical and mental. The state guarantees health and the absence of sickness, but in return it demands obedience to its own dictates. This leads individual nonconformists, such as Mia's brother Moritz, to question the value of a totally state-controlled life and to uphold the validity of individual choice.

In many ways, the world of *Corpus Delicti* resembles that of other dystopian novels such as George Orwell's *1984* (1949) or Aldous Huxley's *Brave New World* (1932) in its vision of a future characterized by the lack of individual freedom. Heinrich Kramer, Mia's antagonist, is a kind of Dostoevskian Grand Inquisitor: himself a nihilist, he grasps for power over other people as a value in and of itself and believes that human beings are unhappy with real freedom.[10] Both Mia and Kramer are nihilists, but Mia's nihilism has led her to an emphasis on individualism and choice, and to a reluctance to argue for any particular point of view, whereas Kramer's nihilism has led him to take on the role of a true believer.

Mia's brother Moritz answers the state's intrusion into his private life with an insistence on personal freedom, and for him the ultimate expression of his freedom is suicide. Since the state claims total control over his life, he removes his life from the state's control: "Yes, I can kill myself. Only if I can also make a decision in favor of death does the decision in favor of life have value."[11] In Moritz's suicide there is an echo of Dostoevsky's novel *Demons* (1873), a book that is centrally concerned with the problem of nihilism, and in which one character, the nihilist Kirilov, proclaims that he will commit suicide "to show my insubordination and my new fearsome freedom."[12]

Like *Spieltrieb*, *Corpus Delicti* also features a female judge named Sophie whose job it is to seek a workable mediation between individual desires and social life. *Corpus Delicti* shows Zeh to be a classic liberal in the sense that she supports human freedom against the state's demands for conformity. However, the novel also shows Zeh to have concerns that go well beyond the individual desire for freedom. This becomes clear in Moritz's emphasis on meaning that transcends personal pleasure. For him, a life without reference to anything but the self is just as meaningless as a life totally dominated by the state.

Spieltrieb

It is in *Spieltrieb* that Zeh addresses the problem of contemporary nihilism most forcefully and articulately. *Spieltrieb* is a contemporary boarding-school novel that bears a resemblance to Robert Musil's *Die Verwirrungen des Zöglings Törless* (The confusions of young Törless, 1906) in its focus on a group of students jockeying for power and position in the microcosm of the school and using their power to blackmail, control, and torment another person. In Musil's novel, three powerful students dominate, torment, and sexually abuse a less powerful student; in *Spieltrieb*, two students — the eighteen-year-old Alev and the fifteen-year-old Ada — blackmail their Polish-born German teacher Smutek (whose name means "sorrow" in Polish). Just as the students in Musil's novel are probably influenced by Nietzschean ideas about nihilism and power, so too Alev and Ada are convinced that the world they inhabit is meaningless, and that only power and domination can add spice to life. Alev and Ada — like Musil's students, in particular his protagonist Törless — are highly intelligent and articulate; unlike many other members of the contemporary younger generation, they read and reflect on thick, difficult works like Musil's *Der Mann ohne Eigenschaften* (The man without qualities, 1921–42), which Smutek has chosen as the primary object of study for his advanced German class. Ada is herself a contemporary incarnation of a person without qualities. She considers "great hatred and also strong love" — i.e., real feelings — "to be a sign of stupidity," and since she was twelve she has believed "that the search for meaning is nothing but a disposable by-product of the human ability to think" (19, 12). At the same time, similar to Ulrich in *Der Mann ohne Eigenschaften*, Ada believes herself to be not so much "an individual being as . . . a distillation of the *Zeitgeist*" (375). In other words, for Ada, as for some of Sibylle Berg's characters, the individual human subject is not, in Emily Jeremiah's words, "stable and intact." In concentrated form, Ada represents the ideas that dominate the contemporary world, and the only value she really believes in is honesty. She proclaims in her final speech to the judge Sophie, "In this transitional state, in a confused and incomprehensible world without rules, there is nothing more dangerous than lies and hypocrisy — and nothing more worthy of respect than honesty" (552). Honesty, for Ada, consists in publicly acknowledging the real state of the world: its lack of moral structure. This condition — nihilism — is the end result of liberalism, and the challenge of the novel will be to recreate some structure without eliminating liberalism.

Spieltrieb also resembles another twentieth-century Austrian school novel, Ödön von Horváth's Nazi-era *Jugend ohne Gott* (Youth without god, 1937), which deals with the conflict between an idealistic teacher and his nihilist students. Although Zeh never overtly refers to *Jugend ohne Gott* in *Spieltrieb*, the novel's central conflict between a teacher and his students recalls the conflict in Horváth's novel. *Jugend ohne Gott* is translated into English as *The Age of the Fish* because Horváth's protagonist and first-person narrator, a history teacher, often sees his students as having the expressionless, soulless eyes of fish. It is precisely as a kind of fish that Ada is often described in *Spieltrieb*. While he is having sexual intercourse with her, Smutek imagines her as a fish: "She was silent like a fish, cold like a fish" (481). Horváth's novel deals with the generational difference between a teacher who tries to communicate humanist values to his students, and a group of students who, because they have long since ceased to believe in such values, view their teacher as hopelessly old-fashioned and even silly. Smutek has the same problem with his students:

> As a teacher Smutek had internalized several insights about German youth that he now recapitulated. The result was not in his favor. These young people had no desires, no convictions, let alone ideals, they were not aiming for a particular profession, wanted neither political influence nor a happy family, no children, no pets and no home, and they longed neither for adventure and revolt nor for the peace and quiet of tradition. (348)

Both *Jugend ohne Gott* and *Spieltrieb* feature a court scene in which a teacher is accused of unprofessional behavior, and both end with the teacher leaving his school and journeying to foreign countries. In *Jugend ohne Gott* the teacher goes to Africa, partly in response to the racism of the students he once taught; in *Spieltrieb* Smutek goes with Ada, his former pupil, to southeastern Europe to explore the place where, for Zeh, contemporary Europe had its formative crisis — "into the wounded heart of Europe, the vivisected core of our history" (564).

Spieltrieb not only reflects the ideas of Nietzsche, Dostoevsky, Musil, and Horváth; it also gives a peculiar twist to contemporary game theory because Alev is an avid reader of Robert Axelrod's book *The Evolution of Cooperation* (1984) and fascinated by the idea of the "prisoners' dilemma." Alev, who asks Ada to read this book and inform herself about game theory, sees his entrapment and subsequent blackmailing of Smutek as a kind of iterative game in which Ada and Smutek, the two "prisoners," ultimately learn to cooperate with each other. Game-playing becomes important for Alev and Ada because in the absence of all values, the pleasure of the game becomes a reason for living. Alev proclaims, "the drive to play replaces religiousness, it rules the stock market, politics, the courts, the media, and since the death of God it has kept us mentally alive" (260). In playing his games, Alev can conceive of himself as a kind of god toying with human figures on a chess board: "After realizing that because of his receptivity to the temptation of power he was not suited to atheism, he was gripped by a new suspicion. If there was supposedly a god whom Alev could not locate in the sky above his head or in the earth beneath his feet or in the intelligence between his ears, then he himself must be god" (212–13). This is another echo from Dostoevsky's *Demons*, in which Kirilov declares: "If there is no God, then I am God."[13]

There is irony in Alev's self-glorification, since he is neither omniscient (as his history teacher Höfi is quick to point out with reference to his grades in school) nor omnipotent. In fact, as Alev readily admits to anyone willing to listen, he is impotent. Although he is physically beautiful and has a personality that attracts both boys and girls, he is incapable of sexual intercourse. Alev's flight into game theory and dreams of omnipotence, then, seems to be motivated at least in part by self-disgust and feelings of inadequacy. When he uses a dildo to put an end to Ada's virginity before her sexual intercourse with Smutek, he confesses to her: "You can surely imagine . . . that I would rather have done this in another way," and since he says this with tears in his eyes, he appears to really feel it.[14] In fact, Alev's concern with other people's sex lives seems largely motivated by his inability to have a sex life of his own. Smutek reacts scornfully when Alev, who sees himself as superior, presumes to give him a lesson about sex and power. Smutek's simple but effective riposte is: "What . . . do *you* know about it?" (412). Alev is so confident of his own power that he never seems to contemplate the possibility that Ada will ultimately fall in love with Smutek, her and Alev's victim. Nor does he take into account the fact that Smutek is physically stronger than he is. When, toward the end of the novel, Smutek beats him up after weeks of blackmail and voyeurism, Alev is surprised, as if, in spite of his intelligence, he had never contemplated this possibility (513).

What Alev, a believer in postmodernism, has failed to understand is the existence of a real world that lies beyond his control. In this real world, power is connected to physical strength and sex is connected to love. The school that Alev and Ada go to is named after Ernst Bloch, the philosopher of hope, and in the end it is the existence of the real world, with its basic human feelings, that offers a glimmer of hope. As Smutek tells Ada toward the end of the novel, "The great thing is that . . . whether you call reality an illusion, shadowboxing, or a language game, it doesn't make the slightest bit of difference" (488–89). Real wisdom, the novel suggests, consists in bringing our conceptions of the world into conformity with the world, and in connecting the older generation with the younger one, Smutek with Ada.

This is precisely what the novel's narrator, the judge Sophie, does. Sophie sees herself as a "mediator between word and world, since these two things have been in trench warfare with each other since language began" (518). Sophie is also a mediator between the two generations, and her presence exerts itself throughout the novel, from the introduction to the end. The novel itself thus comes to have something of the feeling of a language game, since, for instance, a part of Sophie's introduction — a variation on a theme from Musil's *Der Mann ohne Eigenschaften* — reappears later on in the novel as a composition read aloud by one of the girls in Smutek's German class (9–10; 440–41). When they hear this composition, the students in Smutek's class are described as looking at each other blankly, unsure whether this is a piece of "well-done homework" or "a voice from offstage" (442). No doubt with tongue in cheek, Zeh has Smutek assure this girl (clearly a stand-in for the author herself): "You have real talent" (442).

Conclusion

The picture that Zeh gives of the younger generation is quite different from the one given recently by Mark Bauerlein in his book *The Dumbest Generation*.[15] Bauerlein describes contemporary youth as largely ignorant of literature and incapable of serious thought; for them, the World Wide Web and its accessories have become ends rather than means. Bauerlein's "dumbest generation" knows virtually nothing about politics or society. Zeh's young people, on the other hand, are intelligent and conversant with literature and philosophy, and for them the Internet is just one more of many media with which they are familiar. They know about politics, but the world of morality and values is closed to them, and they see most adults as hypocrites because of their inability to admit their own lack of values. Ada expresses this in her reaction to the April, 2002, school shooting in Erfurt when she criticizes the adult world for its platitudes ("We are shocked and deeply moved and hope that the government will do something") and not expressing the reality of the situation:

> Thus the truth went unheard. The fact that the nation had reason for joy was not mentioned. There was cause for nationwide celebrations and for the creation of a legal holiday in view of the fact that shooters like the one in Erfurt didn't mow through the world much more frequently. In spite of the rat-cage crowdedness in which people had to vegetate in this country, in spite of pH-neutral pedagogues who themselves preserved none of the values which it had once been their task to pass on, in spite of the eternal misunderstanding between liberalism and indifference, in spite of a population whose primary concern was getting on each other's nerves, citizens lived day-in and day-out in relative peace with each other. No one gave thanks for that. (199)

These are thoughts that are unlikely to occur to most fifteen-year-olds, and Zeh could be faulted for making her main characters — Ada, Alev, Smutek, and Höfi — into figures who represent primarily philosophical concepts such as nihilism or idealism. In this sense, Zeh is no doubt influenced by her predecessors Dostoevsky, Musil, and Horváth, who had all represented the crisis of modernity and the destruction of traditional values in their novels. The difference for Zeh and her characters is that the crisis of western values is now over a century old and is hence a repetition rather than something new; Zeh's main characters are aware that they are not the first people to have dealt with these problems. Zeh presents a Western world that has come, albeit imperfectly, to live with itself in relative peace, if not in absolute comfort and happiness, in spite of its lack of traditional values. As Commissar Schilf understands, the real question is one of *Weitermachen* (keeping on; 154). In the end, Zeh's characters find a path away from nihilism and toward a cautious, knowing belief in liberalism and basic human values like decency and love: they learn to make a distinction between liberalism and indifference. Their belief, far from being naïve, is presented as the fruit of bitter experience. In *Spieltrieb*, the judge Sophie tells Ada that truth itself is something "that one had to believe in, and among human beings who had lost their ability to believe, there was no more truth. And without truth no judgment" (540). Commissar Schilf asserts something similar: "Someone who fundamentally doubts the essence of reality, doubts himself into despair just like someone who gets lost in a maze." The result is that "whoever believes nothing, can know nothing" (170). Both literature and law, for Zeh, have the function of mediating between reality and the inevitably linguistic ways we interpret it, and of suggesting the existence of a few basic principles in which even skeptical liberals can believe.

Notes

[1] See Patricia Herminghouse, "The Young Author as Public Intellectual: The Case of Juli Zeh," in *German Literature in a New Century: Trends, Traditions, Transitions, Transformations,* ed. Katharina Gerstenberger and Patricia Herminghouse (New York: Berghahn, 2009), 268–84; here, 270.

[2] Cited in Herminghouse, "The Young Author as Public Intellectual," 277.

[3] Herminghouse, "The Young Author as Public Intellectual," 269.

[4] Juli Zeh, *Schilf* (Munich: Random House, 2009), 237. All translations from Zeh's novels are my own. Subsequent page references appear in parentheses in the main body of the text, cited as *Schilf.*

[5] Juli Zeh, *Spieltrieb* (Frankfurt: Schöffling & Co., 2004), 309. Subsequent page references appear in parentheses in the main body of the text.

[6] Sibylle Berg, *Ende gut* (Reinbek bei Hamburg: Rowohlt Taschenbuch Verlag, 2005), 100.

[7] Friedrich Nietzsche, *Der Wille zur Macht: Versuch einer Umwerthung aller Werthe (Studien und Fragmente),* ed. Elisabeth Förster-Nietzsche (Leipzig: Naumann, 1901), 5.

[8] Juli Zeh, *Adler und Engel* (Frankfurt: Schöffling & Co., 2001), 75. Subsequent page references appear in parentheses in the main body of the text, cited as *Adler.*

[9] Juli Zeh, *Corpus Delicti* (Frankfurt: Schöffling & Co., 2009), 88–89. Subsequent page references appear in parentheses in the main body of the text, cited as *Corpus.*

[10] See Fyodor Dostoevsky, *The Brothers Karamazov,* trans. Larissa Volokhonsky (San Francisco: North Point Press, 1990).

[11] Zeh, *Corpus Delicti,* 94.

[12] Fyodor Dostoevsky, *Demons,* trans. Richard Pevear and Larissa Volokhonsky (New York: Knopf, 1994), 619. It is perhaps a testament to the contemporary German preoccupation with nihilism that another recent novel by a younger author takes its title from the same Dostoevsky character. Andreas Maier, *Kirillow* (Frankfurt: Suhrkamp, 2005).

[13] Dostoevsky, *Demons,* 617.

[14] Zeh, *Spieltrieb,* 293. Oskar in *Schilf* acts for similar reasons: he traps his friend Sebastian because of unrequited love. See Zeh, *Schilf,* 279.

[15] Mark Bauerlein, *The Dumbest Generation: How the Digital Age Stupefies Young Americans and Jeopardizes Our Future* (New York: Jeremy P. Tarcher/Penguin, 2008).

5: Daniel Kehlmann, *Die Vermessung der Welt*: Measuring Celebrity through the Ages

Rebecca Braun

WHEN *DIE VERMESSUNG DER WELT* (Measuring the world) appeared in 2005,[1] Daniel Kehlmann could hardly have been described as a new writer. He had already published three other novels, a novella, and a collection of essays, with the most recent previous novel, *Ich und Kaminski* (Kaminski and I, 2003), achieving a print run of thirty thousand copies in hardback alone.[2] However, where the author had spent the previous ten years slowly making a name for himself in publishing circles, now he suddenly became a household name even for those with only a passing interest in German literature. The novel spent thirty-five weeks at the top of the *Spiegel* bestseller list and was quickly translated into over forty different languages, while Kehlmann was awarded numerous prizes and called upon to give countless media interviews. Indeed, over the following months he was repeatedly confronted with his own authorial persona to such an extent that he made the public's interest in the famous author into a guiding theme of both his Göttingen poetics lecture series, *Diese sehr ernsten Scherze* (These very serious jokes, 2007), and his next prose work, *Ruhm* (Fame, 2009). *Die Vermessung der Welt* thus marks the beginning of a new stage in Kehlmann's career that coincides with the point at which he was publicly "made" as a noteworthy young author. He entered into the world of international literary acclaim and the processes of celebrity and intellectual fetishization that this entails.

The spectacular success of *Die Vermessung der Welt* encourages us to think about the nature of what I am terming, following the celebrity studies scholar Chris Rojek, "celebrification."[3] Celebrity, as a product of sophisticated mediation, relies on the way in which a famous person is both socially removed from the public and yet appears so familiar in all the intimate aspects of his or her personality as to be a part of our everyday lives. This curious mix of social distance and personal proximity is maintained by the "celebrifying" media, which prioritize image over substance. Their coverage concerns the way in which a person represents public achievement, rather than offering an in-depth engagement with the achievement itself, and thus for many cultural critics, such as those of the Frankfurt School, celebrity is a fundamentally empty phenomenon that reflects negatively on the nature and quality of human relations in contemporary society.[4] Fame and its allure are by no means restricted to the modern era with its emerging communications industry, of course, but celebrificatory processes have become particularly powerful within today's media-dominated world, where they can significantly determine which images of achievement are widely disseminated and discussed.[5] While there has been a great deal of research into how these images exist within popular culture, the link between celebrity and high culture has been considerably less well investigated. Notably for our purposes, the way in which literary authors can become celebrities of sorts, figures who are subject to mediation and appropriation by a broad-based reading public, has received very little sustained attention.

Kehlmann's recent experiences as a young writer who was suddenly subjected to extensive and prolonged media interest following the success of a novel that very clearly deals with fame can give us some insight into the phenomenon of highbrow, specifically literary, celebrity in the German context. The local specificity of my argument is important here. For unlike the Anglo-American context, German literature has remained relatively resistant to the "middlebrow" and the emergence of bestselling "star authors" that this kind of literary fiction accommodates.[6] This is because in Germany a serious understanding of literature's social purpose was historically dominant well into the 1990s, with the result, on the one hand, that the idea of the author as a popular identificatory figure in the manner of other celebrities has seemed a particularly unlikely phenomenon. On the other hand, however, precisely the author's elite status as a serious cultural figure for the intellectually aspiring has rendered him or her a far more publicly celebrated figure among a broadly based, middle-class, educated cohort than his or her Anglo-American counterparts, and it is precisely this sort of covert celebration within the self-consciously highbrow literary realm that characterizes my understanding of literary celebrity. The significance of celebrity for Kehlmann's literary career goes beyond merely investigating the book's status as a bestseller and the history of its author's media reception, however — the primary way in which Kehlmann scholarship has dealt so far with the question of fame. The idea of celebrity and the aesthetic techniques that underpin the celebrificatory process are, I argue below, what made the book so popular in the first place. It is characterized throughout by an anachronistic celebrificatory gesture, which, for reasons this essay will elucidate, has gone tellingly unnoticed in discussion about the text to date.

Die Vermessung der Welt and Measuring Celebrity as Textual Practice

Recurrent in the numerous early analyses of the novel's success is the contention that its subject matter — the lives of two early nineteenth-century German scientists, Alexander von Humboldt and Carl Friedrich Gauß — makes it an unlikely candidate for mass appeal.[7] Intellectual achievement in general, and mathematical formulae and geophysical exploration in particular, do not obviously lend themselves well to popular public consumption. For many, the book's success must consequently be attributed partly to a quirk in the market, and partly to the unusually entertaining writing style that Kehlmann develops in spite, rather than because, of his subject matter.[8] As the English-language book jacket claims, he "bends time and space to bring these two enlightenment geniuses to life."[9]

Yet Kehlmann's subject matter is only superficially arcane, while his entertaining writing style is in fact a direct result of his choice of content. He is not making any serious attempt to convey complex scientific formulae. Rather, it is the lifestyle of the intellectual as he negotiates the demands of science on the one hand and society on the other that lies at the heart of the text. This is borne out in a heated exchange between Humboldt and Gauß, as the different ways they have led their lives and pursued their widely admired research are contrasted:

> Projects, snorted Gauss. Plans, intrigues. A whole palaver with ten princes and a hundred members of the Academy before you were even allowed to put up a barometer somewhere. It wasn't science.
> Oh, cried Humboldt, so what was science then?
> Gauss pulled on his pipe. A man alone at his desk. A sheet of paper in front of him, at most a telescope as well, and a clear sky outside the window. If such a man didn't give up before he reached an understanding, that, perhaps, was science. (212)

Throughout the text, the two main characters represent two quite different approaches to how they set about mediating themselves and their research to their contemporaries. Humboldt is from a very young age aware of his public image, or, as his elder brother later states, "We were inculcated early with the lesson that life requires an audience" (227). After he has acted out the "correct" display of grief at his mother's death bed and left his visiting card with the great Weimar intellectuals at Goethe's salon, he sets out consciously to leave his mark on the world, for, as he writes to his brother, "The world needs to learn of me. I doubt very much that I am of no interest to it" (41). In so doing, he is particularly aware of maintaining the right kind of lifestyle for popular public consumption, and the way in which he deliberately does this provides a great deal of humor throughout the text. Throughout his Latin American travels, he keeps a diary that edits out any unfavorable elements of his adventures. As he explains to his companion Aimé Bonpland, "he'd thought a lot about the rules of fame. If it was known that a man had had fleas living underneath his toenails, nobody would take him seriously. No matter what his achievements had been" (93). Likewise, he writes regular letters home, to be published in the world press, that detail his exploits, and he places a higher value on ensuring the longevity of his public image than his personal health. Immediately after he has climbed Mount Chimborazo, "Humboldt wrote two dozen letters, in which he made Europe party to the news that he had climbed higher than any mortal who had ever existed. Carefully he sealed each one. Only then did he lose consciousness" (153).

The fictional Humboldt's acute awareness of his public image is what makes Kehlmann's description of this historical character stand out from all other biographical accounts, and it is also what makes the novel so appealing for a contemporary audience. His actions are rendered as readily accessible as those of someone who is deliberately tapping into celebrity processes to further his career. Such cynical manipulation is for most readers a distinct characteristic of the late twentieth century, and it seems amusingly inappropriate to the serious search for knowledge generally believed to characterize the Age of Enlightenment. Indeed, the text makes clear that Humboldt is unusual among his contemporaries. His constant attention to mediating a certain image of himself to a large public audience is not shared by Bonpland, who is little more than a sidekick to Humboldt's burgeoning celebrity in the text. When Bonpland takes exception to the American president's reference to "Herr von Humboldt's journey," remarking "Why not the Humboldt-Bonpland journey? Or the Bonpland-Humboldt journey? The Bonpland expedition?" (180), Humboldt's superior talent at cultivating himself as a celebrity is thrown into sharp relief. Bonpland remains faceless for both his contemporaries and the twenty-first-century reader because he is entirely uninterested in making a particular impression upon anyone. He barely documents anything, composes a farewell letter only under duress, and appears clueless regarding how to deal with the effects of fame when it does finally come, as his unhappy end in Paraguay confirms. Humboldt, meanwhile, attracts ever more media, public, and political attention wherever he lands, thanks to his flawless self-publicity. By the end of his career, he has easily rivaled the Weimar intellectuals in terms of both local political power and international public presence, to the point of having become legendary among the next generation of scientists well before his actual death.

Carl Friedrich Gauß, on the other hand, represents a markedly different approach to managing one's public image and intellectual legacy for the world. Unlike Bonpland, he understands the workings of celebrity only too well. Significantly, he is also endowed with an uncanny ability to view his own times and achievements from the standpoint of the twenty-first century, again bringing an anachronistically contemporary perspective to his sense of self. It is thus not ignorance of the celebrificatory process that makes him reject the trappings of fame but a deep-seated scorn regarding the wider public and the pace of human progress in general. In direct contrast to Humboldt, the lesson he has taken from his youth is that the vast majority of one's contemporaries are woefully incompetent in all matters scientific and that trying to communicate one's higher intellectual insights to virtually any audience is a depressing and ultimately fruitless task. Consequently, he does not seek media dissemination for his discoveries, actually going so far as to neglect to make public those that are of more obviously practical use. When the young Weber encourages him to exploit their early telegraph system to become "rich and famous," Gauß is thoroughly dismissive: "He was already famous, replied Gauss, and actually quite rich too. The idea was so obvious that he was glad to leave it to the numbskulls" (242).

Fame, in fact, seems tediously inevitable for Gauß, who attaches no importance to the opinion of the wider world and would most like to be left alone by it. While Humboldt does his utmost first to make his name and then to maintain it, Gauß focuses solely on his mathematical research, quietly aware of his incredible talent, but only prepared to push himself forward when either his research or his financial circumstances require it. Thus, he convinces Pilâtre de Rozier to let him accompany him on his balloon flight by bluntly stating, "his name was Gauss, he wasn't some nobody, and before long he would be making discoveries that would equal Isaac Newton's. He wasn't saying this out of vanity, but because time was getting short" (52). Purely out of financial necessity, he later turns his attention to astronomy, which duly makes him famous, for, as Gauß is perfectly well aware, "a man who enlarged the horizons of mathematics forever was a curiosity. But a man who discovered a star was a made man" (121). From Gauß's perspective, being admired by the public is a necessary evil of his circumstances, rather like the visions he has of future scientific and technological advances that make living in the present so wearisome. It is an uncomfortable side effect of his great intelligence on the one hand, and of the basic financial realities of his life on the other.

In fact, Gauß's uncanny visionary ability combined with his open scorn for the world in which he lives allows him to function in the text as an outside, criticizing instance with regard to the emerging rules of celebrity and social intercourse by which all the other characters abide. Unlike Humboldt, who is sometimes carried away by his Enlightenment ideals to claim a hasty victory (such as having climbed the highest mountain in the world) or to make a rash projection for the future (the sun would never burn out; 187), Gauß's discoveries and visions are never off the mark and are pronounced with striking authority. Thus, if Humboldt provides an entertaining case study in how one successfully manipulates celebrity processes to further one's scientific and public career, Gauß provides a cold critique of such opportunism. Tellingly, Humboldt eventually learns the perils of embracing celebrity too enthusiastically and is forced to concede that Gauß's horror of attending large receptions may have been well-founded. His Russian journey is hampered from the start by the way his public image precedes him, so that he is barely able to conduct any research at all and is forced instead to attend countless tours, balls, and dinners in his honor. Exasperated and exhausted in Moscow, he concedes that the celebrity circuit with its prioritization of image over substance has overwhelmed his serious scientific persona: "Talk and chatter, whispered Humboldt in Ehrenberg's ear, no science. He must remember to tell Gauss that he understood much better now" (249).

Yet it is not just Humboldt who gains a different perspective on his life by the end of the text. If he in his old age adopts an unexpected degree of humility and gradually comes to realize that pushing oneself into the public eye is not always the best route to realizing one's ambitions, Gauß makes an equal step back into the realm of the ordinary mortal. Increasingly hampered by his ill health and the onset of old age, he begins to grow more tolerant of at least a small section of society (his second wife and son, his young scientific assistant Weber), more accepting of other forms of intellectual endeavor (he starts reading Pushkin and learning Russian), and ultimately quite contentedly philosophical about the passing of time and his own life. With this, both characters make a fundamental shift from the lofty ambition of measuring and, it can be understood, mastering the world to measuring the highs and lows of their own lives. The final, self-aware perspective that the text offers of its two protagonists, explicitly questioning how they have related to the world and evaluating their intellectual achievements, completes its focus throughout on the idea of celebrity. It is not just that both characters reach a position of ironic self-knowledge with regard to the way that they have been, for better or for worse, celebrified within their life and times. For the reader, the text's own dependence on celebrificatory processes becomes apparent in this final shift of perspective, as the very question of perspective is bought into focus. An aesthetic manipulation of celebrity lifts what would otherwise be an entertaining but rather lightweight critique of the phenomenon into a more nuanced engagement with it.

In his essay on Daniel Kehlmann, Robert Menasse describes the aesthetic effect of Kehlmann's texts as making the reader "feel ironic." Generalizing out from Kehlmann's essay on Voltaire, he explains how the texts draw on what he deems a new kind of irony that produces:

> a productive distance, where I don't see myself as complicit with the author in respect to an object (for example in respect of Voltaire), but rather as complicit with the object (with Voltaire) in respect of the

world, which is so completely different to how Voltaire feels it should be. This distance that opens up between me and the world when I identify with Voltaire is what allows me a sense of ironic amusement, ease, and insight into my contemporary situation.[10]

Such a play with distance is one of the main aesthetically noteworthy aspects of *Die Vermessung der Welt*. As a number of critics have observed, Kehlmann employs indirect speech throughout the text precisely in order to avoid the peril of artificial dialogue distancing the reader from the characters. What for these critics is a key feature in Kehlmann's successful manipulation of the historical novel is in my reading more important for the way it allows the text to tap into twenty-first-century celebrity processes. The suggestive nature of indirect speech — summing up the gist of an utterance but not attempting to recreate the actual words used — invites the reader into the minds of the characters to fill in for him or herself how the dialogue is actually unfolding. With this, Kehlmann's text offers a direct conduit into the minds of two of the Enlightenment's greatest thinkers: it allows the reader to shift perspective on his or her world by appropriating an alternative, and quite probably more flamboyant, lifestyle. Furthermore, Kehlmann makes striking use of prolepsis to make further ironic nods to the modern-day reader's world. Gauß repeatedly envisages how society and technology will have developed in three hundred years time, while both Gauß and Humboldt imagine how they will be remembered by later generations. The result of such clear references to the reader's contemporary situation is to make the world of the fictional characters appear oddly foreign and yet humorously familiar at the same time: in identifying with the historically famous characters as they are mediated through the text, the reader can enjoy the process of vicariously consuming the lifestyles of these iconic figures, and in so doing gain a temporary distance from his or her own world.

The way in which the text facilitates personal identification with Gauß and Humboldt amounts to an aesthetic (as opposed to thematic) enactment of celebrificatory processes, directed now primarily at the reader as the consumer of celebrity, for the text's popular public success lies in the way it makes Gauß and Humboldt into exotic figures with whom one can nevertheless identify. In so doing, it makes its own engagement with celebrity more subtle than the simple thematic engagement with fame outlined above could achieve alone. Where Humboldt's vain will to celebrity and Gauß's scornful approach to his admiring public imply, much in the vein of the Frankfurt School, that celebrity is an empty phenomenon that ultimately works against both the interests of true science and public communications of real substance, the text's own celebrity aesthetics tell a rather different story. The success of the text is predicated on the reader enjoying the sense of escapism that consuming celebrity allows, and

Kehlmann's writing style, with his entertaining use of prolepsis and the widespread employment of indirect speech, is directly orientated toward such readerly fulfillment. Iconic figures from the past are brought back to life in a world that is uncannily similar to our present. Repeatedly playing with distance and perspective to titillate its reader, the text thus becomes a sophisticated celebrificatory medium, and Humboldt and Gauß function as startlingly contemporary celebrity figures. Thus, the act of communicating fame emerges from this text as a rewarding creative process for all involved.

Celebrity Intellectuals and Processes of Fetishization in the Contemporary Literary Market

The quirk in the market that some analysts believed to underlie the success of *Die Vermessung der Welt* is thus in my reading the result of a mainstream public readiness to participate in the modern-day phenomenon of celebrity into which Kehlmann's text directly plays. Those who felt that the author was trivializing science or misrepresenting history are not necessarily wrong, but they are off the mark with regard to the significance of his actions.[11] In making Humboldt and Gauss into his protagonists, Kehlmann has chosen two lead figures who unite intellectual seriousness with a certain cultural iconicity that for the modern-day reader invites retrospective celebrification. It is this unusual combination of the highbrow and the lowbrow, in both subject matter and literary form, that makes the text stand out both from other works of literature and from popular fiction. In its thematic focus and aesthetic construction, *Die Vermessung der Welt* is, and was always intended to be, an acutely contemporary text.

In fact, an entertainingly ironic gesture toward its own contemporary context defines much of Kehlmann's work. In discussion, the author has repeatedly drawn attention to his "Kritikersatire" (satire on the critics) *Ich und Kaminski*, which deals with the intellectual emptiness at the heart of the art world, where imposter artists and critics alike can have celebrated careers precisely by blurring the line between derivative work and serious artistic pursuits. Kehlmann was motivated to write the piece because his earlier work *Der fernste Ort* (The farthest place, 2001) had been, in his opinion, entirely misunderstood by a wide spread of literary critics who failed to read past the dust jacket and wrote reviews, albeit positive ones, that quite misrepresented the text. In the resulting 2003 satire, the contemporary art world is shown to be easily manipulated by a charlatan critic who understands that making one's name as a cultural authority is largely a matter of name-dropping and spinning an attractive narrative, and has nothing to do with substantive engagement with the actual art. With this, Kehlmann highlights what Pierre Bourdieu terms the "circle of belief" germane to artistic production and satirically reveals the way it determines how artistic output and artists themselves are valued.[12] People buy into art largely as an intellectual idea and artists can amass considerable symbolic capital simply because the public is prepared to honor them accordingly. This is an inherently fetishizing approach: the artist is celebrated for the way in which he or she apparently single-handedly authors the great work of art while the public remains willfully blind to the many more mundane factors that have significantly facilitated artistic output and in so doing helped "make" the artist. Within this context, Kehlmann infers, the clever critic in today's fast-paced media world is not the one who immerses himself in understanding the artwork, but the one who knows how to profit from the public's willingness to believe in an impression of intellectual authority.

Interestingly, exactly this impression has been created by *Die Vermessung der Welt* in respect of Kehlmann himself. For some readers, the mere fact that he engages with two major scientists of the German Enlightenment is proof of Kehlmann's learnedness.[13] Others have found ample evidence of the young author's serious talent within the literary realm, drawing attention to how well-read Kehlmann is and celebrating the novel's literary style as a subtle variation on, among others, the historical novel, magic realism, and modernist writing. Numerous scholarly commentators have pointed to apparent literary games within the text, such as a veiled reference to the great Latin American authors Carlos Fuentes, Gabriel García Márquez, Mario Vargos Llosa, and Julio Cortázar in the Christian names of the Orinoco oarsmen, and the playful inversion of Kafka's *Das Schloß* (The castle) in Gauß's meeting with Graf von der Ohe zur Ohe.[14] In both cases, Kehlmann is singled out by these supporters as a natural occupant of Bourdieu's field of restricted cultural production — that is, high art — on account of his apparently intellectual credentials. Thus, Kehlmann, largely unheard of in 2004, already has a volume of essays dedicated to him that quickly appeared with his publisher as a companion to *Die Vermessung der Welt* in 2008, as well as an issue of *text+kritik* (2008), the literary critical journal that specializes in gathering together wide-ranging scholarship on notable contemporary writers. Both pieces appear determined to strengthen Kehlmann's standing in the field by roundly asserting his cultural capital as well as placing all the symbolic weight of their respective publishing and academic apparatus behind him.

The point here is not to argue about just how learned or well-read Kehlmann actually is, nor to pass judgment on how successfully the text fits in with recognized literary styles and movements, but to take account of the processes underlying Kehlmann's positioning within the literary realm and to consider what this tells us about the contemporary German literary industry. In Bourdieu's model of the field of restricted cultural production, the fetishizing mode is understood to be both inherent in public engagement with high art, and of necessity denied by all participants in the field. Discussing how we as cultural critics should conceive of the relationship of the celebrated artist to the world of art, he explains:

> It is not merely a matter of exorcizing the "fetish of the name of the master" [Bourdieu refers to Walter Benjamin here] by a simple sacrilegious and slightly childish inversion — whether one wishes it or not, the name of the master is indeed a fetish. Rather, it is a matter of describing the gradual emergence of the entire set of social mechanisms which make possible the figure of the artist as producer of that fetish which is the work of art — in other words, the constitution of the artistic field (in which analysts and art historians are themselves included) as the locus where the belief in the value of art — and in that power to create value which belongs to the artist — is constantly produced and reproduced.[15]

In Germany, literature has historically occupied a special place among the dominant social stratum of the educated middle classes, and the attempt to determine the nation's leading culture (*Leitkultur*) has underlain much of the specifically postwar media coverage of literature, where becoming either a successful author or literary critic was a path to social power and influence for many a self-educated petit bourgeois. This tendency to use literature as a kind of cultural capital that improves one's starting position in the field of cultural production — and thus also ultimately in the field of power — has been evident in many high-profile media debates of the postwar period, most notably in recent times in the attempt made by Frank Schirrmacher and Ulrich Greiner to discredit a whole generation of established authors during the period of German unification. Where that debate was carried out in negative terms, the professional critical discussion of Kehlmann has largely been one of positive superlatives. When asked why his work has been so well received, Kehlmann himself points to two groups of readers who regularly attend his readings but do not usually figure as great purchasers of contemporary literature: people who read according to their own taste rather than follow market trends, and people with a scientific background who appreciate the book's engagement with their general area of interest. This observation is interesting, for it points to one possible motivation among those readers who clearly felt this book was offering something different from other works of contemporary fiction. In engaging with two of Germany's greatest scientists in an accessible literary form that gestures toward more complex traditions, Kehlmann's book thoroughly flatters the average educated middle-class reader. Without actually necessitating any real understanding of science, or indeed literary techniques or movements, the novel offers its readers the cachet of an intellectual content, and it fits into a certain German tradition of education.

People can enjoy the fact that they are able to enjoy a book "about" science and the Age of Enlightenment and that they can recognize various literary references and intertextual games.

Of course, the more broadly popular a work becomes, the more problematic is its ongoing celebration as a work of great literature. As Bourdieu explains, the field of restricted cultural production is not only inherently fetishizing in the way of other celebrity discourses, it is also inherently elitist. It is marked out by its own sense of distinction from popular trends and market capitalist considerations, and so there is a critical point at which financial success and public acclaim begin to count against an author as a truly "literary" writer. As Klaus Zeyringer has observed, these doubts began to set in with regard to Kehlmann the longer his book continued to top the bestseller lists, with the result that prominent TV and print literary critics started publicly downgrading their opinion of *Die Vermessung der Welt*. Where initially its (and by extension the author's) literary and intellectual credentials were roundly praised in clearly fetishizing terms, gradually the book and its author seemed to turn into an ephemeral, lightweight phenomenon that was typical of our age of media hype.[16] With this, their own covert practices of intellectual fetishization are silently renounced and the author's success passed off as the result of celebrity processes that are deemed to exist only in the field of mass cultural production.

However, what the case of Daniel Kehlmann should by now have rendered apparent is the overlap between popular public constructions of celebrity and literary critical fetishization of intellectual achievement. Not only does *Die Vermessung der Welt* openly deal with the celebrification of intellectual achievement in its retrospective portrayal of Humboldt and Gauß, it links this thematic consideration of celebrity to the reader's contemporary situation by the aesthetic celebrificatory processes on which it relies: the reader enjoys consuming Humboldt and Gauß as exotic and yet accessible figures. Furthermore, the way in which the work was publicly received and its author feted encourages us to draw comparisons between scholarly constructions of the text's literary value and mass public celebration of the text as edifying entertainment. What appeals in both instances is the way the text facilitates the expression of a certain kind of lifestyle for those who engage with it, whether this is to enjoy the paradoxical escapist identification that consuming celebrity allows or to contribute actively to creating and maintaining the literary field.

Conclusion

In the context of contemporary German literature, *Die Vermessung der Welt* is unusual within and yet also highly revealing of the wider industry. The text is remarkable for the way it stands on the cusp between high art and popular fiction. For while earlier works have sought to popularize German literature, traditionally an unremittingly elite field of artistic endeavor, they have usually ended up being branded as either "literary" or "popular" in the way they programmatically set about realizing this aim. Thus, the first wave of German pop writing in the 1960s did undermine conventional literary aesthetics, in line with the rebellious mood of the times, but the works which resulted are read and enjoyed by far fewer readers than those of Thomas Mann, Günter Grass, Heinrich Böll, and other more conventional writers. In fact, they were probably only ever of significant interest to those working within the industry, thus remaining firmly within the field of restricted cultural production. The second wave of pop literature in the 1990s was from the start conceived as a much broader market success story, and some of the authors associated with this — for example, Christian Kracht and Florian Illies — have achieved genuine bestseller status. Their texts, however, are for many scholars too opportunistically popular and too obviously rooted in the capitalist processes that their contents describe to function as literary texts with lasting value.

Although Kehlmann has attracted his share of criticism from literary critics suspicious of any widespread public popularity, there seems to be a much greater consensus within the industry that his work is sufficiently intellectual to be considered as literature while it at the same time appeals to a large audience of nonprofessional readers. It has been the contention of this essay that *Die Vermessung der Welt*, the key turning point in Kehlmann's career to date, has managed to prove successful with both groups because of its unusual engagement with celebrity as a contemporary social issue as well as a textual phenomenon. It quite evidently portrays contemporary celebrity processes that are readily recognized by most readers, but these processes are also paralleled within both the text's aesthetics and its own reception history by the far-less-well-acknowledged practices of intellectual fetishization that lie at the heart of the literary field. In this sense, the text and its reception make evident certain characteristics that are not just to be found in the contemporary German literary market, but that actually drive it.

Kehlmann's unexpected success can thus partly be understood in line with the attempt begun by younger authors and their wider publishing apparatus in the mid-1990s to popularize German literature by openly embracing its capitalist context. Kehlmann positions himself within this general market trend while retaining the kind of self-conscious critical distance from his subject matter that tends to characterize more obviously literary works. While the text describes celebrity, and clearly employs its own celebrity aesthetics deliberately, it does not therefore become beholden to the concept in the way that other forms of "lifestyle" fiction have done. Rather, it manages to strike a balance between complicity with celebrity processes and ironic distance from them. In so doing, it helps refine our understanding of how celebrity processes, and in particular processes of intellectual fetishization, can function as a productive part of contemporary culture. For far from displaying the Frankfurt School's distrust of celebrity as a dangerously empty phenomenon, Kehlmann reveals himself to be quite at ease with it, deliberately working with celebrity processes and adapting the creative impetus that underlies them for his literary work. If he is implicitly scornful of the fetishized art world in *Ich und Kaminski,* he clearly accommodates himself with the more entertaining and humorous potential of celebrity as both a ubiquitous social phenomenon and a successful literary aesthetic in *Die Vermessung der Welt.* Looking forward, the 2009 text *Ruhm* represents his most sustained examination yet of the way celebrity processes can be channeled into literary games that play on the reader's sense of reality and the author's calculated manufacture of alternative lifestyles. Indeed, it is tempting to read *Ruhm* as Kehlmann's literary reaction to the fetishizing processes underlying literary celebrity that he experienced firsthand upon the publication of *Die Vermessung der Welt.* That, however, is the beginning of another essay.

Notes

[1] Daniel Kehlmann, *Die Vermessung der Welt* (Reinbek: Rowohlt, 2005).

[2] This is the figure detailed in Gunther Nickel, "Von *Beerholms Vorstellung* zur *Vermessung der Welt:* Die Wiedergeburt des magischen Realismus aus dem Geist der modernen Mathematik," in *Daniel Kehlmanns* Die Vermessung der Welt: *Materialien, Dokumente, Interpretationen,* ed. Gunther Nickel (Reinbek bei Hamburg: Rowohlt, 2008), 151–68; here, 158.

[3] Chris Rojek, *Celebrity* (London: Reaktion, 2001).

[4] For early theorists of celebrity such as Daniel Boorstin, who famously defined the celebrity as "a person who is known for his well-knownness," the phenomenon was directly linked to the kind of criticism of modern society that defines the Frankfurt School; Daniel J Boorstin, *The Image, or, What Happened to the American Dream* (London: Weidenfeld and Nicolson, 1961). This negative understanding of celebrity persists in the work of some celebrity theorists today, for example David Marshall, *Celebrity and Power: Fame in Contemporary Culture* (Minneapolis: U of Minnesota P, 1997).

[5] For a discussion of fame as a concept over the centuries, see Leo Braudy, *The Frenzy of Renown: Fame and Its History* (New York: Oxford UP, 1986). Graeme Turner, *Understanding Celebrity* (London: Sage, 2004) and Joshua Gamson, *Claims to Fame: Celebrity in Contemporary America* (Berkeley: U of California P, 1994) are useful on contemporary celebrity.

[6] On the star author as a concept, as well as the broader American context of middlebrow fiction, see Joe Moran, *Star Authors: Literary Celebrity in America* (London: Pluto, 2000).

[7] Such an assumption is reflected in both the *FAZ* and *Spiegel* interviews with Kehlmann, which begin with a series of questions revolving around why Kehlmann chose his protagonists: "Ich wollte schreiben wie ein verrückt gewordener Historiker," *Frankfurter Allgemeine Zeitung*, 9 February 2006, reprinted in *Daniel Kehlmanns* Die Vermessung der Welt, ed. Nickel, 26–35; "Mein Thema ist das Chaos," *Der Spiegel*, 05 December 2005," reprinted in Nickel, "Von *Beerholms Vorstellung* zur *Vermessung der Welt*," 36–46. (Though not available in English, the titles alone of these two interviews are revealing; they are, respectively, "I wanted to write like a historian gone mad" and "My theme is chaos.")

[8] See Klaus Zeyringer, "Vermessen: Zur deutschsprachigen Rezeption der *Vermessung der Welt*," in *Daniel Kehlmanns* Die Vermessung der Welt, ed. Nickel, 78–94, for an overview of the novel's German media reception.

[9] Daniel Kehlmann, *Measuring the World*, trans. Carol Brown Janeway (London: Quercus, 2007). All subsequent references to this text, which has the same pagination as the US edition published by Vintage, appear as the page number in parenthesis in the text.

[10] Robert Menasse, "'Ich bin wie alle, so wie nur ich es sein kann': Daniel Kehlmanns Essays über Autoren und Bücher," in *Daniel Kehlmann*, ed. Heinz Ludwig Arnold (Munich: text+kritik, 2007), 30–35; here, 32–33. My translation.

[11] These negative reactions are clearly hinted at in some of the questions posed in the *Spiegel* interview, "Mein Thema ist das Chaos." See also Zeyringer, "Vermessen: Zur deutschsprachigen Rezeption der *Vermessung der Welt*," for a description of negative public reactions to the book's scientific content.

[12] See, for example, Pierre Bourdieu, *The Rules of Art: Genesis and Structure of the Literary Field*, trans. Susan Emanuel (Cambridge: Polity, 1996).

[13] Ijoma Mangold referred to Kehlmann as a "Wunderkind" in his presentation speech for the 2005 Candide Prize, which predated the appearance of *Die Vermessung der Welt* by several months. The speech, which is characterized by an admiring tone throughout for the way in which Kehlmann deals with science in literature, sets the tone for many subsequent analyses of Kehlmann's work. It is reprinted in *Daniel Kehlmanns* Die Vermessung der Welt," ed. Nickel, 95–112.

[14] The encomium on Kehlmann written by his lector Thorsten Ahrend is an extreme example of how Kehlmann's intellectual credentials were heavily pushed by his supporters: "No more dogs! Erfahrungen mit Daniel Kehlmann," in *Daniel Kehlmann*, ed. Arnold, 68–72. Mark M. Anderson, Markus Gasser, and Gunther Nickel are examples of just three critics who place Kehlmann firmly within high-brow literary traditions: Mark M. Anderson, "Der vermessende Erzähler: Mathematische Geheimnisse bei Daniel Kehlmann," in Arnold, 58–67; Markus Gasser, "Daniel Kehlmanns unheimliche Kunst," in Arnold, 12–29; Nickel, "Von *Beerholms Vorstellung* zur *Vermessung der Welt*."

[15] Bourdieu, *The Rules of Art*, 291–92.

[16] See Zeyringer, "Vermessen: Zur deutschsprachigen Rezeption der *Vermessung der Welt*."

6: Clemens Meyer, *Als wir träumten*: Fighting "Like a Man" in Leipzig's East

Frauke Matthes

WHEN CLEMENS MEYER'S DEBUT NOVEL *Als wir träumten* (When we were dreaming) hit the German literary market in 2006, the then twenty-nine-year-old author was confronted with unexpected success; the numerous prizes,[1] unfamiliar media attention, and countless interviews must have come — one would think — as a welcome surprise. However, when his writing career took off, Clemens Meyer (b. 1977 in Halle/Saale) did not fit the image of the young writer who had worked continuously on his writing career until finally making it. On the contrary, in 2006 Meyer portrayed himself as a maverick who liked to show off his tattoos, spoke with a slight but noticeable Saxon accent, and boasted of his exposure to the rough side of life by having worked in the construction industry. Although his publisher S. Fischer exploited these characteristics to market this newcomer,[2] Meyer did not wish to be co-opted by the publishing industry. Yet the writer's self-stylization stirred much interest in the media, particularly when it became known that he had studied at the Deutsches Literaturinstitut Leipzig (formerly the Johannes R. Becher-Institut). This traditional creative writing school, founded in 1955, has produced a number of highly successful writers, such as Juli Zeh and Saša Stanišić, and had attracted successful writers as visiting professors such as Ilija Trojanow, Terézia Mora, Ulrike Draesner (all of whom are featured in this volume), and, not least, the winner of the Nobel Prize for Literature in 2009, Herta Müller. Unlike his fellow students, however, Meyer did not seem to wish to adapt to the young literary scene that Leipzig has produced since the mid-1990s, preferring instead to adopt a position outside of this group. Outsiders — that is, characters with whom Clemens Meyer could have identified at the beginning of his writing career — have also been the focus of his writing so far: Meyer is interested in people from the margins of German society, social outcasts who, according to the writer, deserve more literary attention. Such sidelined figures take center stage in Meyer's novel *Als wir träumten* and his collection of short stories *Die Nacht, die Lichter* (The night, the lights, 2008).[3] They present us with a sober and much-needed look on what it means for some youngsters to grow up in East Germany, something that many texts by young East German writers do not provide.

As the novel is set in Meyer's hometown of Leipzig, readers may be tempted to consider it as part of the corpus of autobiographical accounts of GDR and post-GDR childhoods such as Jana Hensel's *Zonenkinder* (Children of the zone, 2002; published in English as *After the Wall*, 2008) or Claudia Rusch's *Meine freie deutsche Jugend* (My free German youth, 2003).[4] These texts attract readers who can identify with the subject matter and therefore often create forms of *Ostalgie* (nostalgia for the former East Germany). Yet it is for its focus on outsiders, on delinquent boys and men, that Meyer's *Als wir träumten* successfully avoids falling into the trap of *Ostalgie* and does not paint a mellow picture of growing up in Leipzig, as does Jana Hensel's work in particular. Her text describes what I call "mainstream" East German youth and leaves out deviant youngsters who disappeared in *Jugendwerkhöfe* (state homes for adolescents with behavioral problems) or youth prisons in order to protect the idyllic world of the GDR.

Yet with his novel, Meyer is not overly distanced from another group of writers of his generation: Jakob Hein and Jochen Schmidt, for instance, take a critical look on what Paul Cooke refers to as "a fragile generation with no fixed points of orientation."[5] Texts such as Hein's *Mein erstes T-Shirt* (My first T-shirt, 2001) or Schmidt's *Müller haut uns raus* (Müller bails us out, 2002),[6] by focusing on the "everyday experience of growing up in the GDR," present us with "a far more matter-of-fact portrayal of life in the GDR."[7]

However, Meyer offers an even more down-to-earth "everyday experience" of youth shortly before and after Germany's reunification than do Hein and Schmidt, and significantly more so than Hensel and Rusch. The fictional quality of his novel allows him to create a distance from his characters and thus to center his narrative on a world that was not openly seen in the GDR, but that increasingly surfaced after the fall of the Berlin Wall. It is through outsiders that Meyer can explore images of manliness and formations of masculinity that were unwelcome in the GDR; through his portrayal of this particular kind of masculinity, Meyer can reveal his characters' search for a belonging that is not tied to a political state but to their homosocial experience. Furthermore, as I shall argue, Meyer links the local world of his characters, which seems to be the exclusive focus of the "ostalgic" texts mentioned above, with the global arena of which the former East Germany is now part. In other words: the novel does not focus on the characters' "otherness" as young people coming from the East, as is suggested by titles such as Jana Simon's *Denn wir sind anders* (Because we are different, 2001),[8] but on their "otherness" due to their criminal acts, as shared by delinquents all over the world.

"The Street Is the School":
Young Delinquent Men

In *Als wir träumten*, Meyer takes his predominantly middle-class readers to a world unknown to most of them: the eastern part of Leipzig, Reudnitz, in the late 1980s and early 1990s. This area is characterized by the Leipziger Premium Pilsner Brauerei, by industry, and by working-class life. Reudnitz is comparable to rundown, though up-and-coming, areas in other large German cities such as Kreuzberg, the Berlin district Andrew Plowman analyzes in this volume. Although the brewery still exists (it now is the Leipziger Brauhaus zu Reudnitz), the industry disappeared after the *Wende* (the political, social, and political changes that took place around the time of the opening of the Berlin Wall), and the area was hit by high unemployment; consequently, parts of the neighborhood became derelict.[9] Meyer's self-stylization as maverick is strongly linked to the setting of his novel: when *Als wir träumten* was praised for its authenticity, Meyer was always quick to comment that he had spent most of his life in the eastern parts of Leipzig — and that he still lives there.

Meyer's novel revolves around a group of working-class adolescents as they grow into young adults. As we, the readers, are carried between the past and present tenses, we learn about the narrator Daniel Lenz, or Danie, and his group of friends. They are: Rico, the boxer, who spends more time in youth prison than in the boxing ring and who leaves the narrative after starting a long prison sentence; Fred, who is proud of his "legendary" crimes (10); Paul, whose collection of sex magazines is the largest in the area; Stefan, or rather Pitbull, who almost beats his father to death and ends up taking drugs; Mark, whose drug addiction kills him; and "der kleine Walter" (Little Walter), who drives head-on into a tree and dies in the collision.[10] Meyer does not develop a tightly plotted storyline, but rather the novel is a succession of Daniel's memories recollected in prison. We read about the boys' school years under the GDR regime, and about their later activities as adolescent gang members and delinquents. The novel opens with a chapter that carries the telling title *Kinderspiele*, "children's games" that the characters play in their early teens and that rapidly turn into reality, into severe violence, and sometimes even death. The immediacy of the narration of events enables the reader to either sympathize with the characters or completely disapprove of their actions. In any case, the reader cannot avoid an emotional involvement.

Als wir träumten focuses on individual fates, and while the political changes of 1989 are closely connected with the social changes they experience, the *Wende* is not central to the boys' passage to manhood. Still, this time of political and social upheaval in Germany forms a significant juncture in the boys' lives: whereas the pre-1989 years appear in Meyer's novel

as a time of innocence, the post-*Wende* years bring devastation and social
decline. It should be pointed out that the coincidence of the start of the
new regime with the beginning of the characters' criminal activities is foremost connected to their age: the boys are between thirteen and fifteen at
the time of the *Wende* and face the end of their childhood after the *Wende*.
In order to come to terms with these developments, Daniel narrates the
events from the perspective of a more mature man in his mid-twenties.
This perspective allows Meyer to introduce the first leitmotif of his novel
that the title already anticipates: the idea of dreaming.

Dreaming relates to the central question "do you remember,"[11]
which guides the reader through the narrative. This question brings back
memories of the boys' childhood and early adolescence, of their innocence, but also of the beginning of their criminal activities, which initially
do not have a major impact. These times, "the old" or "wild times" as
the boys call them, are connected with fun but — significantly — also
with a sense of forlornness. The first chapter ends with Daniel's reflection
on his past:

> There isn't a single night I don't dream about all that, and every day
> the memories dance in my head, and I agonize over the question why
> everything ended up that way. We had a lot of fun back then, that's
> for sure; yet still, whatever we did there was some sort of forlornness,
> which I can't quite explain, inside us. (14)

Meyer allows Daniel to connect his friends' brutality with a sober look at
their actions; even though Daniel was one of boys, as the narrator who
reflects back on their earlier lives, he takes on the position of an outsider
and can thus dismiss moments of sentimentality quickly. Although, to
Daniel, their adolescent activities appear as "strangely dream-like nights of
flying," he does not hide their brutal reality: these nights usually ended
"by landing in the sobering-up cell or on the corridor of the Police
Station South-East, being locked to the radiator with handcuffs" (7). It
would seem that Daniel's narration in the form of "dreaming" is a way of
escaping into a glorified and idealized past, yet his recollecting of his
memories is primarily a means of re-imagining his and his friends' pre-
criminal innocence. Seemingly insignificant details bring this to the fore:
for instance, the characters typically keep giving their *Pionierehrenwort*
(Pioneer's word of honor — the East German equivalent of a Boy Scout's
word of honor), even years after the collapse of the GDR and after leaving
school. By putting such words reminiscent of their childhood into their
mouths, Meyer seems to suggest that his characters do not realize what
they are actually saying. The reader cannot sometimes be sure whether
Daniel and his friends are already men, or still children: they are clearly
grown-ups physically, but emotionally they remain in a state of childlike
irresponsibility.

In his "dreams," Daniel imagines an exclusively masculine world, a world of homosocial relations and gangs as described by Eve Kosofsky Sedgwick:

> in any male-dominated society, there is a special relationship between male homosocial (*including* homosexual) desire and the structures for maintaining and transmitting patriarchal power: a relationship founded on an inherent and potentially active structural congruence. For historical reasons, this special relationship may take the form of ideological homophobia, ideological homosexuality, or some highly conflicted but intensively structured combination of the two.[12]

Meyer does not present his readers with reasons[13] for why his characters have transformed from innocent boys to violent, homophobic, xenophobic, and women-abusing young men whose view of masculinity is based on dominance over weaker men, patriarchal power, and fixed gender as well as social roles — ramifications of what Kosofsky Sedgwick explains in the quotation above. But if we take a closer look at some of the features that characterize homosocial relations in Meyer's late twentieth-century Reudnitz, we can nevertheless discern how his characters perceive manliness.

First, Daniel and his friends are in a gang who fight other gangs, and this is where the majority of the violence that Daniel continuously talks about has its roots. Daniel's gang can exercise this violence because they live in what they call "the ghetto" (10), the area around the brewery, the "Eastside," but his narrative clearly highlights his friends' (subconscious) aspiration to be a little bit more exciting than they actually are, of looking up to New York (the East Side) or the West generally. (But they do not admire Leipzig's west, the *Weststadt,* which is one of their "enemy territories"; indeed, the *Weststadt* is too affluent an area for them.) By establishing their gang and using vocabulary that reinforces their gang culture, the boys seem to be trying to gain access to a global arena, to the masculine globalized world and, despite their pride in their local area, to go beyond their identity as East German boys from Reudnitz. Although being in a gang makes them outsiders in the German society they live in, within gang culture they lose their roles as outsiders and become part of the global picture of rowdy masculinity.[14] Barbara Mennel examines a similar phenomenon in her discussion of Alina Bronsky's *Scherbenpark* (2008; *Broken Glass Park,* 2010) in this volume, albeit focusing on the situation of girls in ghettoes.

The universal dimension of their gang goes hand in hand with the two clearly defined purposes their ghetto around the brewery serves: firstly, and mainly, it excludes others; namely, those who either threaten or (in the case of women) affirm the boys' masculinity. For Meyer's protagonists, these others are differently minded people politically, that is, Neo-Nazis, who also live in Reudnitz and who often get in their way, as well as radicals on the left, the *Zecken* (ticks) who live in Leipzig's south, Connewitz. These others also include supporters of the "wrong" soccer team (that is, 1. FC Lokomotive, or Lok, also called VfB Leipzig for some time in the 1990s — Daniel and his friends are BSG Chemie Leipzig fans),[15] so-called foreigners, and gay people. Above all, others are women: they serve only as an instrument of the boys' pleasure (as prostitutes or — and this is another frequently recurring theme — in the context of pornography) and of proving their masculine prowess. As Kosofsky Sedgwick has written, "women ha[ve] a kind of ultimate importance in the schema of men's gender constitution — representing an absolute of exchange value, of representation itself, and also being the ultimate victims of the painful contradictions in the gender system that regulates men."[16] Indeed, Meyer portrays his protagonists as what Judith Butler calls "compulsory heterosexuals,"[17] which is the basis for their condescending manners and their belief in "acute structural gender inequalities."[18] However, the narrative also introduces female characters in order to highlight how the male characters try to hide their insecurities as men. Their attitudes can be traced especially in prison "where women are present as an idea but not as a social reality."[19] For instance, when playing a prison version of Monopoly with his inmates, Daniel records the following conversation about women:

> Now Frank stood in front of the brothel and had to pay. And he paid. "That was a shag," he said, "all inclusive, sucking, licking and so on. Was a black one, more sort of light brown. Man, her pussy was glowing!" We laughed . . . "You and your Negress," Klaus shouted, "do you know who fucks best? *Fidschi* chicks, Vietnamese women, right?" He patted the *Fidschi* [Vietnamese inmate] on the back. "Honestly, you have . . . well . . . beautiful women." (227)

As women are not physically present in prison, the inmates can objectify them boundlessly and use them, above all, as a means to assert their manhood: they can boast of experiences they might not actually have had and make themselves a little bit more exciting in that way. "Exotic" women play an even more significant role in this context as they also bring to the fore the power relations between "white" men and "foreigners": by orientalizing black and Asian women and by stereotyping their sexual behavior, the young lads are possessive toward them and, by extension, show their power over the "foreign" men in prison — they construct their manliness at the expense of "foreign" women who have sex with German men. However, in prison this is only an imagined construction; the inmates are playing a game, after all. This incident also exemplifies the significance of homosocial experiences (the inmates are laughing when talking about sex, thus showing, or pretending to show, that they all know what Frank is alluding to). Such homosocial experiences are, once again, strongly connected to compulsory heterosexuality. Homosexuals, such as Daniel's cellmate André, are violently excluded from bonding with other inmates, from forming a male society.[20] There is, therefore, every indication that the inmates in *Als wir träumten* regard their masculinity to be under threat; they feel anxious as men. Not having access to women in prison, they cannot physically prove their masculine prowess in that way.

Secondly, the ghetto is an exclusive space; it enables the consumption of drugs, the organization of illegal techno-parties, and, above all, the exercise of violence: "the street is the school" (509), one of the boys makes clear. According to Suzanne E. Hatty,

> clearly, violence is still the prerogative of the youthful male, especially when confronted by the contradictions and paradoxes of thwarted desire and personal and social disempowerment. Reaching deep into the historical and cultural storehouse of masculinity, a young man may still retrieve the ultimate tool of manly self-assertiveness: omnipotence through violence.[21]

For Daniel and his friends, violence is what Anne Campbell has identified as "a measure of being someone in a world where all hope of success in conventional terms is lost."[22] Devoid of, or denying, any parental support, they can only find their masculinity through aggressiveness. Aggressiveness leads to fighting, and thus requires strong bodies. The boys' view of masculinity can therefore only be rooted in their corporeality and the display of their male bodies that the novel frequently thematizes. It is already introduced on the cover of the book through the image of a boxer. Rico's boxing serves as the novel's second leitmotif; boxing prepares the readers for the real fights, the violent actions to come in the boys' later lives that lead to prison. In that respect, Meyer constructs violence as, according to Hatty, a "corporeal experience, involving the collision of bodies, the extension of touch (painful or injurious) into spaces and places where it is not welcome."[23] The focus on bodies is something that Mennel also observes in her discussion in this volume of the ghetto in *Scherbenpark*. In *Als wir träumten*, the body serves as an "instrument,"[24] a "weapon" even, which is only possible because of "the foreign character of their bodies."[25] It enables the boys to detach themselves from their bodies emotionally; the regular occurrences of street fights in the narrative, the frequent descriptions of their bodies in physical conflict, would not allow for a tender relation to their bodies. Feeling pain is seen as effeminate; instead, blood is swallowed and used as an incentive to take an even stronger swipe at one's opponent. Fighting "like a man" is, furthermore, closely tied to the idea of a code (inside and outside the prison), as well as dignity and honor. Physical toughness is needed to keep or defend a man's ("our," 271) or the neighborhood's honor (261). George L. Mosse points out that these notions of will power and courage that make up masculinity have changed little over time.[26] This also holds true for Meyer's protagonists, who do not construct their manliness in an alternative way but adhere to patriarchal concepts that favor men over women, and strong men over weaker ones. The gradual emergence of this attitude reveals the protagonists' development from boys to men and drives the narrative forward.

It does not come as a surprise, therefore, that in prison, Daniel and his fellow inmates — then in their late teens or early twenties — give much attention to their and other inmates' bodies that are endlessly described in an almost cinematic manner.[27] In prison, the body becomes an even more significant "object" than in the outside world; it is the only thing the inmates have control over as they are, in fact, infantilized: like children they are told what to do and when. Furthermore, Yvonne Jewkes's research shows that there also exists "fear among inmates and prison officials," which can be counteracted by building up a strong body; the inmates' built bodies give them "presence and power."[28] Scars and tattoos play a significant role in this context.[29] Daniel observes his fellow inmates in prison: the debt collector "wasn't as tall as the giant and he wasn't as broad as Klaus either, he was of the tough sort, no fat, I had seen that in the showers. He had lots of tattoos, especially on his back" (235). (In this context, it is interesting to note that Meyer himself constructs, or was asked to construct, his masculinity by showing off his tattoos in the photograph on the dust jacket of *Als wir träumten*, as if to ensure the authenticity of his subject matter.) Tattoos and trained bodies give Meyer's men respect from other, that is, weaker inmates; their socially marked bodies make them superior, more powerful, and, above all, honorable men. The correlation of the physical body and abstract values is connected with what Mosse says about "the stereotype of [modern] masculinity," that is, masculinity from the eighteenth century onwards, as "conceived as a totality based upon the nature of man's body."[30] The boys have completely internalized this idea: conflicts are always resolved with fists, never with words. Winning as many conflicts as possible gives them pride and "value" (231–37), and bragging about their violent experiences and the prison sentences they earned as a result of those is a widespread hobby in prison. This "game" affirms their masculinity as it brings a certain degree of invincibility required in the rough prison environment in order to come out unscathed.[31]

It has become clear that the boys' perceptions of masculinity are based on features also to be found in what Jewkes refers to as "underclass cultures": "intergroup loyalty, adherence to a 'code of honour,' a distinctive jargon, display of aggressive toughness, passing initiation rites, opposition to authority."[32] Their ideas of what makes them "real" men help Daniel and his friends create what I call a masculine counter-world — and a sense of (imagined) belonging. As I mentioned before, by contrast to some novels that have emerged in East Germany since the *Wende*, however, *Als wir träumten* does not engage with the trauma caused by a lost "home" that once promised emotional stability.[33] Although Meyer's characters are looking for a sense of belonging, it is not dependent on a political entity or a state, and the notion of a "fractured identity" due to their "fractured history" does not enter the equation.[34] In the chapter "Abschied" (Farewell), the — significantly enough — penultimate chapter, Daniel finds Rico's "Erinnerungsmappe" (memory folder), not long before Rico is caught by the police for the final time in the narrative:

> [Rico] had cut out the article and put it into his memory folder, which he carried with him in his bag. . . . He had a few photos in it, on one of those there were him, Pitbull, who was still called Stefan back then, Walter and myself in front of a Mercedes, we held each other by our hands and laughed, that was at the Fair [the annual Autumn Fair in Leipzig] back then, autumn eighty-nine. Rico also had Walter's and Mark's death notices in his folder, one of the old school magazines, and his notices of dismissal. . . .
> "a swinger club, Danie." . . . He came over to me and put his shirt on. "I said, you know, I wanted to have a big blast one more time, before they nick me." (474)

Looking at the photograph of the then still-fairly-innocent boys, Daniel seems to feel nostalgic, yet his feeling of nostalgia does not relate to the GDR past: the photo happens to have been taken in the autumn of 1989, but the significance of the immense changes of the time do not play a role in Daniel's memories and Rico's "memory folder." Although the boys might still be connected by their memories, they do not linger in them; they simply get on with their lives, like having fun at a swinger club one more time before confronting authority again — here in the form of the police. These regular confrontations signal the gradual descent of some of the boys into criminality and thus structure the novel. Yet, regardless of what kind of stage in the boys' development the narrative describes, it is their more or less serious criminal activities that give them the feeling of belonging to a group, if a delinquent one.

The world of Meyer's characters is a world primarily created in opposition to any form of authority and hierarchy: against the law and the police (although, as we have seen, the boys frequently "lose" and have to go to the Police Station South-East and then to prison), but also against their fathers. In this way, Meyer thematizes the breakdown of patriarchy — a common theme in the GDR's foundational novels as well as post-GDR literature, as Thomas Fox has explored.[35] Meyer's take on this trope, however, reveals the paradoxical development of Daniel, Rico, and their gang and, by implication, the author's divergent depiction of East German youth from most of his contemporaries' portrayals of their young central characters: his protagonists' rejection of authority leads to their patriarchal behavior. In their childhoods, the boys' fathers appear as role models who initiate their sons into militarized manhood; namely, into drinking in their favorite pub, into gambling and other forms of "masculine" behavior, but also into clearly defined spaces, that is, above all into spaces devoid of women and thus based on traditional gender roles. Fathers also "teach" their sons to some extent "to be delinquent," that is, to be tough and aggressive, and to act as risk seekers.[36] Rico's father is even in the military, which was one of the most highly regarded workplaces for men in the GDR.[37] The boys have internalized this kind of militarized behavior, but there is also a real rebellion against their fathers because they do not exist anymore: neither as role models (some fathers have given in to alcohol, for instance), nor, quite literally, as a physical presence. Daniel's father simply disappears; he is probably taken away by the GDR state security service, the *Stasi*. As mentioned earlier, one of the characters, Pitbull, even tries to dispose of his father himself. Furthermore, the world of their fathers, that is, the role of breadwinner, is denied to the boys.[38] Daniel and his friends also have to live with unemployment when they leave school. Although this might appear as a typical East German issue, Meyer does not give a politico-economic explanation for their unemployment. This is yet more evidence that Meyer does not explore the reasons for his characters' behavior, which we as readers nonetheless look for, and especially not those based on the political and social changes in post-*Wende* East Germany. The boys' lives in the ghetto seem to be detached from time and place. Sandra Walklate's comments on the social reality of the street in her study of the connections between gender and crime are thus useful when looking into the delinquent activities of Meyer's characters:

> And whilst the street may have always been a male preserve for different forms of social activity, it takes on a crucial significance in the absence of work and the uncomfortable presence of the alternative: the domestic domain, for which they have no role which they can easily identify. The subsequent involvement, then, of these young men in crime, whether burglary, joy riding, drugs, or rioting, needs to be understood as a product of their economic and social location and their need to express themselves as men.[39]

Although these developments can also be found in Meyer's novel, his protagonists are shown to have developed something in line with what R. W. Connell describes in relation to ethnic minority boys and young men as "protest masculinity."[40] James W. Messerschmidt calls this form of masculinity, with reference to African-American and Hispanic American youths, an "oppositional masculinity born of resistance." This is not an "accommodating masculinity, embodying hegemonic concerns with career and social achievement" as middle-class white males create it.[41] Although

Meyer denies parallels between his characters and ethnic-minority delinquent boys, they do, however, share a number of features.[42] Meyer's protagonists protest because they are marginalized: they live in a socially less affluent area; have, for whatever reason, fewer chances in terms of education (or simply do not seize their chances because they do not want to stand out, but be part of the gang); have no real sense of belonging; and have dysfunctional fathers, if they have any at all. In effect, they are victims of the power relations among men: they are emasculated by the white, male, middle-class society that shuns them. Yet Daniel and his friends desperately want not to be feminized — that is, weakened — so they do what they can do best: show their fists. This becomes their means of "survival." The question remains, however, whether it is their marginalization that turns them into violent criminals, or vice versa.

The novel closes with Daniel remembering the story of how it all began: namely, with the boys' first encounter with Fred, "Leipzig's first car burglar" (506), whom they interview for their school newspaper and who later pulls them into the vortex of violence. In the last chapter, "Als wir Reporter waren" (When we were reporters), all the major themes are introduced to the reader retrospectively: ghettos, drugs, fights, and so on. Yet Daniel ends on a nostalgic note: "It was getting dark outside, Fred lit a few candles, and we moved together and ate and drank and were happy" (518). Meyer leaves us with a slight sadness that is the result of our witnessing the boys' social decline, of our knowledge of what this "happiness" is based on, because although these boys seem to have found a sense of belonging, we are left wondering whether this belonging is founded on the "right" values; namely, those that enable them to become successfully part of society as a whole, whether it can last or only lead to irredeemable forlornness.

A Realistic "Eastside Story"?

The questions remain whether *Als wir träumten* is a realistic novel and whether it reaches beyond a sociological study disguised as a fictional text. The novel's subject matter and its style and language give clues to the answers to these questions. Meyer leads his readers into a world that shatters our sense of placid coexistence. Although readers might be shocked by the boys' actions, it is the sense of forlornness that accompanies the crimes and the "fun" (described earlier) that pushes the novel beyond a voyeuristic look into adolescent delinquency in East Germany. Meyer's sparse, direct style, used when describing the gang's delinquent activities, their violent encounters with other gangs, or the men's bodies, is, in numerous places, reminiscent of watching an action film and ensures the realistic element of his narrative:

"You little bastard," the pig said directly above my head. He had grabbed me by my hair and pushed me with my head into the piss, my piss. . . . I compressed my lips and breathed into my own piss. He let go of me. I felt and heard how he got up and took a few steps back. I lifted my head from the puddle. I turned around. "You know," I said and was glad that there was piss under my eyes, but that pig wouldn't have seen those five tears anyway, "you should fuck your boyfriend properly again." (177)

Meyer describes incidents like these, the conflicts with the police, the fights, and the display of the male body in violent actions in great detail, as with an eye of a camera: he zooms in and out, focuses on particular stills, and manages to make his readers cringe with pain or disgust. Furthermore, some chapter titles are in the style of film titles: "Die großen Kämpfe" (The great fights), "Eastside Story," or "Alle meine Frauen" (All my women). Meyer's "realistic" style is, I suggest, an ideal means of visualizing the past: thinking about the past is like watching a film about it, and, on a meta-level, reading about Daniel's — rather unreliable — memories and his rapid moves between them is like watching a film, too. This raises a number of questions: How do we perceive reality in this day and age? What do we accept as reality — only moments that have been documented on film, even if it is a cinematic experience in our heads only? And can we remember reality only in this way? Susan Sontag remarked that "to reconcile, it is necessary that memory be faulty and limited."[43] Daniel's memories are "faulty and limited," and it is the gaps in his memory and his ability to see beyond the glorification of his and his friends' past that enables him to reconcile with his former delinquent self.

Daniel's narrative (or rather Meyer's writing) guides us toward engaging critically with reality, especially since it does not treat memory in an "ostalgic" or predictable way as some contemporary young East German writers do. His delinquent protagonists — outsiders in (East) German society — do not allow for the same kind of nostalgia associated with the "schöne warme Wir-Gefühl" (nice and warm we-feeling) that Jana Hensel's account of the childhood of a *Zonenkind* (child of the "zone," or GDR) opens with.[44] It is not a novel "about" an "authentic" East German experience, represented here as East German masculinity, but rather the novel looks beyond the surface of delinquency and violence that happens to take place in an East German city,[45] without judging or establishing reasons — which readers might expect to in the social and political circumstances of the time — for the characters' actions. This is the novel's particular strength.

Meyer did not rest on the laurels of his success that *Als wir träumten* brought him. The writer's second publication is the collection of short stories *Die Nacht, die Lichter*, which won him the Prize of the Leipzig Book Fair in 2008. (Interestingly, Daniel uses the phrase "Die Nacht, die

Lichter" [the night, the lights] toward the end of *Als wir träumten*, 511.) Like *Als wir träumten*, most of the stories are set in Leipzig and engage with marginalized characters. In 2010, Meyer published *Gewalten: Ein Tagebuch* (Forces: A diary), a collection of stories based on current political and social events.[46] Yet the recent years of success have transformed Meyer into a more established writer, whose hair has grown longer, and the sleeves of his shirt have become longer, too, in order to cover up his tattoos. Meyer's current, almost feminized self-portrayal in the domestic sphere of his study bears little resemblance with the hypermasculine writer photographed in a derelict factory in 2006.[47] He has learned how to take advantage of the publishing industry — which continues to celebrate the "cult of the author" long after the "death of the author" was pronounced by Roland Barthes and Michel Foucault — as Meyer's versatile marketing shows. Rebecca Braun and Andrew Plowman explore this phenomenon in this volume in their discussions of Daniel Kehlmann's *Die Vermessung der Welt* (2005; *Measuring the World*, 2006) and Sven Regener's *Der kleine Bruder* (The younger brother, 2008), respectively. Meyer's currently less rebellious image makes this clear: he quite happily talks about his books in public now, although his Saxon accent still ensures a sense of authenticity. I do not think, however, or at least do not hope, that Meyer is yet another example of a writer who becomes more interested in his market value and less interested in the stories he regards as necessary to tell, regardless of sales figures. His gripping books speak a different language.

Notes

This article was written as part of my postdoctoral research, which was kindly supported by the Leverhulme Trust with an Early Career Fellowship. I am most grateful to the Trust for its support.

[1] Meyer received, for example, the Rheingau Literatur Preis, Märkisches Stipendium für Literatur, Förderpreis zum Lessing-Preis, Mara-Cassens-Preis, and Clemens Brentano Preis.

[2] See Meyer's portrait on the novel's dust jacket. Clemens Meyer, *Als wir träumten: Roman* (Frankfurt am Main: S. Fischer, 2006). Subsequent page references appear in parentheses in the main body of the text. Unless otherwise noted, all translations from German sources are my own.

[3] Clemens Meyer, *Die Nacht, die Lichter* (Frankfurt am Main: S. Fischer, 2008).

[4] Jana Hensel, *Zonenkinder* (Reinbek bei Hamburg: Rowohlt, 2002); translated as *After the Wall: Confessions from an East German Childhood and the Life That Came Next* (New York: Public Affairs, 2008); Claudia Rusch, *Meine freie deutsche Jugend* (Frankfurt am Main: S. Fischer, 2003). For a comparison of Meyer's and Hensel's texts, see also Kolja Mensing, "Trainspotting in Leipzig-Ost: Clemens Meyer: *Als wir träumten*," *Deutschlandradio Kultur*, 23 February 2006, www.dradio.de/

dkultur/sendungen/kritik/471323/ (accessed 10 December 2009). Here I follow the separation of young East German writers such as Jana Hensel, Claudia Rusch, Jakob Hein, and Jochen Schmidt from older ones such as Ingo Schulze and Thomas Brussig that was established by Paul Cooke in his article "'GDR Literature' in the Berlin Republic," in *Contemporary German Fiction: Writing in the Berlin Republic*, ed. Stuart Taberner (Cambridge: Cambridge UP, 2007), 56–71. This seems to me the fairest basis of comparison in terms of life experiences and the way these writers have grown up. I therefore do not include Schulze, Brussig, and others in my discussion of writing from East Germany.

[5] Cooke, "'GDR Literature' in the Berlin Republic," 67.

[6] Jakob Hein, *Mein erstes T-Shirt* (Munich: Piper, 2001); Jochen Schmidt, *Müller haut uns raus* (Munich: C. H. Beck, 2002).

[7] Cooke, "'GDR Literature' in the Berlin Republic," 67.

[8] Jana Simon, *Denn wir sind anders: Die Geschichte des Felix S.* (Berlin: Rowohlt, 2001). See also Owen Evans on the subject of "otherness" in his article "'Denn wir sind anders': 'Zonenkinder' in the Federal Republic," *German as a Foreign Language* 2 (2005): 20–33.

[9] This holds true for the time when the novel is set; the area has undergone some developments since the mid-1990s, but it remains one of the less attractive parts of Leipzig.

[10] Mensing, "Trainspotting in Leipzig-Ost."

[11] Kai Sina, "Clemens Meyer: Als wir träumten," *Junge Literaturkritik*, 17 May 2006, www.arte.tv/de/M-O/1211930.html (accessed 10 May 2011).

[12] Eve Kosofsky Sedgwick, *Between Men: English Literature and Male Homosocial Desire* (New York: Columbia UP, 1985), 25; emphasis in original.

[13] Cf. Andreas Stirn, "Abturz Ost," *RevolutionundEinheit.de*, 28 April 2009, www.friedlicherevolution.de/index.php?id=49&tx_comarevolution_pi4%5Bcontribid%5D=136 (accessed 10 May 2011).

[14] Cf. Stirn, "Absturz Ost."

[15] For an analysis of how Lok attracts Neo-Nazis, see *Die Zeit*, 3 September 2009, Dossier "Angriff von rechts außen," 15–17.

[16] Kosofsky Sedgwick, *Between Men*, 134.

[17] Judith Butler, "Melancholy Gender / Refused Identification," in *Constructing Masculinity*, ed. Maurice Berger, Brian Wellis, and Simon Watson (New York: Routledge, 1995), 21–36; here, 31.

[18] Stephen M. Whitehead and Frank J. Barrett, "The Sociology of Masculinity," in *The Masculinities Reader*, ed. Stephen M. Whitehead and Frank J. Barrett (Cambridge: Polity, 2001), 1–26; here, 4. Lynne Segal points out that "in jobs sex-typed as male, and with home lives which remain strongly male-dominated . . . the lower working-class tends to produce sharper sex-role distinctions than other classes," Lynne Segal, *Slow Motion: Changing Masculinities, Changing Men*, 3rd rev. ed. (Basingstoke: Palgrave Macmillan, 2007), 222.

[19] Sarah Colvin, "*Abziehen oder Abkacken?* Young Men in German Prisons: Fiction and Reality," *Edinburgh German Yearbook* 2, *Masculinities in German Culture*, ed.

Sarah Colvin and Peter Davies (Rochester, NY: Camden House, 2008), 262–77; here, 265.

[20] On characteristics of *Männerbünde* (male societies), see George L. Mosse, *The Image of Man: The Creation of Modern Masculinity* (New York: Oxford UP, 1996), 142.

[21] Suzanne E. Hatty, *Masculinities, Violence, and Culture* (Thousand Oaks, CA: Sage, 2000), 6.

[22] Anne Campbell, *Out of Control: Men, Women and Aggression* (London: Pandora, 1993), 132.

[23] Hatty, *Masculinities*, 46.

[24] Hatty, *Masculinities*, 119. Hatty refers here to Victor Seidler, *Man Enough: Embodying Masculinity* (London: Sage, 1997).

[25] Hatty, *Masculinities*, 120. Hatty refers to Michael A. Messner, "When Bodies Are Weapons," in *Through the Prism of Difference: Readings of Sex and Gender*, ed. Maxine Baca Zinn, Pierrette Hondagneu-Sotelo, and Michael A. Messner (Boston: Allyn & Bacon, 1997), 257–72.

[26] Mosse, *The Image of Man*, 4.

[27] As the novel is told from Daniel's first-person perspective, readers learn only about his prison experiences.

[28] Yvonne Jewkes, *Captive Audience: Media, Masculinity and Power in Prison* (Portland, OR: Willan Publishing, 2002), 51, 19.

[29] Yvonne Tasker, *Spectacular Bodies: Gender, Genre and the Action Cinema* (London: Routledge, 1993), 2.

[30] Mosse, *The Image of Man*, 5.

[31] Sandra Walklate, *Gender, Crime and Criminal Justice* (Portland, OR: Willan Publishing, 2001), 69.

[32] Jewkes, *Captive Audience*, 51.

[33] See Cooke, "'GDR Literature' in the Berlin Republic," especially 66–67, 68. Cooke specifically refers to Hensel's *Zonenkinder* in the context of the post-GDR nostalgia expressed by young writers.

[34] Anna Saunders, *Honecker's Children: Youth and Patriotism in East(ern) Germany, 1979–2002* (Manchester: Manchester UP, 2007), 165.

[35] Thomas C. Fox, "Post-Communist Fantasies: Generational Conflict in Eastern German Literature," in *Generational Shifts in Contemporary German Culture*, ed. Laurel Cohen-Pfister and Susanne Vees-Gulani (Rochester, NY: Camden House, 2010), 207–24.

[36] Walklate, *Gender*, 57. Walklate refers to Edwin Hardin Sutherland, *Principles of Criminology* (Philadelphia: Lippencott, 1947).

[37] On military education, see Saunders, *Honecker's Children*, 58–68.

[38] Walklate, *Gender*, 67; Walklate refers to Campbell, *Out of Control*.

[39] Walklate, *Gender*, 68; Walklate refers to Campbell, *Out of Control*.

[40] R. W. Connell, *Gender* (Cambridge: Polity, 2002), 144.

[41] James W. Messerschmidt, *Masculinities and Crime: Critique and Reconceptualization of Theory* (Lanham, ML: Rowan & Littlefield Publishing, 1993), 93–96, esp. 95; see also Hatty, *Masculinities*, 117–18.

[42] In an interview with *Spiegel Online*, Meyer points out, "There are similarities regarding solidarity. But in relation to the perverted image of masculinity as it is particularly cultivated in Turkish environments, there are enormous differences": "Unterschicht — was soll denn das sein?" Interview with Florian Gathmann and Jenny Hoch, *Spiegel Online*, 26 February 2008, www.spiegel.de/kultur/literatur/0,1518,536352,00.html (accessed 21 August 2009).

[43] Susan Sontag, *Regarding the Pain of Others* (London: Hamish Hamilton, 2003), 103.

[44] Hensel, *Zonenkinder*, 7. In *Honecker's Children*, Anna Saunders explores the "we-identity" that "has emerged only since confrontation with life in West Germany, and perceptions of Western arrogance and political colonisation, as well as the persistence of economic inequalities between east and west" (5).

[45] Cf. Stirn, "Absturz Ost."

[46] Clemens Meyer, *Gewalten: Ein Tagebuch* (Frankfurt am Main: S. Fischer, 2010).

[47] I am referring to the writer's portrait on the dust jacket of his first book and the portrait accompanying the interview "Ich hab' es richtig krachen lassen," interview with Jan Brandt, *Frankfurter Allgemeine Zeitung*, 11 March 2008, http://www.faz.net/-00myv8 (accessed 10 May 2011).

7: Saša Stanišić, *Wie der Soldat das Grammofon repariert*: Reinscribing Bosnia, or: Sad Things, Positively

Brigid Haines

THE BALKAN REGION IS SUBJECT TO its own kind of Orientalism in the Western imagination. The birthplace of European civilization, it has nevertheless frequently been mythologized as Europe's less civilized other.[1] The eruption of violence in the former Yugoslavia in the 1990s did nothing to dispel this trend. Indeed, it has been argued that even such engaged recent commentators as Peter Handke, W. G. Sebald, Norbert Gstrein, and Juli Zeh struggle to move beyond the stereotypes of exotic yet tragic Balkan otherness.[2] In *Wie der Soldat das Grammofon repariert* (2006; *How the Soldier Repairs the Gramophone*, 2008), however, the other writes back, representing, in the author's own words, "sad things, positively." This novel, loosely based on the author's own experience, concerns the Bosnian conflict of 1992 and its aftermath. Despite evoking a tragic set of events, it is hugely energetic, often humorous, and ultimately life-affirming. It does not shirk the horror of the war, even though it does not represent it directly. Rather, it approaches it obliquely in a number of ways, building into its aesthetic the knowledge that time, like life, moves on. That Stanišić's "sad things, positively" self-description appeared on Twitter, the microblogging social networking site, and in English, are symptomatic of the positive outcome of his own personal story as well; namely, his transformation from child refugee into global bestselling author and multilingual citizen of the world.

Wie der Soldat das Grammofon repariert met with rave reviews both at home in Germany and abroad, particularly in the English-speaking world when Anthea Bell's translation appeared in 2008; it has been translated into some twenty-eight languages. Critics found it an exhilarating read, fast-paced and vivid. Its labyrinthine, patchwork, or symphonic structure, its mixing of genres — part family novel, part migration story, part war memoir, with shades of magic realism — and its bold incorporation of elements of the tragic, the picaresque, the absurd, the surreal, the comic, the melancholic, the lyrical, and the naive drew widespread praise. Stanišić was hailed as a major new voice, "an exceptionally talented, impish and caring writer who has walked to the edge of the abyss," his "crazy-quilt novel" celebrated as "a bold, questing work of art deeply rooted in the complex history of a blood-soaked, bone-planted land."[3] The *Guardian* reviewer called it "a wonderfully inventive and impressive novel."[4] With *Wie der Soldat das Grammofon repariert*, Stanišić won the Publikumspreis of the Ingeborg-Bachmann-Preis in Klagenfurt, was a finalist for the Deutscher Buchpreis in 2006 and, in 2008, was the youngest ever winner of the Chamisso Preis for German writing by authors whose mother tongue is not German.

Stanišić is one of a number of writers who have moved from the former Eastern Bloc to the German-speaking countries since the fall of communism and are contributing collectively to the *Osterweiterung* (Eastern expansion) of, or "Eastern turn"[5] in, contemporary German literature. Together, such writers as Ilija Trojanow (featured in this volume) and Dimitré Dinev from Bulgaria, Artur Becker and Radek Knapp from Poland, Zsuzsa Bánk and Terézia Mora (featured in this volume) from Hungary, and Vladimir Vertlib (featured in this volume) and Wladimir Kaminer from Russia constitute a new wave of German writing, distinct from — though sometimes thematically similar to — Turkish-German literature and other *Migrantenliteratur* (migrant literature). In writing of their homelands, they are capitalizing on the interest of Western readers in the countries "lost" for forty years behind the Iron Curtain, but are also staking a claim in the project of redefining Europe, insisting on broadening out both historically and geographically the Cold-War definitions of Europe based on the Franco-German heart of the European Union. Europe, they insist, is ancient, dynamic, and complex; its peoples are shaped by empires, whether the Ottoman Empire, Austria-Hungary, the Soviet Union, the Third Reich, or global capitalism.

Yet like many of these writers, Stanišić's pedigree is also distinctly German in that, like many of the best contemporary writers, he attended the Deutsches Literaturinstitut Leipzig. He rejects the label "immigrant literature" as "simply wrong, because it is wrongly simple," objecting also to the patronizing assumption that authors who do not write in their mother tongue enrich the host literature, and adding that a language is "the only country without borders."[6] After coming to Germany as a fourteen-year-old in 1992 with his family to escape the fighting in his home town, Višegrad, he attended both high school — where he was encouraged to write by a teacher who spotted his promise — and university in Heidelberg. He has worked as a teaching assistant at Bucknell University in the United States, and as writer-in-residence for the city of Graz. The author of many short stories, as well as a work of fantasy (with Stephanie von Ribbeck), *Aus den Quellen des Harotrud*, and a play, *Go West*, which was staged in Graz in 2008, he currently lives in Berlin and is a keen blogger, tweeter, and soccer fan, a theme that emerges in the novel.

This chapter will show how, through its innovative narrative form, through employing sport as theme and metaphor, and through intertextuality, *Wie der Soldat das Grammofon repariert* registers the violent collapse of Yugoslavia, and brings the story of Bosnia, "perhaps the only true representation of Yugoslavia,"[7] up to date. Engaging the reader in a debate about how to represent the shock of war and displacement without succumbing to despair, it shows how identities are continuously renegotiated in postcommunist Europe. Neither sentimentalizing nor exoticizing Bosnia or former Yugoslavia, it nevertheless creates a space to mourn what has been lost while still insisting on the dynamic potential of historical forces.

The Limitations of Fiction: Representing Bosnia

At the silent heart of the novel lie the genocidal events that occurred in the Bosnian town of Višegrad in 1992 when Serbian soldiers went on the rampage against the Muslim population. While other atrocities during the Bosnian war, such as the Srebrenica massacre, have become iconic, what happened in Višegrad, though shocking in the extreme, is less well known. Višegrad, a town on the river Drina near the Serbian border, was strategically important because of the hydroelectric dam on the river and because it was on the main route connecting Belgrade in Serbia and Sarajevo in Bosnia. Ed Vullamy of the *Guardian* describes the events:

> Night after night, truckloads of Bosnian Muslim civilians were taken down to the bridge and riverbank by Bosnian Serb paramilitaries, unloaded, sometimes slashed with knives, sometimes shot, and thrown into the river, dead or in various states of half-death, turning the turquoise of the Drina red with blood. As well as the slaughter on the bridge, hundreds of Muslims were packed into houses across Visegrad and incinerated alive, including women and children. Visegrad was, too, the location for the one of the most infamous rape camps, at a spa called Vilina Vlas, where Muslim women and girls were violated all night, every night, to the point of madness and sometimes suicide.[8]

The ethnic cleansing was horribly effective: while Višegrad's population before the war was nearly two-thirds Bosniak and less than one-third Serb, by the end of the war, it was virtually a Serb-only town and remains so today. What happened there was symptomatic of the Bosnian war in general — a genocidal conflict orchestrated from the outside that turned communities against themselves and ended with a re-mapping of the area that seemed to some to hand victory to the aggressors.[9]

These events are not portrayed directly, however, but via the first-person testimony of a child narrator, Aleksandar Krsmanović,[10] who is close to the fighting without witnessing it directly or, at the time, understanding its causes. Escaping with his family to Germany, he catalogues his memories into lists, researches the war, and returns years later, hoping to fill in the gaps in his knowledge. By using a child narrator who matures, Stanišić brings the reader close to the intimate, rather than the macro-political, causes of the hostilities, and invites the reader to reflect on the dislocations of exile and the painful processes of coming to terms with the loss of a homeland.[11]

The very few negative reviews of *Wie der Soldat das Grammofon repariert* accuse Stanišić of kitsch and whimsy but are, I believe, based on a misreading of his narrative technique.[12] It is true that in the opening chapters, the author plays with bucolic Balkan stereotypes and risks the sentimentality that can attend a child narrator, especially one as naïve as Aleksandar, despite all his precociousness. The scenes, however, are crafted to show that the hatred of the other that emerged with frightening speed at this period came from tensions that had always been present. One of the earliest scenes, for example, is set at a village party thrown by Aleksandar's grandparents to inaugurate a new outdoor toilet. The food at the feast is lavishly described; there is much jocularity and merrymaking; the scene, like much of the novel, has the ring of magic realism. But the incipient nationalism surfaces when one of the guests objects to the gypsy songs being sung, insisting that they should be singing patriotic Serbian songs instead. The child narrator does not understand that the future of his country is at stake; rather, at this stage, he is still inspired by and devoted to the memory of his beloved grandfather, Slavko. Slavko is associated throughout both with Josip Tito's vision of a multiethnic, federal, communist Yugoslavia, and with the transformative gift of storytelling, which Slavko bequeathed to Aleksandar shortly before he died. The narrative undermines Slavko's dual legacy by a pattern of references to, for example, the hostility between Aleksandar's father and his uncle Miki, and to the sadness of his mother that the boy's gift with invention can do nothing to alleviate. The ethnic tensions that were latent but contained in Bosnia until Yugoslavia started to break apart are shown to exist in the most private of spaces: the family. Aleksandar's mother is Bosniak, his father and radicalized nationalist uncle are Serbian. When the family flees to neighboring Serbia and the car is searched at the border, the mother says "I'm the weapon they're looking for" (113).[13] Aleksandar discovers that he himself effectively embodies Yugoslavia, and that while this used to be an unproblematic identity, it is now in crisis. In one of the key statements from the novel, he realizes that he is "a mixture. I'm half and half. I am a Yugoslav

— which means, I'm disintegrating" (41).[14] While Aleksandar does not disintegrate, however, the family never recovers. In exile, his father, always a gloomy critic of Yugoslavia's leaders, criticizes the Dayton Accord that effectively partitioned Bosnia along ethnic lines, and the now-adult Aleksandar has to grapple with the knowledge that his uncle Miki, who in the toilet scene is just about to join the Serbian army, became one of the perpetrators. From the start, then, the apparent idyll of ethnic harmony is undermined.

This is reflected in the narrative form that progressively challenges Slavko's utopian manifesto on the holistic power of storytelling. After the family's flight to Germany, the linear narrative fractures and becomes a kaleidoscope of pieces and fragments that refract rather than represent the fighting directly. The novel apparently consists of twenty-eight chapters, most of which have long titles reminiscent of Grimmelshausen or Cervantes that refer, somewhat elliptically, to the events contained in them. For example, the chapter describing the family's terrifying stay in the Višegrad cellar while the fighting rages overhead, where Aleksandar meets the Muslim girl Asija, is called "What we play in the cellar, what the peas taste like, why silence bares its fangs, who has the right sort of name, what a bridge will bear, why Asija cries, how Asija smiles" (86). But when this norm is broken, unpredictability sets in: several chapter headings after the move to Germany consist merely of a date, the content being a letter written by an increasingly desperate Aleksandar to Asija, the lost girl who becomes the focus of his longing. Another chapter contains the transcripts of Aleksandar's calls to various numbers in Sarajevo in his search for Asija. A novel within the novel, with its own contents list, further disrupts the reading experience. Entitled "When Everything Was All Right, by Aleksandar Krsmanović, with a foreword by Granny Katarina and an essay for Mr. Fazlagić" and dedicated to Grandpa Slavko, it represents Aleksandar's attempt to capture his memories, both idyllic ones of fishing in the Drina, and compromising and shaming ones — as, for example, when the young Aleksandar joined in rejecting the friendship of the visiting Italian dam engineer, Francesco, in a collective act of homophobia. The final chapters return to the narrative present, recounting Aleksandar's visit back to his homeland and resuming the chronology of events.

Aleksandar's is far from being the only voice represented. The polyphony serves to incorporate some of the testimony that Aleksandar himself, with his limited perspective, cannot give. The text incorporates monologues from, for example, Aleksandar's mother, still enraged by her dead father's drunkenness; the rabbi cruelly taunted by the soldiers (this chapter heading incidentally consisting simply of three dots); Asija bewailing the destruction of her village; and the soldier lamenting his lost beloved. Aleksandar's formerly silent grandmother speaks of her newfound sense of liberation in the United States, while his friend Zoran bears witness to the throwing of bodies into the river and the suicide of Ííka Hasan, an unwilling perpetrator of this act until he can take no more of it (247). In Aleksandar's imaginative essay, the river herself, whom Aleksandar envies because she can see so much, laments that she has had to carry away so many corpses, cannot hide, close her eyes to crimes, or save anyone at all (184).

The increasingly polyphonous and fractured novel is styled as a *Künstlerroman* (artist's novel), reflecting Aleksandar's development from a naïve storyteller confident of his own powers into a postmodern writer who accepts the limitations of fiction, the incompleteness and instability of memory, the possibilities of fluid identities, and the strategic necessity of silence. The novel's chaotic structure and inventiveness reflect "the splintering of the glass of Aleksandar's perception and life course"[15] and his attempt to find an adequate means of expressing his loss and bewilderment as he works through his politically induced crisis of identity, distancing himself from the utopian aspect of his grandfather's aesthetic while simultaneously preserving memories and a belief in the power of invention. Slavko's credo was that "the most valuable gift of all is invention, imagination is your greatest wealth" (1), but Aleksandar is soon silenced by his grandmother's grief at Slavko's funeral, and he expresses his impotence in a rant against death and closure, taking his cue from his artist father's belief that "a painter must never be satisfied with what he sees" but rather must "reshuffle and rebuild reality" (13). Stanišić shows that mimesis is not adequate, and neither is pure narrative, which tends to closure. Aleksandar resolves to be "a soccer-playing, fishing, serial artist of the Unfinished" (13). Just as he then paints pictures that are unfinished, so too the kaleidoscopic structure of the remainder of novel after the catastrophic intrusion of war represents aspects of reality without attempting completeness or closure. Years later, the closer he returns to the scene of his greatest fear, the cellar, the more his memory lists compiled in exile — of smells, of buildings in the town, of girls, of silences, of his unfinished paintings, and of questions he did not dare to ask in the cellar — are intercut into the narrative. His desire upon returning is to fill in the gaps, but despite the fact that he has become a good listener, some people in the aftermath of conflict do not want to talk and even think it is better not to — for example, the wife of the teacher, glad that her now-demented husband can hide from both memory and the terrible present. Zoran's endless repetitions of the trauma scene and his angry rejection of Aleksandar as a stranger who should be glad of it (244) are painful, as is Aleksandar's shame when he cannot defend his mother's name to the old policeman, still in office, who had been involved in the massacres. Stanišić provides no closure, except tentatively in terms of Aleksandar's own personal healing process: the novel's last words, "yes, I'm here" (277) affirm his acceptance of the present moment and the realization that there is no way back.

Ideals and Identities: Sport

Sport is employed as a thematic thread providing connections across the fragments; in one key stand-alone episode, it also serves as a metaphor for the fighting. Soccer has recently played a positive role in the construction of a West German, and then a German, identity, as for example in F. C. Delius's *Der Sonntag, an dem ich Weltmeister wurde* (The Sunday I became a world champion) and the film *Das Wunder von Bern* (The miracle of Bern), not to mention the 2006 World Cup fever that provided the mass spectacle of Germans waving their flags without embarrassment or irony for the first time in fifty years. In contrast, Stanišić's sporting references chart the breakup and disappearance of Yugoslavia, and the transformation of Bosnia, and catalogue the effects this has on the identities that are constructed out of that state and that republic.

Some of Stanišić sporting references are trivial and humorous, and some deathly serious, a mix that reflects the comic-tragic border crossings of the novel itself. Early in the novel, sport functions as a sign of harmony, leisure, and healthy competition, though there is always an edge. Aleksandar's passions are playing soccer with his friend Edin, fishing in the river Drina, storytelling, and painting. But as he registers the disappearance of normality in the buildup to war, the sporting references become more sinister. An excellent fisherman with a love of tall fishing yarns, he wins a local championship but cannot attend the final contest because it is too near the fighting. When the soldiers arrive, their idea of sport is to fish with a hand grenade, kill a horse by tipping it off the bridge into the river, and shoot a dog, showing off to local children; the purity of sport becomes abased. In the cellar, as the radio now names his town up above as the scene of fighting, Aleksandar destroys his own marbles, perhaps signifying his child's understanding that the possibility of play is suspended. When his family hurriedly load the car and leave, he is not allowed to take his soccer ball, so he gives it to his friend Edin. His last view through the rear view mirror is of Edin chalking goalposts on a wall and taking some shots, clinging to normality. Later, his friend Zoran, who remains behind, reports that no one plays anything any more and the sports hall is full of people, prisoners or refugees, he is not sure which. When Aleksandar returns years later to a shattered country where the Muslim population has gone and the perpetrators of ethnic cleansing, including his own uncle, walk the streets unchallenged, the goalposts have been removed from the school playing field.

The key sporting scene in the novel is set up to function as a microcosm of the Bosnian war, in line with Stanišić's aesthetic of showing rather than telling. Placed late in the novel and narrated in the third person, it has no framing authorial comments to guide the reader. During a ceasefire in the fighting between the Serbian and the Territorial Defense forces over a strategically important route to Sarajevo, a soccer match is held. It is the third such match; the Serbs have won the previous two. Before it starts, two players from opposite sides who are old school friends, Kiko and Mikimaus, embrace over the body of a dead comrade. During play, with the Serbs two-nil up, the Territorial Defense player Meho accidentally kicks the ball into the woods, which are mined. Ordered to fetch it, he shits himself but succeeds, after some tense moments, in retrieving the ball. Afterwards, he cries as he borrows clean trousers from the dead comrade. On returning to the match, he discovers that the ceasefire has finished and the Serbs, under their brutish commander, General Mikado, have turned their guns on their opponents. When one of the Territorial Defense players dithers, he is shot dead by the Serb goalie. The desperate Territorial Defense captain, Dino Zoff, fearing for the lives of the rest of his men, challenges Mikado to let them continue the game, promising that if his side wins, no one will die. The challenge is accepted, and the match continues. One death and several goals later, Mikimaus, the normally silent, giant farm boy — who only realized that he was a Serb when the war was looming and who is only in the war in order to escape the drudgery of farm work — leads a mutiny of the Serbs against their own captain in the name of fairness, insisting that a wrongly disallowed goal stand and the match be continued. The result is a draw, but a victory for sporting values.

With its obvious echoes of those famous fraternizations between German and British troops who discovered a common humanity on the Western front on Christmas Day 1914, Stanišić has also constructed the scene to bring out the peculiarities and absurdities of the Bosnian conflict: both sides speak the same language, they often know each other, their personal motivations have nothing to do with the strategic aims of those directing the fighting from afar. The scene shows the bewildering speed of events and the — even for a war situation — grotesquely deadly stakes and carelessness with human life. One could also comment on the particular brutality of the Serbs, though it is shown to be chance that they grab their weapons first when the ceasefire ends. Mikimaus's mutiny restores fair play in, and proper closure to, the game, which serves to highlight the messiness, open-endedness, and stalemate of the actual fighting.

It is worth considering why, when much of the novel is autobiographically inspired, Stanišić invented this match.[16] Four characteristics of soccer are its relative simplicity (the only requirements are a ball and two improvised goals), its near universality (it is played all over the world), the fierce loyalty local teams engender, and the fact that it is the national sport for a majority of the world's countries.[17] Its simplicity and universality make it suitable for metaphorical use, but Stanišić also uses soccer to chart the disappearance of Yugoslavia and the transformation of Bosnia, and to trace the changing identity of his protagonist as he migrates West. Vic Duke and

Liz Crolley argue that soccer "captures the notion of an imagined community perfectly,"[18] and that the politics of soccer in relation to the state is most straightforward where the state "overlaps to a large degree with the nation."[19] Yugoslavia, however, was never that simple. On the one hand, its leaders aspired to creating a national identity, and the success of its national soccer team no doubt helped.[20] Bosnians, incidentally, because of the multiethnic nature of their republic, had the largest stake in this collective project. Yet the country was actually composed of a variety of nations held together in a federation under a communist system, and the nationalism of the various ethnicities was often expressed through club loyalties. These tensions are explored in what follows.

Aleksandar is a Red Star Belgrade fan who, though brought up in a secular household, has been known to pray for his team's success in the mosque. Red Star, one of the most successful teams in former Yugoslavia, were a Serbian team strongly associated with Serbian nationalism, whose supporters, led at one stage by the warlord Arkan, were involved in a famous riot with Dynamo Zagreb fans in 1990 just before Croatian independence. Praying for this team in a mosque is therefore a gesture heavy with ironies that Stanišić characteristically does not draw attention to. For Aleksandar, there is no contradiction, however, because of his mixed parentage that only becomes troublesome as the state is threatened. He is not the only Red Star fan for whom his team allegiance does not map seamlessly onto his ethnic identity. Before venturing into the forest on his potentially deadly mission during the soccer match, Meho, who is playing for the Territorial Defense, the Bosniak (Muslim) side, takes off his precious Red Star Belgrade shirt, and entrusts it to Marko on the other side. When asked by Marko how he, a Bosniak, can support a Serbian team, Meho reacts with an expression of unswerving loyalty that Nick Hornby himself would recognize: "I don't care where the team I support comes from, the lads are only playing soccer" (214). When Meho is shot, his precious Red Star shirt, with all that it symbolizes of potential unity across and beyond the newly imposed ethnic boundaries, and of the ability of sport to rise above nationalism, is also destroyed.

But Aleksandar is not like the old men he meets in Sarajevo years later, who mourn the good times when the Yugoslav team was great — 1962 in Chile — and bemoan the loss of a national side: "if we were still all one country . . . we'd be unbeatable today" (203). Even though, as his friend Kiko puts it in one of the most telling sporting metaphors, the whole country was relegated when war threatened (225), Aleksandar, with the adaptability of youth, moves on. He develops a new team loyalty in Germany, to Schalke 04. He continues to fish, and spends his time playing Sensible Soccer on his friend's PC. Meanwhile, his mother in the United States takes up ice-skating and looks forward to attending an American football game. While the old men remembering 1962 see only the negative

— "Sixty-two in Chile . . . the country was doing all right, and when a country is doing all right sport doesn't do badly either. Now it's like this: shit here, shit there" (203) — Aleksandar is not stuck in the past. But interestingly, his national affiliation, it seems, does not transfer to Germany. Rejecting the glib discourse of German multiculturalism that suggests that he is well-integrated, he notes that he backs five national teams. He doesn't name them — he leaves this comment hanging — but presumably they are Bosnia, Serbia, Croatia, Macedonia, and Slovenia. Yugoslavia may have disappeared as a state, but that is not the end of its story.

Endless Reinvention: Intertexts

Sporting references thus contribute continuity and resonance to the fractured narrative and to Aleksandar's continuously renegotiated identity; so too does the use of intertextuality. Stanišić draws on at least three intertexts in order to deepen and enhance his search for the meaning of the events in Višegrad. While Aleksandar does not witness the killing, the burning of houses, the carting off of women to rape camps, and the throwing of bodies into the river from the town's famous bridge, his friend Zoran, who stays behind, does. In a ranting but lyrical phone call to Aleksandar, he expresses his despair at the breakdown of society and his hatred of the soldiers responsible for the atrocities and of Aleksandar for leaving. His reference to Paul Celan's famous Holocaust poem "Todesfuge" (Death Fugue), "I like to read. Death is a German champion and a Bosnian outright world champion" (124),[21] serves as a stark reminder that genocide, which post-Holocaust Europeans tend complacently to believe occurs only in such far off places as Rwanda, can still occur here. How that can be is the central question that the adult Aleksandar investigates in the second half of the novel. His quest is indicated in the poem he cites by the Bosnian poet Mak Dizdar:

> Who is that, what is that? Forgive me!
> is it,
> Where does it come from,
> Where is it going,
> This country
> Of Bosnia?
> Tell me! (198)

The question posed here of the history and future of Bosnia is answered progressively through references to a third, and the primary intertext, Ivo Andrić's Nobel-Prize-winning novel, *The Bridge over the Drina* (1945). Andrić (1892–1975), a Croatian Catholic by birth, who was imprisoned by the Austrians during the First World War and later worked as a civil servant and ambassador for Yugoslavia, is revered by Bosnians of all ethnic groups. His novel chronicles the history of Višegrad through its famous bridge, from its building in the sixteenth century by an Ottoman vizier to the First World War. It is a story of empires and of the peoples subject to them: the bridge was built as a statement of Ottoman power but becomes a symbol of timeless endurance when the Ottoman empire declines and retreats, to be replaced by the Austrian empire. The different peoples of the town enjoy varying fortunes depending on the macro-political situation over the centuries.

Stanišić's novel functions as a homage to and conclusion of Andrić's, though it is quite different in tone and scope. Andrić's tone is wise and knowing, his perspective sovereign and detached. The events he depicts all occur in Višegrad, where the bridge and the townspeople continue to endure even when the wider world is engaged in the "war to end all wars." Stanišić's fractured aesthetic and chaotic structure reflect the bewilderment of the victim of historical violence rather than the detachment of the bystander; his protagonist builds a new life in a global arena, returning to find the town and Bosnia itself radically transformed.

The intertextual references work on a number of levels. First, certain incidents and images, often connected to the bridge, act as literary echoes to any reader familiar with the iconic Bosnian novel, suggesting continuity across the ages. These include the sight of women washing blood from the bridge after acts of violence, the trepidation about whether the bridge will survive the fighting (it always does), accidental drowning in the river, suicide by drowning, and the grisly and bestial topos of murder by skewering (246).[22] Secondly, Andrić is metonymically present in the novel in the fact that his statue in the town is destroyed by the Serbian forces. The novel's reproduction of this violent historical event unequivocally signifies rupture, the impossibility of the vision of an enduring, ethnically diverse Bosnia and a federal Yugoslavia that Andrić espoused and promoted in his life and works. The references to the eponymous gramophone bear this out, too: for Andrić, the gramophone signifies modernity, cosmopolitanism, and the power of art in the last uneasy years before the outbreak of the First World War: "Everywhere the gramophone ground and churned out Turkish marches, Serbian patriotic songs or arias from Viennese operettas, according to the tastes of the guests for whom it played. For men would no longer go where there was neither noise, glitter nor movement" (226). For Stanišić, it signifies violence and violation: in the cellar, a Serb soldier repairs an old-fashioned gramophone he has found by kicking it. But in the third and most powerful use of intertextuality, Stanišić's postmodern aesthetic incorporates some of Andrić's modernist insights into the catastrophic effect of macro-political events on the relations between — and on the psyches of — those subject to them. Thus, when the mood turns sour in Stanišić's toilet party, the reader is reminded of the sudden intrusion of communal violence in *The Bridge over the Drina* where, retreating before the advancing Austrians, the Muslim population takes revenge on one of their number who has been outspoken in pointing out the futility of resistance by nailing his ear to the ground: "So in a few moments there took place what in any one of those moments would have seemed impossible and incredible" (120). And when Aleksandar's father rails against the Dayton Accord for carving up Bosnia, he is like Andrić's townspeople in 1913, looking at a map showing the future partition of the Balkan Peninsula, "They looked at the paper and saw nothing in those curving lines, but they knew and understood everything, for their geography was in their blood and they felt biologically their picture of the world" (229).

Stanišić's novel echoes many of the themes of this volume: like Bronsky, he writes of assertive young identities within an increasingly global culture; like Berg, he questions what it means to be German; like Vertlib, he writes of migration with a surprising lightness of touch. Like many of the authors represented here, he employs a self-conscious playfulness and postmodern polyphony, unashamedly offering publishers the "new readability" they seek after decades of introspective and aesthetically challenging German fiction. Most interesting is the comparison with Mora's *Alle Tage*. Both novels express the sense of displacement and loss arising from the breakup of Yugoslavia, and stretch the novel form in order to adequately represent the effects of the shock of war. Biendarra's argument that Mora refuses to celebrate the possible liberatory effects of diaspora that are glibly championed by some critics partially holds true for Stanišić as well. For what is remarkable in Stanišić's text is the immutability of the sense of loss and of the brute fact of nationalism at the heart of Bosnia past and present. Nevertheless, the differences are striking, for while Mora's text is deliberately generalized, and her protagonist remains traumatized, set apart from his new surroundings, able to speak but not to communicate, Aleksandar proactively seeks ways to convey the specificity of his experience and of those around him, with the result that he does not remain isolated between cultures but evolves along with them.

According to his Nobel citation, Andrić asked "what forces . . . act to fashion a people and a nation";[23] so, too, in *Wie der Soldat das Grammofon repariert*, does Stanišić. But while Andrić's epic novel is built around the solidity of the bridge and highlights the impotence of individuals to influence their fate in the age of nation-states, Stanišić's postmodern novel, even as it charts the death of Yugoslavia, takes its cue from the fluidity of the river itself that allows for endless reinvention. Resisting Andrić's fatalism and Mora's pessimism, Stanišić finds a way to write about sad things, positively.

Notes

This article was generously supported by the Arts and Humanities Research Council under their Research Leave Scheme.

[1] Maria Todorova, *Imagining the Balkans* (New York: OUP, 1997).

[2] Boris Previšić, "Poetik der Marginalität: Balkan Turn gefällig?," in *Von der nationalen zur internationalen Literatur: Transkulturelle deutschsprachige Literatur und Kultur im Zeitalter globaler Migration*, ed. Helmut Schmitz (Amsterdam: Rodopi, 2009), 189–203.

[3] Donna Seaman, "War and Bigotry from a Child's Eye View," *Los Angeles Times*, 15 June 2008, articles.latimes.com/2008/jun/15/books/bk-seaman15 (accessed 31 March 2010).

[4] Josh Lacey, "Rage among the Ruins," *The Guardian*, 5 May 2008. Links to further reviews can be found on Stanišić's personal website, www.kuenstlicht.de/rezensionen.html (accessed 31 March 2010).

[5] See Michaela Bürger-Koftis, ed., *Eine Sprache — viele Horizonte: Die Osterweiterung der deutschsprachigen Literatur. Porträts einer neuen europäischen Generation* (Vienna: Praesens 2009), and Brigid Haines, "The Eastern Turn in Contemporary German, Swiss and Austrian Literature," *Debatte: Journal of Contemporary Central and Eastern Europe* 16, no. 2 (2008): 135–49.

[6] Saša Stanišić, "Three Myths of Immigrant Writing: A View from Germany," wordswithoutborders.org/article/three-myths-of-immigrant-writing-a-view-from-germany/ (accessed 31 March 2010).

[7] Misha Glenny, *The Fall of Yugoslavia. The Third Balkan War* (London: Penguin, 1992), 162.

[8] Ed Vulliamy and Nerma Jelacic, "The Warlord of Visegrad," *The Guardian*, 11 August 2005, www.guardian.co.uk/world/2005/aug/11/warcrimes.features11 (accessed 31 March 2010).

[9] Noel Malcolm, *Bosnia. A Short History* (London: Macmillan, 1994), 252.

[10] Saša is a diminutive form for Aleksandar, showing the closeness of author and protagonist.

[11] Maria Motter, "Ohne Kunstblatt," www.falter.at/web/shop/detail.php?id=6598 (accessed 31 March 2010).

[12] See, for example, Iris Radisch, "Der Krieg trägt Kittelschürze," *Die Zeit*, 5 October 2006, www.zeit.de/2006/41/L-Stanisic, and Sam Munson, "The Naive Fiction of Saša Stanišić," *The New York Sun*, 23 April 2008, www.nysun.com/arts/nave-fiction-of-saa-stanii-263/75158/ (both accessed 31 March 2010).

[13] Saša Stanišić, *How the Soldier Repairs the Gramophone*, translated by Anthea Bell (London: Weidenfeld & Nicolson, 2008). Quotations are taken from the English translation unless otherwise indicated. (Editor's note: The term "football" has been replaced throughout with "soccer," as is the case also with the American version of Bell's translation published by Grove Press.)

[14] The last key sentence, which is unaccountably missing from Bell's translation, is my translation.

[15] Unpublished interview with the author, 29 May 2008.

[16] A survivor whom Stanišić interviewed about life in the trenches told him that fraternization and trade in goods between the two sides did occur but that they did not play soccer because they did not have a ball. Unpublished interview with the author, 29 May 2008.

[17] Vic Duke and Liz Crolley, *Football, Nationality and the State* (Harlow: Longman, 1996), 1.

[18] Duke and Crolley, *Football*, 4.

[19] Duke and Crolley, *Football*, 5.

[20] As Jonathan Wilson reminds us, "There was a time when Yugoslavia was the Brazil of Europe," *Behind the Curtain. Travels in Eastern European Football* (London: Orion, 2006), 98.

[21] The allusion is much clearer in the original: "Ich lese und liebe das Lesen, der Tod ist ein Meister aus Deutschland, er ist gerade ein Meister aus Bosnien," Saša Stanišić, *Wie der Soldat das Grammofon repariert* (Munich: Luchterhand, 2006), 147.

[22] See also Ivo Andrić, *The Bridge over the Drina*, trans. by Lovett F. Edwards (London: Harvill Press, 1995), 48–50.

[23] nobelprize.org/nobel_prizes/literature/laureates/1961/press.html (accessed 31 March 2010).

8: Ilija Trojanow, *Der Weltensammler*: Separate Bodies, or: An Account of Intercultural Failure

Julian Preece

A Necessary Novel

ILIJA TROJANOW'S *DER WELTENSAMMLER* (The collector of worlds, 2006),[1] a novel in three long chapters about the Victorian explorer Richard F. Burton, was welcomed in the review sections of the highbrow German-language press. In fact, its author, already well known for his travel writing and journalism, soon came to be feted as a new literary star. Ilija Trojanow has good looks and well-developed communication skills and is ready to take sides in public debates. A further selling point is his fascinating and unique personal backstory, which is often summarized on book covers and in newspaper profiles. Born in Bulgaria in 1965, his family fled the communist regime when he was seven years old, finally settling in Nairobi, Kenya, where he attended first an English-speaking school, then the Deutsche Schule, where he learnt German for the first time and took his Abitur (graduation diploma). After studying in Munich, he lived in Bombay and Cape Town before settling recently in Vienna. Contemporary cosmopolitan Germany is tempted to see an ideal image of itself reflected in such a writer. Austrians are reminded of a time when the peripheries of the Habsburg Empire produced many of their most celebrated poets and thinkers. Trojanow's *Der Weltensammler* was a novel that all the German-speaking countries perhaps needed to read in 2006. It was received both as an original *Abenteuerroman* (adventure novel, the term that appears most frequently in reviews) and as a contribution to discussions about race and identity in the wake of the American "war on terror" and particularly of the ongoing German debates about immigration and the value of culturally heterogeneous societies.[2]

What was missed in the broadly positive assessments of the novel and its unlikely hero for a German-language novel is that it enacts the opposite of contemporary liberal thinking on interculturality. Trojanow's Burton is not the role model for interaction between East and West that he appears at first sight to be. In fact, by the end he has more or less failed. In this chapter, I wish to focus on a specific and as yet unexplored theme in the novel; namely, the body as a source of metaphor and identity. A discussion of the body will highlight a feature that has not been fully recognized in critical discussion of the novel hitherto. I aim to retrace the journey that Burton travels in his novel (which is intellectual and emotional as well as physical) in order to show up the limits of his endeavors to transcend cultural barriers.

For all its apparent celebration of postcolonial hybridity and cross-cultural osmosis — which Burton practices with consummate skill and feeling and evident satisfaction — *Der Weltensammler* is about qualified failure. We last see the hero at the end of chapter three, physically broken, ravaged by malaria, at loggerheads with John Hanning Speke after both men have lost the respect of the local Africans. Throughout the novel, Burton's physical state is an indicator of his mental well being in alien climes and the success or failure of his series of missions. While he was mildly injured in Arabia, where he takes on the guise of doctor, he had earlier returned seriously ill from India, after initially feigning sickness in order to be relieved of his duties. A true servant of the Empire must learn to master his own body, at least in public and for the sake of outward appearances. For example, General Napier, Burton's commanding officer, experiences pain with every step on account of wounds suffered in battle and cannot sleep on account of rheumatism, but even though "half a cripple" (203), he sticks it out. Burton implies that the role Napier plays in the British Empire is the real cause of his poor health. "Does not the responsibility which is bestowed upon you for a country which is so complex, so incomprehensible, so many-sided, weigh you down sometimes?" (205) Napier appears only to half-understand the question and replies that exercising power is never unpleasant. Napier denies his body, which Burton never does.

Der Weltensammler is Trojanow's third novel, after the semi-autobiographical *Die Welt ist groß und Rettung lauert überall* (The world is large and salvation lurks everywhere, 1996, filmed in 2008) and the co-authored *Autopol* (1997).[3] It took him some seven years to write, researching on location in India, Africa, and Arabia, but the material had preoccupied him even longer. He has also already produced a number spin-offs and sequels, which either give an account of his research or take the Burton story further.[4] Trojanow trod in Burton's footsteps by taking himself on a pilgrimage to Mecca. His book-length report on his experience, which he writes as a believer and in the tradition of Arabic Mecca travel narratives, is a contribution to the better understanding of Islam in the West.[5]

Ideal Alter Ego?

Trojanow himself is a multilingual traveler, who abhors being pinned down when asked about his primary cultural or national allegiances, and this historical biographical novel about a traveler and writer who has fascinated him since his boyhood in Kenya is something of an idealized autobiography. As an adventure hero, Burton's greatest feat for Trojanow has been to elude all definitions, which in itself is a Romantic reaffirmation of individual uniqueness. His Burton explores identities and linguistic personae by testing reactions in a series of encounters with the resident populations in colonial British India and Ottoman Arabia, where the novel's first two chapters are set. In the third chapter, set in as yet uncolonized East Africa on an expedition to find the source of the Nile, Burton is presented through the eyes of the leader of the African bearers, Sidi Murbarak Bombay, who has been on similar expeditions with the likes of the American Henry Morton Stanley. *Der Weltensammler* is structured around of a series of such narrative reversals. In each chapter, representatives of the subject colonial or native peoples give accounts of Burton's activities, passing on their memories to a scribe (Burton's erstwhile Indian servant Naukaram) or reminiscing to family members (the elderly Sidi Mubarak Bombay). In the Arabian chapter, the Ottoman authorities' investigation into the purpose of Burton's presence on their territory is the counternarrative. This is one way that a postmodern author can relativize the truth claims implicit in a work of fiction.[6]

Trojanow shows how all sides in intercultural encounters create images of each other that, even when placed side by side, do not make a complete picture. In the first two chapters, there is always a gap because a piece of information is missing that results in a mystery or an unanswered question. This strategy changes in the third chapter as Bombay presents himself as an expert on Burton, though he is repeatedly challenged by his wife, who witnessed some the events herself and has heard him tell his tales many times before. As the trio of chapters are framed by discussions that occur immediately after Burton's death on whether he was Catholic, as his widow claims, or Muslim, as others suspect, the novel does not conclude with epistemological closure. Trojanow's Burton keeps everyone guessing in and after death.

Post-Orientalism and the Iraq War

Der Weltensammler was published at a time when the Iraq War still dominated relations between East and West — that is between the Muslim world, which encompasses all three regions where Burton travels, and western Europe and North America. All three German-speaking countries were also preoccupied with political discussions on how their white populations should engage with immigrants with different skin colors and from different cultures. In Austria and Germany, these took place in the shadow of the Holocaust, in Switzerland within a long historical tradition of individual freedom and respect for human rights. All three countries have far-right parties with varying levels of popular support that are opposed to multiculturalism and resent the presence of other races. Trojanow shows that cultures can learn from and respect each other. He was not the only German-language writer to be taking on such big international themes in the mid-2000s. Reviewers associated him with Daniel Kehlmann and Feridun Zaimoğlu, who published superficially similar and equally ambitious novels around the same time.[7] In April 2006, the *Frankfurter Allgemeine Zeitung* devoted one of its Sunday "Topics of the Week" to German novels set in remote corners of the globe ("Chinese deserts and African torture camps, Mecca and Tibet, India, Algeria, the Antarctic and Rumania"), which its critic took to be a welcome sign of openness and a new internationalization.[8]

One of Trojanow's themes is the perception and inevitable multiple misperceptions of one culture by another. In India, Burton has some fun telling General Napier what the natives really think of their British rulers, which he has found out by wandering among them as an ideological agent provocateur (contemporary parallels abound). Disguised as a market seller called Mirza Abdullah, who wins the confidence of his customers with his generous measurements, he provokes a discussion of the recent British defeat in Afghanistan in 1842 when "Sixteen thousand of these Unbelievers pulled out of Kabul, only a single one of them made it to Jalalabad" (191). Needless to say, his listeners find this British military tragedy no bad thing. In the next chapter, Trojanow reports on the marauding Wahhabis — today the austere rulers of Saudi Arabia — who as Bedouin tribesmen attacked pilgrims on their way to and from Mecca for centuries. One of the governmental achievements of the Wahhabi regime after the fall of the Ottoman Empire has been to ensure the safety of pilgrims, who no longer have reason to fear such attacks. Not all changes are for the better, however, and not all contemporary traditions have any basis in history. Unlike today, when Saudi women are not permitted to drive cars, in the 1850s the male Wahhabis thought nothing of riding alongside women who did not cover their faces. "The women did what the men did. They rode their own dromedaries or sat on little saddle cushions behind their men. They did not value the veil and they did not behave in any way like the weaker sex" (315). In their attempts to discover Burton's intentions in Mecca, the Ottomans torture his companions, only to find out that the infliction of physical pain is a most unproductive method of gaining accurate information. Readers in the early twenty-first century will likely think of the treatment of Islamic terror suspects at Guantánamo Bay or Abu Ghraib. The

East African chapter recalls the journey upstream in Joseph Conrad's *Heart of Darkness* (1902). Instead of a parable of colonial cruelty, however, Sidi Mubarak Bombay gives us a tale on the limits of linear western thinking.

Literary Tradition

In contrast to the best-selling novels by Kehlmann and Zaimoğlu, which either have German characters or are set partly in Germany, the most German thing about *Der Weltensammler* is the language, which Trojanow chose over his native Bulgarian and also English, which he learnt as a child before German. His reasons for this choice will hearten those fearful that German cannot compete in today's Anglophone globalized culture. For Trojanow, German has more "art": "From flowing sensuousness to mathematical exactitude, it has everything. Besides, in no other language do you have so much scope for making playful insinuations with compound nouns."[9] At the same time, his literary references in his essays are to international and Anglophone literature. In the interview cited, he reports that he reads Stendhal and Dostoevsky, Sterne and Swift. Günter Grass is the only German author that he refers to — and Grass has also placed himself in a tradition that includes Sterne and Swift. Similar to Grass's *Die Blechtrommel* (1959; *The Tin Drum*, 1961), *Der Weltensammler* features picaresque adventure, linear narrative, flashback, and a hero who engages in trickery and deceit and is a master of disguise and transformation. The two novels share, too, a sensual approach to experience and the joy of telling tales that exist in more than one version.[10]

Trojanow also reworks the master narratives that ideologically underpinned nineteenth-century European colonialism and continue to influence contemporary discourse. *Der Weltensammler* is not simply another account of the exploits of Sir Richard Francis Burton, whose life has attracted up to a dozen English biographers, but a patchwork narrative of a set of encounters between representatives of different worlds, whether they be called West and East, Christian and Muslim or Hindu, colonizers and colonized, or first and third worlds. A postmodern, post-Saïdian novelist working at the beginning of the twenty-first century can only carry this through knowingly, that is, with irony. All the interactions between Burton and the people he meets belong to a by now well-known repertoire that reaches back either to a source like *The Arabian Nights* or to set of stock situations and characters from colonial history or more recent postcolonial novels. The narratives in the novel thus float on top of Burton's own writings, which are Trojanow's first point of reference, as well as Orientalist and post-Orientalist discourses in their many and variegated forms. These include the discourses of master and servant, in which the duplicitous servant traditionally turns the tables on his master and has a superior grasp of what is going on, or that of colonial ruler and native mistress who instructs him in the art of love. The narrative techniques of embedding tales within tales, foregrounding the tellers of the tales, and setting one version off against another are all familiar from *The Arabian Nights*, which Burton translated into English in its entirety. There are also motifs borrowed from this classic orientalizing work, such as that of the stranger moving through the city in disguise in order to hear new tales or pick up information (in *The Arabian Nights*, the Caliph, Haroon al Rashid, does this; in *Der Weltensammler*, it is Burton,). Other reworked ingredients are little more than clichés — the sensual promise of the East that is offset by its chaotic inscrutability, the false self-presentation of the British civilizers as fair-minded, the Oriental as despot or as homosexual, and even the white man deceiving his hosts in Mecca. Like many other highly original novels, *Der Weltensammler* is not original at all.

The Body as Boundary

Der Weltensammler begins with its hero's dead body, which has just been administered the last rites at the insistence of his widow. When alive, Burton uses his body in India, Arabia, and Africa for a variety of purposes. The body is apparently irreducible, what all humanity has in common before language and culture intervene to produce difference. It is decorated, controlled, and enjoyed according to different customs. Burton changes his own physical appearance, having himself circumcised and coloring his skin with walnut oil to pass for a Muslim. He learns to walk, sit, and hold himself like an Oriental rather than an Englishman. Burton's interaction with other cultures is physical in a number of ways. He tests his own bodily endurance and discovers the limits of sensual experience. He first encounters the Indian other as body to his disembodied mind and gaze. When he first lands in Bombay, he is disgusted by the smells of bodily waste, stepping onto a "quai that was built on top of rotten fish, above a layer of dried urine and bilious liquid" (22). As he passes through the teeming crowd in a rickshaw, "A child with no skin is held up to him" (23), presumably in the hope that the white man can cure it. The houses appear to him to be suffering from gangrene and "The few buildings of stature looked like guards in a leper colony" (23). The German word for leper (*Aussätziger*) implies a person who has been "placed outside," who lives beyond the pale of the social mainstream, which has historically been the lot of lepers. On his first walk through the city, his guide is a medical orderly (*Sanitäter* in German, which has connotations of policing public hygiene). They see real lepers begging. One is holding up the traffic by walking naked, his dark skin smeared in fat, and brandishing a sword. When he stumbles, the crowd that he has been threatening jump on him, punching and kicking. The newcomer Burton is disoriented and unsure what the scene means but is advised not to intervene by his frightened guide.

The city of Bombay is all body. It sometimes "burped" and "everything smelt as if marinated in gastric juices" (31). To cap Burton's first impressions of decay and disease, he sees crows pecking at a corpse in front of his hotel. As the sector of the city inhabited by the British is maintained to more hygienic standards, the Carnac Road becomes "the border between the brain of the Empire and its bowels" (25). The India of the native inhabitants is identified with excretion and the smell of digestive processes. It is also rich, fertile, and at times highly desirable. The Indians see the British as "parasites who are sucking out the country's blood" (193). Such a vampiric transaction presupposes the existence of a British body but this is repressed or denied. The Ottomans suspect that the British intend to annex the Arabian Peninsula (the German *einverleiben* signals making another thing a part of one's own body).

Sex is associated by the British with native culture, which is why Burton is advised at dinner on his first evening to avoid relations with native women. Indian women combine all the worst features of the place, being "dire" (*fatal* in German) like the climate, "limited" like the servants, and "septic" like the streets (25). Burton is sexually as well as culturally promiscuous and muses that the intimacy that is entailed by conversing with another in the same language would be compared with sex by his fellow British: "They are sure to think that sharing a language is like sharing a bed" (26). The British cannot be expected to practice what they preach, of course. Men in colonial service learn what little Hindustani they know from their mistresses, but the resulting comedy is lost on them: "One of them spoke exclusively in the imperative; another always used the female conjugation — everyone knew, he was copying what his native lover said" (52). Burton's rewarding physical relationship with Kundalini is emblematic of his productive interaction with India as a whole, but his refusal to grant her dying wish by marrying her in a private ceremony shows up the limits of his engagement with India and Indians.

There is, however, another side to Indian disorder, violence, and bodily stench, and that is the delights that can be accorded the senses by sweet fragrances, narcotics, and sex. All of these are more readily available to a young British officer in the colonized Orient than in his own country. Burton's second walk through Bombay is to a brothel. Following his new servant Naukaram to a premises where he consumes a "wonder drink" (36), he is led to a bedroom where one of the women makes love to him as he has never been made love to before. When it comes to sex,

Burton is not so very different from his compatriots. In Baroda, Naukaram soon procures him Kundalini, who had worked as a sacral prostitute in the Hindu temple. She now instructs her new master in the art of being a good lover, just as his guru Upanitsche teaches him Sanskrit. Kundalini teaches the first English translator of the *Kama Sutra* to give as well as to receive. The best joke in the novel is that Burton's Oriental sex lesson adds up to no more than assimilating the information that women can experience a sexual climax. But Kundalini will not share food with him, refuses to spend the night in his bed, and will not let him kiss her. She and Burton do not have children because she applies a herbal concoction as a contraceptive. He, too, keeps his distance. She asks to marry him only on her deathbed when she is wasting away from a mysterious disease, but he refuses. Through her, Burton's learning and his encounter with India are eroticized. As she sits astride his "pulsating astonishment" in an ostensibly dominant physical position, Kundalini teaches him about local life and wisdom by telling him stories. Like Schererazade in the bed of the Sultan, she delays his sexual satisfaction until she reaches the end of her tale.

After Kundalini's unexpected death, the grieving Burton surrounds himself with apes, with whom he performs the social ceremony of taking tea. He intensifies his spying missions. Subjecting himself to the pain of an adult circumcision, he aims to join the indistinguishable nonindividualized mass of native bodies ("A rising in the breath of the universe. Almost a nothing," 185) in order to disprove what Upanitsche has told him — that he can "discard his disguise at any time," whereas "We are prisoners of our skin. Fasting is not the same as starving" (212). When he is arrested by mistake by the British, he undergoes more pain, preferring to let himself be sodomized by a truncheon under interrogation than give away his true identity to his interrogators. Burton has now become the marked, feminized native body. In a letter to his brother and sister in which he first mentions a homosexual brothel, Burton declared himself to be "no longer even sure of his genders" (110). As a spy, his greatest success is to identify this brothel as the locus for the exchange of secret military information, which has been causing the British problems for some time. Yet his superiors are so scandalized by the results of Burton's investigations that they deny the news can be true. What is even more scandalous is that the British officers are letting themselves be sodomized in this establishment, thus subverting (in play, so to speak, and in secret) the imperialist and patriarchal order. Their changing places with either the woman or the native male must be wrong, in the eyes of the officers Burton reports to, for no other reason than that it has security implications for the Empire. Throughout this chapter, the British project what they reject about their own physicality onto India and the Indians. Burton weaves his way between the two sides but, by rejecting Kundalini, shows himself ultimately to be a prisoner of his British identity.

The Cultural Hybrid as Failure

The next leper (in the sense of *Aussätziger*) that appears in the novel is known as The Bastard of Baroda, whose story is told in a subchapter entitled "Son of Two Mothers" (178–82). He is an alter ego for Burton, and by extension for Trojanow, too. The illegitimate son of an Irish deserter and a native woman from beyond the North-West Frontier, he is an embarrassment to the British, though they are nevertheless grateful for his services as legal interpreter when they need them. Caught between cultures, he has a facility for intercultural communication. He learnt English from his father and also knows many of the Indian native dialects. The figure of the "Anglo-Indian" or "Euro-Asian" is familiar from English novels set in colonial India, such as George Orwell's highly critical *Burmese Days* (1934). The similarities between Trojanow's and Orwell's novels cannot be coincidental: anticolonial critique has its own novelistic tradition and Orwell is its classic exponent. James Flory, Orwell's antihero, could be taken as a Burton manqué: He, too, keeps a Burmese mistress and shows more respect for Burmese culture than his compatriots deem acceptable. He shares some of Burton's cultural and linguistic interests, though little of his flair. He is similarly concerned with another such "bastard" or hybrid, Dr. Veriswami, who is held in contempt by the British officers and who himself reacts by despising the Indian/Burmese half of his background and exalting all things British, often arguing with Flory over the merits of the two cultures. In contrast to Burton's retreat to Britain at the end of the first chapter in *Der Weltensammler*, Flory, at the end of *Burmese Days*, commits suicide after his mistress creates a scene in front of the young Englishwoman he hopes to marry. Flory's attempts to exceed his role in the colonial police service by interacting with the host culture thus end in worse failure than Burton's.

Burton twice takes pity on the Bastard of Baroda. He rescues him after he has been beaten up for mimicking the British by taking tea outside the regimental mess on the Queen's birthday. He later gets him released from prison after he is arrested for parading through the streets in a suit made from scraps of the union jack. Burton, who is rumored to number a gypsy among his recent forebears, recognizes part of himself in this outcast, but so surely do his British compatriots. As it was common to take an Indian mistress, and such relationships inevitably resulted in mixed race children, figures such as the Bastard of Baroda and Dr. Veriswami showed them an image of themselves that they did not want to see displayed in public.

The Healer as Imposter

If sex is the currency of exchange in the first chapter, in the second it is medicine. The novel thus moves from the erotic to the medical body. Burton, still calling himself Mirza Abdullah, travels as a dervish or holy man who has developed skills as a healer. He has a mission to reach Mecca and calculates that he is less likely to arouse suspicion if he takes such an active role. Mecca is the holy site that legendarily makes pilgrims whole when they drink water from the spring of the *zamzam*. Yet when he gets there, Burton is so appalled by the death and suffering he sees that he recommends hospitals be set up for pilgrims. Mirza Abdullah, alias Burton, is a fraud as dervish/doctor, and depends on the confidence tricks of the medical quack down the ages and across the cultures. The healing properties of the *zamzam* water are evidently not all that they are cracked up to be, either. There is international interest in the public health of the region because epidemics can cross borders, yet this concern is only apparently altruistic or humanitarian — the Ottomans believe that it is likely to be an excuse for imperialist military intervention and, in any case, that diseases are more likely to travel in the other direction.

Burton's pretended profession is also a source of thrills as it grants him access to that secret realm denied to other men in Muslim lands, but he reaches the limits of his effectiveness when he flees a harem (the Arabic word for women's quarters) in fear of exposure. His female patient is in distress that, as a newlywed wife, she has failed to become pregnant, which could result in her husband taking her life. Burton is surely ashamed that what for him is an elaborate joke may have life or death consequences for her. As she lies half undressed before him, apparently imploring him to undertake a gynecological examination, he notices that he has become aroused. One could put it another way: he has reacted to her nonempathetically and he could not offer her a treatment in any case. At this point he runs away.

Betrayal and Final Defeat

Readers of the novel are not always sure how the three chapters fit together to make a meaningful whole. At the end of his Indian spying mission in chapter one, Burton refuses to reveal the names of his native sources because he had sworn that he would not betray them. While he argues that his loyalties are not divided, but rather doubled, he does reveal that British officers frequented the homosexual brothel. When, in the second chapter, he uses his linguistic skills to assume a false identity in Egypt and Arabia, and was moved as a Muslim by his experiences at Mecca, there is still a difference from chapter one. Here, his betrayal is the other way round: by publishing his bestselling account of their pilgrimage on his return to Britain, he causes his native friends to be arrested, and some of them tortured, since his fellow pilgrims are identifiable from what he has written about them. The difference between his love affair with Kundalini, for all that she was in an economically subservient position, and his failure to engage meaningfully with the frightened married woman in the harem, is surely of the same degree. There is thus between the first two chapters a movement away from empathy with the host culture to alignment with the British, which is to be intensified in the third. By the time of his expedition to find the source of the Nile, Burton appears to make little effort to understand his environment or blend in with it. What is more, he is engaged in an imperialistic mission, motivated by personal glory, and an unabashed proponent of the British Empire, shouting at Sidi Mubarak Bombay that the suspicious tribesmen in a region they are passing through should be grateful if the British colonized them: "Do you not comprehend . . . what a monumental sacrifice we would be making were we to settle in your country, and what a wonderful blessing it would be for you?" (434).

Despite this progression, Trojanow retains the bipartite narrative structure in the East African chapter, and Sidi Mubarak Bombay is if anything an even more sympathetic observer of Burton than his Indian servant Naukaram or the Mecca pilgrims. Nonetheless, he is obliged to keep his distance, observing from the outside. Naukaram was more ambitious and returned to Britain with his master, but his experiences were not happy and he soon took to his heels. Bombay is looking back on his life from a position of understanding and is conveying to his children and grandchildren that the British are not as crazy or their behavior as incomprehensible as they are inclined to believe. Bombay has become acculturated to the British at the same time as Burton has moved steadily in the opposite direction. His imam, in fact, has no doubt that Bombay is now biased in their favor: "The unbelievers have turned your head. . . . Everyone knows that! You spent too much time with them, you were too close, you were at their mercy and that did you no good" (357). Bombay explains why the British want to be the first of their tribe to reach the source of the Nile, but has to begin by saying what they mean by "source" since the whole idea of prioritizing the longest tributary and measuring its entire length by identifying an origin is alien to them. Bombay also has to account for why Burton's fellow explorer, John Speke, engages in destructive behavior by shooting animals that he is not going to eat. Unlike the earlier two chapters, there is no attempt on Burton's part to make physical or sexual contact with a native person, but the chapter ends with Bombay making love to his wife.

On their return from the African interior to the coast, the expedition passes by a diseased village in which all the inhabitants suffer with vastly bloated limbs; some of the men are characterized by inflated testicles and vanished penises. Burton and his party make no attempt this time to intervene medically. There is a further sign that relations are breaking down and mutual respect is diminishing. The African bearers mock the European explorers by telling Speke made-up names for landscape features that he believes he is discovering and claiming for his queen by naming them. The idea comes to the bearers while they are drunk on banana beer, and their made-up names are either willfully obscene or inspired by bodily functions. A lake is Great Emptying of the Bladder, two hills are The Tits of the Fat King, and a ravine becomes Where a Man Pushes In and a Baby Comes Out. They have recognized what has been clear in Trojanow's novel since its hero first set foot in Bombay — that the British identify the locals and their land with sex, bodily functions, and physicality. By giving the narrator of this chapter the same name as the Indian city where Burton began, Trojanow indicates that the city is talking back, and doing so finally in a language that the British can half-understand.

Conclusion

Burton has enacted in this novel a milder version of what Trojanow has described in *Gebrauchsanweisung für Indien* (Instruction manual for India: India, 2006) as the switch in British behavior and historiography with regard to India. Eighteenth-century British writing on India reflected a pre-Imperialist interest in foreign cultures that showed respect for their difference and resulted in intermarriage and intermingling. That changed with the rise of the idea of empire. The antithesis of Trojanow's books was written by James Mill, father of the liberal philosopher, in 1817. Mill never visited India, did not know any of the languages that were spoken there, and even rejected on principle earlier writings in English on India. He asserted his opinions as a priori correct, and his purpose was to demonstrate the inferiority of all things Indian. His three-volume *History of British India* was an instant classic and much of the misinformation and prejudice that he put into the world can be felt to this day.[11] Trojanow's Burton is no more a second Mill than the historical Richard Burton was an apologist for white supremacy, but *Der Weltensammler* shows Burton unable and unwilling to transcend the distinctions between cultures and religions that so fascinated him. Whether this has a direct contemporary relevance is perhaps beside the point. Trojanow is bound by his historical sources, or at least has decided not to contradict them. He could not have made Burton's behavior into a blueprint for today's troubled relations between East and West. What surely outshines Burton's personal failure is Trojanow's literary success in fashioning a narrative in which an exploration of empathy for the other is the red thread that weaves the various strands and sections together.

Notes

German and English transliterations of Trojanow's name differ; the German is used throughout this chapter.

[1] Ilija Trojanow, *Der Weltensammler* (Munich: Deutscher Taschenbuch Verlag, 2008). References are to this edition and translations are my own. The published English translation is Iliya Trojanov, *The Collector of Worlds. A Novel of Sir Richard Francis Burton*, trans. William Hobson (London: Faber and Faber, 2009).

[2] Ingo Arend, writing in the left-leaning weekly *Freitag* exclaims, "Blessed is the country and its literature that counts such world travelers among its own," and ends his review by wondering whether the xenophilia of Trojanow's hero could be a model for intercultural dialogue in our own times; see Arend, "Einer von ihnen. Ilija Trojanows Roman Der Weltensammler ist ein Plädoyer für die Aneignung des Fremden," *Freitag*, 5 May 2006. See also the interview with Trojanow, "Kulturen kämpfen nicht," *Neues Deutschland*, 17 January 2007. Newspaper articles in this chapter were provided by the Innsbrucker Zeitungsarchiv and page numbers were not available.

[3] Ilija Trojanow, *Die Welt ist groß und Rettung lauert überall* (Vienna/Munich: Hanser, 1996), and (with Rudolf Spinder) *Autopol* (Munich: Deutscher Taschenbuch Verlag, 1997). The film of *Die Welt ist groß*, an international co-production directed by Stephan Komanderev, was released in 2008.

[4] Ilija Trojanow, *Ein Nomade auf vier Kontinenten: Auf den Spuren von Richard Francis Burton* (Berlin: Eichborn, 2007); *Oberammergau: Richard F. Burton zu Besuch bei den Passionsspielen*, bilingual edition, trans. Susann Urban, *Oberammergau. A Glance at the Passion-Play* (Hamburg: Arche, 2010).

[5] Ilija Trojanow, *Zu den heiligen Stätten des Islam. Als Pilger nach Mekka und Medina* (Munich: Malik, 2004); in English as *Mumbai to Mecca: A Pilgrimage to the Holy Sites of Islam*, trans. Rebecca Morrisson (London: Haus, 2007).

[6] See Stephanie Catani, "(Re-)Thinking History: Ilija Trojanows *Der Weltensammler*," *Angermion* 2 (2009): 91–108.

[7] Daniel Kehlmann, *Die Vermessung der Welt* (Hamburg: Rowohlt, 2005) and Feridun Zaimoğlu, *Leyla* (Cologne: Kiepenheuer & Witsch, 2006).

[8] Volker Weidermann, "In acht Romanen um die Welt," *Frankfurter Allgemeine Sonntagszeitung*, 2 April 2006. As a subject of literature, films, travel books, autobiographies, and other writings, Africa has remained highly fashionable. See Dirk Göttsche, "Der neue historische Afrika-Roman: Kolonialismus aus postkolonialer Sicht," *German Life and Letters* 56 (2003): 261–80.

[9] Quoted by Alexandra Kedveš, "Gebrauchsanweisung fürs Globetrotten. Der Schriftsteller Ilija Trojanow in Zürich," *Neue Zürcher Zeitung*, 17 June 2006.

[10] Ilija Trojanow, "Oscar in Afrika. Nairobi 1982" is a veiled tribute to *Die Blechtrommel,* in *Der entfesselte Globus. Reportagen* (Munich: Hanser, 2008), 18–22. Trojanow elsewhere presents Grass's failure to interact with the people of Calcutta in his account of six months that he and his wife spent there — documented in Grass's *Zunge zeigen* (Show your tongue, 1988) — as the antithesis of what he himself sets out to do: "Auf den Spuren von Günter Grass: *Zunge zeigen* in Kalkutta," in *Der Sadhu an der Teufelswand. Reportage aus einem anderen Indien* (Munich: Sierra, 2001), 152–60.

[11] Ilija Trojanow, *Gebrauchsanweisung für Indien* (Munich: Piper, 2006), 74–75.

9: Sibylle Berg, *Die Fahrt*: Literature, Germanness, and Globalization

Emily Jeremiah

T HE QUESTION OF CONTEMPORARY German national identity is uniquely
vexed. The legacy of National Socialism, the ongoing effects of reunification, the challenges of multiculturalism and of globalization — all of
these combine to create a fascinating case study: "Germanness" is a shifting construct that is fraught with difficulties. It is a matter that has been
hotly and widely debated within Germany over the past decades.[1] The
discursive construction and contestation of Germanness have logically
formed the subject of numerous discussions in German literary and cultural studies, which examine, among other topics, memory and history,
East and West Germanness, Turkish-German culture, Jewish identities,
and gender and nation.[2] This chapter aims to contribute to such investigations through a reading of Sibylle Berg's 2007 novel *Die Fahrt* (The journey), in particular by building on work concerning globalization and
Germanness.[3]

Debates about national identity have complex histories and contexts,
nowhere more so than in the Berlin Republic. Because of the especial difficulty of the German case, and the self-reflexivity manifested in the
numerous political and popular discussions of German national identity in
recent decades, Germany has been described by Stephen Brockmann as
"postnational," that is, as a nation in which the very concept of nation is
open to question.[4] Owing to its horrific history, Brockmann argues,
Germany is well positioned to attempt the creation of an unconventional
national identity, one that involves as much self-questioning as it does self-
affirmation.[5] Berg's questing, questioning novel is German in Brockmann's
postnational sense. At the same time, however, Brockmann's deployment
of the term "Germany" must be carefully scrutinized, for it performs a
homogenizing gesture. Which Germany is in fact well positioned to be
questioning and creative? Arguably, it is only a small minority of Germans
that is so positioned and/or minded. A quizzical stance is perhaps the
preserve of a privileged few. And fantasies of fixity and security undeniably
persist in the German context, with *Heimat* in particular serving a con-
solatory function.

Heimat — "home(land)" or "home region" — is a floating signifier in German culture that connotes "shelteredness and harmony."[6] It is an intrinsically conservative construct involving idealized notions of family and nature, in which these are strongly marked with conventional assumptions about gender.[7] It is an idea of continuing relevance in the Berlin Republic, as Peter Blickle asserts and as Berg's novel critically implies. For Blickle, *Heimat* remains a formative and all-pervasive element of German culture, constituting a crucial aspect of German self-perceptions.[8] *Heimat* has a complex relationship with German nationality, however. While it has historically been used to yoke together a "nation of provincials," as Celia Applegate has demonstrated,[9] it is also an antinational construct — albeit one that paradoxically has served to support a broad and not clearly defined nationalism.[10]

A renewed attachment to this trope or dream is in evidence. In postunification East Germany especially, provincialism and consciousness of *Heimat* have been reasserting themselves steadily.[11] The East German turn to *Heimat* can be linked to the questions of *Ostalgie* — a nostalgically indulgent view of the GDR past — and of an Eastern *Trotzidentität*: a defiant assertion of a specifically East German identity in opposition to hegemonic West German values and assumptions.[12] Discourses surrounding "home" and "belonging" are thus continually reworked to fit shifting contexts and agendas. In the Berlin Republic as a whole, the reliance on *Heimat* can be viewed as key to the German reaction to "the shock of globalization"[13] — Berg's novel both acknowledges this shock and undermines attempts to lessen it through *Heimat* fantasies. The predilection for such fantasies can itself be seen as an interesting example of glocalization, involving as it does a local or national response to global forces.[14] But one cannot simply read *Heimat* as standing for the national, as opposed to the global; *Heimat* connotes regionalism as much as, or indeed more than, it does nation.[15]

Heimat thus demonstrates the difficulty of disentangling the many factors involved in the construction of (German) identity — regional, national, and global. This last term is crucial for a reading of Berg's novel, which constitutes a response to and a comment on a globalized world, one characterized by the erosion of national borders, ever-more-sophisticated communication technologies, and increased ease of travel.[16] In this context, the nation — a relatively recent construct — is arguably less salient than before. But as Craig Calhoun argues, the nation still holds significance, with nationalism remaining a powerful force.[17] Pitting the global against the national is in any case not a helpful move, since both are at work in the construction of the postmodern (German) subject, along with regional identity, gender, ethnicity, sexuality, age: a list that inevitably concludes with "an embarrassed etc."[18]

Die Fahrt engages with the issues of nation and/or postnation in instructive ways. It undermines globalization as an ideal, exposing its discontents.[19] But it does not flee from the world at large to take refuge in idealizations of Germanness or *Heimat*. Instead, it offers a complex vision of transnational, interconnected subjects. It puts forward and practices what might be termed a nomadic ethics — a way of conceiving ethical relationality that accounts for and indeed welcomes mobility and multiplicity — in particular by means of its form and technique. The novel shows that the global and the national are intertwined, making a renewed case for the glocal. Indeed, literature in general both demonstrates and enacts the meshing that the term "glocal" implies. Literature involves an encounter between self and other, decentering unitary models of (national) identity and promoting a vision of the subject as fluid, multiple, and relational.

Berg and Pop Literature

Sibylle Berg was born in 1962 in Weimar and now lives in Zurich. In 1984, she left the GDR for West Germany, being *freigekauft* (bought free of the regime). In 1997, she published her first novel, *Ein paar Leute suchen das Glück und lachen sich tot* (A couple of people seek happiness and laugh themselves to death). Berg is the author of six novels altogether, as well as of essays, newspaper columns, and plays. In 2008, she won the Wolfgang Koeppen Prize. The four novels that precede *Die Fahrt* present thematic concerns and formal techniques that are revisited by the later novel; they have also helped to construct Berg's persona and her status as a writer of *Pop-Literatur*.

   Ein paar Leute consists of numerous short chapters narrated by or from the point of view of various characters whose lives overlap; such criss-crossing and multiplicity led one critic to comment: "Promiscuity has become form, so to speak."[20] Such "promiscuity," also found in *Die Fahrt*, implies multiplicity and interactivity; the subject is not static, but always on the move and encountering others. Moritz Baßler likens Berg's technique here to that of films such as Jim Jarmusch's *Mystery Train* and Robert Altman's *Short Cuts*, thus drawing attention to the text's filmic qualities: swift changes of scene and the use of montage.[21] Such cinematic techniques are reprised in *Die Fahrt*. The laconic, ironic tone and black humor of Berg's first novel are also echoed in later works. Again like *Die Fahrt*, *Ein paar Leute* features characters aimlessly on the move. Characters seek love and fulfillment but are foiled, failure and frustration are the norm, and most of the protagonists die in gruesome ways. The text also includes a number of pronouncements on the state of the world. This is a world of unreality, insubstantiality, a world of no fixed values and of mindless, rampant consumerism.[22] Berg has been described as "an expert in cynicism,"[23] and her work is in general shot through with bleakness. *Ein paar Leute* refuses easy identification; the narration here is self-reflexive, the jokey narratorial asides drawing attention to the constructedness of the literary text and creating an alienating effect. However, the briskness and humor of the novel mean that it is extremely readable,[24] like *Die Fahrt* but unlike certain of the later works.

Sex II (1998), for example, features a deracinated protagonist who wanders through a city over a period of twenty-four hours, observing, and seeming to enter the consciousness of, many of its inhabitants; her first-person narrative is interrupted by third-person passages telling of the experience of these others. The characters — if they can be termed such — are summed up brusquely at the beginning of their respective sections: for example, "Rosa, 33. Teacher, does creative writing, falls in love a lot. Unhappily. Not particularly contented, no reason to be."[25] The figures encountered are in the main failures, perverts, and depressives. The stagnant nature of the novel's plot, und the unremitting blackness of its vision, make for a forbidding read. *Amerika* (1999) is similarly deflating: the America of the title is a site of fantasies that are to remain unrealized for the novel's characters; again, disappointment and failure reign. *Die Fahrt* will explore further the disappointment inherent in dreams of escape. Like these earlier works, it, too, features numerous characters, whose very numerousness involves a challenge to ideals of uniqueness and individuality, let alone heroism. In *Die Fahrt*, however, such a challenge opens up new ways of conceiving subjectivity and ethics.

Ende gut (2004), in contrast, offers very little hope. It features a heroine who cannot be described as such unproblematically; the work itself alludes to and undermines the notion of literary heroism.[26] It is a polyphonic text, consisting of numerous disembodied pronouncements by various subjects. There is no unifying narrative voice here, and the text is disorienting, even off-putting. Voices seem simply to emerge, clashing and canceling each other out. The work thus stages postmodernist uncertainty, demonstrating the crisis of values that it explicitly thematizes. It strongly recalls the work of Elfriede Jelinek at points, with caustic observations about sex and family, and mocking citations of dominant discourses; Jelinek is, in fact, mentioned in the text (36). *Ende gut* functions, among other things, as a radical deconstruction of the novel. Within the text, other novels are mentioned dismissively; one character has been given a book by Günter Grass as a present: "Wasn't up to much," is her comment (79). Authors like Nick Hornby, John Irving, and Jonathan Franzen are name-checked, but they stand only as brands, comparable to the many other labels that are mentioned here. This is a grotesque and surrealist text, featuring apocalyptic, gory scenes. It alludes often to Islamist terrorism and millennial anxieties. It is comparable in vision to the work of Michel Houellebecq, who is mentioned here and elsewhere by Berg.[27] Like previous works, it addresses the state of the world, with characters offering such analyses as: "we are the generation that is nothing" (100). This is a world replete with information, which has a paralyzing effect on its consumers. Bodies have become impotent in this posthuman world — human beings are insignificant. *Die Fahrt*, too, portrays human subjects as insignificant, adrift, and bewildered.

Berg's savageness is often accompanied by playfulness, evident also in her self-presentation. Berg can be seen as a sophisticated and savvy marketer of her work and her brand. She has a stylish website and is an enthusiastic tweeter on Twitter.[28] The cover of Berg's first novel features a head-and-shoulder shot of the author lying in bed, apparently naked under the sheets, holding a cigarette and looking at the camera. The author's image — youthful, sexualized — is integral to this book as product. The author is quoted on the back of the 2008 Reclam edition as claiming the book is perfect for depressive nineteen- to twenty-five-year-olds. On the one hand, Berg is here mocking discourses associated with marketing and advertising; on the other, she is assisting in the cultivation of her own brand, associating it with a saleable youthful melancholy.

A similar ambivalence is at work in the author biography in *Ende gut*, which reads: "Sibylle Berg, born not so long ago in Weimar . . . has since her debut novel been considered the 'mother' [*Übermutter*] of new German literature. She could do without that." This (self-)description positions Berg teasingly both inside and outside contemporary literature. It also alludes to the question of her age, suggesting a discomfort with generational positioning; Berg was born not long ago, but is now already an *Übermutter*. The description ends: "Sibylle Berg lives in Zurich because it's so nice there." This bland explanation serves to suggest deeper and more complex motives, raising the question of Berg's relationship to her homeland — a question pertinent to a reading of *Die Fahrt*. The issue of biography is perhaps especially salient when it comes to considering Berg's latest novel, which features a writer living in Switzerland.[29] Berg teasingly offers up self-portraits, but as is the case with the cover of *Amerika*, which features a heavily made-up, elaborately costumed Berg,[30] such images are self-consciously artificial and partial.

Berg has thus cultivated a strong but subtle and playful brand. She is associated with the label *Pop-Literatur*, being included, for example, in Baßler's book *Der deutsche Pop-Roman* (The German pop novel). *Pop-Literatur* is a term that is hard to pin down, but for Thomas Ernst, contemporary pop literature in German appears to be a reaction to a changed world, one characterized by the dissolution of national borders and by Americanization.[31] This description certainly applies to Berg's work, which can also be set convincingly alongside other German-language texts that have been labeled "pop." *Ein paar Leute* is comparable to Ingo Schulze's *Simple Storys*, whose interlocking stories owe a debt to Raymond Carver and to Robert Altman. Berg's spare prose, disaffected characters, and allusion to brands recall Christian Kracht's *Faserland*, itself influenced by the work of Bret Easton Ellis. And Berg's citationality is reminiscent of Thomas Meinecke's *Tomboy*, for example, which alludes relentlessly to academic discourse and popular culture. Thus, Berg can plausibly be seen as a practitioner of intertextual, international pop.

Die Fahrt

Die Fahrt constitutes a return to the accessibility of Berg's first novel; both texts offer a humorous and sprightly narrative that is not entirely suffused in cynicism and gore. It is a softer work than most of its predecessors and has even been accused of being moralistic.[32] The novel has been recognized as marketable; it formed the basis of the podcast for the 2007 Frankfurt Book Fair. But for all its palatable and commercial qualities, this is a probing and questioning novel.

Die Fahrt is also a dizzying work; it is multiperspectival, its third-person narration hopping in and out of different points of view, as well as multi- and transnational. The numerous characters encounter one another, clash, part, or miss each other, in locations that include Germany, Iceland, Israel, China, India, the United States, and the United Kingdom. Characters are most often on the move, in pursuit of or in flight from something that remains obscure. Globetrotter Helena exemplifies this tendency: "Helena . . . was constantly searching for something that she found more meaningful than herself."[33] We have here a shifting set of subjects characterized by restlessness and rootlessness. Characters search for meaning in the context of lives that seem arbitrary and pointless — a vision familiar from other of Berg's texts. As one character in *Die Fahrt* reflects: "Most people just kind of end up in a life" (92).

With its focus on mobility, Berg's novel can be seen as a product and an enactment of globalization, but it is skeptical regarding the benefits of unlimited movement. It wittily critiques facile discourses on globalization in which disembodied subjects roam the globe unproblematically with the aid of technology;[34] such discourses are subjected here to irony, in particular through the figure of Frank. Frank, who is approaching middle age and leads a dull and isolated life in Berlin, a city depicted as overly gentrified, soulless, and fragmented. He keeps in contact with far-flung acquaintances and friends via the Internet; his promises to go and stay with such contacts are never realized (15–16). Frank's isolation serves to expose contemporary communication technologies as inadequate substitutes for meaningful, sustained relationships. Frank has never had a *Heimat*, we are told, because "You don't find a homeland on the Internet or by means of frantic toing and froing" (17). This assertion points, again, to the isolation and rootlessness of the contemporary global subject, but it also mounts a challenge to *Heimat*, revealed here as an absent referent.

Saskia Sassen has observed that the contemporary emphasis on transnationalism and hypermobility has given rise to a widespread feeling of powerlessness among local actors, and a sense that resistance is futile.[35] Berg's Frank lacks a sense of agency, having long ago given up on the idea of changing the world, and he can thus be seen as a disempowered local actor (17); this sense of passivity and despair is familiar from other of Berg's works. Failing to find *Heimat* on the Internet, Frank opts for frantic toing and froing. Experiencing a sense of restlessness one week, he concludes that he has been struck by "Reiselust" (a desire to travel), and books a trip to Shanghai on the Internet — a decision he immediately regrets. On his way to the airport, Frank considers turning back, but chides himself that his life will otherwise be totally predictable. He then wonders what would be wrong with that. Frank boards the airplane but then flees, exhilarated (118). The ideal of joyous mobility, of liberating nomadism, is thus undermined. While habit and the everyday can be deadening, the novel points out, they also serve a useful protective function; another character, Ruth, leaves Berlin for Tel Aviv, where the absurdity of her existence becomes even more undeniable than before since it is not glossed over by the comforting if empty rituals of social life (167). Frank does eventually leave Berlin, however, to find a *Heimat* in Iceland, where he experiences a sense of peace and a loving relationship with Ruth, cut short by his death from cancer. There is no happy end here, then, but Frank at least glimpses happiness — away from Germany.

Leaving Germany is not necessarily a solution for all. Helena, who hates her life, takes refuge in ceaseless travel, and in "tantra, reiki, the works" (26, 27). She takes a consumerist, superficial view of other cultures — we are informed that she has visited nearly all the countries covered by the Lonely Planet series (27). Her ignorance means that she receives insults in a foreign tongue with uncomprehending humility: "She had smiled when the locals insulted her, and when they said you ugly piece of white sausage, she nodded . . . and thanked them humbly, using the few sentences she'd picked up beforehand from the guidebook" (27). In India, Helena exemplifies colonial attitudes common among Western visitors, who overlook the country's realities (141). Such visitors hold patronizing attitudes toward the "natives," satirized elsewhere by Peter, the proprietor of a hotel in Sri Lanka: "you sweet little natives, just you stay innocent now, or what we think of as innocent" (93). Helena's realization that Indians are people comes as a shock to her, countering as it does her habitual othering (146). Her naivety leads her into absurd and perilous situations, as when she finds herself living among Brazilian gold-diggers — who offer a fitting symbol of the largely hopeless questing of the novel's protagonists (66). Rather than finding herself through travel, Helena in fact loses part of her self, feeling that travel has transformed her into a person she does not yet know (271). Helena's journeying could be seen as representative of Germany's search for a new "global" identity — a search that here seems futile and ridiculous.[36] Helena eventually finds a home in an alternative community in Füssen, Bavaria: a comically bathetic conclusion to her international exploits (342).

Travel, then, is often disappointing, as well as ethically dubious. Tourism is a superficial "viewing of foreign lives" (48), fueled by a desperate and misguided desire for authenticity (44). Peter is irked by what he terms the "We-want-to-live-like-the-natives-lot" (93). Mobility — more precisely, travel for the purpose of leisure — is a shameless luxury. For slum-dweller Amirita, there is "no elsewhere" (148). Amirita dreams of being an air hostess, a dream that appears cruelly impossible and that highlights the injustice of the world order (151).[37] Thus, the novel undermines illusions of unhampered mobility and escape, asserting economic and existential realities. The quotidian is inevitably demanding and draining (37). Banality is inescapable, as Frank realizes: "everywhere looked like something" (16). For most people, in any case, what is important is food, family, and TV: daily, local practices and pleasures (37). Habit might be deadening, but it is also useful in maintaining mental health. While contemporary — popular and academic — discourses might affirm mobility as a lifestyle choice, or as paradigmatic of new and radical ways of being and thinking, it is not necessarily healthy, and is in any case only open to a privileged few.

The myth of globalization as a source of wealth and freedom for all is undermined in the novel, as dreams of a better life are shown to founder. Gulzada, for example, moves to New York from Kyrgyzstan and is soon disillusioned (223). As Sassen points out, the global city does not offer a level playing field to its players: "Global cities are sites for the overvalorization of corporate capital and the further devalorization of disadvantaged economic actors."[38] New York is indeed viewed by one character in *Die Fahrt* as a lethal money-making machine (212), and the narrator refers explicitly refers to "globalization's losers" (148). Globalization results in sterile homogenization; in Vienna, Pia observes: "Mango and Zara . . . Schlecker and Nordsee . . . was there no end to it?" (224).

Heimat and/or Germanness?

Heimat has acted as a refuge from globalization in the German context — and it is a myth that is punctured here. Germany is depicted in uncomfortable terms. Returning to Germany after a long absence, Pia detects a specifically German form of "joylessness" in evidence (281).[39] The German flags she observes in Bayreuth, where the Wagner festival is being held, provoke fear in her — a detail that implies discomfort with German nationalism (282). Pia asks herself: "Just what has become of the Germans?" — a rhetorical question that can be seen as emblematic of the quizzical Germanness that Brockmann identifies (284). Return to Germany does not bring about fulfillment and peace, as it does in the traditional *Heimat* narrative.[40] German nationalism is lampooned here. Flag-waving soccer fanaticism gives Germans a sense of being and belonging: "and everyone was finally someone, an us" (224). National identity is in fact a matter of chance, the narrator points out (229). The narrator observes of the fans: "the globalized population of the world reeled through the summer and played at nationalism" (224), thereby undermining a sense of national belonging; in fact, the population is "globalized."[41]

Germanness remains, however, as a restrictive and exclusionary construct. Ruth, a German Jew, travels from Berlin to Tel Aviv, but once she is there — no longer *anders* (other) as a Jew — she finds herself adrift. She returns to Germany, perhaps accepting her Germanness (169, 189). However, this decision is complicated when Ruth finds herself "at home and very foreign" (264), and considers alternative places to live. Numbing herself with medication, she attempts to imagine a better life for herself in Berlin. The chapter ends with an ellipsis, perhaps suggesting that a German-Jewish identity is unimaginable. Ruth leaves Germany again, to find love with the dying Frank in Iceland. Jenny, who is German-Chinese, offers another case study of alienation. While she deems herself German, she is often complimented on how good her German is or asked how things are in her country, when "her country was Germany, whether she liked it or not" (129). Jenny goes to China on a quest to understand her father and herself. Her impressions are not favorable and she wishes to go home, yearning for "democracy, civilization, all of that" (162). There is here a typically wry and nuanced treatment of nationality: Jenny might not like Germany, and other Germans may act in a way that excludes her, but it is her country and other countries might not be more to her liking.

Such a nuanced approach is also evident in the handling of the issue of multiculturalism. Fatma is the only Muslim girl in her class in a German school, "and somehow she was nothing" (292): a criticism of German intolerance and xenophobia. Yet naïve liberal discourses concerning multiculturalism are also critiqued. Pia, in Whitechapel, views her surroundings with distaste, and reflects, in light of the Muslim women around her: "bollocks to multiculturalism if it meant you'd have to put on a veil" (317).

Aesthetic, Ethics, Identity

The novel's technique shores up its message. The narrative often relies on comic exaggeration or distortion (see, for example, 38, 251). In addition, it frequently practices a deadpan citation of dominant assumptions: for example, "Helena was a woman and equipped with faulty visual-spatial ability" (183). German notions of leisure and pleasure are wittily deconstructed when Füssen is described as being "what the average German means by a 'Nice Place'" (286). The novel is citational, then, quoting discourses to undermine them. In this way, it opposes what the narrator sees as a habitual, widespread lack of self-questioning. People are described as acting as they think adults act, and it is this failure to question that renders the world so dreary (20). Such an adoption of de rigueur attitudes is found in the mothers in a Berlin café who are "terribly environmentally aware and thick" (17). The use of "and" here, and in the description of Helena above, has a jolting effect that troubles common-sense notions of logic and causality: in the first case, by ironizing biologistic conceptions of gender, with their facile explanations of human behavior, and in the second case by hinging together usually unrelated notions (environmentalism and stupidity), and so overturning a widely held liberal view that environmental awareness is the mark of superior intelligence and of moral stature. Here, it is a sign of superficial trendiness.

The novel explicitly asks where ideas come from, concluding they come from television and one's parents and neighbors (180). Ideology is a fashionable indulgence. Peter, we learn, used to be left wing: "communism, Mao, squatting, nuclear power demos — the works" (93). It is clear to Peter now that he had just wanted to be different; in fact, his faddish adoption of causes only makes him into a stereotype. Received wisdom is bandied about and unquestioningly assumed. As one character, Pia, learns, one can question oneself, and the result can be liberating. One can avoid holidays if one does not enjoy them, or put aside books that are not to one's taste, but self-scrutiny is necessary for the establishment of one's true desires and inclinations. Thus, as Pia perceives: "The reward for the effort involved in questioning oneself is personal freedom" (181). The novel's mocking citationality upholds and heightens its critique of received wisdom.

Similarly, the critique of individualism found in the work is mirrored and strengthened by its multiperspectival form. When Helena realizes that Indians are real, the narrative point of view switches to that of Amirita, one such real Indian, who looks on Helena with scorn. This shift in perspective reflects and enacts a challenge to the colonial gaze that is elsewhere denounced (146). It also challenges the notion of the individual subject as stable and intact. One character, Brian, mounts a critique of individualism, asking when individuals first began to deem themselves such (96). Individualism involves unhealthy delusions of grandeur. According to Brian, it arises from excessive consumption of the media, therapy, and the fact that stardom now seems available to all (97). Helena, who has grown up in the context of "individualism contingent upon underpopulation," has to confront the fact in India that, were she to die, it would not signify much (143). In this way, Western individualism is contextualized and critiqued.

Brian also offers an interesting perspective on the notion of difference, a key term in critical theory of recent decades. According to Brian, uniqueness and difference are wrongly prized, and indeed illusory: "The human being is a replaceable part of a large mass" (97). Difference, then, should not be fetishized, being always relative. The novel's form — the use of *erlebte Rede* (free indirect discourse) and numerous points of view, the mobile network of characters — also suggests that individual identities are porous and overlapping, or "nomadic," in Rosi Braidotti's sense.[42] The subject is not stable or discrete, but rather shifting and relational. The novel's technique recalls Sara Ahmed's description of identity formation as taking place through encounters between subjects.[43] The text proposes and practices a relational nomadic ethics, for relationality is ultimately celebrated here. While the characters' quests for meaningful relationships are largely ridiculous and unsuccessful, the questing itself is perhaps not so derisory. In the opening chapter of the novel, the recently widowed Gunner reflects: "After all, life was only bearable with another person" (13). The novel ends with Ruth and the dying Frank entwined in bed in Gunner's house (345).

Different viewpoints do not necessarily cancel each other out, then; there is the possibility that (fleeting) mutual understanding can be achieved. The multiplicity and mobility of postmodern subjectivity does not necessarily spell the end of beneficial connections to others; rather, an ethics built on this very multiplicity and mobility can emerge. Literature is one site where this ethics can be explored and enacted. The use of photographs in *Die Fahrt* — images of landscapes are interspersed throughout — points up the acts of representing and communicating, and highlights the relationality inherent in them, and the dialogue between writer and reader(s). According to her publisher's website, Berg traveled extensively in order to research this novel;[44] the photos thus function as a reminder of the authorial presence, hinting at a Flickr-style sharing of Berg's experiences while traveling that is in keeping with her status as a tweeter. In this way, the author is alive — this contrary to Barthesian pronouncements regarding the death of the author — and implicated in her work. The author/text, author/protagonist divide can thus be seen to be challenged, and (authorial) subjectivity shown as interactive and dynamic.

Conclusion: "Glocal" Literature

Literature arises from the particular experiences of an individual writer — albeit one who is to be understood as a relational subject-in-process. It usually involves specific local or national settings and is written in a certain language — in this case, German, which is spoken in Germany and Switzerland (enabling Berg's mobility and granting her a readership, potentially, in both countries) but is not a global language with the reach of English. Most often, literature is initially marketed and consumed in one country. In this way, it is perhaps always to some extent local.[45] But there are numerous ways in which literature can transgress national boundaries and highlight or enact hybridity: by featuring mobile characters with diverse or mixed backgrounds; by alluding to texts from other national contexts; by foregrounding or featuring multilingualism or translation; by being consumed in different settings; by being translated.[46]

In this way, literature can blur, or anyway relativize, national/regional/cultural differences and enable the realization of what Berg's Brian understands as our shifting, overlapping selves. Literature can be seen to enact glocalization, rendering global — or anyway other — experiences and ideas homey. Beth Linklater indeed argues that glocalization, originally a business term meaning "the adaptation of the global to the local in the production of a new form of hybrid," is highly appropriate as a way of thinking about literature.[47] Literature both demonstrates and encourages the relationality of subjectivity, and is thus extremely pertinent to a globalized world, in which there is a constant, dynamic tension between self and other and between familiarity and strangeness; Arjun Appadurai describes global cultural processes in terms of "the infinitely varied mutual contest of sameness and difference."[48] Berg's novel both explores and participates in this contest.

Notes

[1] As Anne Fuchs notes, "the meaning of being German remains a contested issue in contemporary German discourse." Anne Fuchs, *Phantoms of War in Contemporary German Literature, Films and Discourse: The Politics of Memory* (New York: Palgrave Macmillan, 2008), 3.

[2] See, for example, Anne Fuchs, Mary Cosgrove, and George Grote, eds., *German Memory Contests: The Quest for Identity in Literature, Film, and Discourse since 1990* (Rochester, NY: Camden House, 2006); Paul Cooke, *Representing East Germany since Unification: From Colonization to Nostalgia* (Oxford and New York: Berg, 2005); Tom Cheesman, *Novels of Turkish German Settlement: Cosmopolite Fictions* (Rochester, NY: Camden House, 2007); Linda E. Feldman and Diana Orendi, eds., *Evolving Jewish Identities in German Culture: Borders and Crossings* (Westport, CT: Praeger, 2000); Patricia Herminghouse and Magda Mueller, eds., *Gender and Germanness: Cultural Productions of Nation* (Providence, RI: Berghahn, 1997).

[3] See here Renate Rechtien and Karoline von Oppen, eds., *Local/Global Narratives*, *German Monitor* 68 (Amsterdam: Rodopi, 2007); Stuart Taberner, ed., *German Literature in the Age of Globalisation* (Birmingham, UK: Birmingham UP, 2005).

[4] Stephen Brockmann, *Literature and German Unification* (Cambridge: Cambridge UP, 1999), 192. Historian Mary Fulbrook agrees that, since 1945, Germany (divided and reunified) has been almost continually preoccupied with debates about its identity and history. Mary Fulbrook, *German National Identity after the Holocaust* (Cambridge, Polity, 1999), 2, 3.

[5] Stephen Brockmann, "'Normalization': Has Helmut Kohl's Vision Been Realized?" in *German Culture, Politics, and Literature into the Twenty-First Century: Beyond Normalization*, ed. Stuart Taberner and Paul Cooke (Rochester, NY: Camden House, 2006), 17–29; here, 28.

[6] Peter Blickle, *Heimat: A Critical Theory of the German Idea of Homeland* (Rochester, NY: Camden House, 2002), 17.

[7] See here Elizabeth Boa and Rachel Palfreyman, *Heimat — A German Dream: Regional Loyalties and National Identity in German Culture 1890–1990* (Oxford: Oxford UP, 2000), 23, 26; Blickle, *Heimat*, 71, 82, 83.

[8] Blickle, *Heimat*, 1, 4, 151.

[9] Hence the title of her book: Celia Applegate, *A Nation of Provincials: The German Idea of Heimat* (Berkeley and Los Angeles: U of California P, 1990).

[10] See here Blickle, *Heimat*, 47.

[11] This was Applegate's 1990 verdict, *A Nation of Provincials*, 246. See also Blickle, *Heimat*, 47.

[12] See here Paul Cooke, "Performing 'Ostalgie': Leander Haussmann's *Sonnenallee*," *German Life and Letters* 56 (2003): 156–67; here, 156–57; Cooke, *Representing East Germany*, 8.

[13] See here Andrew Plowman, "'Was will ich denn als Westdeutscher erzählen?': The 'Old' West and Globalisation in Recent German Prose," in *German Literature in the Age of Globalisation*, ed. Taberner, 47–66; here, 48.

[14] Compare Stuart Taberner, "Introduction," in *German Literature in the Age of Globalisation*, ed. Taberner, 1–24; here, 13.

[15] See here David Clarke, "Introduction: Place in Literature," in *The Politics of Place in Post-War Germany: Essays in Literary Criticism*, ed. David Clarke and Renate Rechtien (Lampeter: Edwin Mellen Press, 2009), 1–24; here, 18.

[16] Compare the following definition: "Globalization refers to the fact that more people across large distances become connected in more and different ways": Frank J. Lechner and John Boli, "General Introduction," in *The Globalization Reader*, ed. Frank J. Lechner and John Boli (Oxford: Blackwell, 2008), 1–5; here, 1.

[17] Craig Calhoun, *Nationalism* (Buckingham: Open UP, 1997), 2.

[18] Judith Butler, *Gender Trouble: Feminism and the Subversion of Identity* (New York: Routledge, 1990), 143.

[19] A reference to Saskia Sassen, *Globalization and Its Discontents: Essays on the New Mobility of People and Money* (New York: The New Press, 1998).

[20] Moritz Baßler, *Der deutsche Pop-Roman. Die neuen Archivisten* (Munich: Beck, 2002), 80. All translations from German sources are my own.

[21] Baßler, *Der deutsche Pop-Roman*, 81.

[22] Sibylle Berg, *Ein paar Leute suchen das Glück und lachen sich tot* (Stuttgart: Reclam, 1997); see, for example, 46, 57, 97, 170.

[23] In a text concerning a television program featuring Berg, online at www.3sat. de/dynamic/sitegen/bin/sitegen.php?tab=2&source=/specials/98550/index. html (accessed 9 November 2009).

[24] On discussions of the "new readability" as a desirable feature of new German fiction, see Taberner, "Introduction," in *German Literature in the Age of Globalisation*, 15.

[25] Sibylle Berg, *Sex II* (Stuttgart: Reclam, 1998), 78.

[26] Sibylle Berg, *Ende gut* (Reinbek bei Hamburg: Rowohlt Taschenbuch Verlag, 2005), 15.

[27] See Stephan Maus, "Madame Berserker singt den Blues. Von Anfang an gut: *Ende gut* von Sibylle Berg," *Süddeutsche Zeitung*, 14 February 2005, www.stephan-maus.de/serendipity/archives/36-Sibylle-Berg-Ende-gut-SZ.html (accessed 15 July 2010). See also Berg, *Ende gut*, 26. Houellebecq features in Sibylle Berg, *Das Unerfreuliche zuerst. Herrengeschichten* (Cologne: Kiepenheuer & Witsch, 2001).

[28] See www.sibylleberg.ch/flash/ and https://twitter.com/SibylleBerg (accessed 9 November 2009).

[29] Sibylle Berg, *Der Mann schläft* (Zurich: Hanser, 2009). Iris Radisch speculates that the narrator has "a little bit of Sibylle Berg in her." See www.zeit.de/2009/37/ L-B-Berg (accessed 15 July 2010).

[30] Sibylle Berg, *Amerika* (Hamburg: Hoffmann und Campe, 1999).

[31] Thomas Ernst, "German Pop Literature and Cultural Globalisation," trans. by Heather Fleming, in *German Literature in the Age of Globalisation*, ed. Taberner, 169–88; here, 170.

[32] See Kristina Maidt-Zinke, "Mit Hass im Aug sieht man besser," *Süddeutsche Zeitung*, 9 October 2007, www.buecher.de/shop/buecher/die-fahrt/berg-sib-ylle/products_products/content/prod_id/22818044/ (accessed 15 July 2010).

[33] Sibylle Berg, *Die Fahrt* (Reinbek bei Hamburg: Rowohlt, 2009), 26. Subsequent page references appear in parentheses in the main body of the text.

[34] See Sara Ahmed et al., Introduction, in *Uprootings/Regroundings: Questions of Home and Migration*, ed. Sara Ahmed et al. (Oxford: Berg, 2003), 1–19; here, 1.

[35] Sassen, *Globalization*, xxviii.

[36] Compare Taberner, Introduction, in *German Literature in the Age of Globalisation*, 14.

[37] See here Ahmed et al., Introduction, in *Uprootings/Regroundings*, 5.

[38] Sassen, *Globalization*, xx.

[39] Compare Berg, *Ende gut*, 39.

[40] See here Boa and Palfreyman, *Heimat*, 25–29.

[41] Compare Berg, *Ende gut*, 40.

[42] Rosi Braidotti, *Nomadic Subjects: Embodiment and Sexual Difference in Contemporary Feminist Theory* (New York: Columbia UP, 1994).

[43] Sara Ahmed, *Strange Encounters: Embodied Others in Post-Coloniality* (London: Routledge, 2000), 7.

[44] www.kiwi-verlag.de/36-0-buch.htm?isbn=9783462039122#inhalt (accessed 15 July 2010).

[45] See Beth Linklater, "Germany as Background: Global Concerns in Recent Women's Writing in German,' in *German Literature in the Age of Globalisation*, ed. Taberner, 67–87; here, 73.

[46] Thus far, Berg has had a novella translated into English: *By the Way, Did I Ever Tell You . . .* (Zurich: JRP Ringier, 2007). The work is illustrated by Andro Wekua and Rita Ackermann and edited by Raphael Gygax; it is not clear from the publicity material who translated it. An English-language description of *Die Fahrt* and an extract from the novel translated into English (by Franklin Bolsillo Mares) are available on the Web: www.litrix.de/buecher/belletristik/jahr/2008/diefahrt/buchbesprechung/enindex.htm (accessed 15 July 2010).

[47] Beth Linklater, "Germany as Background," 73.

[48] Arjun Appadurai, "Disjuncture and Difference in the Global Cultural Economy," in *The Globalization Reader*, ed. Lechner and Boli, 95–104; here, 104.

10: Julia Franck, *Die Mittagsfrau*: *Historia Matria* and Matrilineal Narrative

Valerie Heffernan

WHEN JULIA FRANCK WAS AWARDED the German Book Prize in 2007, she was by no means a newcomer to the literary scene. The author had already published three novels and two collections of short stories before her epic tome *Die Mittagsfrau* (literally, Lady Midday, the noonday witch, 2007; published in English as *The Blind Side of the Heart*, 2009) earned her Germany's most prestigious literary award. In selecting Franck's novel, the jury members were unanimous in their praise of its "vivid use of language, narrative power and psychological intensity," calling it "a novel for long conversations."[1] Franck's powerful depiction of a woman who, against the backdrop of war-torn Germany, comes to the momentous decision to abandon her seven-year-old son at a railway station certainly provides plenty of material for discussion.

Prior to the publication of the novel that earned her the prize, Franck was quite well known in Germany as one of the writers of the so-called *Fräuleinwunder* generation, the "wonder girls" of contemporary German literature. Volker Hage originally coined the term in a 1999 article in *Der Spiegel* that drew attention to a group of young women writers, including Karen Duve and Kathrin Schmidt, who were taking the literary scene by storm and whose candid writing, in his view, showed that they had no fear of clichés or strong emotions.[2] Whether or not Hage's observations about this new generation of women writers were correct, the label of the *Fräuleinwunder* stuck, and it shaped how contemporary women's writing in German was read and marketed in the years following the publication of his somewhat problematic article.[3] Publishers and magazines alike complemented interviews with writers and discussions of their literature with glossy photos that promoted the writers as a phenomenon in themselves, the bright stars of Germany's literary future. Despite the fact that Julia Franck's name was never mentioned in Hage's article, she has always been depicted by the media as one of Germany's wonder girls.

Franck herself has always argued very strongly against the notion of a *Fräuleinwunder*, asserting that it is nothing more than a marketing label and that it actually undermines the legitimacy of contemporary writing by women.[4] Against this, she links her writing to a more general hope that women will begin to play a more dominant role, not just within the family, but through the family in the wider arena.[5] Correspondingly, Franck's writing often tends to focus on female figures that do not fit conventional gender roles or patterns of behavior. Her literary world is inhabited by strong-minded women who are solitary figures and who learn early in life to rely on themselves.

The publication of *Die Mittagsfrau* in 2007 brought an end to all discussions of Franck's work as mere *Fräuleinwunder* and launched the author onto a European stage. This novel is inspired by an episode from Franck's own family history: her father was abandoned at a small train station outside of Berlin shortly after the end of the Second World War. It was in fact the quest to understand what might have happened to cause her paternal grandmother to walk away from her child — at a time when others were desperately searching for their families — that motivated her to write the novel:

> When I had my first child seven years ago, it became a burning question for me to understand what could drive a woman to abandon her child, to be so convinced that that child would be better off anywhere else than with her. . . . I find her decision to turn her back on her motherhood and her relationship to her child both strange and unsettling. I wanted to explore it and to try to come up with a story for this woman.[6]

Clearly, the driving force in the writer's decision to focus on this episode in her family history is her fascination with an act that seems to fly in the face of all that society and culture deem to be natural and instinctive to a mother. It is also telling that Franck reports that this issue only began to haunt her when she herself became a mother. The author's comments suggest that *Die Mittagsfrau* can be read as a more general exploration of motherhood, its expectations and demands, its possibilities and its limitations.

Like many writers of her generation, Franck is concerned with depicting the personal stories of her protagonists against the backdrop of the turbulent and, at times, violent history of Germany in the first half of the twentieth century. Her epic narrative begins in Bautzen, a small town outside Dresden, in 1913, a year before the outbreak of the First World War, moves to Berlin in the roaring twenties and concludes more than four decades later in the remote countryside of what by then is East Germany. The novel thus depicts a period in German history that is characterized by some of the most intense and destructive conflicts ever witnessed, the Holocaust against the Jewish people, immense political and economic instability, and massive social upheaval and transformation. However, as this essay will show, the historical aspects of the novel are less important that its examination of the meaning of motherhood in the contemporary era. In both aspects, *Die Mittagsfrau* taps into current trends in literature and culture, and in both Franck offers a new and different perspective on these issues.

Franck's *Historia Matria* of Germany

This is one of many contemporary novels that engage with historical discourses by focusing on the compelling story of one remarkable character.[7] Franck's epic novel tells the remarkable story of Helene Würsich through two world wars, and as such, it involves a broader investigation of German history in the early twentieth century. In an interview about her earlier novel *Lagerfeuer*, Franck acknowledges that her writing engages with historical discourse. Her understanding of history is influenced by Carlo Ginzburg's concept of microhistory, which she sees as "a very good way of understanding the past."[8] The Italian historian Ginzburg's approach to historiography grew out of a dissatisfaction with conventional historical models, which to his mind focused on grand narratives and great heroes instead of the lived experience of the individual, especially where that individual does not fit normative patterns. Against this, he and other Italian historians sought to move the subject of historical enquiry from the center to the margins, to the "little people" who are often lost or exploited in the processes of modernization and historical advancement.[9] As such, microhistory is not dissimilar in approach from what is known in Germany as *Alltagsgeschichte* or the history of everyday life, and in the Anglo-Saxon world as history from below.[10] Believing that that the fate of individual historical agents can reveal much about wider historical trends, microhistorians focus their attention on borderline figures and outsiders, who would not usually be subjects of historical enquiry; through examining their relationships and interactions with the community, they claim to be able to reconstruct a richer and more inclusive picture of that community. Franck emphasizes that microhistory allows us to understand "how history becomes history. And how the history of a society can be mirrored in a very private, personal history."[11]

Interestingly, the Mexican microhistorian Luis González suggests that microhistory could alternatively be termed *historia matria*, a type of maternal history. In contrast to the metahistorical narrative of the *patria* or fatherland, González uses the term *matria* to encompass what is conventionally seen as the small, weak, feminine, sentimental world of the mother — the family and the home — and thus his *historia matria* focuses on that which has been ignored in historiography: the maternal.[12] If Franck's interrogation of the past can read as an analysis of German twentieth-century history, it could be argued that hers is an *historia matria*, since it is evidently the domestic sphere that is her focus. She approaches the history of two world wars from a different angle than that presented in conventional history books. Her novel depicts this era from the point of view of the women left at home: the wives who lie awake at night worrying about their men fighting on the front, the mothers who must work hard to earn a living in order to feed their families, the daughters whose dreams of a bright future are shattered by the harsh realities of war.

It is significant that the historical events of the period covered in *Die Mittagsfrau* are only ever referred to in an oblique way and never overshadow the personal histories of the novel's protagonists. This is evidenced by the fact that years and dates are seldom mentioned. The reader can only discern the time in which the happenings in the novel take place through allusions to certain historical and cultural landmarks: Helene's presence at the Berlin première of Brecht's *The Threepenny Opera*;[13] newspaper boys shouting the news of a fire in the Reichstag building (308); Helene's concerns at how the newly passed Nuremberg Laws protecting Aryan blood might affect her (313); or her attendance at the celebrations to mark the opening of the Reich autobahn between Berlin and Stettin (345).

Equally, the description of certain characters serves as an indicator for the reader of particular social groups and political trends that would have been prominent in Germany of this era. The depiction of Helene's father in his hussar's uniform serves as a textual marker for German imperialism and the outbreak of the First World War. By the same token, the rise of the National Socialists is not dealt with in a direct way in *Die Mittagsfrau*, yet tall, handsome Wilhelm Sehmisch, with his fair hair and blue eyes and his weakness for blondes, is immediately identifiable to the reader as the Nazi of the piece. Moreover, the changing fortunes in the 1920s and 1930s of Aunt Fanny, a Jewish cousin of their mother's who offers Martha and Helene a home in Berlin, reveal much about the economic instability of the Weimar republic and the situation of Jews in Germany during these years. When we first encounter Fanny, she is the stereotypical rich Jewish heiress who can afford to spend her days lounging around her luxurious home, recovering from her excesses of the night before. However, in the course of the 1920s, as the economic crisis is becoming more acute, Fanny is obliged to sell more and more of her possessions to make ends meet. After Helene's move to Stettin with her new husband in 1935, she loses contact with her aunt. A reader aware of the historical backdrop will already have assumed what Helene eventually learns in the most veiled terms; namely, that Fanny was "taken away" (384) by the Nazis.

By contrast, *Die Mittagsfrau* undertakes an *historia matria* in that it concentrates on how history is made in the home — in the daily business of surviving wars; in tending to the needs of the population at home; in healing the sick; in giving birth to, and raising, the next generation. Helene and her sister Martha are presented from the outset as strong female characters who are active in shaping their fate. While their father is away fighting in the First World War, the task of supporting the family and running the household falls to them. In Berlin of the 1920s, they and women like them are the stereotypical new women, playing an active role in the workplace and driving forward social progress. As nurses, Martha and Helene contribute to the war effort at home during the Second World War; their hands save the lives of many civilians injured in the allied bombings, and they do what they can for the wounded. As a mother, also, Helene has a crucial role to play in the progression of history; on one occasion, another woman emphasizes the importance of this: "Thank God women like you are still having children" (378).

It is evidently through the character of Helene that *Die Mittagsfrau* engages most obviously with the historical events of the early twentieth century; she is the exceptional individual of Franck's *historia matria*. Helene's fate represents the fate of many mothers, daughters, and sisters who lived during this turbulent phase in Germany's recent past. Her premature confrontation with responsibility and financial hardship, her tragic and premature loss of a loved one, her struggle to look after her child during the war, and her repeated rape by Red Army soldiers after the fall of Berlin in 1945 reflect the experiences of many German women during this time. Yet *Die Mittagsfrau* emphasizes her heroism in facing down these challenges and taking control of her fate. By surviving these difficult years in Germany's history and by making difficult, at times even scandalous decisions that enable her to extricate herself from her circumstances, she manages to shape her own history and thereby alter in some small way the course of historical events. The personal histories of exceptional individuals such as Helene may not be at the forefront of conventional historical analysis of this period in time. Nevertheless, stories such as hers contribute to a richer and more inclusive image of twentieth-century German history.

Motherhood as Matrophor

In justifying their decision to award the 2007 German Book Prize to the author, the jury described *Die Mittagsfrau* as a novel that tells the disturbing story of a mother who abandons her child "against the background of two world wars."[14] The jury's appraisal of the novel is appropriate, since it emphasizes that the historical discussion is merely the backdrop to Franck's interrogation of the maternal role. Indeed, although many reviews of *Die Mittagsfrau* have highlighted its engagement with Germany's recent history, most reviewers focus more on Franck's complex protagonist and her depiction of motherhood in the novel.[15] For many, it is the image of seven-year-old Peter standing by his suitcase in a train-station, waiting in vain for his mother to return, that is the most powerful impression that emerges from the novel.[16]

Franck's negotiation of the maternal role in *Die Mittagsfrau* both reflects and feeds into a cultural climate in Germany in which concerns about motherhood are ubiquitous. During the first decade of this century, the German media landscape has been concerned to the point of obsession with the country's falling birth rates and, all too often, the reason given for the perceived crisis in maternity is German women's decision to prioritize career over family.[17] Some contributions to the media discussions about the changing roles of mothers in contemporary Germany have generated heated debate, such as Eva Herman's bestselling *Das Eva-Prinzip* (The Eve principle, 2006), in which the TV personality blames the feminist movement for women's reluctance to have children, and controversially advocates a return to traditional gender roles.[18] The following year, the well-known German feminist Alice Schwarzer published *Die Antwort* (The answer, 2007) — the title of which implies that it is intended as a response to Herman — in which she argues that men are just as capable of bringing up children as women, and women are just as entitled to find fulfillment through their careers as men.[19] Schwarzer's ideas were greeted with as much enthusiasm as Herman's, indicating the range of opinions that characterize discussions of motherhood in Germany today.

That a woman writer should opt to interrogate the question of what it means to be a mother in her writing is in itself nothing new. Women's writing has long been concerned with motherhood, mothering, and maternity and all of their cultural manifestations. In particular, the relationship between mothers and daughters plays a central role in literary texts by women, especially when they are based on or include autobiographical elements.[20] German literature of the late twentieth century features many instances of strong mother figures, who are often depicted in very negative terms. Among the more striking examples of this genre are Elfriede Jelinek's *Die Klavierspielerin* (1983; *The Piano Teacher*, 1988) and Anna Mitgutsch's *Die Züchtigung* (1987; *Punishment*, 1988), both of which feature very domineering and cruel mothers.[21] Rebecca Dakin Quinn uses the term "matrophor" to express "the persistent nature of maternal metaphors in feminism";[22] one might argue in the same vein that women's writing is also pervaded by the matrophor. In this sense, Franck's novel does not represent a new departure, but continues a practice in women's literature of interrogating the characteristics and the boundaries of the motherly role.

Franck's treatment of motherhood can thus be read as a contribution to a certain cultural climate in Germany and to a tradition in recent

German literature by women.[23] The author also shows that she is conscious of the wider implications of addressing ideas such as motherly love and maternal instinct in her literature, since they go to the heart of debates about a woman's rights and responsibilities:

> While I was working on the book, I very quickly found myself dealing with the theme of feminism. I soon became aware that it is so taboo for us when a woman abandons her child because we assume from the outset that the most important person for a child is its mother and that she can never leave it.[24]

Die Mittagsfrau questions assumptions such as this and attempts to construct a narrative that might explain, if not justify, an action that in society's eyes seems to defy explanation. While the novel probes the expectations that society places upon mothers, there is certainly some truth in the suggestion expressed in *Der Spiegel* that its main character Helene is "an attack on the traditional image of woman."[25] Like Alex in Karen Duve's novel *Taxi* (2008) or Anita in Ulrike Draesner's *Mitgift* (2002), Helene is difficult to categorize in conventional terms, and this often makes her a problematic literary heroine.

Helene's difficult relationship with her own mother has an enormous impact on her perception of what it means to be a mother. Selma Würsich is anything but a conventional mother; her mental illness, exacerbated by the loss of five infant sons, prevents her from developing any bond with her last, unplanned and unwanted child. Helene's repeated attempts to reach out to her mother are greeted with coldness and indifference:

> While Mother shouted at her daughters, cursing them, complaining that she'd given birth to a couple of useless brats, Helene kept on and on repeating the same thing like a prayer: May I comb your hair? Her voice quivered: May I comb your hair? As a pair of scissors flew through the air she raised her arms to protect her head: May I comb your hair? (27)

As Martha tells Helene, it is as if their mother's heart has gone blind, so that she simply cannot see people any more. The unsympathetic motherhood that Helene is faced with throughout her childhood ultimately evokes mistrust, fear, and even repulsion in her, and it is easy to understand how a child confronted with such a negative image of mothering would grow up to become an adult with fundamentally ambivalent feelings about what it means to be a mother.

The narrative makes reference to a number of other female characters in Helene's life who act as maternal figures, and at times some of these seem to offer a more positive image of the maternal role. Some volunteer to play the role of mother, such as the Sorbian housemaid Mariechen; she attempts to compensate for Selma's indifference by taking care of Helene as if she were her own child. It is Mariechen, for example, who names the baby Helene when Selma shows no interest in her newborn child, and she even attempts to breastfeed Helene when her mother pays no attention to the baby's cries. Equally, Helene looks to others for the tenderness and attention denied her by her mother. Her sister Martha seems to play the strongest maternal role in Helene's life, and she responds to Helene's need for mothering by taking on the conventional tasks associated with a mother, looking after her younger sister and encouraging her to follow her dreams of becoming a doctor.

Given Helene's own experience of mothering, we can well imagine the ambivalent feelings her own pregnancy evoke in her. It is telling that Helene opts to terminate her first pregnancy, despite the fact that her beloved Carl has already expressed his hopes of having children with her. Her second pregnancy, this time to her husband Wilhelm, is equally unwelcome. Despite her reluctance, there is evidence that Helene does all she can to be a good mother to her son. She breastfeeds her baby until she is sick and physically exhausted; she worries about leaving him when she has to go to work. Nevertheless, her difficulties with her role as mother are highlighted throughout the narrative. Her feelings toward her son are often presented in quite negative terms; Peter is compared to an octopus whose tentacles surround her and squeeze the last breath out of her (405), and she has neither the time nor the energy to cope with his need for her. As the text emphasizes, "Helene had never been a Mama or a Mummy" (406).

The simplicity of the language in *Die Mittagsfrau* has led many critics to describe Franck's writing as cold and detached.[26] In fact, the starkness of the language in this novel is arguably crucial to its depiction of Helene's mothering. The bare prose, rather than indicating a lack of emotion, creates a constant tension that suggests an underlying depth of emotion. For example, the words used to describe the moment when Helene comes to her momentous decision are stark but by no means devoid of feeling: "She had to make a decision, she knew that; no, it was not exactly a decision, it was just something she had to do" (407–8). The fact that this crucial moment in the development of the narrative is presented in such bald terms does not detract from the novel; on the contrary, the simplicity of the language points to impossibility of encapsulating in words the complex issues involved in Helene's decision.

The shifting narrative perspective of *Die Mittagsfrau* adds an additional dimension to the novel's portrayal of motherhood. The prologue and epilogue are portrayed from Peter's point of view, and they offer a very different view of Helene than the intimate picture of her that emerges in the main part of the narrative. Indeed, the difference is so marked as to suggest that Helene presents an entirely different persona to others, even to her son. This double personality is marked by her two names; in private, she is Helene, but to the outside world, she is Nurse Alice, the resilient but aloof Aryan woman who works hard and appears impervious to the pain and suffering she witnesses every day at the hospital. The passages written from Peter's perspective depict a strong, beautiful, capable, but emotionally distant woman who seems unable to offer her son the kind of love and affection he craves so desperately. Peter describes his mother as "the most beautiful mother in the world" (4), but even as a seven-year-old, he cannot fail to notice that the expression in her eyes is "icy" (13). The narrative perspective produces a curious doubling effect: the presentation of two experiences of mothering, both from the child's point of view, accentuate the parallels between Helene's own experience of being mothered and the kind of mother she later becomes.

It is precisely this shift in narrative perspective that is critical to Franck's novel and that makes her depiction of motherhood so powerful and so complex. It is especially significant that the point of view moves from Helene to Peter at the crucial point when Helene makes the decision to abandon her child. We observe her deliberate, measured actions in packing his clothes and preparing his suitcase for the move, but from the moment they leave Stettin, we witness everything through the eyes of seven-year-old Peter, who has no understanding of why his mother has abandoned him. In refusing her readers access to Helene's thoughts at this decisive moment in the narrative, Franck demands that they decide for themselves whether or not her actions can be justified. Thus, the narrative perspective both enables the reader to view Helene's monumental decision from all angles and forces him/her to take a stance on her action.

Die Mittagsfrau as Matrilineal Narrative

One of the criticisms leveled at Franck in the reviews of *Die Mittagsfrau* is that the male figures in the novel appear clichéd and rather one-dimensional, more caricatures than fully rounded characters.[27] Indeed, we need only compare the rather simplistic depiction of Helene's father with the much more complex characterization of her mother to conclude that the male characters play only supporting roles in the action. By contrast, it is clearly the female figures that dominate the action and drive the plot of Franck's novel. Both in Bautzen and in Berlin, Helene is surrounded by strong women who demonstrate through what they say and what they do that they can steer their fate without the help of their male counterparts. This situation and the way in which these female characters react to and interact with each other suggest that *Die Mittagsfrau* can be read as what Tess Cosslett calls a "matrilineal narrative." Cosslett defines the matrilineal narrative as "one which either tells the stories of several generations of

women at once, or which shows how identity of a central character is cru-
cially formed by her female ancestors."[28] Yi-Lin Yu elaborates this definition and, interestingly, she points out that "women writers' preoccupation
with female family relations often leads to the relative obscurity of father
figures in most matrilineal narratives."[29]

Cosslett's concept of the matrilineal narrative provides a useful framework for analyzing *Die Mittagsfrau*, as it emphasizes the effect that the
female figures in Franck's narrative have on Helene's development. Helene
is clearly seen as part of a female lineage, and her female relatives have an
enormous influence on her character and her sense of her own identity.
Thus, while Selma Würsich's deficient mothering of her younger daughter
obviously shapes Helene's view of motherhood, her difficult relationship
with her emotionally distant mother is clearly also central to her development as an individual and, by extension, to the unfolding of the events
depicted in the narrative. The effect on her that this rejection has throughout her life in expressed most powerfully in the answer that "burst[s] out
of her" when Wilhelm proposes. Her response is: "Something like me isn't
supposed to exist at all" (312). Her mother's maltreatment of her has left
her doubting not only her own ability to be a good mother but even her
own value and worth as a person.

Nonetheless, Helene's later replication of her mother's behavior in her
own mothering of her son is reflective of the "strong sense of identification
between mothers and daughters" that Yi-Lin Yu sees as central to the matrilineal narrative.[30] Despite Helene's efforts to distance herself both physically and emotionally from her mother, there is a sense that she is carrying
on her mother's legacy, indeed, that this is almost inevitable. We can only
really get an insight into why and how Helene makes the decision to abandon her child by understanding her relationship with her mother. Her
model of mothering may be lacking in every way, but it is what she has
grown up with. Helene's ambivalence about taking on the motherly role
is obviously rooted in a fear that she will repeat the cycle and become the
kind of mother that her own mother was. The fact that her fears are confirmed reinforces the similarities in their characters.

We might also argue that Helene's unusually strong bond to her older
sister Martha merits closer attention in the context of the matrilineal narrative, since Martha also plays a central role in Helene's development.
Certainly, she is her most important influence in her formative years, and
Helene owes her upbringing to Martha more than to anyone else. Through
their years in Berlin and after Helene's marriage to Wilhelm, they remain
very close; Martha is always the first person Helene turns to, and it is her
opinion and approval that she seeks more than anyone else's. We might
even go so far as to say that Martha is the love of Helene's life. Her devo-
tion to her older sister goes beyond mere familial love and gratitude to the
older sister who has mothered her in place of her mother. Helene's first

sexual experiences are with Martha, and she compares her subsequent lovers to her. In the epilogue to the novel, we learn through seventeen-year-old Peter that his mother is not in a position to accept him back into her life, as there is no room for him in the tiny apartment she shares with her sister. Thus, where once Martha stepped in to replace Helene's mother, she now takes the place that rightfully belongs to her child.

Conclusion

The matrilineal narrative is often associated with texts that have an auto-biographical impetus;[31] women writers use it to trace their own development as individuals and as subjects and to understand themselves as part of a historical progression or familial chain. Julia Franck's acknowledgment that her exploration of female lineage in *Die Mittagsfrau* is both connected to an endeavor to understand an episode in her family past, and provoked by her own experience of becoming a mother, suggests that her novel can also be read in this light.

Through the complex female characters that Franck creates in this novel, she explores the possibilities and limitations of maternal influence. Through her matrilineal narrative, she explores how women can shape the characters of the women around them to the extent that they can actually alter the course of events. Furthermore, her *historia matria* also considers this idea on a wider scale; it examines how women — mothers, daughters, and sisters — contribute to shaping the course of history. Her novel reflects issues that preoccupy other contemporary writers: the relationship between the individual and history, the function and meaning of motherhood today, the relationship between the past and the present. At the same time, she takes a unique stance on these issues. The narrative structure of the novel, and in particular the shift in narrative perspective, allow for the fact that there are always a number of different ways of looking at an issue, and each individual has something to add to the discussion. Franck's novel offers a rich and detailed image of a very difficult era in recent German history. By approaching it from the maternal perspective, she adds a new aspect to the discussion and a new dimension to contemporary German literature.

Notes

[1] Claus Setzer, "Julia Franck is awarded the German Book Prize 2007 for her novel *Die Mittagsfrau*," Press release of the Deutscher Börsenverein, 5 October 2007, available on www.boersenverein.de/de/135031 (accessed 19 August 2010).

[2] Volker Hage, "Ganz schön abgedreht," *Der Spiegel* 12 (1999): 244–246.

[3] For an overview of the phenomenon of the *Fräuleinwunder* and its appropriateness for contemporary German literature by women, see Heike Bartel and Elizabeth Boa, eds., *Pushing at Boundaries: Approaches to Contemporary German Writers from Karen Duve to Jenny Erpenbeck* (Amsterdam: Rodopi, 2006). See also Christine Caemmerer, Walter Delabar, and Helga Meise, eds., *Fräuleinwunder literarisch: Literatur von Frauen zu Beginn des 21. Jahrhunderts* (Frankfurt: Peter Lang, 2005) and Heidelinde Müller, *Das "literarische Fräuleinwunder." Inspektion eines Phänomens der deutschen Gegenwartsliteratur in Einzelfallstudien* (Frankfurt: Peter Lang, 2004).

[4] Julia Franck, "The Wonder (of) Woman," trans. Alexandra Merley Hill, *Women in German Yearbook* 24 (2008): 235–240; here, 236.

[5] Wiebke Eden, "Julia Franck: 'Beim Schreiben ist man mit sich und der Geschichte allein,'" in *"Keine Angst vor großen Gefühlen." Die neuen Schriftstellerinnen* (Berlin: Edition Ebersbach, 2001), 23–32; here, 31.

[6] Julia Franck, in Susanne Geu, "Schreiben zum Überleben. Interview," *ZEIT online*, 10 October 2007, www.zeit.de/online/2007/40/interview-julia-franck (accessed 10 July 2010). My translation.

[7] Other novels discussed in this volume that deal in a similar way with specific epoques in German and European history include Vladimir Vertlib's *Das besondere Gedächtnis der Rosa Masur* (2003), Terézia Mora's *Alle Tage* (2004), and Saša Stanišić's *Wie der Soldat das Grammofon repariert* (2006).

[8] Julia Franck, in Stacey Knecht, "Interview with Julia Franck," *The Ledge*, an independent platform for world literature. Available on www.the-ledge.com/HTML/conversation.php? ID=28&lan=uk (accessed 10 June 2010).

[9] Georg G. Iggers, *Historiography in The Twentieth Century. From Scientific Objectivity to The Postmodern Challenge* (Middletown, CT: Wesleyan UP, 1997), 102.

[10] For an in-depth discussion of the similarities and difference between these three strands of historical analysis, see Sigurður Gylfi Magnússon, "Social History — Cultural History — Alltagsgeschichte — Microhistory: In-Between Methodologies and Conceptual Frameworks," *Journal of Microhistory* (2006), available on www.microhistory.org/pivot/entry.php?id=20 (accessed 10 June 2010).

[11] Knecht, "Interview with Julia Franck."

[12] Luis González y González, "El arte de la microhistoria," *Invitación a la microhistoria* (México: Edición Clío, 1997), 11–47; here, 16. Carlo Ginzburg also uses the phrase "matria history" as an English translation of González's terminology in Carlo Ginzburg, John Tedeschi, and Anne C. Tedeschi, "Microhistory: Two or Three Things That I Know about It," *Critical Inquiry* 20, no. 1 (1993): 10–35; here, 12.

[13] Julia Franck, *The Blind Side of the Heart*, trans. Anthea Bell (London: Random House, 2009), 229. Subsequent page references appear in parentheses in the main body of the text.

[14] Setzer, Press Release of the Deutscher Börsenverein.

[15] See for example Elmar Krekeler, "Das erkaltete Herz," *Die Welt*, 29 September 2007; Antje Korsmeier, "Blindheit des Herzens," *Die Tageszeitung*, 29–30 September 2007; Katharina Döbler, "Peterchens Mutter," *Die Zeit* 6 September 2007; Matthias Schreiber, "Düstere Lichtgestalt," *Der Spiegel*, 17 September 2007; Nico Bleutge, "Meisterin der Handarbeitskunst," *Neue Zürcher Zeitung*, 17 October 2007.

[16] See for example Christoph Schröder, "Das abgestorbene Innenleben," *Frankfurter Rundschau*, 18 September 2007; Jörg Magenau, "Eine duldsame Frau," *Falter*, 12 October 2007; Stefan Tolksdorf, "Die Erblindung eines Herzens," *Badische Zeitung*, 6 October 2007. It is noteworthy also that Random House opted to use this image for the cover of the English translation of Franck's novel.

[17] Media reports on this subject range from the moderate, such as a themed issue of the *Spiegel* magazine entitled "Wieviel Mutter braucht das Kind?" *Der Spiegel* 9 (2008), to the sensational headline of a German tabloid, "Baby shock: We Germans are dying out!" *Bild-Zeitung*, 15 March 2006.

[18] Eva Herman, *Das Eva-Prinzip. Für eine neue Weiblichkeit* (Starnberg: Pendo, 2006).

[19] Alice Schwarzer, *Die Antwort* (Cologne: Kiepenheuer & Witsch, 2007).

[20] Norgard Klages, *Look Back in Anger: Mother-Daughter and Father-Daughter Relationships in Women's Autobiographical Writings of the 1970s and 1980s* (New York: Peter Lang, 1995), 11–12.

[21] A useful and interesting analysis of mother-figures in the literature of this era is provided by Emily Jeremiah, *Troubling Maternity: Mothering, Agency, and Ethics in Women's Writing in German of the 1970s and 1980s* (Leeds: Maney/MHRA, 2003). See also Katharina Aulls, *Verbunden und Gebunden. Mutter-Tochter-Beziehungen in sechs Romanen der siebziger und achtziger Jahre* (Frankfurt: Lang, 1993) and Renate Dernedde, *Mutterschatten — Schattenmütter. Muttergestalten und Mutter-Tochter-Beziehungen in deutschsprachiger Prosa* (Frankfurt: Lang, 1994).

[22] Rebecca Dakin Quinn, "An Open Letter to Institutional Mothers," in *Generations: Academic Feminists in Dialogue*, ed. Devoney Looser and E. Ann Kaplan (Minneapolis: Minnesota UP, 1997), 174–82; here, 179. Astrid Henry also develops the idea of the matrophor in her book *Not My Mother's Sister. Generational Conflict and Third-Wave Feminism* (Bloomington: Indiana UP, 2004). I am grateful to Hester Baer for bringing this term to my attention.

[23] Alexandra Merley Hill offers an insightful overview of this debate and Julia Franck's engagement with it in "'Female Sobriety': Feminism, Motherhood, and the Works of Julia Franck," *Women in German Yearbook* 24 (2008): 209–28.

[24] Anke Dürr, Ulrike Knöfel, and Claudia Voigt, "Weder Muse noch Madonna," *Der Spiegel* 28 (2008): 136–39; here, 139. My translation.

[25] Dürr, Knöfel, and Voigt, "Weder Muse noch Madonna," 139.

[26] Franck comments on this criticism of her language, which she links to readers' and critics' expectations of women's writing: "I don't think my novels are cold

— on the contrary. My language is just very clear. But readers would rather a female writer give them a happy ending, or at least offer them comfort," Knecht, "Interview with Julia Franck."

[27] See, for example, Christoph Schröder, "Das abgestorbene Innenleben," *Frankfurter Rundschau*, 217, 18 September 2007, and Karl-Markus Gauß, "Die Kälte des Sommers," *Die Presse*, 6 October 2007.

[28] Tess Cosslett, "Feminism, Matrilinealism, and the 'House of Women' in Contemporary Women's Fiction," *Journal of Gender Studies* 5, no. 1 (1996): 7–17; here, 7.

[29] Yi-Lin Yu, *Mother She Wrote. Matrilineal Narratives in Contemporary Women's Writing* (New York: Peter Lang, 2005), 3.

[30] Yu, *Mother She Wrote*, 3.

[31] Cosslett, "Feminism, Matrilinealism, and the 'House of Women,'" 9.

11: Alina Bronsky, *Scherbenpark*: Global Ghetto Girl

Barbara Mennel

IT HAS BECOME A MAINSTAY of globalization theory that local and global are not mutually exclusive categories. Global forces produce locally inflected culture, which does not exist outside of networks of transnational exchange. Within this dialectic of the nexus between global and local, literature has retained a privileged status. Literature's dependence on language situates it as integral to national culture, especially in the case of Germany, which historically has defined itself as a *Kulturnation* (cultural nation). Yet national literature nonetheless responds to, incorporates, and partakes in global networks of production and circulation of culture. Thus, when Alina Bronsky's *Scherbenpark* (2008; *Broken Glass Park*, 2010) tells the story of its main character Sascha Naimann, a teenage immigrant girl in the Russian ghetto of an unnamed German city, the text circulates within the boundaries of German-language literature but simultaneously echoes and engages with global impulses.[1] *Scherbenpark* refracts and revises Germanness through a literary account of contemporary migration from Russia to Germany reliant on a binational model of chronological temporality and geography organized around nation-states and participates in a discourse that centers on the figure of the girl as a global phenomenon. The pseudonym "Alina Bronsky" names an emerging, yet successful, author whose novel can be explicated comprehensively only in a multilayered and multidimensional framework of transnational and intermedial intertextuality.

Scherbenpark tells the story of seventeen-year-old Sascha Naimann, who lives in a high-rise populated by Russian immigrants on the outskirts of a German city. Two years prior to the time of the novel's action, Vadim — her mother's second husband and father of Sascha's younger siblings Anton and Alissa — had shot and killed her mother and her German boyfriend. Sascha's mother had filed for divorce when Vadim had hit Sascha in the face with a belt while trying to beat Anton. The children continue to live in the apartment where their private horror took place with the help of Vadim's cousin Maria from Novosibirsk. Sascha fantasizes about killing Vadim. When she sees a newspaper article sympathetically describing

Vadim's life in jail, she seeks out the article's author, Susanne Mahler at the newspaper. Her boss, Volker Trebur, apologizes for her and offers Sascha help. Sascha requests that he take her to his home, where she meets his sixteen-year-old son Felix, with whom she has sex, even though she has feelings for his father. Later, Volker makes sexual advances toward Sascha but then apologizes. While Volker and Felix are on vacation, Sascha meets a young man, also named Volker, who turns out to be a right-wing extremist. After she has sex with him in the park, she takes him to a group of young Russians, led by her nemesis and neighbor Peter, who beat him up, and then she skates around town in a self-destructive daze. When the newspaper subsequently reveals that Vadim has committed suicide in jail, Sascha takes out her frustration in a fight with her neighbors, which leaves her unconscious and hospitalized. Volker and Felix take her home and visit Maria, Anton, and Alissa. Sascha steals away from the ensuing harmonious moment to travel to Prague.

The novel evinces national, binational, and transnational dimensions, including migration from Russia to Germany, the reimagination of Europe, and the global explosion of girl culture. *Scherbenpark* partakes in a current global phenomenon of literature and cinema by and about girls that validate their experience and perspective, often, but not always, associated with the ghetto as a result of migration. Since the modern ghetto appears as a space of male criminality, the figure of the global ghetto girl appropriates signifiers of masculinity. This commodified and reified figure circulates in transnational media networks, intervening into national discourses and in that process changing gender configurations. The contemporary global presence of the figure of the girl speaks to an important shift away from the singularity of the male as a paradigmatic figure to negotiate socio-historical shifts, such as transnational migration, the collapse of the Eastern Bloc, and the new global world order.[2]

The increased digital and electronic communication that has accompanied globalization produces an intermedial exchange. Films and books about self-confident and independent girls from around the world circulate in transnational networks that cut across different media: girls produce and are produced by zines and blogs, music and videos, literature and film. Books collect blogs by girls, such as Riverbend's *Baghdad Burning: Girl Blog from Iraq* (2005) or are written as e-mail exchanges, such as Rajaa Asanea's *Girls of Riyadh* (2008), both part of the phenomenon of recent global blockbusters that center on the figure of the girl.[3] Thus, my discussion of *Scherbenpark* offers a close reading of the novel in the context of national and global literature and film that bespeak the recent phenomenon of the "global ghetto girl."

The protagonist, Sascha, signals a reconfiguration of national literature both in terms of gender, youth, and an ethnic understanding of "Germanness." It is particularly the works produced in what Leslie

Adelson has termed "the literature of migration" that show a "preponderance of interventions into and beyond national archives of twentieth-century German culture."[4] National literature signals high culture, whereas global cultural production names popular entertainment for consumption. *Scherbenpark* follows conventions of the ghetto discourse, echoes chick lit, and dialogues with transnational migration narratives. Yet, despite its proximity to popular genres and media, it differs substantially from the highly gendered genre conventions that dominate the current entertainment market, such as chick lit, chick flicks, or the male-dominated ghetto film. The book's ironic and irreverent style captures the attempts of the first-person-narrator Sascha to ward off trauma instead of working through it, and to access codes of masculinity to cover over her vulnerability.[5] The novel advances a disillusioned, postfeminist, minoritarian suspicion of institutions and their apparent alternative, the ethnic minority group that constitutes itself in a defensive relationship to the host country, often reproducing particularly traditional and patriarchal structures. *Scherbenpark*'s textual construction of its main character Sascha Naimann and her brash narrative of a violent and traumatic life in the Russian immigrant ghetto functions in a set of interrelated contexts that account for the local articulation of global changes in representation of gender and genre, produced, I argue by shifts in intersecting transnational and national cultural markets.

The Global Girl

The subject of the girl emerged in global film and literature during the 1990s, and continued to be commodified and circulated in the first decade of the twenty-first century. Cinematic examples include Niki Caro's *Whale Rider* (2002) from New Zealand, Maria Meggenti's *The Incredibly True Adventure of Two Girls in Love* (1995), and Jason Reitman's *Juno* (2007) from the United States.[6] This trend's Western European equivalents from France and the United Kingdom focus on second-generation immigrant girls portraying young North Africans in France, as in Faïza Guène's *Kiffe Kiffe Tomorrow* (2004), and South Asians in Britain as in Gurinder Chadha's *Bend It Like Beckham* (2002).[7]

These contemporary literary and cinematic productions have their roots in anarchic forms of rebellious girl culture. Rebecca Munford sees "girl culture" as an "eclectic and politically grounded phenomenon," "far more" so than the dominant media acknowledges.[8] Ednie Kaeh Garrison defines "girl power" as a "young feminist (sub)cultural movement that combines feminist consciousness and punk aesthetics, politics and style."[9] This post-second-wave-feminism girl culture articulates itself across the different media of zines, music, magazines, film, web-based projects, blogs, home videos, and literature. This contemporary "global girl" echoes its predecessor, "the modern girl," a global phenomenon that emerged during the 1920s and 1930s in cities around the world.[10] The Modern Girl Around the World Research Group argues that "the Modern Girl was distinguished from other female figures and representations by her continual incorporation of local elements with those drawn from elsewhere," which they entitle "multidirectional citation."[11] The particular interface between popular forms of culture and serious social concerns connects the global modern girl to its new incarnation.

Scherbenpark captures the global girl's existence in a postfeminist world, in which young women are sexually liberated but the political issues of second-wave feminism, such as domestic violence and the division of labor, have neither been eradicated nor resolved. Angela McRobbie proposes that "postfeminism actively draws on and invokes feminism as that which can be taken into account in order to suggest that equality is achieved."[12] Sascha, for example, incorporates the qualities that define post-second-wave-feminism girls as an independent, out-spoken, and pro-sex young woman. Typical for a postfeminist world, female collectivity does not offer Sascha solidarity in her confrontations with German cultural institutions, nor guide her through the painful process of maturation, nor assist her healing from her personal and familial trauma. For Sascha, these are solitary processes.[13] At the same time, the novel accords domestic violence, the mobilizing topic of the second women's movement, a central place in the novel's narrative at the root of Sascha's trauma.

Scherbenpark portrays the generation of the daughter instead of the mother. By portraying continuing domestic violence against women, the novel also points to the limits of the success of feminism and the uneven access women have to its promised achievements. At the core of Sascha's trauma lies Vadim's murder of her mother and the violence against his children. Sascha contrasts with the seemingly successful Susanne Mahler, who works at the newspaper and cares less for the female victim than for advancing her career with a story about the perpetrator. For Sascha, neither a political ideology of feminist liberation nor of social integration can provide an avenue out of her psychological, material, and social entrapment.

The Global Ghetto

The ghetto is *en vogue* — all around the world. *Scherbenpark*'s "ghetto" as an imaginary spatial construction is both locally specific — reflecting Russian immigration to Germany after 1989 — and circulating globally as a commodified global signifier for marginality that simultaneously exceeds its local and specific meaning. The imaginary site of the ghetto reflects the complex spatial interplay between local specificity and global address, and between deterritorialization and reterritorialization. Ghettos as spatialized constructions appear increasingly with a double function, invoking specific locales but circulating globally precisely because they are excluded from the imaginary space of the nation. Neill Blomkamp's South African film *District 9* (2009), a science fiction film about the discrimination against aliens that takes place in a ghetto reminiscent of the townships outside of Johannesburg, South Africa, is a case in point.[14]

Cinematic and literary depictions of the urban ghetto as a result of migration center on the authentic social experience of communal destitution, in instances to be overcome by a singular hero. In the 1990s, African-American cinematic depictions of the postindustrial, criminal urban ghetto produced what critic Jacquie Jones labeled "the new ghetto aesthetic," which took place in the "contemporary urban ghetto."[15] Those films denied substantial roles for female characters.[16] Jones argues that films such as Mario Van Peebles's *New Jack City* (1991) and John Singleton's *Boyz n the Hood* (1991) responded to a "marketability" of accounts of criminal young black men.[17] Ghetto literature and film have undergone a process of commodification similar to the successful popular novels about girls in global circulation, exemplified by Fernando Merielles's Brazilian film *City of God* (2002) and Pierre Morel's French *Banlieue 13* (2004).[18] Recent ghetto films indicate the increasing commodification of the ghetto-film genre, in which the space of the ghetto is reduced to a backdrop for genre cinema: action in *Banlieue 13* and science fiction in *District 9*. The signifier of the ghetto is dislodged from its origin and emptied out of meaning. Men inhabit and dominate the limited spatial territory of the ghetto in spectacles of masculine action, from chases through the urban landscape in *Banlieue 13* to shoot-outs in *City of God* and *District 9*. Based on the dialectic relationship between global and local, Germany films — such as Fatih Akın's *Kurz und schmerzlos* (1998; released to English-speaking audiences as *Short Sharp Shock*), Lars Becker's *Kanak Attack* (2000), and Detlev Buck's *Knallhart* (2006) — rewrite the ghetto film conventions in the context of Turkish migration to Germany.[19]

The few films that emphasize young women in the ghetto illustrate the attempts to appropriate the genre for women, while undoing its strong reliance on fetishized masculinity. Ghetto films centered on girls symptomatically reproduce ghetto films' thorough inscription of the associations of femininity with domesticity and masculinity with violence. For example, in successful films centered on girls in Latino barrios — for example, Allison Andres's *Mi Vida Loca* (1993) and Patricia Cardoso's *Real Women Have Curves* (2002) — the choices for young women vacillate between sexuality linked to pregnancy, portrayed in the former, or labor and higher education, celebrated in the latter.[20] In Germany, Bettina Blümner's *Prinzessinnenbad* (Pool of princesses, 2008) reflects this trend of girl-centered ghetto narratives by following the life of three teenage girls in Berlin's Kreuzberg, the neighborhood most emblematic of migratory populations in Germany.[21] *Prinzessinnenbad* emphasizes the authentic look at the ghettoized ethnic neighborhood through the convention of the long-term documentary. This genre straddles the ethnographic gaze inscribed by those with access to the means of cultural production and its attempt to lend a voice to its subjects whose life stories the film portrays.

Coming-of-Age in the Imagined Community

Scherbenpark's force derives from the global presence of the girl, a figure endowed with dynamic rebellion against tradition and convention, particularly as they are expressed as prohibitions for young women. In the complex interconnection between global and local, and national and transnational, the dynamics of globalization enable a rewriting of the relationship of gender and nation in the context of German literature. Globally, minority literature has intervened in the form of coming-of-age-narratives portraying a process of maturation in tandem with questions of assimilation, especially in relationship to young women. The identity-formation of developing subjectivity functions as an allegory for emergent ethnic writing, when an imaginary coming of age metaphorizes writing oneself into nationhood.[22]

Coming-of-age-novels often include sexual awakening, and *Scherbenpark* depicts a protagonist undergoing a maturation process, something that in German national literature has traditionally centered on paradigmatic male characters that embody the nation. Traditionally, the model protagonist for a coming-of-age novel or *Bildungsroman* is male, from Wilhelm Meister and Anton Reiser to Demian, Hans Castorp, and Felix Krull, reflecting the historical difference in access to education, travel, inheritance, and the public sphere between men and women. However, as Birte Giesler points out in her discussion of the relationship of gender and the *Bildungsroman*, scholarship throughout the twentieth century has contested the literary history's account of the genre's paradigmatic male characteristic.[23] The global presence of girls productively intervenes into national discourses about gendered genre conventions.

Benedict Anderson, in his foundational *Imagined Communities: Reflections on the Origin and Spread of Nationalism*, emphasizes the "central importance of print-capitalism" for the imagined community of the nation.[24] He focuses on the genre of the novel centered on the figure of the "solitary hero," the focal point of the "national imagination."[25] Anderson does not reflect critically on his description of the male-gendered hero as the projection site for the imagined community of the nation. The maleness of the characters that Anderson invokes to buttress his argument about the centrality of the novel for the project of the imagined community is not coincidental but integral to the ability of those figures to model national consciousness in print culture. In one of Anderson's examples, the novel's hero is "a young man who belongs to the collective body of readers" and thus can embody the particular nation's "imagined community."[26] Anderson suggests that "the imagined community is confirmed by the doubleness of our reading about our young man reading," in this case, the newspapers.[27] This literary configuration creates "calendrical coincidence . . . which provides the essential connection — the steady onward clocking of homogeneous, empty time," a feature Anderson interprets as essential to imagining the nation.[28]

In *Scherbenpark*, newspapers, journalists, and print news also feature centrally, intersecting with Sascha's life and motivating important plot lines. But here, the newspaper does not validate or mirror the main character; in contrast, Sascha repeatedly experiences news as traumatic, officially inscribing her subaltern status as a young immigrant woman in Germany. To highlight this difference, it is worth noting that Sascha does not read the newspaper to remain informed about national news. Instead, the news interferes with her life, doubling the original attack and emphasizing her disenfranchised position in the public sphere, which turns the killing of her mother into an object of an exploitative gaze.

When Sascha, the young, female, solitary heroine who embodies a differently imagined community of Germany, is revictimized by national news, she confronts the source of her psychic injury by searching out the author of the article, Susanne Mahler. In contrast to Anderson's ideal model of the newspaper as neutral source for information and of the reader as uncontested identification figure, the encounter between Sascha and Susanne illustrates the contestation and negotiation that produces and reflects narratives that shape imagined communities. Susanne combines the privileged access of the German-born intellectual with female subordination as Volker's intern.[29]

In *Scherbenpark*, media functions in a complicated web around Sascha. Her mother worked for a small newspaper with ads, where she met her German boyfriend:

> And she [Sascha's mother] did start living, and she bumped into Harry. She met him in the offices of the little local paper in which her column on Russian-Germans appeared . . .
> My mother was very proud of that job. (33)

The "little local paper" at which Sascha's mother worked and published her bilingual column provided her with a forum to express her creativity and gave her limited access to the public sphere. *Scherbenpark* covers a range of media in a complex field, more decentralized and differentiated than Anderson maps it out. As diverse members of the imagined community, the differently situated characters have unequal access to the public sphere.

Talking Back: Local Girl, Global Music

Scherbenpark consciously engages with a global ghetto discourse by recirculating the ghetto aesthetic of recycling and participating in the African-American tradition of "call and response." Sascha talks back to famous U. S. hip-hop artist Eminem, outdoing his song with her own hyperbolic promise of violence, mimicking the convention of battling rap. Sascha confronts the globally commodified text from the perspective of a girl in Germany claiming the tradition because of her own liminal status as an outsider. The icon of the hard rapper, an appropriation of an African-American art form, embodies the global circulation of ghetto culture. Eminem's song "I'm sorry, Mama," presents a sarcastic apology to his mother, which Bronsky contrasts to Sascha's aggressive promise of revenge on Vadim. The text contrasts the gender configuration of the son's address of his mother with the stepdaughter's fantasmatic confrontation with her stepfather in a bilingual exchange:[30]

> *I'm sorry, Mama*, says Eminem.
> You'll be sorry, Vadim, says Sascha.
> *I never meant to hurt you.*
> I'm really going to hurt you.
> *I never meant to make you cry.*
> I promise I will make you cry.
> *But tonight I'm cleaning out my closet.*
> What are you cleaning out, Marshall? Your cabinet?
> I'm cleaning mine out, too — my cabinet of poisons. (157–58)

The address of the abusive stepparent enters into a competitive dialogue of globally circulating ghetto culture and its localized response, in which the genders are crisscrossed. Bronsky appropriates the masculinist discourse with the voice and the body of a girl and self-reflexively points to the performative aspect of ghetto discourse, despite its proclaimed authenticity. Here the character Sascha, whose name performs masculinity, "calls out" Eminem by his bourgeois first name Marshall, undermining his claim to authentic ghetto-credibility. The text performs a double function, simultaneously participating in the tradition of battle rap, in which two hip-hop artists outdo each other with hyperbolic and sometimes insulting word play and verbal prowess, and at the same time undoing the assumed claim to authenticity associated with ghetto aesthetics. Improvisation is integral to battle rap, which is also called "freestyle," of which Eminem's *8 Mile* is an example. Bronsky's literary depiction of Sascha's freestyling captures this tradition but also constitutes a gap to the visceral and affective immediate presence of rap, even though the text continues the cadence of rap, retaining its rhythm to reflect its roots in spoken word, returning the commodified and circulating text to its originary dialogic exchange.

While Bronsky stages the imaginary verbal competition between Eminem and Sascha, which defines rap culture, the address of Sascha's threat is Vadim. The reference to a "poison cabinet" appropriates the posture of violent revenge with the poetic invocation of feminine means. The intertexual references resignify the trope of violent revenge in a text about a young girl dealing with death as a result of interpersonal violence, a staple of ghetto narratives. Ghetto films such as *Boyz n the Hood* portray retributory violence in an excessive visual display. *Scherbenpark* inserts a female and local voice into the global discourse, emphasizing the fantasy of violent retribution as a vehicle of psychological survival that is neither meant to be acted out nor to be political program.

Music is one of the intermedial references that function in Sascha's world but also situate the novel in a global network of cultural exchange. While Eminem's rap partakes in global commodified ghetto culture, a reference to the Russian postpunk band Nautilus Pompilius functions in a binational framework as melancholic attachment to the lost homeland via the loss of the mother.[31] Through these different cultural musical inscriptions, which make use of the songs' original texts, the novel aligns the mother with the melancholy for the past and the lost homeland, refracted through the access to music that is mobile in global networks.

Sascha's encounter with the music of the band Nautilus Pompilius is staged in conjunction with her repeated psychological injuries.[32] One day Sascha picks up her younger sister Alissa from her friend Katja, Peter's little sister. Peter opens the door, and Sascha and Peter engage in their usual aggressive exchange before Peter reveals that his mother will not allow Katja to visit Alissa in their apartment because it was the site of the murder. He distances himself from his mother's position, which opens a window into the possibility of him as a sympathetic character, once situated in the domestic setting. However, his remarks deeply hurt Sascha, who violently mourns the loss of her mother and ruthlessly defends her younger siblings. Just as Sascha registers the different psychic injuries, she hears the band's song "I Want to Be With You" coming out of Peter's apartment:

> I know the song.
> *The drunken doctor*
> *Told you*
> *That you*
> *No longer exist.*

The fire department says
Your house
Has burned down.
. . .
The song hits me like a punch in the gut.
There's no way Peter really listens to the music of this long-forgotten
Russian goth band. My mother liked them . . .
How is it possible, I wonder, that here — in an apartment that reeks
of coal, that's scrubbed spic and span, a place where every piece of
furniture is draped with a doily, where there are plastic flowers in vases
on the windowsills, where the walls are covered with the type of hor-
rible pictures of pink children that you can get three-for-ten-bucks at
the supermarket — that here of all places, this music is played?
In a strange room
With a white ceiling
A right to hope
And a belief
In love.
I stare at the checkered curtains.
We never had curtains. My mother hated them . . . She always wanted
to have the windows open. The sun should come in. (143–44)

Scherbenpark's account of Sascha's interior narrative seamlessly shifts
between her observations and the song, creating a fluid relationship
between her own subjectivity and the enigmatic text, which turns catastrophe into poetry. The second stanza announces the more hopeful topics of
love and hope. The song's positive note, emerging out of the catastrophe
portrayed in the song and the strange places that it evokes, links to Sascha's
mother, who is also tied to space and sun, foreshadowing Sascha's later
departure. It is incomprehensible to her that Peter has the same taste in
songs as her mother because it questions the world as she has configured
it in order to cope with the death of her mother. Her mother's indiscrim-
inate love for different forms of music — which included a sentimental
attachment to the new wave, postpunk band Nautilus Pompilius from their
homeland — becomes tainted if the enemy Peter listens to it.

The Active Female Body and the Masculine Pose

Sascha's irony functions to ward off her psychological injury, capturing the
complex positions that young women have to negotiate in defining their
roles in a web of desires and social expectations of femininity that implies
vulnerability. But the irreverent tone, intended to cover over Sascha's
vulnerability, paradoxically reveals her pain. For example, when Sascha sees
the newspaper's headline about Vadim, she describes her reaction as
follows:

> On this morning, my heart suddenly freezes — just for a second —
> then it kicks on again and jumps into my throat and flutters there like
> a bird in distress. I gasp for breath and try to swallow in order to get
> my heart back down where it belongs. (49)

The novel performs a warding off of emotions that distances the voice
of the narrator from the traditional femininity integral to chick lit, but
also points to the gap between the narrator's femaleness and access to
formations of masculinity. Sascha Naimann has a name like a man but is
a girl: "My name is Sascha Naimann. I'm not a guy, even though
everyone in this country seems to think so when they hear my name"
(13).

While Germans cannot read her gender correctly because of a linguistic mistranslation, *Scherbenpark* also deconstructs masculinity by
ironically reflecting on the self-stylization of the "cool pose" of ghetto
masculinity.[33] Sascha describes Peter: "The Marlon Brando of Our
Russian Ghetto. Long black eyelashes that give his face a feminine note.
Which is probably why he lifts weights so obsessively" (140).[34] By pointing to the cinematic and historic construction of the young, male rebel
in global circulation, such as James Dean and Marlon Brando, the text
deconstructs the notion of authentic masculinity, which appears as medi-
alized poses. In contrast to Sascha's ironic gaze at Peter, the text does not
offer a description of Sascha's body, substituting instead dynamic movement, when she runs or skates.

Related to ghetto discourse's emphasis on the body, Sascha copes
with trauma through physical action and verbal jousting. Reflection and
memory, associated with working through a traumatic past, appear as
privileges she cannot afford in her fierce dedication to her survival.
Traditional ghetto narratives center on the male body as the vehicle of
self-assertion in the absence of access to institutional or material
resources,[35] which finds expression in the oral tradition of hip-hop and
the recycling in contemporary rap. *Scherbenpark*'s fashioning of the
female body as a vehicle of aggressive acting out in relation to a traumatic
past differs strongly from the German memory discourse that privileges
working through as an internalized process. Sascha does not take pleasure in physical activities, but engages in them to flee what haunts her, an
attempt that the text ironizes:

> I run three times around the Emerald and then head off. I'm drag-
> ging. I haven't run in a long time and wouldn't have today if I hadn't
> woken up with a sick, tense feeling. I try to run away from this feeling
> but just end up with stitches in my sides. (48)

But the physical activity throws her back onto her body and its banal
physical existence when all she can achieve is a mild form of exhaustion
because she is out of shape.

The emphasis on the active body when Sascha runs, roller-skates, and bikes, extends to her ability to fight verbally and with her fists. Her relationship with Vadim is a "battlefield" (47) in which she is victorious. At the heart of *Scherbenpark*, like in other ghetto texts, lies violence, both individual and structural. This includes, in addition to rough language, fighting. Sascha has to fight for herself because patriarchal protection can neither be found in the violent immigrant, nor in the emasculated but privileged liberal German. The depiction of the male characters approximates stereotypes of violent, drunk immigrants from the East in contrast to emasculated liberals in the West. The reproduction of outdated discriminatory representation of masculinity to carve out a space for a popular account of liberated minority femaleness is reminiscent of the scandal that surrounded the ground-breaking, now feminist classic, Alice Walker's *The Color Purple* (1982), a book that was accused of reifying the myth of the black rapist in order to stage the development of a black feminist subjectivity.[36]

The novel portrays Sascha's necessity to fight physically for survival but also the limitations of her ability to do so. When Sascha is running through her neighborhood, she encounters Peter and his group of friends who are mad because Sascha is not afraid of them:

> "Girls like you need to be smacked around," he says, breathing heavily. "And ones like your mother. It's fucked up that you're not scared of anything. I think we need to change that." . . .
> I ram my elbows into his ribs, rip myself free, jump to the side, and bend down. I had already seen it gleaming — an empty brown beer bottle. I grab it and brandish it above my head . . .
> He puts out his arms. I slash at his face with the bottle.
> But I've misjudged it.
> The bottle doesn't break. It's still whole. And it flies out of my hand, slipping between my sweaty fingers. I've barely hurt Peter at all. He just grunts, puts his hand up to his face, and then lunges at me. I'm thrown back by the weight of his body and my head hits the wall.
> That's when I begin to scream. At first I don't know myself what I am screaming. It's a word. A name.
> I am screaming for Volker. (151–52)

For girls, the possibility of appropriating signs of masculinity is ultimately limited. Yes, access to femininity does not guarantee survival through protection, neither as a realistic strategy, nor as a fantasy offered to girls. Sascha screams for Volker but he is not there to rescue her. The contemporary possibility of appropriating attributes formerly deemed to be masculine defines contemporary global girl culture as a result of second-wave feminism, and differentiates it from chic lit. Important texts such as Niki Caro's *Whale Rider* (2002), Gurinder Chadha's *Bend It Like Beckham*, and Lucia Puenzo's *XXY* (2007) negotiate girls' attempts to access and integrate notions of masculinity.[37]

In contrast to chick lit, Sascha negotiates her femaleness not in the framework of sex or heterosexual gender, but in relationship to the memory of her mother. She is unable to embrace heterosexual femininity because her mother and Maria represent victimization — the former of violence, and the latter of domesticity. But she cannot identify with masculinity, either. While Vadim embodied destructive violence, she slowly comprehends that Volker inhabits an unreflected heterosexual male privilege when she realizes that Volker also knew her mother and had an affair with Susanne Mahler.

Closure and Departure

The space of the ghetto includes spatial restriction, and thus Sascha's maturation coincides with her departure from their apartment, the scene of violence. After she has returned from the hospital, Volker, Felix, Maria, Anton, Alyssa, and Sascha sit around in their living room and have a good time, and their happiness enables Sascha to leave. The novel's concluding two paragraphs are peaceful but refuse a traditional happy ending. In the novel's penultimate section, Sascha first addresses her dead mother without naming her: "Hello, you, and you, too, Harry, I say" (218), but lists her name Marina a little later for the first time in the novel (220). Sascha apologizes for not having taken the photo of her mother into the hospital with her and that she has not thought about her in the hospital, except once when she was happy that her mother did not have to watch her. The novel's depiction of warding off trauma not only refers to the violence that centrally shapes the narrative events, but also Sascha's mourning the loss of her mother. *Scherbenpark* does not end in a stereotypical romantic happy ending but in Sascha's coming to terms with the loss of her mother, which allows her to mature.

Thinking about her mother's journeys as a young person, Sascha decides to travel to Prague.[38] She leaves Volker and his son behind with Maria and her siblings: "There's nothing left for me to do here. I feel as if they will all be all right now even without me" (219). Once Volker and Felix are in her apartment, she does not have to carry the responsibility for her siblings anymore. Volker and Felix fulfill their important function not as romantic interests for her but as substitute caretakers for her family, reversing gender stereotypes. Once they are present, she can leave:

> It would be an exaggeration to say I'm in a good mood. But something is singing inside me — and the words aren't Eminem's.
> In the foyer I stumble over my rollerblades — and then over Anton's. I can't imagine ever putting those things on again. I put on my sneakers and listen to the voices wafting in from the living room as I tie the laces.

. . .

I throw my backpack over my shoulder, turn my baseball cap backwards, and head out into the sun. (221)

The positive open end continues Sascha's process of moving, not haunted by the past and looking forward into the future. She travels east, following in the footsteps of her mother. This departure is enabled by Volker and Felix's visit to the space of the ghetto, instead of a forced assimilation by Sascha into Germany.

The departure of the hero at the end of ghetto narratives constitutes a staple genre convention. But in contrast to the heroes of *City of God* and *Boyz n the Hood*, who are the sole survivors of the ills of the Brazilian favela and American inner-city, and who disavow their affective relationship to the social networks left behind, Sascha's departure is enabled by her coming to terms with her care for her family. *Scherbenpark* participates in the global circulation of literature about girls and narrative conventions of ghetto aesthetics. However, while the text relies on formulaic conventions, which enable the genre's popular success, it also moves beyond a simplistic reproduction of genre traditions. The simultaneous appropriation and rewriting of popular textual conventions enables the text to straddle the global with the local and intervene in transnational and national discourses about gender and immigration. *Scherbenpark* endows the literary figure of the global ghetto girl with a forceful subjectivity that appropriates popular textual conventions to open up traditional depictions of gender, and thus subtly change the literary depiction of historical change at the points where the local and the global meet.

Notes

[1] Alina Bronsky, *Scherbenpark* (Cologne: Kiepenheuer & Witsch, 2008); quotations are taken from the English translation, Alina Bronsky, *Broken Glass Park*, trans. Tim Mohr (New York: Europa Editions, 2010). According to the German publisher's webpage, the translation rights have also been sold to Italy and Poland: www.kiwi-verlag.de/476-0-current-news-on-our-titles.htm (accessed 1 August 2010). While this reflects the global appeal of the novel, there is also a particularly local national appeal, expressed in the many school invitations and the stage version at the Junges Deutsches Theater at the Deutsches Theater, Berlin, in the fall of 2010. Here, the authenticity of Russian migration is reintroduced when German youth of Russian background act with professional actors on stage. See www.deutschestheater.de/junges_dt/mitmachen/scherbenpark/ (accessed 1 August 2010).

[2] See, for example, Anke S. Biendarra's essay "Terézia Mora, *Alle Tage*: Transnational Traumas" in this volume, which discusses a novel that could also be

read as part of an "Eastern turn," and that is organized around a male character named Abel.

³ Rajaa Alsanea, *Girls of Riyadih: A Novel* (London: Penguin, 2008); Riverbend, *Baghdad Burning: Girl Blog from Iraq* (New York: The Feminist Press, 2005).

⁴ Leslie Adelson, *The Turkish Turn in Contemporary German Literature: Toward a New Critical Grammar of Migration* (New York: Palgrave, 2005), 5 and 12.

⁵ For an extensive discussion of an example of a ghetto narrative that foregrounds masculinity, see Frauke Matthes's contribution to this volume, "Clemens Meyer, *Als wir träumten*: Fighting 'Like a Man' in Leipzig's East."

⁶ Niki Caro, dir., *Whale Rider* (2002); Maria Meggenti, dir., *The Incredibly True Adventure of Two Girls in Love* (1995); Jason Reitman, dir., *Juno* (2007).

⁷ Faïza Guène, *Kiffe Kiffe Tomorrow*, trans. Sarah Adams (Orlando: Harvest, 2004); Gurinder Chadha, dir., *Bend It Like Beckham* (2002).

⁸ Rebecca Munford, "'Wake Up and Smell the Lipgloss': Gender, Generation and the (A)politics of Girl Power," in *Third Wave Feminism: A Critical Exploration*, ed. Stacy Gillis, Gillian Howie, and Rebecca Munford (New York: Palgrave, 2004), 142–53; here, 143.

⁹ Ednie Kaeh Garrison, "U. S. Feminism — Grrrl Style! Youth (Sub)Cultures and the Technologics of the Third Wave," *Feminist Studies* 26, no. 1 (2000): 141–70; here, 142.

¹⁰ In German literary history, this is particularly associated with Weimar Republic author Irmgard Keun, whose books include *Kind aller Länder* (1938), *Nach Mitternacht* (1937), *Das Mädchen, mit dem die Kinder nicht verkehren durften* (1936), *Das kunstseidene Mädchen* (1932), and *Gilgi — Eine von uns* (1931).

¹¹ The Modern Girl Around the World Research Group (Alys Eve Weinbaum, Lynn M. Thomas, Priti Ramamurthy, Uta G. Poiger, Madeleine Yue Dong, and Tani E. Barlow), "The Modern Girl as Heuristic Device: Collaboration, Connective Comparison, Multidirectional Citation," in *The Modern Girl Around the World: Consumption, Modernity, and Globalization*, ed. The Modern Girl Around the World Research Group (Durham: Duke UP, 2008), 1–24; here, 4.

¹² Angela McRobbie, "Notes on Postfeminism and Popular Culture: Bridget Jones and the New Gender Regime," in *All About the Girl: Culture, Power, and Identity*, ed. by Anita Harris (New York: Routledge, 2004), 3–14; here, 4.

¹³ Sascha's solitary existence contrasts to the male bond described by Matthes in Meyer's *Als wir träumten*.

¹⁴ Neill Blomkamp, dir., *District 9* (2009).

¹⁵ Jacquie Jones, "The New Ghetto Aesthetic," *Wide Angle* 13:3–4 (1991): 32–43; here, 32.

¹⁶ The domination of visual culture in the global circulation of this genre has its effect also on the style of writing, analyzed as cinematic by Matthes in her discussion of Meyer's *Als wir träumten*.

¹⁷ Mario Van Peebles, dir., *New Jack City* (1991); John Singleton, dir., *Boyz n the Hood* (1991).

[18] Fernando Merielles, dir., *City of God* (2002); Pierre Morel, dir., *Banlieue 13* (2004).

[19] Fatih Akın, dir., *Short Sharp Shock* (1998); Lars Becker, dir., *Kanak Attack* (2000); Detlev Buck, dir., *Knallhart* (2006). See also Barbara Mennel, "Bruce Lee in Kreuzberg and Scarface in Altona: Transnational Auteurism and Ghettocentrism in Thomas Arslan's *Brothers and Sisters* and Fatih Akın's *Short Sharp Shock*," *New German Critique* 87 (2002): 133–56.

[20] Allison Andres, dir., *Mi Vida Loca* (1993); Patricia Cardoso, dir., *Real Women Have Curves* (2002).

[21] Bettina Blümner, dir., *Prinzessinnenbad* (2008). See also Jaimey Fisher, "Kreuzberg as Relational Place: Respatializing the 'Ghetto' in Bettina Blümner's *Prinzessinnenbad* [Pool of princesses, 2007]," in *Spatial Turns: Space, Place, and Mobility in German Literary and Visual Culture*, ed. Jaimey Fisher and Barbara Mennel (Amsterdam: Rodopi, 2010), 421–46.

[22] This section is influenced by a discussion with Kenneth Kidd, specialist of children's and young adult literature. Important feminist texts about Latina girls growing up in the United States include Julia Alvarez, *How the Garcia Girls Lost Their Accents* (New York: Plume, 1991); Sandra Cisneros, *The House on Mango Street* (New York: Vintage Books, 1989); Esmeralda Santiago, *When I Was Puerto Rican* (Cambridge: Da Capo Press, 1993). Taking a different theoretical approach, the comparison between Turkish-German and Chicana literature as bilingual and bicultural is central to Azade Seyhan, *Writing Outside the Nation* (Princeton: Princeton U P, 2001).

[23] Birte Giesler, "Julchen Grünthal — ein Bildungsroman," particularly the section entitled "Bildungsroman und Geschlecht," in *Literatursprünge: Das erzählerische Werk von Friederike Helene Unger* (Göttingen: Wallstein, 2003), 210–29. I thank Birte Giesler on her feedback on an earlier and shorter version of this paper as a talk.

[24] Benedict Anderson, *Imagined Communities: Reflections on the Origin and Spread of Nationalism* (London: Verso, 1983), 18.

[25] Anderson, *Imagined Communities*, 30.

[26] Anderson, *Imagined Communities*, 30.

[27] Anderson, *Imagined Communities*, 30.

[28] Anderson, *Imagined Communities*, 31.

[29] Interestingly, according to Suzanne Ferriss and Mallory Young, the main characters of chick lit are often single women in their twenties and thirties balancing demanding careers and personal relationships and who are often employed in the media industry and publishing. Thus, one could read Susanne Mahler as a typical character for chick lit, and Sascha as constructed in contrast to her. Suzanne Ferriss and Mallory Young, "Introduction," in *Chick Lit: The New Woman's Fiction*, ed. Suzanne Ferriss and Mallory Young (New York: Routledge, 2006), 1–13; here, 3.

[30] In the German original, Eminem's song text is in English and italicized, while Sascha's response in German and the narrative voice is non-italicized. The English

translation retains the italics but cannot retain the bilingual quality of the original German:

> *I'm sorry, Mama*, sagt Eminem.
> Dir wird es leid tun, Vadim, sagt Sascha.
> *I never meant to hurt you.*
> Und wie ich dir wehtun will.
> *I never meant to make you cry.*
> Doch, du wirst heulen, versprochen.
> *But tonight I'm cleanin' out my closet.*
> Was machst du da sauber, Marshall? Deinen Schrank?
> Und ich sortiere meinen — den Giftschrank.
> Bronsky, *Scherbenpark*, 201.

[31] I thank Ingrid Kleespies for sharing her insight on Nautilus Pompilius. The song, one of the most famous ones by the band, is originally in Russian, and its text appears in *Scherbenpark* in German and in *Broken Glass Park* in English. Reading the loss of the Russian mother would be another entry into a reading along the lines of a binational emphasis in the context of the "Eastern turn" of German literature, as outlined by Biendarra in the opening of her essay in this volume.

[32] *Scherbenpark* does not include either of the titles of the two songs in its text.

[33] See Richard Majors and Janet Mancini Billson, *Cool Pose: The Dilemmas of Black Manhood in America* (New York: Touchstone, 1993).

[34] This presents an intriguing parallel to Matthes's reading of the main characters of *Als wir träumten* as affirming their masculinity to ward off social emasculation, which could otherwise be read as feminization. Sascha's inner voice repeatedly uncovers those kinds of psycho-social mechanism.

[35] See also Matthes's article in this volume.

[36] Alice Walker, *The Color Purple* (Orlando: Harvest, 2003).

[37] Lucia Puenzo, dir., *XXY* (2007). These three films offer different narrative trajectories about the motivations for girls to desire masculinity and the ways in which their access to masculinity enables or disables self-actualization. A comparative discussion goes beyond the scope of this article. What is important to me here is to point out that contemporary texts represent the investment in the possibility that masculinity is available to girls at all.

[38] Her desire to travel to Prague because she wants "to go someplace" where she does not "understand everything around" her "for a change" (220) also creates a parallel to Abel's loss of all languages except to say "that's good" in "the local language" in Mora's *Alle Tage*. See Biendarra's article in this volume.

12: Karen Duve, *Taxi*: Of Alpha Males, Apes, Altenberg, and Driving in the City

Heike Bartel

TAXI (2008), BY THE HAMBURG-BORN AUTHOR Karen Duve, tells the story of Alex, a young female taxi driver in Hamburg during the six years of her work for the taxi company Mergolan before the novel ends in a car crash. The simple plot might suggest that almost nothing happens in this text, which deals with the protagonist's various encounters with passengers inside the taxi and with (mostly) men outside the taxi and features a surprise ending. However, *Taxi* is more than a drive-through: it is an accomplished literary portrayal of the individual in a postmodern cityscape. Drawing on cultural theories analyzing how people engage with the city and its inhabitants, this essay will explore Duve's images of taxi driving as a metaphor for postmodern life.[1]

Taxi (2008) is not only the story of a female taxi driver in Hamburg, it is also a literary tour through Duve's recent work. *Taxi* features unusual characters from her previous books: the dwarf Pedsi from the fairy-tale parody *Die entführte Prinzessin: Von Drachen, Liebe und anderen Ungeheuern* (The kidnapped princess: Of dragons, love, and other monsters, 2005), who is smitten with the chambermaid Rosamonde. She, in turn, is tall and good-looking like the female protagonist in *Taxi*, and like her has to overcome inner and outer obstacles before she finally realizes her love for a smaller man. *Taxi* also features characters resembling the mean taxi drivers from the children's book *Weihnachten mit Thomas Müller* (Christmas with Thomas Müller, 2003) who brutally kick a poor lost teddy bear, who cannot pay his fare home, out of a taxi and into the freezing night; and, finally, a chimpanzee that seems to have jumped right out of Duve and Thies Völker's *Lexikon der berühmten Tiere* (Encyclopedia of famous animals, 1997) and into Alex's taxi.

These three perhaps lesser-known works already highlight the wide array of literary genres Duve engages with and draws upon in *Taxi*. It is characteristic for her writing that none of these three books stays within the traditional boundaries of fairytale, encyclopedia, or children's story, respectively, but treat their templates with irony: Pedsi laments his unrequited love for the tall Rosamonde in New Age psychoanalytical jargon; the teddy bear's taxi-driver introduces a realistic brutality to the Christmassy children's story that is underlined by his bumper-sticker "DEATH PENALTY FOR TAXI MURDERERS"; and the *Lexikon der berühmten Tiere* mocks the traditional value of an *enkuklios paideia* (all-round education) by devoting its entries to characters from so-called "low culture" generally assumed to have very little educational value, like advertising, comics, or television. Typically for Duve's writing, all three texts straddle the thin line between mirroring and critically reflecting upon aspects of both form and content of the narrative modes, a technique that also appears in *Taxi*.[2]

By comparison, Duve's earlier acclaimed and best-selling novels *Regenroman* (Rain novel, 1999; published in English as *Rain: A Novel*, 2002) and *Dies ist kein Liebeslied* (2002; *This Is Not a Love Song*, 2005) present a different approach in dealing with genres and boundaries. The representation of violence, particularly the rape of Martina, in *Regenroman*, and the depiction of the self-harming, disordered protagonist Anne Strelau in *Dies ist kein Liebeslied*, seem to oppose the playfulness and irony of Duve's take on fairytales and children's stories. Elizabeth Boa comments on the "extended metaphor intertwine[d] with precise detail of contemporary life" in *Regenroman*, and highlights its "mood and mode shift . . . between the comic and the horrific, the parodic and the straight, between realism and traces of the fantastic, of fairy tales, of myth, or of comic-book violence."[3] It is against the background of similar perspectival shifts, as well as Duve's approaches to the themes and techniques of crossing boundaries, playing with genres and clichés, and intertwining the realistic and the fantastic, that we embark on our ride in *Taxi*.

The Taxi and the City

Arguably Duve's most autobiographical novel, *Taxi* consists of episodic narration of the gritty, dull, yet strenuous life of Alex, a young female taxi driver in the mid and late 1980s. The city through which Alex drives her taxi with the number "twodoublefour" is Hamburg, and Duve's writing is clearly informed by her own experience as a Hamburg taxi driver for thirteen years. The streets and landmarks really exist, the routes are correct and can be mapped out, and the photo of Duve in her taxi-driving days on the back cover of the novel in particular seems to position the text as authentic, autobiographical, and nonfictional. However, various features punctuating the narrative suggest that taxi driving can be read as a metaphor for postmodern life. Echoing the style of Duve's previous work, *Taxi* plays with allusions to different forms of writing and introduces from the start a dynamic tension between the "real" and literary constructed that culminates in the fantastically real or real fantastic ending.

With its focus on a city, *Taxi* evokes the numerous contemporary German-speaking novels and films dealing with the city, particularly the city of Berlin.[4] In comparison with these approaches to the German capital that is loaded with architectural markers for Germany's national self-perception, the city of Hamburg seems to be freer from the "explosion of symbolism" that Frank Trommler attributes to Berlin.[5] Although Hamburg's cityscape may not have an internationally recognized emblem on the scale of Berlin's Brandenburg Gate, it has landmarks that summon up Germany's past and present socio-cultural and historical life. True to the reality of taxi driving in Hamburg, the novel evokes particularly the city's stereotypes, which include Hamburg's trade-mark, the Reeperbahn, in the infamous red-light Sankt Pauli district; the harbor; the famous zoo, Hagenbeck Tierpark; and the Springer Verlag building, home to the *BILD-Zeitung*, which confirms Hamburg's reputation as media metropolis.

Most of these places are viewed from the taxi driver's perspective: waiting outside on the thresholds without venturing inside. In its mapping of the city-space through the eyes of a taxi driver, the novel adopts a perspective that does not facilitate an engagement with the city as a whole. The city is presented as fragmented, broken into the street names and the codes for pick-up points that are given over the radio to the drivers who are addressed by their taxi numbers. Places are first and foremost addresses, distances are measured by numbers ticking away on the taxi meter, and Alex's pathways through the city are unpredictable, dictated by the choices of her passengers. This results, despite the frantic and stressful search for the best route between two places, in a considerable lack of spatial interconnectedness. As taxi driver, Alex functions literally as a vehicle to accommodate other people's destinations without having any herself.

The fragmented character of Duve's portrait of life and the city is underlined by the radio messages announcing new fares that constantly interrupt the conversations of the waiting taxi drivers. Printed in bold letters, they punctuate the text visually: **"Twodoublefour, Hütten thirty-three for Himmler."**[6] Form and content are intertwined: the monotony, repetitiveness, and the long waits are reflected aesthetically in the form that constantly repeats the same dialogues and situations, stages monotony and exhibits unfulfilled, wearisome waiting through its over 300 pages. The reader is effectively drawn into this experience of boredom and aimlessness but may also eagerly anticipate change or get annoyed with the completely aimless protagonist. Like Anne Strelau in *Dies ist kein Liebeslied*, Alex does not fit the traditional literary role of a heroine, or even anti-heroine. She appears neither likeable nor particularly unlikable; if anything, her apparent lack of ambition is slightly irritating to a reader expecting a protagonist to develop, and to acquire knowledge or insight throughout the novel. Also, like Strelau in Duve's *Anti-Bildungsroman* (anti-coming-of-age novel), Alex does not undergo an educational process but stays literally in the same position behind the wheel of her taxi throughout the novel.[7] In fact, she is getting worse rather than better at her job. Consequently, the turning point at the end is not initiated by her but happens by chance. In her disengaged and aimless motion through her life and the city, Alex appears to be the direct opposite of Lola in Tom Tykwer's film *Lola rennt* (Lola runs, 1998; released in the United States as *Run Lola Run*), who masters with a clear purpose, abundant energy, and on foot the obstacle course of people and places that is the reunified city of Berlin. While Lola may be viewed as representing the new Berlin,[8] Alex delivers a representation of modern Hamburg, albeit one that is deliberately fractured and distorted through the perspective of a taxi driver.

Theorists such as Zygmunt Baumann and Richard Sennett emphasize the role of technology, particularly the technology of motion, in the process of disengaging the individual from his or her surrounding space.[9] According to Sennett, motion has become a means to an end in itself: "we now measure urban spaces in terms of how easy it is to drive through them, to get out of them."[10] Drawing parallels between the disconnected motion through urban space and the disengaged consumption of mass media, Sennett describes the urbanite as a "traveller" who "like the television viewer, experiences the world in narcotic terms; the body moves passively, desensitized in space, to destinations set in a fragmented urban geography."[11] Alex's life as a taxi driver fits this description perfectly, particularly toward the end of the novel when, after five years of taxi driving at night, she is burnt-out, depressed, drugged by constant lack of sleep, and hallucinates passengers waving or obstacles in the road. The image of driving through the city brings together the reality of life as a taxi driver with theoretical approaches to a postmodern notion of the individual. Thus, reflecting so-called real life and critically reflecting upon it reveal themselves as two sides of the same coin.

The Taxi and Time

The portrayal of time in the novel is intrinsically connected with the lack of interconnectedness and engagement on a spatial level. The division of the book into two chapters, "1. Part 1984 — 1986" and "2. Part September 1989 — June 1990" sets a distinct time frame of six years. The three years between 1986 and September 1989 are simply covered by the first sentence of the second part: "And then five years had gone and I was still driving a taxi . . . The tours merged into one blur of lights, streets, cigarette smoke and always the same conversation" (145). The time and experiences of her taxi-driving life are melting together, unaffected by events. However, the subheadings of the novel alert the reader to a shift in perspective, and the explicit time span indicates a distinct historical backdrop. The second heading, in particular, highlights a period that is marked by international events leading to the fall of the Berlin Wall in autumn 1989 and German unification in October 1990. On the level of the first-person narrator Alex, however, these historical events are not explicitly addressed, let alone commented on or celebrated. They only register on her radar as far as they concern her taxi-driver existence: she notes when the first East German *Trabi* cars appear in the streets or a young East German man asks for a free ride because the queue was too long to receive his *Begrüßungsgeld*, the welcome money paid by West Germany to visitors from the East until the end of 1989. Further important national and international events in the 1980s are introduced in a similarly uninvolved manner. The nuclear disaster of Chernobyl on 26 April 1986 is only registered through the half-informed discussion among the taxi drivers about whether it is safe to drink milk, which mirrors public fears in the aftermath of the environmental catastrophe. From an equally disengaged viewpoint, the media event that changed the landscape of television — the introduction of commercial television in Germany in 1984 — is noted only through Alex's annoyance at the interrupting advertisements. Her lack of reaction supports Sennett's theory of "freedom from resistance," which describes the disengaged, passive, and desensitized postmodern individual regarding his or her lack of interaction with the surrounding world.[12]

What Alex does not consciously notice is, however, highlighted through a shift in narrative perspective. The two subheadings, particularly the second, mark a rare shift away from the first-person narrator Alex and her tunnel vision to allow a more distanced voice to come through. This recalls Duve's *Dies ist kein Liebeslied*, where the reader is confronted on the first pages with a similar meltdown of time in the shape of a breathtakingly fast tour through national and international, politically relevant and less important events of the 1980s:

> Meanwhile Bayern Munich football [soccer] club won the German championship eight times. All the people I knew bought watches with digital displays and swapped their flares for tight jeans or tapered pants. Iran denounced the USA as the Great Shaitan, and MTV began its programs with "Video Killed the Radio Star" by the Buggles. British soldiers marched into Afghanistan, American soldiers marched into Grenada.[13]

The speed and grotesque combination gives this accumulation of events a dry wit and irony that encourages the reader to view critically the relationship, or lack of it, between the disengaged individual and the deeply engaging political, historical, or socio-cultural matters. *Dies ist kein Liebeslied*, and to some extent *Taxi*, can be seen as citing as well as critically engaging with the trends that mark a *Neue Deutsche Popliteratur* (new German pop literature), a seemingly politically disengaged contemporary version of pop literature with a particular emphasis on the consumer culture, brand names, fashion styles, and the mass media obsession with the so-called "Generation Golf."[14] In a manner that seems to fit Moritz Baßler's evaluation of the authors of the German pop novel as the new archivists, both *Dies ist kein Liebeslied* and *Taxi* accumulate events, facts, and names taken seemingly uncritically from the immediate surroundings.[15] However, both texts also go beyond the associations of this genre; while they do not take an explicitly critical stance, neither do they display the "politische Gehaltlosigkeit" (political emptiness) rightly or wrongly attributed to *Neue Deutsche Popliteratur*.[16] Although Duve's writing is, as Peter Graves observes, by no means "fuelled by some didactic intent," "her writing convinces precisely because it does not . . . have a palpable design on us."[17]

People as Dirt

For most drivers in the modern age, cars represent sealed private spaces in which they glide through their environment; they protect their passengers from the surrounding world and especially from other human beings. Car users appear shielded by layers of centrally locked metal against any intrusion of their mobile personal space by others, while air-conditioning and stereo systems prevent any smells and sounds from intruding. Cars seem to present the solution for the modern individual, particularly in crowded cities, to deal with the physical presence of other human beings that can be experienced as threatening, according to Sennett.[18] Elizabeth Boa and Rachel Palfreyman stress the secluded nature of driving in their study *Heimat: A German Dream.* They refer to a chauffeur-driven figure in Martin Walser's novel *Seelenarbeit* (1979) as a "symbol for the postmodern condition," "listening in a mobile space bubble to sounds emanating from a virtual space filled with the ghostly traces of instruments and voices transported from some other time and somewhere else."[19] Drawing on Anthony Giddens's term "disembedding," Boa and Palfreyman highlight a "process of disconnection" emphasized by the advent of the motor car, which is characterized by "the 'lifting-out' of social relations from local contexts."[20]

Alex's experience of driving at reckless speed through the deserted city by night while listening to loud music can be viewed as a form of lifting-out. However, this only applies to tours without passengers; in her role as taxi driver, the car cannot predominantly entail the element of locking the outside world out. On the contrary, it mostly means being locked in with an ever-changing and random cross section of the city's inhabitants. In the "Kapsel" (capsule) — as Alex describes her taxi — contact with others is, in fact, condensed and intensified:

All night I sat in this small rolling capsule, the doors opened and shut, and people got in and out and brought their unfamiliar smells and their moods with them, and in the beginning I was defenseless. (30)

Alex experiences the close spatial proximity of her passengers as an intensive bodily experience, an inescapable assault on her senses. "Dreck" (dirt) is what she sees her passengers bring into the confined space of the taxi. Not just dirt from the city on their shoes and clothes but dirt that is perceived by Alex as intrinsically bodily, as coming directly from the people, crumbling from their bodies, escaping through the pores of their skin and the orifices of their bodies and exhaled with their stinking breath (29–30). Her passengers are mainly perceived through and as this "Dreck," which Alex feels covers not only the steering wheel and the inside of her car but ultimately herself also. Unlike Travis Bickle, the male protagonist in Martin Scorsese's *Taxi Driver* (1975), Alex's response to the "scum of this city" — as Bickle calls New York's inhabitants — is not a violent, gun-shooting rampage. Her reaction to Hamburg's dirt is not Bickle's (male) aggression aimed at others but a defense mechanism aimed at her (female) self: vigorous and repeated hand-washing in an attempt to flush the dirt down the sink. These descriptions of repetitive hand-washing, and an episode of vigorous body-scrubbing, sit uncomfortably close to an obsessive-compulsive disorder that is reminiscent of the behavior of the female protagonists in *Regenroman* and *Dies ist kein Liebeslied*. However, Alex's defense mechanism for dealing with enforced closeness is replaced in later episodes by a neglect of personal hygiene when she drifts into depression and stops washing herself, and thus not only succumbs to her own dirt but also to the "Dreck" of her passengers.

Alex's reaction to the close bodily proximity of her passengers and their "Dreck" can be read through Winfried Menninghaus's theoretical study as *Ekel* (disgust): "The fundamental schema of disgust is the experience of a nearness that is not wanted. An intrusive presence, a smell or taste is spontaneously assessed as contamination and forcibly distanced."[21] In Alex's case, it is the sense of smell that is assaulted most.[22] Breathing somebody else's breath, smoke, or odor as a form of forced consumption becomes particularly prominent in an episode where a female passenger with bad body odor enters the car:

She sat down on the backbench with her legs spread, slowly lifted her long black skirt and fanned the air with the hem. The stench became overwhelming. . . . The fat woman sucked greedily on her cigarette, filling her soot- and slime-encrusted lungs. Then she exhaled the smoke with relish through her big black nostrils. The smoke drifted over to me. . . . I didn't want to have inside me something that had just been inside that woman. But the smoke slipped into my mouth like a genie. (192–93)

In her study on the aesthetics of disgust, Katie Jones describes the complex interconnection of disgust, intimacy, and attraction:

> The object of disgust is perceived as contagious: we avoid contact with it in order to avoid being tainted with disgustingness, as though the real source of our disgust were the idea that the rejected object could become all too easily part of us. In this respect, disgust involves a more intimate attitude towards its elicitors than other aversive emotions, such as fear or dislike. Indeed, the fact that we sometimes choose to imagine disgusting things . . . indicates . . . an element of attraction.[23]

In Alex's encounter with her fat female passenger, the disgust reaction clearly has sexual overtones. The woman's vapors are connected with her sexuality, the smell is omitted from what is underneath her black skirt. Furthermore, the smoke coming from her nostrils that slips "like a genie" into Alex's mouth and her protestations "I didn't want to have [it] inside of me" evoke images of forced sexual intercourse. It echoes the "Get the hell out. Get out, get out!" that Alex screams during unprotected sex when, against her wishes, her lover ejaculates inside of her, exposing her to his bodily fluids and leaving her vulnerable to sexually transmitted diseases or an unwanted pregnancy (223). Alex's inability to establish relationships — or allow "Nähe" (closeness) in Menninghaus's terms — is magnified and intensified by her job that enforces spatial closeness with others. However, this inability is also mirrored in her numerous affairs with men, in which sex plays an important role yet intimacy hardly ever occurs.

The moving capsule that is Alex's taxi not only exposes her to her passengers' smells but also to their moods and emotions. During her first months as a taxi driver, Alex is, in her own words, defenseless and experiences the close encounters with the ever-changing passengers as an emotional rollercoaster ("Gefühlsachterbahn"; 30). Within very short spaces of time, she is engulfed in emotions of loss and sadness when she drives an elderly woman who has just picked up the belongings of her beloved deceased husband from a hospice, and then minutes later is exposed to the sexual assaults of two drunk male passengers, only to have to be on guard when driving a threatening brute immediately afterwards. "Inside the tiny interiors of the cab . . . drivers and passengers enact human dramas," is Graham Hodges's depiction of the emotional strain of taxi driving.[24] Duve employs metaphors from the field of driving and movement to describe this emotional overload in *Taxi*: being forced to fully step on the "emotional brakes" and having to change direction at great speed from one minute to the next (31). Alex's human emotions are equated with the taxi she is driving, reducing the individual to a reactive mechanism and exposing the inhuman conditions of her work, life, and the city.

In this state of being emotionally overwhelmed, defenseless, and completely lacking orientation, Alex falls not exactly in love but into a relationship with her taxi-driving colleague Dietrich, whom she doesn't "even like very much" (32). Unsurprisingly, this relationship fails to provide a sense of direction, let alone fulfillment. Moreover, this most private realm is restricted by the rhythm of their taxi-driver jobs. Dietrich and Alex meet and kiss for the first time during the quiet period shortly after eight and just before ten in the evening, only to be out driving again when business picks up after ten. Their jobs with the Mergolan taxi firm bind them together, they are connected through radio and have a similar daily pattern that brings them to the same places. The notion of the romantic relationship that potentially has the power to introduce fulfillment and happiness loses this potential by being consumed by the job that, in turn, emphasizes Alex's inability to achieve and sustain closeness. Her statement, "Above all it's really important to me that I don't have to be with anyone for more than ten or twenty minutes" (118), applies to her relationships with men just as much as with her passengers.

Mirroring Alex's inability to find a different job is the fact that she does not manage to get out of her unwanted relationship with Dietrich for the best part of the novel. Once she has moved into the apartment below him, she finds herself completely incapable of finding a new job, apartment, or boyfriend. She feels forced to stay with Dietrich for years simply because she lacks the energy to get out of this life and relationship, despite having sex with a neighbor and with Marco, an old classmate with dwarfism. Alex's inability to interact with people socially and emotionally, coupled with a complete lack of drive to get away from them, is a fatal combination that affects her disastrous relationships with men and reveals her job as taxi driver as the worst possible career choice for her. Closely intertwined as they are, both her job and her relationships have the effect of diminishing her, as she states: "And if I stayed together too long with someone, I would turn into what this person expected of me, and only a little shrunken mummy of what I really was remained" (34). Tellingly, she shrinks by ten kilos within the first two months of driving a taxi, thus highlighting Duve's literary engagement with issues of body weight and eating disorders as self-destructive female behavior in reaction to a hostile environment, which were extensively explored in the author's first two novels in the figures of Martina and Anne. Only Alex's friendship with Marco, the man with dwarfism, seems to offer an alternative to her unfulfilled affairs. Yet even their relations are not free from abusive behavior on both sides. In depicting this relationship that combines physical dis-

ability and various psychological hang-ups, yet fulfilled sex and intellectual compatibility, Duve both cites and breaks with numerous clichés and
assumptions at the same time. At the end of the novel, it is Marco who
provides the focal point for Alex that may well mark a turning point in
her life.

Intellectuals, Alpha Males, and an Ape

More than Duve's other work, *Taxi* engages with feminist issues in the
form of the problems and stereotypical attitudes encountered by the protagonist as a woman in her working and private life. On one level, *Taxi*
can be read as the tragic portrayal of an aimless woman who is shaped by
male expectations and fantasies. For Dietrich, a failed artist, Alex is the
muse that inspires his work and can be manipulated, modeled, and
reshaped to his liking, giving him control over her body even after they
finally separate: "He didn't really care about my character. He was probably sitting upstairs in his apartment, working on one of the pictures of
me again. Painting the boobs bigger or the bum smaller" (259). In addition to art, literature is another tool to shape the female protagonist
according to male expectations. Dietrich embarks on a mission to educate
her and brings her piles of books to read: Henry de Motherlant's
Erbarmen mit den Frauen, titles by August Strindberg, Ernst Jünger,
Friedrich Nietzsche, Otto Weininger, and Peter Altenberg, and a book of
photos by Leni Riefenstahl (54–55). However, in *Taxi*, unlike other literary works, particularly German educational novels, the process of reading
does not mark the beginning of the protagonist's self-knowledge and
understanding of the world.[25] Moreover, these misogynistic books initiate
a process that discourages and diminishes the (female) reader: "Every
book opened a door to a desirable world full of new ideas and strange
thoughts, and every book upheld the view that I and my kind were infe-
rior and repulsive. The more I read the lower I felt" (55). Here, *Taxi*
seems to engage with a socio-cultural dimension of female subordination
that uses literature as its tool: like several of the drivers, Alex aspires to
write, but a male-dominated literature and philosophy serve to hinder the
female protagonist in the fulfillment of her educational novel. A mistrust
of another type of book is found in the novel's mocking of the publisher
Suhrkamp and its highly intellectual status, to which most of the male taxi
drivers aspire as failed intellectuals and authors — "downtown Descartes
and freeway Foucaults" in the words of Risa Mickenberg.[26] Duve's witty
skepticism and sarcastic view of the educational value of these books is
echoed in her style of writing that stays clear of didactic intent or prescrip-
tive concepts, although the author writes with a clear opinion regarding
socio-cultural and political matters from feminist to environmental issues.

However, the novel also engages on a different, more subtle and aesthetically productive level with other literary texts. *Taxi* skirts Günter Grass's *Die Blechtrommel* (1959; *The Tin Drum*, 1961) with its enigmatic dwarfish Oskar Matzerath, maneuvers around various literary genres from autobiography to the fantastic, and finally crashes with an evocation of Kafka's "Ein Bericht für eine Akademie" (Report to an academy) in the ape who becomes a passenger.

The misogynist attitudes Alex experiences on an intellectual level are crudely mirrored in the brutal face of Hamburg's sex industry, which reveals itself in the pimps, prostitutes, and sex customers who form the majority of Alex's nightly passengers. The protagonist's personal experiences, cultural and philosophical aspirations, and the brutality of the sex industry all come together and accumulate in the small space of Alex's taxi, putting its female driver at the receiving end of both physical and mental abuse, sexual and verbal assaults. Here, Duve's portrayal of the city is unforgiving and exposes the "urban nightscape" as dominated by sexism, the exploitation of women, and a culture of drunken violence that is not exclusive to Hamburg in the 1980s.[27]

Throughout the novel, Alex's only attempt to make sense of and analyze this environment is to compare it with the world of apes, the only area in which she is truly an expert, constantly furthering her knowledge through reading. She recognizes the "aura of brutal dominance" that marks the behavior of an aggressive pimp — but is also displayed by "many businessmen, politicians and even newspaper editors" — and identifies him as an "alpha-male" (16). However, exposing the laws of the urban jungle as the laws of great apes does not help Alex in any way to deal with them, and a low point of the novel is reached when a brutal attack by such an alpha male coincides with the news of the violent murder of the gorilla conservationist Dian Fossey in Rwanda. Alex's fascination with apes pays off, though, in a completely unexpected twist of the story that crosses the boundaries from the realistic into the fantastic and brings a long-awaited turning point at the end of the novel.

The End

The end of the novel could be described with a term coined by J. R. R. Tolkien as a "eucatastrophe," a sudden and fantastic turn of events at the end of a story that saves the protagonist.[28] The ending of *Taxi* has elements of the fantastic although it is not so far removed from reality that it completely loses its grounding; moreover, the ending stretches the plot — so far utterly believable — to the utmost. The realistic reflection of urban life seems to turn into the distorted image in a fairground mirror when two passengers from a traveling circus, the home of fantastic illusions, distortion, parody, and exaggeration, bring a radical turn of events. After years of reading about apes, Alex's last passengers are a chimpanzee and his brutal keeper who holds the obviously mistreated animal on a tight dog leash. The world of apes that served Alex as a guide to understand and explain human behavior now enters her reality in form of this jumping, unpredictable circus-chimp dressed in a stripy jumper and pants. In a move that subverts the story of *King Kong*, the white woman Alex abducts the ape and, in an uncharacteristically decisive move apparently inspired by Dian Fossey, decides to head for Africa with the rescued chimp. Her dreams of an idyllic life of returning to nature and living in tree-nests in the jungle of Tanzania are, unsurprisingly, wrecked. The behavior of the chimp echoes Duve's parodic revelations about Tarzan's chimp-companion Cheetah in *Lexikon der berühmten Tiere*. The animal had to be replaced regularly "because chimps become ill-tempered and unpredictable after a few years."[29] Just as Duve's *Lexikon* breaks with the myth of Cheetah as Tarzan's best friend by describing how Tarzan actor Mike Henry ended up in the hospital after having been brutally smacked in the face by Cheetah actor Dinky, Alex's new companion does not behave as desired. He becomes violent, grabs the steering wheel, and causes the taxi to crash. He escapes, leaving the car a complete write-off but Alex unharmed. In a move that repeats Duve's literary style of bringing literal and metaphorical meaning together, the accident marks a radical turn of events. Nature, personified by the mistreated primate, literally takes over and catapults Alex out of her car and her machine-driven existence.[30] With her taxi license confiscated and her taxi crashed, Alex has to turn a new corner in her life. Although the written-off taxi means insurance money for her employer, which will save the run-down company, her career as a taxi driver is well and truly over.

After years of driving by night and spending the days with the curtains closed, the novel ends with a sunrise and Alex, listening to birdsong, on the way to the man she now realizes is her true love. Aesthetically, Duve employs here the trademark elements of a clichéd fairytale happy ending: the liberated female, the rising sun marking a new start, the cheerfully tweeting birds, the waiting lover, and the promise of living happily ever after. However, by evoking clichés but not completely serving them, the car-crash ending brings the conventional and the unconventional to collision point. In a twist that at the same time evokes and contrasts the stereotypical sickly sweet finale of the Disney-style fairytale, "Snow White" does not marry the tall and handsome "Prince Charming," but chooses Marco, the man with dwarfism. With this unusual and by no means trouble-free coupling of Alex and Marco — two characters who are both outsiders in a conventional order — the novel mocks the inherent cliché of its own ending. Yet at the same time it seems contrived to uphold some of the force of this cliché as Duve offers a glimpse of fulfillment in this relationship that pushes at the boundaries of stereotypical expectations and standardized perceptions.

Realistic and fantastic at the same time, Duve's ending confirms a style of writing that plays with the confines of genre and cliché, masters the tension between the seemingly real and the imaginary, and employs references that evoke possible readings but do not point to one clear signification. Finishing on the fine line that separates critique from pastiche, the novel leaves it to the reader to make up his or her own mind: whether to read the ending as a promise of an escape for the postmodern individual into a world of fulfillment, human mutuality, and wholeness, or to recognize a grotesque mirroring of this very world that nevertheless offers new perspectives.

Taxi confirms Duve's position within contemporary German literature as both accessible and innovative. Less playful than *Lexikon der berühmten Tiere* or the illustrated adventures of the teddy bear Thomas Müller, the novel assumes a much clearer position as a critical parody of clichés than *Die entführte Prinzessin*. *Taxi* upholds the expertise Duve shows in *Dies ist kein Liebeslied* by presenting a seemingly noncommitted and nondidactic pop novel featuring an aimless antiheroine, yet still delivering a critical reflection of postmodern society and its troubled individuals.[31] As in *Regenroman* and *Dies ist kein Liebeslied*, Duve places the main focus on a dysfunctional female protagonist and her futile struggle to function in a supposedly normal life. With its use of extended metaphor (explored in the theme of taxi driving through an urban cityscape) and exploring perspectival shifts (especially between protagonist and narrator) *Taxi* displays Duve's accomplished style that contributed to the success of her critically acclaimed *Regenroman*. At first glance a novel simply about taxi driving, *Taxi* reveals itself with closer reading as a text of many layers, impressive depth, and critical insight without losing the dark humor and seemingly aimless air that is the author's trademark.

Notes

¹ Elke Brüns specifies three discourses in the novel with regards to gender, primates, and the individual in relation to his or her work — "misogyne[r] Gender-Diskurs," "Primatenordnung," "Subjektformation des arbeitenden Menschen" — and the following essay will touch upon all three aspects: Elke Brüns, "Mensch und Tier in Karen Duves Roman *Taxi*," *Gegenwartsliteratur* 8 (2009): 218–37; here, 220.

² This has gained Duve criticism, and particularly with regard to *Die entführte Prinzessin*, Lyn Marven remains uncertain whether the book "masks a return to

problematic values, or is critical of these even while citing them." Lyn Marven, "Writing by Women in the Berlin Republic," in *Contemporary German Fiction. Writing in the Berlin Republic*, ed. Stuart Taberner (Cambridge: Cambridge UP, 2007), 159–76; here, 161.

[3] Elizabeth Boa, "Lust or Disgust? The Blurring of Boundaries in Karen Duve's *Regenroman*," in *Pushing at Boundaries. Approaches to Contemporary German Women Writers from Karen Duve to Jenny Erpenbeck*, ed. Heike Bartel and Elizabeth Boa (Amsterdam: Rodopi, 2006), 57–72; here, 58.

[4] For a wider overview see, for example, Katharina Gerstenberger, *Writing the New Berlin. The German Capital in Post-Wall Literature* (Camden House: Rochester/Suffolk, 2008); Matthias Harder and Almut Hille, eds., *"Weltfabrik Berlin": Eine Metropole als Sujet der Literatur* (Würzburg: Königshausen und Neumann, 2006); Susanne Ledanff, "Bildungsroman versus Großstadtroman. Thesen zum Konflikt zweier Romanstrukturen," *Sprache im technischen Zeitalter* 78 (1981): 85–114; Franziska Meyer, "'und dabei heißt es immer aufbruchstimmung': Das Verschwinden einer Metropole in ihren Texten," in *Pushing at Boundaries*, ed. Bartel and Boa, 167–84; Ulrike Zitzlsperger, *ZeitGeschichten: Die Berliner Übergangsjahre. Zur Verortung der Stadt nach der Mauer* (Bern: Lang, 2007); Godela Weiss-Sussex and Ulrike Zitzlsperger, *Berlin: Kultur und Metropole in den zwanziger und seit den neunziger Jahren* (Munich: Iudicium, 2007).

[5] Frank Trommler, "Introduction," in *Berlin: The New Capital in the East: A Transatlantic Appraisal*, ed. Frank Trommler (Washington: American Institute for Contemporary Germanic Studies, 2000), 1–5; here, 1.

[6] Karen Duve, *Taxi* (Berlin: Eichborn, 2008), 57. Subsequent page references appear in parentheses in the main body of the text. All translations are my own but I have gratefully drawn on Lyn Marven's suggestions and on the draft translation of *Taxi* by David Dollenmayer, kindly made available through the publisher, Eichborn.

[7] Frank Degler and Ute Paulokat, *Neue Deutsche Popliteratur* (Paderborn: Fink, 2008), 102.

[8] See Margit Sinka, "Tom Tykwer's *Lola rennt*: A Blueprint of Millennial Berlin," *glossen* 11 (2000), http//www.dickinson.edu/departments/german/heft11/lola. html (accessed 1 August 2010).

[9] Zygmunt Baumann, *Postmodern Ethics* (Oxford: Blackwell, 1993); Richard Sennett, *Flesh and Stone: The Body and the City in Western Civilization* (London: Faber and Faber, 1994).

[10] Sennett, *Flesh and Stone*, 17–18.

[11] Sennett, *Flesh and Stone*, 18.

[12] Sennett, *Flesh and Stone*, 18.

[13] Karen Duve, *This Is Not a Love Song*, trans. Anthea Bell (London: Bloomsbury, 2005), 1.

[14] Florian Illies, *Generation Golf. Eine Inspektion* (Frankfurt am Main: Fischer, 2001). The term refers to the West German generation born between 1965 and

1975, and takes its name from the (at that time) highly popular Volkswagen Golf Mark II convertible, in a metallic paint, as a way of noting this generation's materialism.

[15] Moritz Baßler, *Der deutsche Pop-Roman. Die neuen Archivisten* (Munich: Beck, 2002).

[16] Degler and Paulokat, *Neue Deutsche Popliteratur*, 11.

[17] Peter Graves, "'The Novels of Karen Duve: just 'chick lit with . . . grime' and dragons?" in *Pushing at Boundaries*, ed. Bartel and Boa, 27–40; here, 38.

[18] Sennett, *Flesh and Stone*, 21.

[19] Elizabeth Boa and Rachel Palfreyman, *Heimat — A German Dream. Regional Loyalties and National Identity in German Culture 1890–1990* (Oxford: Oxford UP, 2000), 203.

[20] Boa and Palfreyman, *Heimat*, 203. By situating their discussion in the chapter entitled "Postmodern Nomads: The End of Heimat?" the authors indicate the difficulties of applying a concept of *Heimat* to the postmodern individual.

[21] Winfried Menninghaus, *Disgust. Theory and History of a Strong Sensation*, trans. Howard Eiland and Jöel Golb (Albany: State U of New York P, 2003), 1.

[22] See Preece's contribution in this volume for further literary examples of attacks on the sense of smell and an engagement with the aesthetics of disgust. In Ilija Trojanow's *Der Weltensammler*, the stench of many individual bodies merges into one vile smell, the "burp" of the city of Bombay that is described as a "body" with all its bodily functions, one which is getting too close for comfort to the protagonist, yet also holds a strong sexual attraction.

[23] Katie Jones, "Representing Repulsion: The Aesthetics of Disgust in Contemporary Women's Writing in French and German" (unpublished doctoral thesis, University of Nottingham, 2009), 11–12.

[24] Graham Russell Hodges, *Taxi! A Social History of the New York City Cabdriver* (Baltimore: The John Hopkins UP, 2007), 5.

[25] See, for example, Ralph-Rainer Wuthenow, *Im Buch die Bücher oder Der Held als Leser* (Frankfurt am Main: Europäische Verlagsanstalt, 1980); Heike Bartel, "Von Jonny Rotten bis Werther: Karen Duves *Dies ist kein Liebeslied* zwischen Popliteratur und Bildungsroman," in *Pushing at Boundaries*, ed. Bartel and Boa, 89–106.

[26] Risa Mickenberg, *Taxi Driver Wisdom*, photos by Joanne Dugan (San Francisco, CA: Chronicle, 1996), back cover.

[27] Compare Paul Chatterton and Robert Hollands, eds., *Urban Nightscapes: Youth Culture, Pleasure Spaces and Corporate Power* (London: Routledge, 2003).

[28] For a definition of the term "eucatastrophe," see David Sandner, *Fantastic Literature. A Critical Reader* (Westport, CT: Praeger, 2004), 308.

[29] Karen Duve and Thies Völker, *Lexikon der berühmten Tiere* (Munich: Piper, 1999), 149.

[30] Brüns points out parallels to Kafka's short stories where, in the reading of Deleuze and Guattari, animals play a central role to introduce a "Fluchtweg" (escape route) for the subject. Brüns, "Mensch und Tier," 235n39.

[31] At the time of preparing this article for printing, Karen Duve's book *Anständig Essen: Ein Selbstversuch* (Decent food: A self-experiment) (Berlin: Galiani, 2011) had just been published. Here, the motif of animals and their relationship with "modern man," which plays an important role in many of Duve's texts, takes center stage in the author's critical assessment of society's eating and consumer habits and the animal suffering caused by it. Mixing the narrative styles of novel and report of a self-experiment, the text is another example of Duve's ability to push at the boundaries of literary genres and deliver a clear message appealing to the reader's consciousness in a style of writing characterized by dry humor, self-irony, and a refreshing lack of any hint of preaching.

13: Yadé Kara, *Cafe Cyprus*: New Territory?

Kate Roy

WINNER OF THE GERMAN BOOK PRIZE 2004 for most successful debut novel for *Selam Berlin* (2003), which also earned her the 2004 Adelbert-von-Chamisso Förderpreis (promotional prize), Yadé Kara is a commercially successful Turkish-German writer. Kara, a "staunch West Berliner,"[1] who had a diverse career as a journalist, actress, teacher and manager in four metropolises before becoming a writer, was born in Çayırlı, eastern Anatolia, in 1965 and moved to Germany with her parents as a child. In her thoughtful and at times critical[2] Chamisso Prize acceptance speech, she compares her coming to Germany and her identity as a Berliner to Adelbert von Chamisso's circumstances, writing:

> As a child, Adelbert left France and fled the French Revolution; I left Turkey as a child and fled Anatolian earthquakes.
> We both came to Berlin. Adelbert lived at the castle as a page to Queen Friederike Luise; I lived a few streets away from the castle in a typical old Berlin building.
> He learnt to read, write, and speak German at the Prussian Court; I learnt at a West Berlin elementary school.[3]

Kara belongs to the "second generation"[4] of Turkish-German women writers, and her work has enjoyed popular success while developing a distinctive style that sets her apart from many of her contemporaries, not least in the work's narration through a male protagonist.[5] I will argue that despite these differences, however, her work, and in particular her second novel, *Cafe Cyprus* (2008), forms part of a new trend of (female) Turkish-German writers whose texts are reterritorialized on ideological concepts such as religion, family, and nation. While the majority of these authors focus on peppy, entertaining, yet ultimately orientalizing narratives of "harmless" Turkish-German family lives,[6] for Yadé Kara reterritorialization takes the form of a very concrete notion of identity politics, mouthed by characters in her work, and jarring in the mouth of the supposedly apolitical narrator Hasan, who in *Selam Berlin* seemed more inclined toward description than programmatic statement. This reterritorialization is even more developed in *Cafe Cyprus*, set in London in the early 1990s, than in *Selam Berlin*, set in Berlin between the fall of the Wall and reunification; *Cafe Cyprus* thus presents an interesting response to citizenship debates in early twenty-first-century Germany.

The "marketability" of identity politics is, however, seemingly demonstrated in the novel's positive reception: it has been termed "an appeal against intolerance and xenophobia — regardless of which culture these might come from," whose protagonist Hasan "becomes . . . the beacon of hope for a more tolerant society."[7] Yet these (rather sweeping) celebratory comments perhaps also suggest that reviewers do not know quite what to make of the novel's content, and that they, misled by Hasan's move to London, are not alive to the interplay with twenty-first-century Germany that the narrative seems to offer — a reception comparable to that which Julian Preece's chapter in this volume sketches for Ilija Trojanow's *Der Weltensammler* (which arguably forms another very telling "British prism," albeit through historical figure rather than location).

Termed by Kara "a classic *Bildungsroman* [coming-of-age novel], 'A young person goes out into the big wide world, learns something, achieves something, becomes more and more mature,'"[8] it is in fact Hasan's observations of London that drive the narration of *Cafe Cyprus*, and not the plot or character development. Hasan finds himself several jobs, working first at a kebab stand with his old friend Kazim from Berlin, then also, to earn more money for his English classes, at Ali's Supermarket on Green Lanes and at the eponymous Café Cyprus, a "subsidiary" of the supermarket. On Saturdays he sells retro jackets at Portobello Market with new friend Khan. He shows his mother and cousin Leyla the sights when they (separately) come to visit. He falls in love with the fashion student Hannah, who apparently leaves him to go to New York toward the end of the novel — he then falls out of love, and back in love when Hannah sends a cryptic message in the closing pages announcing her imminent return. Yet Hasan's only great epiphany, the "something" that he learns (and builds into a kind of political manifesto) is that the people he terms "the new Londoners" are his kindred spirits, and that along with the "new" Berliners and Parisians they are all "pioneers and border crossers in Europe" who drag the old continent forward with them, ignoring its protests[9] — something he has been repeatedly observing and transmitting in a more sophisticated manner through his descriptions of Londoners and the connections these make throughout the novel.[10] What interests me here is why there might be a need for this explicit political statement on Hasan's part, and I will explore this reaction as both a response to the reception of *Selam Berlin* and to contemporary political events in Germany.

Selam Berlin and Beyond:
Negotiating "Identity" Terrain?

Kara's first novel *Selam Berlin* was received by the press as "the Turkish answer to the *Wende*," yet also as the first great *Wenderoman* (novel dealing with the radical changes in Germany around the time of the opening of the Berlin Wall in 1989) in its own right.[11] It tracks the changing atmosphere in Berlin, both the city's turbulent times between the fall of the Wall and German reunification, and the reflected turbulence within the narrator's family. Indeed, the Wall narrative effectively becomes the background of the novel, while its effect on the family takes center stage, as Hasan discovers that his father has another family on the other side of the wall. Here, Kara and Hasan intervene in German history, infiltrating a supposedly German-German historical event. This act of placing the family narrative in the foreground, and having it make connections with an interactive history, produces a literal making of space in "German" narratives of that history, otherwise ordered spatially in terms of the geography and time of the nation-state. The functioning of Berlin here suggests the manner in which location works not just as a backdrop in Kara's work,[12] but as an active part of the narrative, as *Cafe Cyprus* also shows.

For Petra Fachinger, Kara has "'made it to the centre' without compromising the subversive potential that characterises . . . the creative works of the members of 'dritte Ethnie.'"[13] *Die dritte Ethnie* (the third ethnicity) is Maxim Biller's term for the children of immigrants in Germany whose creative endeavors are charged "with a specific kind of energy, the energy of those who are at the margin and are either attempting to make it to the centre, or, in an oppositional move, proclaim the margin as the centre."[14] Kara has certainly made it to the "mainstream" in terms of commercial success and relatively widespread recognition, yet the notion that this has come without compromising her works' subversive potential invites skepticism, as does the associated notion that simply proclaiming the margin as the center, or "demonstrating that there are more than two different value systems, one Turkish and one German, set against each other," is "subversive."[15]

Certainly, Yadé Kara herself seems to seek to avoid the label of "Turkish-German author,"[16] yet the subject matter and subsequent reception of *Selam Berlin* and their focus on "a Turkish-German perspective" on "the aftermath of the fall of the Wall,"[17] as well as the marketing of both novels, owe much to "ethnic" labeling. Indeed, Moray McGowan goes so far as to say that *Selam Berlin* "entertainingly[,] if somewhat mechanically, rehearses sociological or ethnographic facts about Turkish culture in Germany," and suggests, furthermore, that this is the feature that enhances the novel's marketability.[18] The tension between the drawbacks and perceived benefits of "labeling" is well expressed by journalist and writer Iris Alanyalı in her review of *Selam Berlin*:

> [Kara's] reticence, bordering sometimes on the grotesque, is reminiscent of the typical fear of so many assimilated members of a minority — however large it may be — who face the public with an artistic work for the first time. Petrified of being reduced to their biographical characteristics, they play these down — because they suspect and fear that it is precisely this aspect that has sparked public interest.[19]

This tension between cashing in on the appeal of the exotic (on the part of the publishers) and the fear of being reduced to it (on the part of the author) pervades not only Kara's interviews,[20] but also her work. Her publisher, Diogenes, as mentioned in some early press reviews, reacted very quickly to sign her up, suspecting her "Turkish" *Wende* novel might become a cult classic.[21] Postpublication, Kara found herself peppered with questions that Hasan had already answered in *Selam Berlin*. Hasan had said, "Actually I had it all . . . I was like a rubber ball, bouncing back and forth between East and West, ha,"[22] yet in *Die Nacht des blauen Sofas* (The Night of the Blue Couch), filmed at the Leipzig Book Fair 2004, Christhard Läpple and Yadé Kara discuss her views on questions she is nonetheless often still asked, particularly the question that originally prompted Hasan's response above: "What are you really, German or Turkish? Well?" Kara answers:

> I can understand if people . . . I mean, most people on this planet grow up just with one language or in one cultural group and through this globalization the process has really begun now where people are now at home in several languages or several cities.[23]

It seems therefore significant that in Kara's second novel, *Cafe Cyprus*, Hasan leaves Germany and travels to London, seeking anonymity: "Oooooh, was I glad to get away from that backwater Berlin. Here, in London's anonymity, it was freer, calmer, and easier" (*CC*, 171). However, a tension between the "content" of the novel and its outward presentation remains in the publishing house's choice of cover, a generic Turkish tea glass (Kara would have preferred something more "urban"),[24] and title, *Cafe Cyprus*.[25] Indeed, this second novel was even launched at the Frankfurt Book Fair 2008, where Turkey was the fair's main focus.

Planes of Politics

Cafe Cyprus is by no means (just) a text confined to the London of the early 1990s, but rather a text that engages, both subtly and directly, with contemporary debates about German citizenship. From 1913 to 1999,

German laws of citizenship were based on *jus sanguinis*, where "ethnic" Germans received citizenship rights even if their ancestors had left Germany hundreds of years before and they did not speak German, whereas children born in Germany to non-German parents were not entitled to citizenship rights. Tom Cheesman discusses this apparent incongruity and how it came to prominence in the politics of the 1990s, in particular after a spate of violent xenophobic and racist attacks in Germany were reported on by the international media.[26] Cheesman refers here to incidents such as those at Mölln (1992) and Solingen (1993), neither of which, perhaps surprisingly, is mentioned in *Cafe Cyprus*.[27] The citizenship laws were finally modified in 1999, and these modifications came into effect on 1 January 2000, following which second-generation migrants have had dual citizenship until the ages of 18–23, when they must "choose" whether they wish to retain German citizenship or that of their parents. Since January 2005, the law has forbidden dual citizenship, leading Cheesman to comment that

> the denial of dual citizenship is symbolically very significant. It enshrines a refusal to accept "foreigners" as anything but either rank outsiders, or assimilated insiders. Following the compromise reform of the citizenship law, the categorical distinction between "Germans" and "foreigners" has in fact become stricter.[28]

This, I would argue, may explain the return of Turkish/German stereotypes and the preoccupation with the "intercultural" in popular literature by "new" writers. Karin Yeşilada has introduced us to "the nice Turkish girl next door," for whom fitting in and showing how "German" she is is paramount.[29] *Cafe Cyprus*, which postdates the legislation, seems to engage with it in two different ways: its deterritorialization of 1990s London takes on the debate from within, challenging fixed identity positions and celebrating the infiltration of "others" into the "traditional" image of the British capital, while its discourses on minority politics, by creating separate and "militant" minority subject positions, play back into and enshrine the very discourse of self and other — that is, the discourse of majority and minority.

A Deleuzian approach can illuminate these de- and reterritorializing dynamics in *Cafe Cyprus*, thus rescuing the novel both from the simplistic praise it has received (as, for example, a "300-page plea for tolerance and cosmopolitanism")[30] and from its outright dismissal as being full of stereotypes — Cheesman has referred to its predecessor as "rarely escap[ing] the realm of cliché."[31] Deterritorialization and reterritorialization are not the polar opposites they might sound; indeed, as its name suggests, the former "is tied to the very possibility of change immanent to a given territory,"[32] where territory is an established environment, constituting, for example, place, nation, language, or even a concept. Deleuze and Guattari explain the relationship as follows: "The function of deterritorialization: D is the movement by which 'one' leaves the territory"; reterritorialization serves to block this movement, and "anything can serve as a reterritorialization, in other words, 'stand for' the lost territory; one can reterritorialize on a being, an object, a book, an apparatus or system . . ."[33]

The distinctions between Deleuzian minor politics and minority politics are useful for understanding how *Café Cyprus* works. According to Deleuze, politics is not reducible to the political sphere, but is an engagement with the social totality. This notion of a minor politics, as outlined by Nicholas Thoburn, does not imply a political program or position, but rather a practical and active interplay with the situation at hand.[34] While minority politics is politics in the sense of fighting to overcome marginalization, stereotyping, and discrimination (i.e., resistance) — making the margins the center, and still concerned with identity — minor politics is politics in the sense of engaging creatively with the dynamics of these constraints.[35] It is not an (existing) identity,[36] but rather a creative and challenging tendency within identities, practices, and languages, in constant engagement with the major rather than ensconced in its own political space (like a minority subgroup). The minor therefore is not a minority subgroup, but a renunciation of subject positions.[37]

Minor and minority politics, like de- and reterritorialization, are usually co-present, and this is certainly the case in *Café Cyprus*, where the novel succeeds in deterritorializing the city of London to construct a heterogeneous space/time that intervenes in identity-positioning and the German citizenship debates, yet almost simultaneously takes recourse to identity politics and an enunciation of subject positions. We could conclude that the novel thus ends up asserting a minority politics rather than a minoritarian politics, a position that may have encouraged some of the "praise" it has received, as, for example, "a moving and provocative handbook,"[38] praise that is well-meaning but that, at the same time, in its language unconsciously illuminates the limitations of the text.

Space: London Is Deterritorialized

When a text is "located" (in space or time), it is usually viewed as historically and geographically situated. Such an approach involves reading location in a text as extensive, taking it as a representation of referents (spatial and temporal) in the world we know, and attributing to them conventional meanings. I will show, however, that in the presentation of apparently fixed entities, time and space are nonetheless dispersed: a notion expressed in the idea that location can be a trajectory rather than a fixed point, so that references to space and time open up the narrative to assemblages that go beyond the text. This is to read location as intensive, noticing the connections made "outside" the work itself: with the (informed) reader, and with other spaces and times. In *Café Cyprus*, London functions not so much as a setting, but rather as a tool for the discussions of identities within it: what London (as open location) facilitates is more important than the narrative/plot itself. Through the opening up of the unknowability of London, its flexibility in time and space, the narrative becomes more than the sum of its parts, making productive connections that point beyond its setting. When Hasan evokes the eternal city cliché — "it had all always been here, before me, and after me it would still be standing here, and nothing moved me more" (*CC*, 331–32) — his statement about the city of London also seems to point to the flexibility of location in its invocation of past, present, and future.

Hasan's travels around the city might be seen as creating his personal London or favorite London spaces. The limitation of the concept of "personalizing city space," however, is that it subjectivizes space, fixing it in relation to a subjectivity (and vice versa), rather than demonstrating how spaces are transformed by those who pass through them — who are in turn transformed. If we look, in contrast, at what Hasan's mapping of places does, London could also be seen as activated through Hasan's presence, for himself and for the reader — as a multicultural London certainly, a London predominantly composed of "others," who have infiltrated and thus transformed its historical center: for example, in their travels on the tube — and ultimately as a space that comments on identity positions for the German multicultural debate.

The novel's focus, through Hasan, on "how firmly some images are stuck in people's heads," referring to the image of London from Hitchcock films, and how this image, "long since passé," is still cherished on the continent (*CC*, 14), seems to hint at its German audience: London, with its "history of 'peopling,'" has long been regarded as a multicultural city in the English-speaking world.[39]

The milieu[40] of London is created by Hasan's travels, where his journey through areas of London and his description of their associated characters activates different spatial trajectories that make further connections with the issue of fixed identities. The example of Café Cyprus itself is perhaps the clearest indication of this. The Cypriot customers of this London café literally repeat the Cyprus conflict of 1974, playing it out time and again with the props they have on hand. Within the café, Cyprus's infamous Green Line, prior to 1974 a temporarily erected frontier, "converted into an impermeable physical partition" in that year, following the Turkish intervention,[41] is re-erected:

> Sometimes the old men piled the whole of history on the table. Here Makarios (tea glass), there Lefkoşa (teaspoon), there Girne (matchbox), there the Turkish army (ashtray). Sometimes the tabletop

wasn't big enough for an accurate reenactment of the military and
political events of the hot summer of 1974. . . . So the old guys used
the whole room. The counter was Cyprus, the blue linoleum on the
floor the Mediterranean, the old chairs Turkish ships, the ventilators
thousands of Turkish paratroopers. . . . Factions that I'd never
known existed emerged during these coffee sessions. An invisible
Green Line separating Northern Cyprus from Southern Cyprus ran
through Café Cyprus. Greek Cypriots held sway at tables in the
right-hand corner of the café, and Turkish Cypriots at tables in the
left. There was a tacit understanding that no one crossed this line.
Right at the back of the café sat a small group of Greek and Turkish
Cypriots. . . . Ali Bey called this group the "Aristotle and Plato fac-
tion." They were the more moderate Cypriots from both sides who
commented on the Cyprus conflict, rivalries, and other disagree-
ments in general and had a philosophical approach to the whole
predicament. (*CC*, 50–52)

The echoes within this passage are more complex than a simple reading as a
testimony to London's history of immigration and diverse suburbs might
imply. Nicosia, as divided city, has a clear parallel with Berlin that is further
enhanced by the patrons themselves — "Of course they'll be reunified. After
all, East and West Berlin united and brought down the Wall . . . Ask *Haraç
Hasan*, he comes from Berlin doesn't he" (*CC*, 52–53). That the café is
located in the British capital is similarly no accident: not only because the
Cypriots, with their British passports, relocated to the United Kingdom after
the turmoil, but also because prepartition Cyprus was crucial to British
interests in the region as a gateway to the Middle East. Significantly, for
Calame and Charlesworth, the British colonial authorities fostered ethnic
divisions, which in turn served their own interest in "legitimiz[ing] a permanent presence on the island."[42] For the purposes of the novel, it is the café's
nonnegotiable identities that are paramount, evocatively brought to life in
Hasan's energetic description of the futile reenactments that "reproduce
already established forms and rhythms," copying the past "as faithfully as
possible," representing it.[43] They become particularly significant when the
café and its clientele are ultimately rejected by Hasan. He intentionally
avoids its uncomfortable atmosphere later in the novel, before the café and
its customers disappear from the narrative altogether, abandoned for the
"future" of London: Londoners who have transformed the city, rather than
"parroting" the effects of the past,[44] "I let myself be carried by this London
of Bengalis, Rastas, Pakistanis, Indians. . . . Bit by bit, through dogged, hard
work, they'd made London their new home. Yeah, I wanted to stay here and
get ahead, after all, I still wanted to conquer London" (*CC*, 375).

An episode ostensibly pointing to the future has similar resonances.
Hasan's girlfriend Hannah's father, a former Jewish Istanbulite, and current resident of leafy Kew (*CC*, 268), is working on the Potsdamer Platz

projects. He gives his views on the plans for the "whitening" of the Reichstag: "They can cover a building made of concrete, steel, and stone in white, but not the past" (*CC*, 272–73). Given that the novel is apparently set in the early 1990s, the reference is oriented toward the Germany of the future — the Reichstag was wrapped by artists Christo and Jeanne-Claude in June 1995, prior to its renovation by Sir Norman Foster and its reuse for political functions — yet Hasan's reaction is simply to reject the obvious implications of the Reichstag's past: "for me, the Reichstag was an old building" (*CC*, 273). Instead, his Reichstag is recast as the site of the family barbecues and soccer games of his childhood. This different repetition of the old/new seat of German power is subversive in its transformation of an imposing, loaded monument, depoliticizing its well-known history and transforming its context in the relaxed seating of Hasan's family and the other "Turkish" picnickers in front of it. They are always already there: "Big deal! That's just the way it was" (*CC*, 273).

Britain's own history of colonialism and immigration is intertwined with Hasan's narrative as the "new Londoners" infiltrate British history, as they repeat it differently through (for example) the monumental Circle Line — which forms a ring around the historic center of London and provides the title for two of *Cafe Cyprus*'s chapters — on their tube journeys. Hasan's descriptions of his fellow passengers in the tube — descriptions that pervade the novel — resonate with the following comment, made by the British-Iranian character Khan, for whom the tube renders everyone "equal":

> a trip on the Circle Line is like a tour through English history [. . .]. Events and places line up like a chain. Westminster Cathedral . . . Houses of Parliament . . . Buckingham Palace — seat of the Royal Family, Victoria Station — she married Albert, brought a whole load of children into the world, shaped nearly a whole century, colonized and took a whole load of nations prisoner, made them England's servants. And this Circle Line brings it all *into one line*. (*CC*, 127)

Yet even the iconic Circle Line and its implications are not fixed in London. The "haggard guys in tracksuits" spotted by Hasan in the cafés at Victoria Station, whom he guesses to be "Yugoslavians," blend, through his narration, seamlessly into "the 'railway station Turks' from the seventies" now retired and traveling between "Anatolian villages and German cities" (*CC*, 100–101). Similarly, the old men and women working on the tube "who . . . had left Caribbean islands with a great view of the sea" become "the old Anatolians from Kottbusser Tor who went off to the factories in the early morning" (*CC*, 325).

The novel's opening and closing pages, tied together by the underground system, similarly point beyond their settings. The novel begins with the antiapartheid song "Gimme hope Jo'anna" (1988) by Guyanese-

British reggae musician Eddy Grant, alluding to both apartheid (from the root "separateness," the ultimate segregation along ethnic lines) and optimism.[45] We could read the inclusion of this song merely as a nod to pop lit, yet it seems to have wider-reaching implications when read in conjunction with the closing passages of *Selam Berlin* and the impetus of *Café Cyprus* itself. *Selam Berlin* ended with the words:

> From far off I heard the sound of fireworks. It was coming from the direction of the Reichstag. And I knew that at this moment the Liberty Bell was ringing and the flag was being raised. And at midnight two German states would become one Germany again. I warmed my hands with the cigarette and suddenly knew what was going on in my life . . . Ha! (*SB*, 382)

This passage has been read positively by Fachinger as reflecting Hasan's "self-confidence and independence from cultural and societal constraints."[46] Yet in light of *Café Cyprus*, it seems clearer that Hasan's response to reunification's immediate effect on his Berlin is in fact negative: reunification — and explicitly, the changing attitudes and atmosphere in a Berlin now the scene of "Neo-Nazi marches" (*CC*, 11) — prompt Hasan to leave Germany. In view of this, could we see the song's inclusion as a rebuke?

The "Hope" in the song's title seems to suggest optimism for Hasan's new beginning in London, or indeed an optimistic response (through the whole passage's connection with the tube) that other forms of dealing with subject positions are possible. Hasan sings this song as he goes down the steps to the tube station at Charing Cross. Here he first encounters Ron, the busker of Caribbean origin who returns again and again as a refrain, usually in the trains of the Circle Line, at its stations, or in the immediate environment of these stations. The act of going down from the historical monument of Charing Cross and the readily associable, clichéd image of a line of London's black cabs waiting above ground to the busker below, who, carried away by his own music, is getting the feet of all the passers-by tapping ("they jiggled to his beat and danced to his rhythm"; *CC*, 7) implies that the traditional image of London will be turned on its head, and, arguably, that this narrative of an apparently "new" London will be turned toward Germany — a significant act to open the narrative.

The novel ends with Hasan emerging from the tube to attend the Notting Hill Carnival, where the busker Ron is again present, and his effect on those around him is repeated: "Ron needed just three minutes to pull people's feet out from under them and drop them into dreams and images of the wilderness. Thunderclouds over the dense urban jungle" (*CC*, 374–75).

This connection to the Notting Hill Carnival is possibly more ambiguous than Kara intended, given the origins of the event as a protest against racist attacks, and its subsequent part-transformation into something of a programmatic cliché, marketing ethnicity. For Kara herself: "Carnival is . . . the celebration of the new London that has risen up bit by bit since the Second World War!"[47] Susanne Cuevas writes that the Notting Hill Carnival has been key for Black British, and in particular for those of Caribbean origin, "as a symbol of reclaiming the streets and black cultural expression."[48] Carnival postdates the 1958 antiblack riots in the area, and the idea for it was conceived in the 1960s by local community leaders who sought to "bring together the ethnically diverse local populations" and revamp Notting Hill's "negative image," as well as to create awareness about local issues such as housing problems. Cuevas argues that particularly since the 1970s Carnival has been a focal point for "black political activism and cultural representation," especially for the Caribbean British community.[49]

What Cuevas also draws attention to, however, is Carnival's increasing draw as a London tourist attraction, its commercialization and commodification, leading community leaders to bemoan the loss of its "political and oppositional edge."[50] Significantly, Cuevas also notes that Carnival does not make an appearance in the London texts by Black British and British Asian writers that she discusses, probably because "by definition, Carnival marks a temporary suspension of normality."[51] Following Cuevas's analysis, the Carnival ending is thus more fitting and more ambiguous than even Kara gives it credit for: indeed, we could see it as mirroring both the positive — in its symbolic resistance — and the negative — in its marketing of ethnicity and commercialization — aspects of *Cafe Cyprus* as a work of literature.

Identities Reterritorialized

In Kara's *Cafe Cyprus*, the reply to the "new" infiltration of categorical distinctions in German identity politics, aptly described by Cheesman, is manifested differently to that of the assimilating chick lit, with its adherence to these categories of "German" and "Turkish" — and, through another "watershed" for Turkish-German identity, the aftermath of German reunification. As we have seen, Hasan's "emigration" from Germany exemplifies his rejection of the state (past and present) that created the identity categories he repudiates: "I thought about leaving because I often had the feeling that the new Berlin and I were leaning against each other like cards and could slide apart any second" (*CC*, 11–12). It is therefore perhaps not surprising that Hasan's voice becomes more strident in response:

> On London streets, seeing a foreigner who'd grown up in another culture and language meant just looking at him, nothing more. No sizing him up, no judgment. In Berlin on the other hand I was

pigeonholed on account of my black hair, my clothes, my shoes, and my Turkishness. People looked at me and thought "Oh, a foreigner! Turk! Kreuzberger!" (*CC*, 64)[52]

Hasan's explicit reference to exterior perceptions has created a shift in his self-description, from describing himself as a rubber ball bouncing between "East" and "West" (in *Selam Berlin*) and, surprisingly evocatively, as an egg: "I am like this egg . . . an all-rounder that can do loads of things" (*CC*, 166),[53] he moves to long explanatory monologues addressed to the reader:

> because lots of people can't handle "multiple identities"! And how could you expect them to? Most of them could only speak one language and spent most of their lives in only one country, one city, or one village. Most knew only one culture, one language, one area, and one way of dealing with people. Most people had only one dimension. I was 3-D. I mean, I was at home in German, Turkish, and now English too. I could compare everything, see all the pros and cons, weigh them up, bugged by the weaknesses of some and blown away by the strengths of others. It was a continuous learning process. The good thing about it was that I could pick out the best bits and make them my own and carry them around with me. (*CC*, 167)

This explicit and almost militant formation of self-identity, opposed to a group identity comprising "most people," echoes Kara's words from her interview with Läpple at the Leipzig Book Fair. Fachinger has argued that "Hasan is not burdened by his dual cultural heritage,"[54] and while his approach to it in these passages is positive (even if his response does rather evoke the "identity supermarket" that Feridun Zaimoğlu shuns in *Kanak Sprak*), by merely categorizing his experience as privileged, better, and different he does nothing to challenge the categorization of majority and minority; if anything, his words uphold it.

The latter phases of the novel are notable for Hasan's realization of a group identity, created in somewhat repetitive passages that adhere to "models" for all their apparent "newness":

> Sukjeet was right, we were the new Berliners,[55] Parisians, and Londoners, working in Kreuzberg, Barbès, and Southall in banks, offices, shops, and restaurants, bringing our energy, our enthusiasm to the business and driving everything forward. We were the new Bohemians, conquering the scene bit by bit. We made new images, new languages, new practices, a new character, and called the old one into question . . . never before had there been a mix like us on European soil. . . . Oh yeah, we were pioneers and border crossers in Europe. . . . We went our own way and pulled Europe along with us, sometimes it came limping, sometimes dragging its feet, sometimes screaming and throwing itself on the ground like a little kid. Big deal! (*CC*, 317–18)

This passage's vocabulary of "new Europeans" and "new Londoners" seems paradoxical in its rhetoric: the repeated "new" downplays the duration of the existence of Hasan's Londoners and Berliners, cleverly evoked in some earlier passages.[56] Yet the passage is perhaps intended to reference Rushdie's notion of "newness." As John McLeod explains, for Rushdie, locations such as Brixton are those where "newness comes into the world," a happening that McLeod, like Hasan, attributes in part to London youth "drawn from those with ancestral connections to once-colonized countries."[57] "Newness" seems to come then in the creation, or recognition, of a group identity that involves the notable shunning of ethnic identity in favor of a young, "city" identity. While this is seemingly a positive subject position, it still brings to mind resistance to marginalization in the suburbs and names it evokes, and in its passionate opposition to the majority, "Europe." The repetition of "we," and in particular of "we were," the *representation* of a collective minority position, reterritorializes the passage in identity politics. As Christian Jäger warns, "every form of minority *being* points to the power of definition of the majority and preserves this, affirms it."[58] While "proclaim[ing] the margin as the centre"[59] in *Cafe Cyprus* thus poses a challenge to categorical distinction in ethnic terms, it nonetheless leaves the way open for "identity categories" to be seen in the same old terms of "majority" and "minority."

A Grounded Nomad?

The trajectory of the narrator Hasan in *Cafe Cyprus* both deterritorializes the city of London in space and time (through past, present, and future references to Berlin and Cyprus, for example), creatively engaging with "fixed identities" at all turns, and reterritorializes firmly on identity politics in its efforts to proclaim the "margins" as the "new" Europe, its vocabulary maintaining an oppositionality that problematizes any straightforward idea of "new" as a resoundingly positive solution. By settling into a European discourse, the novel reerects exclusive territorial boundaries that it has also rendered unstable. Both dynamics in the novel engage with early new millennium Germany. Here, the initial territorialization is reflected in the law of a "major" European power, the denial of dual citizenship and the strengthening of notions of "Turkish" and "German" (a dual positioning Kara has always rejected), creating a space in which only an ironic cosmopolitanism can be possible, as Cheesman has stated.[60] Spaces described by Hasan in London intervene in this debate, destabilizing notions of "either/or," yet the narrative is reterritorialized in Hasan and his language, entrenched in familiar terms of identity politics that stand for the "territory" of the citizenship debates, casting doubt on Fachinger's assertion that with Kara, "Turkish-German writing [. . . has] broken free of [its . . . niche]."[61]

Indeed, the sweeping praise that *Cafe Cyprus* has received seems far more reminiscent of McLeod's reading of Graham Huggan's postcolonial exotic; namely, that "all forms of postcolonial resistance and counter-value are always readily commodifiable by global capitalism as exotic spectacle."[62] Cheesman's "consumerist cosmopolitans" have welcomed Hasan and the other "new Europeans" with open arms, only to read their resistance as spectacle and instead "romanticize" them "as nomads, hybrids, new potentials."[63] Predictably termed a "modern nomad" by the publishing house and reviewers,[64] Hasan has moved cities in *Cafe Cyprus*, but *Selam Berlin* was arguably nomadic to a greater degree in making space in a "German" narrative of history by showing that "Turks" were always already a part of it, and by being able to formulate this through the "open" identity of "Berliner"[65] plain and simple, and not "new." *Cafe Cyprus*, like other texts discussed in this volume — in particular Sibylle Berg's *Die Fahrt*, Terézia Mora's *Alle Tage*, and to a certain extent Trojanow's *Der Weltensammler* — ultimately throws into question readings of "generic" transnational mobility as automatically freeing up notions of identity. What distinguishes Kara's case, however, is that this process functions as an unconscious aside to the novel's predominant preoccupations, which are in fact seeking to advocate the very opposite. Hasan, I would argue, can no longer claim a nomadic subjectivity in *Cafe Cyprus*. The first premise of nomadic subjectivity is creativity, the "porous" and "shifting and relational" identities Berg's *Die Fahrt* is shown to have created in Emily Jeremiah's chapter in this volume. Kara's narrative, in contrast, in rejecting identities of "rank outsiders" and "assimilated insiders" for its subjects, becomes caught up in its pursuit of new, stable, and still predominantly oppositional (European) subject positions, taking part in the same old debate instead of transforming the argument itself.

Notes

I am grateful to the IGRS (School of Advanced Study, University of London) for a Sylvia Naish Research Fellowship, which supported the research for this article.

[1] "Yadé Kara im Gespräch mit Christhard Läpple," in *Die Nacht des blauen Sofas: von der Leipziger Buchmesse 2004*, moderated by Wolfgang Herles, Mainz: ZDF, aired 29 March 2004. All translations are my own, unless otherwise indicated.

[2] See, for example, the following, where Kara hints at the patronizing nature of the celebration — through ethnicization — of "niche" authors and their "enrichment" of German-language writing: "Today, some groups might call Adelbert von Chamisso a 'Franco-German writer' or a 'diasporic writer' and find his unique perspective interesting, etc., etc. For me, Adelbert von Chamisso is beyond all that:

he's an all-rounder who proved himself as a writer, a poet and, a naturalist. And, for me, he is above all a *Berliner*," in "Yadé Kara," in *Viele Kulturen — eine Sprache: Adelbert-von-Chamisso-Preisträgerinnen und Preisträger 1985–2009*, ed. Frank W. Albers and Irene Ferchl (Stuttgart: Robert Bosch Stiftung, 2009), 40–41; here, 41, original emphasis. See also Tom Cheesman on Feridun Zaimoğlu's skepticism about the "Adelbert-von-Chamisso-thingamajig," Tom Cheesman, *Novels of Turkish German Settlement: Cosmopolite Fictions* (Rochester, NY: Camden House, 2007), 149.

[3] "Yadé Kara," in *Viele Kulturen*, ed. Albers and Ferchl, 41.

[4] I use the term here in a very basic sense in terms of timing of publication, and must own that I share Margaret Littler's and Tom Cheesman's skepticism of the term's usefulness in any "classification" of Turkish-German writers. See, for example, Margaret Littler, "Intimacy and Affect in Turkish-German Writing: Emine Sevgi Özdamar's 'The Courtyard in the Mirror,'" *Journal of Intercultural Studies* 29, no. 3 (2008): 331–45; here, 335, 343–44n11. Tom Cheesman in particular warns against the "teleological tendency in some recent commentaries on German-Turkish writing which celebrate the youngest writers as the most 'advanced,'" "Juggling Burdens of Representation: Black, Red, Gold and Turquoise," *German Life and Letters* 59, no. 4 (2006): 471–87; here, 471, 475.

[5] For a discussion of the possibilities open to Kara as a result of this choice, see Lyn Marven, "Crossing Borders: Migration, Gender, and Language in Novels by Yadé Kara, Jeannette Lander and Terézia Mora," *Gegenwartsliteratur* 8 (2009): 148–69; here, 151–57.

[6] See Karin Yeşilada's excellent article "'Nette Türkinnen von nebenan' — Die neue deutsch-türkische Harmlosigkeit als literarischer Trend," in *Von der nationalen zur internationalen Literatur: Transkulturelle deutschsprachige Literatur und Kultur im Zeitalter globaler Migration*, ed. Helmut Schmitz (Amsterdam: Rodopi, 2009), 117–42.

[7] chr, "Stress im Multikulti-Cafe: Yadé Karas Zweitling," *Saarbrücker Zeitung*, 17 October 2008.

[8] Petra Pluwatsch, "Die Liebe ruft — das Leben auch. Zwischen den Kulturen: Yadé Kara erzählt in 'Cafe Cyprus' von der Weltoffenheit," *Magazin des Kölner Stadt-Anzeiger*, 1–2 November 2008.

[9] Yadé Kara, *Café Cyprus* (Zurich: Diogenes, 2008), 317–18. Further references to *Cafe Cyprus* will appear in the text as *CC*.

[10] Compare also Kara's comments in an interview: "It was during her studies in London that she first realized that there were many other young people like her: Indians, Chinese, West Indians, Turks, Pakistanis, whose families, now into their second, third, fourth generations, were living in Europe's major cities and 'represent something totally distinct and new.' '50 years ago in Berlin,' she says, 'you wouldn't have come across people like me.'" Kara, in Pluwatsch, "Die Liebe ruft."

[11] See for example: "We've been waiting for years for the great 'Wenderoman,' and finally a young Turkish author has produced it." Annemarie Stoltenberg, "Die

türkische Antwort auf die Wende," *Hamburger Abendblatt*, 30 August 2003. Iris Alanyalı also terms the novel a "Berlin *Wenderoman* from a Turkish point of view." Iris Alanyalı, "Ein Leben im Transit," *Die Welt* (*Die Literarische Welt*), 24 May 2003, 2.

[12] Petra Fachinger has also noted that "in *Selam Berlin* Berlin signifies more than mere geographical setting," and this forms the basis of Lyn Marven's argument that "Berlin offers an alternative identity and space for negotiation and cultural inclusion." Marven also discusses the historical participation of Turks in Berlin's (literary) history. See Petra Fachinger, "A New Kind of Creative Energy: Yadé Kara's *Selam Berlin* and Fatih Akın's *Kurz und schmerzlos* and *Gegen die Wand*," *German Life and Letters* 60, no. 2 (2007): 243–60; here, 247 and 249; and Lyn Marven, "'Kanacke her, Almanci hin. . . . Ich war ein Kreuzberger': Berlin in Contemporary Turkish-German Literature," *Edinburgh German Yearbook* 1 (2007): 191–207.

[13] Fachinger, "A New Kind of Creative Energy," 260.

[14] Ethnic Germans form the first *Ethnie*, and first-generation immigrant authors form the second. Fachinger acknowledges, however, that she has some reservations about Biller's thesis. Fachinger, "A New Kind of Creative Energy," 243–44.

[15] Fachinger, "A New Kind of Creative Energy," 243 and 260.

[16] See also note 2 above, where Kara seems to reject "diasporic positioning" altogether.

[17] Fachinger, "A New Kind of Creative Energy," 260.

[18] Moray McGowan, "Turkish-German Fiction since the mid-1990s," in *Contemporary German Fiction: Writing in the Berlin Republic*, ed. Stuart Taberner (Cambridge: Cambridge UP, 2007), 196–214; here, 200.

[19] Alanyalı, "Ein Leben im Transit," 2. The chapter on Trojanow in this volume suggests a similar complex dynamic.

[20] Compare with "She'd like you to take an interest in the book's 'story,' not in Hasan's roots. But it is precisely his origins and their shaping of his point of view that make the content even more interesting." Cornelia Geissler, "Damals im Westen," *Berliner Zeitung*, 11 March 2003.

[21] Volkhard Bode, "Good Bye Bosporus," *Börsenblatt für den Deutschen Buchhandel*, 28 May 2003. See also Franz Josef Görtz, "Ihr Liebling Kreuzberg," *Frankfurter Allgemeine Sonntagszeitung*, 16 March 2003, 49. Significantly, Anke S. Biendarra's chapter on Mora in this volume opens with a reference to publishing houses' increased interest in works by authors of "hyphenated" (as she terms it) or non-German origins, alluding to their heightened marketability in an environment of increased preoccupation with transnational writing.

[22] Yadé Kara, *Selam Berlin* (Zurich: Diogenes, 2004), 223. Further references to *Selam Berlin* will appear in the text as *SB*.

[23] "Yadé Kara im Gespräch mit Christhard Läpple," in *Die Nacht des blauen Sofas*.

[24] Personal correspondence with the author.

[25] This was one of a number of working titles Kara proposed to her publishers, who had the final choice (personal correspondence).

[26] Cheesman, *Novels of Turkish German Settlement*, 2n2.

[27] Interestingly, they *are* mentioned in *Selam Berlin*, in a passage that suggests the retrospective narration of that narrative (*SB*, 120).

[28] Cheesman, *Novels of Turkish German Settlement*, 19.

[29] Yeşilada, "Nette Türkinnen von nebenan," in *Von der nationalen zur internationalen Literatur*, ed. Schmitz.

[30] Pluwatsch, "Die Liebe ruft."

[31] Cheesman, *Novels of Turkish German Settlement*, 96.

[32] Adrian Parr, ed., *The Deleuze Dictionary* (Edinburgh: Edinburgh UP, 2005), 67.

[33] Gilles Deleuze and Félix Guattari, *A Thousand Plateaus: Capitalism and Schizophrenia*, trans. Brian Massumi (London: Continuum, 2004), 559–60.

[34] Thoburn stresses that "minor politics is not a set of programmatic rules of a correct 'Deleuzian politics.'" Nicholas Thoburn, *Deleuze, Marx and Politics* (London: Routledge, 2003), 13.

[35] Thoburn, *Deleuze, Marx and Politics*, 43.

[36] Thoburn, *Deleuze, Marx and Politics*, 8.

[37] Thoburn, *Deleuze, Marx and Politics*, 7; Deleuze and Guattari, *A Thousand Plateaus*, 117–18. Indeed, Deleuze and Guattari identify three basic modes: "The majoritarian as a constant and homogeneous system; minorities as subsystems; and the minoritarian as a potential, creative and created, becoming." Deleuze and Guattari, *A Thousand Plateaus*, 117.

[38] Nicole Rodriguez, "Aufsehen erregender 'Ratgeber': Yadé Kara 'Cafe Cyprus,'" in www.hr-online.de, Frankfurt, 30 August 2008.

[39] John McLeod, *Postcolonial London: Rewriting the Metropolis* (London: Routledge, 2004), 18. Godela Weiss-Sussex's research on Anna Jokl suggests that the concept of "multicultural London" does not constitute a new image of London in German literature, either, but that the positive response to it *is* new. Weiss-Sussex, "Das Leben als Gewebe: Anna Jokls 'Die Reise nach London,'" London in German Literature Symposium, Centre for Anglo-German Cultural Relations, Queen Mary, University of London, 18 December 2009.

[40] A milieu is a space that is journeyed through, made up of qualities, substances, powers and events. See, in particular, Gilles Deleuze, "What Children Say," in *Essays Critical and Clinical*, trans. Daniel W. Smith and Michael A. Greco (London: Verso, 1998), 61–67.

[41] Jon Calame and Esther Charlesworth, "Nicosia," in *Divided Cities: Belfast, Beirut, Jerusalem, Mostar, and Nicosia* (Philadelphia: U of Pennsylvania P, 2009), 121–42; here, 133. Calame and Charlesworth additionally note that "rather than fulfilling its ostensible purpose — to provide time and space for gradual reconciliation and negotiation — partition seemed to encourage further animosity and segregation between the two rival communities," and furthermore, that "ethnic

homogenization on either side of the Green Line became almost total." Calame and Charlesworth, "Nicosia," 134, 141.

[42] Calame and Charlesworth, "Nicosia," 127.

[43] Claire Colebrook, *Gilles Deleuze* (London and New York: Routledge, 2002), 119.

[44] Colebrook, *Gilles Deleuze*, 119.

[45] Katy Derbyshire makes a similar point in her "love german books" blog entry of 14 November 2008, http://lovegermanbooks.blogspot.com/2008/11/turn-again-hasan-kazan-caf-cyprus.html (accessed 1 August 2010).

[46] Fachinger, "A New Kind of Creative Energy," 253.

[47] Personal correspondence.

[48] Susanne Cuevas, *Babylon and Golden City: Representations of London in Black and Asian British Novels Since the 1990s* (Heidelberg: Winter, 2008), 83.

[49] Cuevas, *Babylon and Golden City*, 83.

[50] Cuevas, *Babylon and Golden City*, 83n60.

[51] Cuevas, *Babylon and Golden City*, 117.

[52] The irrevocable linking of "Kreuzberger" and "Turk" in this quotation is interesting because "Kreuzberger" and "Turk" were not necessarily one and the same in *Selam Berlin*: see Marven on Hasan in *Selam Berlin*: "he sees himself neither as a marginalized Turk in Germany, nor a Germanized Turk, but — typical for a Berliner — as a Kreuzberger." Marven, "Kanacke her, Almanci hin," 194.

[53] Compare Kara's deliberately "non-Multikulti" description of Adelbert von Chamisso in note 2. Both this quotation and the following quotation from *Cafe Cyprus* were translated by the German-to-English workshop group (led by Shaun Whiteside) at the British Centre for Literary Translation Summer School 2009, where Yadé Kara was a writer-in-residence. I am grateful to the BCLT for a bursary which enabled me to attend.

[54] Fachinger, "A New Kind of Creative Energy," 243.

[55] In terms of this vocabulary and its connections, it is interesting that Hasan makes a distinction between *Neuberliner* ("New Berliners," those recently arrived from the provinces) and *die neuen Berliner* ("the new Berliners" with transformative potential).

[56] John McLeod, for example, uses the term "new Londoners" to refer to the new inhabitants of Brixton in the 1950s, the parents or grandparents of the generation Hasan refers to as "new." McLeod, *Postcolonial London*, 2.

[57] McLeod, *Postcolonial London*, 191.

[58] Christian Jäger, "Grenzkontrollpunkte: Methodologische Probleme des Transitraums und der 'kleinen Literatur,'" in *Transitraum Deutsch: Literatur und Kultur im transnationalen Zeitalter*, ed. Jens Adam, Hans-Joachim Hahn, Lucjan Puchalski, and Irena Światlowska (Wroclaw: Neisse Verlag), 41–51; here, 43. Italics mine.

[59] Fachinger, "A New Kind of Creative Energy," 244.

[60] Cheesman, *Novels of Turkish German Settlement*, 20.

[61] Fachinger, "A New Kind of Creative Energy," 245.

[62] McLeod, *Postcolonial London*, 13.

[63] See Cheesman's concept of Atlanticist consumerist cosmopolitanism, and in particular his references to the *Heimat Kunst* festival of 2000, in *Novels of Turkish German Settlement*, 50–51.

[64] This was no doubt inspired by the following passage from *Selam Berlin*: "I didn't want to tie myself down, hold myself back, put down roots. The nomad in me was driving me to new places, spaces, cities and streets. I wanted to go further west, to London, New York, San Francisco — or east? To Tokyo, Tehran, Tashkent. Airports, train stations, hotel rooms. Neither here nor there, just away. Yeah, that's what I wanted, hey ho, let's go!" (*SB*, 382).

[65] The flexibility of the "Berliner" identity is detailed by Marven in "Kanacke her, Almanci hin."

14: Sven Regener, *Der kleine Bruder*: Reinventing Kreuzberg

Andrew Plowman

T HE PUBLICATION IN 2008 of Sven Regener's *Der kleine Bruder* (The younger brother) marked the completion of a trilogy of works devoted to the story of a figure named Frank Lehmann, which has ranked among the critical and commercial successes of recent German writing. The initially garrulous but passive Lehmann had first appeared in *Herr Lehmann* (Mr. Lehmann, 2001; published in English as *Berlin Blues*, 2003) as a bartender living and working in the alternative subculture of the Kreuzberg district of West Berlin on the eve of the fall of the Wall in 1989. This first novel crystallized central political and literary concerns and was adapted to film by the director Leander Haußmann in 2003. On the one hand, *Herr Lehmann* offered a Western counterpart to the trend toward *Ostalgie* (nostalgia for the former East Germany) and a grudging acceptance of the imperative of normalization after 1990. The novel bid a nostalgic farewell to Kreuzberg's subculture while acknowledging also that this was an anomaly that would have no place in a unified German capital. On the other, it epitomized the quality of "readability" central to recent literary debates, which it furnished with an iconic moment when the normally highbrow critic Marcel Reich-Ranicki declared on the TV show *Das litera-rische Quartett* that the work had made him laugh aloud.[1] Despite being published first in the sequence, *Herr Lehmann* was set last. Named after a housing estate in his native Bremen, *Neue Vahr Süd* (2004) looked back at Frank Lehmann's conscription into the Bundeswehr prior to his departure to West Berlin in the early 1980s. *Der kleine Bruder*, finally, deals with Frank Lehmann's arrival in Kreuzberg immediately after his discharge from the army and presents him as a more dynamic figure than the previous texts. The novel tells how Lehmann arrives in Kreuzberg in the hope that his elder brother Manfred, who is a sculptor, will help him land on his feet. However, his brother has disappeared. In the process of searching for him, Frank succeeds in establishing himself.

This chapter places *Der kleine Bruder* in the context of the media interest that surrounded Sven Regener as an emerging writer and it offers a reading of the work as the final part of the Frank Lehmann trilogy. What makes Regener an interesting case study of an emerging figure on the literary scene — and a revealing contrast to Daniel Kehlmann, who, as Rebecca Braun shows in her chapter, slowly built his literary reputation before finding widespread fame with the publication of *Die Vermessung der Welt* (2005; *Measuring the World*, 2006) — is the prominence he had enjoyed already prior to *Herr Lehmann* as the singer of the rock band Element of Crime, which was formed in 1985 and named after the 1984 film by Lars von Trier. The chapter begins by showing how, against the background of a trend toward "pop" literature in the Federal Republic, Regener's celebrity as a musician shaped the reception of his work and in reviews, interviews, and profiles, and provided a framework within which its meanings and his own relation to it were negotiated. Reluctant to engage in the reflection on the nature of celebrity that for Braun characterizes Kehlmann's novel, Regener in his statements about his work has refused the suggestion that Frank Lehmann was an extension of his own cult persona as a musician, and the reading of *Der kleine Bruder* suggests that the narrative of personal development that it offers seeks to affirm both the figure of Frank Lehmann and his fictional distance from Regener himself. While it ascribes to Lehmann pragmatic qualities, the narrative of his search for his brother is nonetheless intimately connected to the cultish and mythic space of alternative scene of Berlin-Kreuzberg in the 1980s. The chapter continues by showing how it opens out the terrain of this district and resurrects the subculture that flourished there. In the skewed chronology of the Frank Lehmann trilogy, *Der kleine Bruder* partially retracts the sober conclusion of *Herr Lehmann*, and the Kreuzberg scene of the 1980s is revived — not in a valedictory tone, as in the earlier novel, but rather self-consciously as performance and simulacrum of the original scene.

Regener, Pop, and the Affirmation of Herr Lehmann

A striking feature of the reception of the Lehmann trilogy has been the contest between reviewers and interviewers, on the one hand, and Sven Regener, on the other, over its meaning and Regener's relation to it. If it is scarcely surprising that perceptions of Regener's writing have been shaped by his role in popular music, his response has been to assert the discrete character of his musical and literary activity. A critical model that throws Regener's stance into relief is provided by Dirk Niefanger's recent work on the proper name of the author. Niefanger has examined how writers associated with pop literature in the 1990s such as Benjamin Stuckrad-Barre or Christian Kracht have staged themselves in the media as "stars" of a type more familiar from the music industry than the literary sphere. To explain how this process shapes the understanding of these authors' works, Niefanger offers a development of Foucault's concept of the classificatory function of the author's name. Here, he argues, the name is collapsed into the text, becoming a "label" that serves the purposes of product differentiation, provides information, and underwrites expectations about it.[2] By contrast, what Regener's many public pronouncements about the Frank Lehmann novels suggest is his refusal to accept the wholesale collapsing into them of attributes or "labels" associated with his name as a rock musician.

While Regener's "star" status as a rock musician has generated interest in his writing, it has also seen it endowed with cult qualities and promoted its alignment with pop literature. Breaking with its punk and English-language origins, Regener's band Element of Crime became noted with albums like *Psycho* (1999) and *Romantik* (2001) for reflective German-language lyrics and a sound reminiscent of the *chanson* that prominently featured Regener's trumpet and his gravel voice.[3] It is clear from reviews and interviews that the band's "cult" reputation in the music scene has facilitated the labeling of Regener as a cult writer and Frank Lehmann as a cult figure.[4] The marketing appeal of such claims is self-evident, but these claims are hardly borne out by the mainstream scale of Regener's commercial success, which has seen *Herr Lehmann* sell over 1.7 million copies and both *Neue Vahr Süd* (remarkably for a six-hundred-page novel) and *Der kleine Bruder* top bestseller lists.[5]

The tendency to align Regener's work with pop literature was particularly apparent with respect to *Herr Lehmann*, which appeared relatively soon after key pop texts like Kracht's *Faserland* (Land of fibers, 1995) or Stuckrad-Barre's *Soloalbum* (1998). For reviewers, *Herr Lehmann* was Regener's own "solo album": a literary "summer hit," a collection of episodes crafted like pop songs, each with its own "chorus" and "solo," and an assault on the boundaries between rock music and literature underlined by the "gig"-like character of his public readings.[6] A recurrent feature of the reception of the whole trilogy has been the conflation of its author's star persona with his protagonist in a manner characteristic of the public engagement with pop texts.[7] Typically, commentators have seen Frank Lehmann's melancholy disposition as an extension of a central trait of Regener's songwriting and interpreted Lehmann in turn as an autobiographical figure.[8]

In dealing with the media, Regener has in turn proven an astute figure, willing to accept the interest in him as a star with modesty and to embrace the language associated with pop to describe his characteristic "Lehmann sound."[9] With their male protagonist who (until *Der kleine Bruder*) avoids responsibility, the essential gender differences they posit, and their often ironic tone, the Frank Lehmann novels draw on a vein of internationally popular fiction that is exemplified by Nick Hornby in English but has been given a German twist also by figures like Frank

Goosen, the author of *Liegen lernen* (Learning to lie down, 2001).[10] Whether the novels' classic style of narration, in the third person but using free indirect discourse to construct Frank Lehmann as their focalizer, truly exemplifies a pop aesthetic is less certain. There are, if one follows Sabine von Dirke's recent attempt at a precise definition of the phenomenon, manifest contiguities — for instance, the novels' focus on daily life and, at least in *Der kleine Bruder*, the mobilization of an aesthetic of the surface.[11] Yet it is harder to see in Regener's novels the characteristic de-emphasis of plot and character, the formal emulation of the electronic media, or the demonstration of a new understanding of the function of the author in a media society.[12] On the contrary, Regener has proven, on the face of it, an altogether more conservative figure in his insistence on the discrete nature of his activities as a musician and as a writer. As he put it in 2008, though not for the first time: "Writing songs and lyrics is simply a different discipline from writing novels. . . . In the way that bowling and golf are different."[13] In his statements, this pose is coupled with the expression of the refusal of the tendency to fold his rock-star persona into his writing and to conflate the author and protagonist of the Lehmann works. Regener has stated his case calmly, as for instance when he explained to the *Stuttgarter Zeitung* in 2004 that, while he was himself familiar with aspects of Frank Lehmann's life, he would never dream of writing an autobiographical work.[14] He has asserted it more bluntly, too, explaining to the *Frankfurter Rundschau* (also in 2004) that *Neue Vahr Süd* was "nicht meine Scheiß-Autobiographie" (not my goddamn autobiography).[15]

The story in *Der kleine Bruder* of how Frank Lehmann successfully establishes himself in Berlin-Kreuzberg — in less than forty-eight hours — itself offers a fictional intervention in the contest over Regener's work. While the novel's narrative of personal development largely retracts the somber and downbeat conclusion of *Herr Lehmann*, it also challenges widely held assumptions about the figure of Frank Lehmann and marks the fictional difference between protagonist and author. Indeed, the reception of the novel shows how Regener sought to use the text to assert his authority over and his distance from his literary creation. On the one hand, it was not lost on reviewers how the previously seemingly indolent Frank Lehmann had now discovered, as Ursula März put it in *Die Zeit*, a surprising capacity for activity.[16] On the other hand, this unexpected turn offered Regener the opportunity to provide an explanation, and his explanation emphasized the practical and unmusical disposition that differentiated Frank Lehmann from him. As he observed in *Sonntag* around the same time, making a barbed aside at some of the comments expressed about *Herr Lehmann*: "He likes what he is doing. . . . I find it regrettable that a literary figure is thought to be a good-for-nothing who does not develop simply because he works in a bar and likes it."[17]

The motor of the plot is Lehmann's search for his brother Manfred, whom he knows as Manni, but who is known in Berlin-Kreuzberg as Freddie. The narrative picks up where *Neue Vahr Süd* left off, with Lehmann and his companion Wolli driving along the transit route from the Federal Republic to West Berlin, each with the intention of starting a new life — Wolli in a house occupied by punks, Frank Lehmann with the help of his brother. It ends with the discovery of Freddie's whereabouts after Frank moves, with Karl and other new friends from his brother's communal living situation in the apartment of the bar owner Erwin Kächele, to a new apartment above his future workplace, the Einfall bar. In the intervening time, the major developments include Frank Lehmann's discovery of his vocation selling drinks and his acquisition of a fresh set of values. He discovers his vocation at a raucous musical performance after the original vendor of beer cans is injured by a projectile. Having stepped in to save the day, he loses himself in mastering the intricate movements of stacking and selling the cans, which are described at length:

> He sold und sold, until his head was spinning from turning round for fresh supplies, and so he stacked all the remaining packs of beer on the ground next to him in such a way that he could scoop them up with a single movement and . . . swing them onto the table so that the surrounding plastic split at the point where he was holding them . . . and then he sold and sold, and felt peaceful thinking of nothing else.[18]

The novel echoes Lehmann's claim in *Herr Lehmann* that his work selling drinks is a job that consists in giving a purpose (literally, "life-contents" or *Lebensinhalt*) to other people's lives.[19] However, it grounds this claim in a pragmatic vision of self-realization for Lehmann himself. Likewise, *Der kleine Bruder* gives a definitely positive twist to Lehmann's embrace of the idea that he encounters in Kreuzberg that everything is *scheißegal* (all the same).[20] As he sells the beer cans at the gig, this apparently apathetic cast of mind appears as the enlightened acceptance that one take things — "at least those that are positive" (71) — as they come.

Lehmann's pragmatic self-realization is thrown into relief by two other figures in the novel. The first is Wolli, with whom he drives to Berlin. Unlike Lehmann, Wolli has visited Kreuzberg before, having attended a musical event for conscripts and soldiers of the reserve organized by the Communist League of West Berlin (he plays tuba). On this occasion, he had recognized that the communist cells that were part of the landscape of radical politics after 1968 were in decline, and he opted to become a punk. On the transit route, Wolli advises Lehmann on life in West Berlin from his position of privileged knowledge: "You can't do anything wrong here. . . . Living in Berlin is like playing tuba: the main thing is that you just let go!" (18). Yet Wolli fails to settle among Kreuzberg's punks and finally he borrows money from Lehmann to return to Bremen. The other figure is Freddie, who remains an elusive figure as Frank searches for him. The other inhabitants of Erwin Kächele's apartment barely know him, and there is no trace of his metal artwork either in his rented atelier or in the nearby Galerie Plastik. Freddie turns up at the close in an anonymous hotel near the Kurfürstendamm (or Kudamm), West Berlin's famous shopping boulevard, where he is participating in trials for the pharmaceutical company Secumedic to raise cash to move from Berlin to New York. In the novel, Frank Lehmann displaces Freddie. Greeted initially as Freddie's brother, he takes Freddie's place in his apartment, and by the close is known rather as "young Lehmann" (234).

Implicitly, the novel also underlines the fictional distance of Lehmann from Regener that he had asserted in his comments on the text. The sense of purpose that Lehmann finds in serving drinks is pointedly coupled with a lack of interest in the musical scene where Element of Crime had its roots. An example is the musical performance where, the text notes laconically, the music being played "was not his thing" and Lehmann rather concentrates on serving (71–72). If this lack of interest makes Lehmann an unusual figure in the Kreuzberg represented in the text, his relation to his environment, after all, exhibits something of the "sympathetic" irony that Robert Menasse ascribes to the prose of Daniel Kehlmann. For Menasse, this is less the conventional literary irony that exists in the distance between the surface of the text and its meaning. Rather, it rests on an act of identification between the reader and a central figure with the productive distance — the "feeling ironic" described by Braun in her chapter — that defines that figure's relation to the world.[21]

Mapping Kreuzberg in *Der kleine Bruder*

The narrative of Frank Lehmann's personal development is intimately tied to the space of Berlin-Kreuzberg in which it unfolds. The pragmatic character ascribed to Frank Lehmann in *Der kleine Bruder* stands in marked contrast to the novel's direct appeal to the cultish qualities associated with the Kreuzberg milieu. From the 1960s until the 1990s, it was in the postal area of Kreuzberg SO36, rather than in the more slightly more affluent Kreuzberg SO61, that the district's famous alternative subcultures flourished.[22] The character of SO36 was decisively shaped by the fact of the Berlin Wall, which enclosed it on three sides: along the river Spree to the north and along the right-angle formed by the Landwehrkanal to the southeast and the south.[23] This transformed a once-busy neighborhood near the historic center of Berlin into an enclave on the margins of West Berlin and led to the departure of some of its traditional working-class population and the neglect of its housing stock. On account of its demilitarized and inter-Allied status, West Berlin as a whole was a magnet for young men from the FRG who were keen to avoid conscription. Kreuzberg SO36, in particular, became a favored destination for bohemians in the 1960s, political radicals after 1968, and a plurality of groups attracted to living out alternative lifestyles from the late 1970s into the 1980s.[24] These groups lived, often squatting in unused apartment buildings, alongside a growing immigrant population and the remainders of the working-class population in what has become known as the "Kreuzberg mix."[25]

According to the ethnologist Barbara Lang, symbolic narratives about Kreuzberg SO36 have lent the area a mythic dimension. A recurring topos is its construction as doubly "other" — politically and culturally alien to West Berlin in the same way that West Berlin was exterritorial to the FRG. This twofold otherness underlined the meaning of SO36 as a site where individuals broke decisively with the past and practiced radical forms of self-fashioning.[26] Since 1990, Lang claims, this myth has been inflected by the knowledge of the decline of the area's alternative subcultures.[27] Narratives such as Kits Hilaire's *Berlin dernière* (1990) — and *Herr Lehmann*, too — have cast SO36 in a nostalgic light and invoked the prospect of its gentrification after 1990. If gentrification, too, has emerged as a powerful motif in discourses about Kreuzberg, this has, despite the efforts of urban planners and of government, only fitfully been realized.[28]

The narrative of *Der kleine Bruder* is marked by a relative unity of space and time. Following his arrival at the novel's start, Lehmann leaves Kreuzberg SO36 only once near the end to speak to Freddie. His search for Freddie turns him from a first-time visitor to West Berlin, entranced by the lights of the Kudamm, into a Kreuzberg inhabitant who opts finally to avoid the glitzy commercialism of the center. What is so striking compared to *Herr Lehmann*, however, is the relative lack of nostalgia with which *Der kleine Bruder* treats what Lang calls the "Kreuzberg myth." Where *Herr Lehmann* looked back wistfully at an anomaly destined to be consigned to history, *Der kleine Bruder* reaffirms the Kreuzberg SO36 of the early 1980s and reinscribes it within the space of the district. The novel reasserts its marginal status, maps out its terrain, and vividly brings parts of its subculture to life, though less in a spirit of mourning for a lost utopia than in a playful (re-)performance or simulation of the original scene. The context in which it implicitly does so are the dominant spatial-political discourses since the 1990s about the unification of Berlin and its transformation into the capital of the FRG and a modern metropolis.[29] Here, too, less visibly than *Herr Lehmann*, the novel raises the specter of the demise of the alternative scene near the end.

The opening account of Frank and Wolli's journey through the GDR serves to reestablish the separation of West Berlin from the rest of the FRG. The "very dark darkness of the transit route" (6) appears as a long tunnel, at the end of which the bright lights of the border checkpoint at

Dreilinden emerges out of the darkness with the alien appearance of "a freshly landed space ship" (9). Beyond this, there is more darkness, until suddenly West Berlin rises as a forbidding concrete mass next to the motorway (13).

In turn, Kreuzberg is positioned marginally within West Berlin. Frank and Wolli enter Berlin without a street map and in the absence of signs pointing to their destination must follow the directions either to the International Congress Center or to the Kurfürstendamm and the district of Wilmersdorf (11). They pick the latter and the Kudamm appears to be as much of a tunnel as the transit was, albeit, with its lights, an initially alluring one. The would-be Kreuzberger Wolli's explanation that the Kudamm is a destination for tourists rather than for locals prompts from Lehmann the bemused riposte that neither he nor Wolli can claim to be locals. Though Wolli fails to find his place in Kreuzberg, Lehmann does, and in the final words of the text affirms its separation from the commercialized center of West Berlin. As he leaves Freddie's hotel near the Kudamm, he glances around, musing that "it is time I got out of here" (282).

The lack of a street map is significant for the treatment of SO36 in the novel. Without a map to chart its topography and situate it with respect to surrounding areas, Lehmann is compelled to trace out the syntax for the area himself as he traverses it on foot in search of Freddie. This search provides him with "a feeling of how everything fits together" (179) and creates an urban landscape in which significant locations anchor a network of interconnected streets. Named streets mark out the topographical parameters occupied by Kreuzberg's alternative scene. At the very center stands the occupied house in the Naunynstraße, from which the narrative unfolds the terrain and to which Lehmann returns several times. First, this is where he drops Wolli off to join the punks in the rear of the house. He returns there upon learning that Freddie has his atelier in the front, which houses an artists collective. It is here, lastly, that the self-styled leader of the collective reveals to Lehmann that he owns the property and that its occupation by the artists had been a *Hausbesetzungssimulation* (simulated house squat; 185) ruined by the arrival of the punks to squat for real.

From the Naunynstraße, Lehmann's search widens to cover all of Kreuzberg SO36. It takes him from Erwin Kächele's apartment in the Reichenbergerstraße to the club Die Zone (the zone) in Oranienstraße, where the musical performance takes place, and from the Galerie Plastik in the Dieffenbachstraße, which once exhibited Freddie's artwork, to the corner of the Wiener Straße and the Ohlauer Straße, the location of the Einfall bar and the apartment into which he, Karl, and others finally move. Predictably, the name of the club, Die Zone, gives rise to a comic misunderstanding when the new arrival Frank assumes that Karl is taking him into the GDR — "the zone" was a pejorative term used in the West for

GDR as the former Soviet occupation zone. This misunderstanding high-lights the inward-looking character of Kreuzberg's alternative scene, which was a world in itself. Significantly, however, the novel repeatedly retraces the borders of SO36 to the GDR along the Berlin Wall. Near the Pfuehlstraße, for example, Frank and Karl make out the row of lights behind the Wall on the other side of the River Spree near the site of the ruined Oberbaumbrücke. On another occasion, they ascend one of the viewing platforms on the Western side:

> Frank had always imagined that the city just continued behind the Wall, but now he saw for the first time how wide the corridor was which had been drawn between the houses to make room for fields of sand, paths, walls, fences, watchtowers, and tall lamps that bathed everything in an unreal yellow light. The other city was more than a hundred meters away. (192)

In the novel, this scene offers an uncharacteristically sober moment of reflection on the border at the edge of Kreuzberg SO36 as a scar running through a divided city.

Within the parameters mapped out thus, the episodic narrative offers what one reviewer aptly describes as an "ethno-typology" of Kreuzberg's diverse cultures and subcultures.[30] An episode in the Krahl-Eck pub, for instance, affords a glimpse of the life world of the district's working-class population, though in a spirit of inverse snobbery the Krahl-Eck turns out to be a favored haunt of the leader of the art collective in the Naunynstraße. With its standing-height tables, Frank Lehmann recognizes it as a place for "other, older, and local people" that serves various kinds of schnapps and the traditional *Schmalzbrot* (bread and drippings; 102). The old-fashioned music playing here includes Freddie Quinn's 1963 hit "Junge, komm bald wieder" (Come home soon, my son), in which a young man who has gone to sea relates his mother's pleas to return home. This song serves as an ironic comment both on Freddie's disappearance and on Lehmann's departure to begin a new life in Berlin. The novel also points to the inter-face between Kreuzberg's immigrant population and its alternative subcul-tures in restaurants and in a network of stalls selling kebabs and beer. (The beer is the local Schultheiss rather than his favored Beck's from his native Bremen, which Lehmann recognizes as a commodity absent from Kreuzberg.) Though Karl and the Turkish man in the stall where he takes Lehmann seem familiar with one another, this is, as in *Herr Lehmann*, a limited and regulated point of contact between an immigrant and a German population that, for Regener, existed in parallel worlds and did not otherwise meet.[31]

Like *Herr Lehmann*, *Der kleine Bruder* strips the alternative subcul-tures of Kreuzberg SO36 of their political impetus.[32] Even into the late 1980s, the radical and anarchist currents that gave the district its distinct character were capable of erupting into violent protest.[33] In running jokes about the suspicion that outsiders are undercover policemen or the assumption that Lehmann's military haircut makes him a principled deserter from the army, however, *Der kleine Bruder* defuses antiestablishment politics. Rather, the text foregrounds an increasingly pluralistic experimentation with alternative lifestyles that was an expression of — but also became disassociated from — these politics.[34] Regener's Kreuzberg SO36 also comprises figures who undercut the claim to alternative, experimental lifestyles. These include the bar owner and entrepreneur Kächele, who proves quite conventional when his girlfriend becomes pregnant and he dissolves the cooperative living situation in his own apartment, offering Frank and Karl the one over the Einfall instead. However, the novel foregrounds two elements of Kreuzberg's alternative scene in particular: the punk subculture around Wolli and the artistic scene around the absent Freddie.

Lehmann's major encounter with the punks comes when he and Karl stumble into the Honka bar. Here, to intolerably loud music, the assembled punks perch on their stools like sinister black birds, staring in a fashion so hostile that Lehmann wonders whether permission is needed to enter. The punks appear in the text as suspicious, indolent, and greedy. Silence follows when Karl enquires whether there is anyone working in the bar who can help him. The punks complain bitterly at the artists in the Naunynstraße when these cut off the electricity to the rear of the house because they did not want to *mitbezahlen* — help pay for the punks (119). It is they who push Wolli into leaving by forcing him to pay into all manner of funds and kitties until he is bled dry. These include funds for provisions and for "winter preparations" (which to Frank Lehmann sounds like something from the Eastern Front under National Socialism; 194–95).

The other milieu that characterizes the image of the Kreuzberg of the early 1980s in *Der kleine Bruder* is its artistic subculture. With Freddie being a sculptor, Frank Lehmann's search inevitably involves encounters with a range of figures: aspiring artists like Karl, who hopes to exhibit his own constructions in the upcoming Skin of the City exhibition; artists-cum-performers like the collective in the Naunynstraße, which doubles up as an avant-garde rock band; or exhibitors like Almut in the Galerie Plastik. What defines the activities of this scene in the novel are above all the aspects of "performance" and "simulation" (234, 185) that they put into play. Beyond the fact that many activities engaged in by these figures are staged, the self-fulfilling and performative impulse at their heart is spelled out to Lehmann by Karl when he explains to him: "Art is when someone says it is art. . . . If needs be, I can say this. . . . Then it is art" (201). The idea of simulation comes into view, of course, in the simulated house squat staged by leader of the collective in the Naunynstraße — a simulation turned into a reality by the presence of the punks in the back of the house. While the narrative focus on the pragmatic point of view of Frank Lehmann makes for a sometimes bemused and quizzical treatment of Kreuzberg's artists, *Der kleine Bruder* also and self-consciously acknowledges how — in the Skin of the City exhibition, for instance — their practices shaped and sustained the "Kreuzberg myth."

Indeed, it is precisely as "performance" and "simulation" that *Der kleine Bruder* itself largely dispenses with the valedictory tone of *Herr Lehmann*. Where *Herr Lehmann* bids the Kreuzberg of the 1980s a nostalgic farewell in the knowledge of its demise, *Der kleine Bruder*, on the one hand, projects West Berlin as a stage or film set (*Kulisse*, 14) on which Frank Lehmann acts out the process of his self-realization and on which Kreuzberg SO36 is brought back to life. On the other hand, the resurrection of SO36, which proceeds as a mapping out of the terrain and its repopulation with elements of its subcultures, has something of the quality of what Baudrillard names the "simulacrum." With the simulacrum, it is no longer "imaginary coextensivity" that governs the relationship between the territory and the map but rather the "resurrection [of referentials] in a system of signs" or a "substituting [of] signs of the real for the real itself."[35] In the way it unfolds the terrain of SO36 as simulation, or dramatizes the slippage of sign and reality in the simulated squat, *Der kleine Bruder* is Regener's work that most closely mirrors the aesthetics of the surface in German-speaking pop literature.[36] Yet here, in the end, the knowledge of the demise of the alternative subcultures of Kreuzberg cannot be banished and it returns as an element of a historical reality that pierces the seamlessness of the performance or simulation of the Kreuzberg scene. The manner of Freddie's discovery is in itself indicative of the limitations of a Kreuzberg that appears in the novel as entirely male-dominated. It transpires that Chrissie, Kächele's niece, had known all along where Freddie was, but had kept silent because no one had presumed that she as a woman was worth asking. But it is Freddie's prediction, under the influence of the psychotropic drugs he is testing, which offers a baleful reminder of the rupture to come. "Berlin is too small," he intones, declaring his intention of making for the wider horizons of New York. "In a few years it will be all over, then it will be like [the provincial town of] Verden an der Aller here" (279).

Notwithstanding the shadow cast here, *Der kleine Bruder* still offers an upbeat ending as Lehmann returns from the Kudamm to Kreuzberg. When it appeared in 2008, the novel thus offered a largely affirmative conclusion to the Frank Lehmann trilogy as a whole, and perhaps a curious one in view of its lopsided chronology, in which *Der kleine Bruder*, which plays in the early 1980s, sets itself against the more sober conclusion of the earlier *Herr Lehmann*, which ended later with the fall of the Wall. It is fascinating to consider this fact and the affirmation of Lehmann that it offers, as this chapter did at the outset, in the context of the negotiation, beyond the text, of its author's celebrity as a rock musician and emerging writer. However, its treatment of Frank Lehmann's quest for personal identity and its engagement with the memory and meaning of Berlin Kreuzberg before 1989 are what in the end makes *Der kleine Bruder* a memorable novel. On the one hand, the novel offers an affirmation of Lehmann that resists the interpretation that this figure performs the cult and celebrity status of Sven Regener as the author of the text. On the other hand, Lehmann appears as the lynchpin of a performance or simulation of the Kreuzberg scene of the 1980s in all its mythic dimensions as the novel lays claims to cult status for its protagonist in his own right.

Notes

1 *Das literarische Quartett*, ZDF, 17 August 2001.

2 Dirk Niefanger, "Der Autor und sein Label. Überlegungen zur *fonction classificatoire* Foucaults (mit Fallstudien zu Langbehn und Kracauer)," in *Autorschaft. Positionen und Revisionen. DFG-Symposium*, ed. Heinrich Detering (Stuttgart: Metzler, 2002), 521–39; here, 521–22. See also Florian Hartling, *Der digitale Autor. Autorschaft im Zeitalter des Internets* (Bielefeld: transcript Verlag, 2009), 84–85.

3 "Piaf statt Punk. Zu Besuch bei Sven Regener — Vom Element-of-Crime Popstar zum Teilzeitschriftsteller," *Rheinischer Merkur*, 4 January 2002, 31; no author given.

4 "Piaf statt Punk," 31.

5 Jan Ulrich Welke, "Das Leben ist eine Geisterbahn. Sven Regener komplettiert mit 'Der kleine Bruder' seine verblüffende Lehmann-Trilogie," *Stuttgarter Zeitung*, 4 September 2008, 31.

6 Marius Meller, "Unser Sommerbuch: Sven Regener greift mit seinem Debüt, dem Kiez-Roman 'Herr Lehmann' zu einem neuen Instrument, zur Prosagitarre," *Frankfurter Rundschau*, 30 August 2001, 19; Thomas Steinfeld, "Aber dann, aber dann: Kreuzberger Hosenträger sind lang. Sven Regener kehrt bei Herrn Lehmann, dem Zapfer, ein und spendiert ihm einen Roman und zwanzig Biere," *Süddeutsche Zeitung*, 17 August 2001, 15.

7 Niefanger, "Der Autor und sein Label," in *Autorschaft*, ed. Detering, 522.

8 For instance, "Piaf statt Punk," 31.

9 "Mein Sound. Mit 'Der kleine Bruder' schließt Sven Regener seine 'Herr Lehmann'-Trilogie ab. Ein Trip ins alte Westberlin," *Neues Deutschland*, 16 September, 2008, 10; no author given.

10 Andrew Plowman, "'Was will ich als Westdeutscher erzählen?': The 'old' West and globalisation in recent German prose," in *German Literature in the Age of Globalisation*, ed. Stuart Taberner (Birmingham: Birmingham UP, 2004), 47–56; here, 57.

[11] Sabine von Dirke, "Pop Literature in the Berlin Republic," in *Contemporary German Fiction: Writing in the Berlin Republic*, ed. Stuart Taberner (Cambridge: CUP, 2007), 108–34; here 109.

[12] von Dirke, "Pop Literature," in *Contemporary German Fiction*, ed. Taberner, 110.

[13] "Im Gespräch: Sven Regener. Wieso kann man Romane nicht singen, Herr Regener?," *Frankfurter Allgemeine Zeitung*, 23 August 2008, "Bilder und Zeiten," Z6.

[14] "Rauchende Trümmer. Sven Regener hat seinen Romanhelden wiederbelebt," *Stuttgarter Zeitung*, 8 September 2004, 25.

[15] "Bloß kein Lampenfieber. Sven Regener, Autor des Erfolgsromans 'Herr Lehmann' über die Kunst der Sinnlosigkeit und die Melodie der Worte," *Frankfurter Rundschau*, 8 July 2004, 30; no author given.

[16] Ursula März, "Abschied vom Lehmannismus. Der vermutlich letzte Teil von Sven Regeners Lehmann-Trilogie," *Die Zeit*, 1 October 2008, 60.

[17] "'Wer gegen Schwaben ist, ist auch Rassist.' Die Multikulti-Lüge, der Kiez-Muff und die kleine Welt der Spiegel-Redakteuren. Wer sich das Denken zu einfach macht, bekommt mit Sven Regener zu tun," *Sonntag*, 24 August 2008, 51; no author given.

[18] Sven Regener, *Der kleine Bruder* (Frankfurt am Main: Eichborn, 2008), 70. All translations are my own. Subsequent page references appear in parentheses in main body of the text.

[19] Sven Regener, *Herr Lehmann* (Frankfurt am Main: Eichborn, 2001), 58.

[20] Compare Regener, *Herr Lehmann*, 87.

[21] Robert Menasse, "'Ich bin wie alle, so wie nur ich es sein kann': Daniel Kehlmanns Essays über Autoren und Bücher," *text+kritik* 177 (2008): 30–35; here, 32–33. I am grateful to Rebecca Braun for drawing my attention to the way Menasse's comments on Kehlmann could be made fruitful for a reading of Regener's work.

[22] See also Barbara Mennel, "Political Nostalgia and Local Memory: The Kreuzberg of the 1980s in Contemporary German Film," *The Germanic Review* 82, no. 1 (2007): 54–77; here, 57–58.

[23] Barbara Lang, *Mythos Kreuzberg. Ethnographie eines Stadtteils 1961–1995* (Frankfurt am Main: Campus Verlag, 1998), 17.

[24] Lang, *Mythos Kreuzberg*, 103–5.

[25] Mennel, "Political Nostalgia and Local Memory," 54–55.

[26] Lang, *Mythos Kreuzberg*, 26 and 46.

[27] Lang, *Mythos Kreuzberg*, 44.

[28] Ingo Bader and Martin Bialluch, "Gentrification and the Creative Class in Berlin Kreuzberg," in *Whose Urban Renaissance: An International Comparison of Urban Renaissance Strategies*, ed. Libby Porter and Kate Shaw (Abingdon: Routledge, 2009), 93–102; here, 102.

[29] Karen E. Till, *The New Berlin: Memory, Politics, Place* (Minneapolis: U of Minnesota P, 2005), 31–40.

[30] Maike Albath, "Sven Regeners Lehmann-Trilogie: 'Trink, Brüderlein, trink.' Jeder Szenenwechsel beschert dem verblüfften Frank Lehmann die Bekanntschaft mit weiteren charakteristischen Kreuzberger Gewächsen," *Frankfurter Rundschau*, 6 October 2008, 22.

[31] "Wer gegen Schwaben ist, ist auch Rassist," 51.

[32] Stefano Beretta, "Kreuzberg 36 und die Bremer Lehrjahre: Zu Sven Regeners Romanen *Herr Lehmann* und *Neue Vahr Süd*," in *Gedächtnis und Identität: Die deutsche Literatur nach der Vereinigung*, ed. Fabrizio Cambi (Würzburg: Königshausen & Neumann, 2008), 99–109; here, 103.

[33] Beretta, "Kreuzberg 36," in *Gedächtnis und Identität*, ed. Cambi, 103.

[34] Lang, *Mythos Kreuzberg*, 155–58.

[35] See "Simulacra and Simulations" in Jean Baudrillard, *Selected Writings*, ed. Mark Poster (Stanford: Stanford U P, 1988), 166–84; here, 167.

[36] See also Frank Degler and Ute Paulokat, *Neue Deutsche Popliteratur* (Munich: W. Fink, 2008), 112.

15: Kathrin Schmidt, *Du stirbst nicht:* A Woman's Quest for Agency

Sonja E. Klocke

IN THE FALL OF 2009, Kathrin Schmidt found herself in the limelight when she was awarded the prestigious German Book Prize for her novel *Du stirbst nicht* (You are not going to die). This honor suggests that Schmidt, previously known only to a small audience, now emerges as an eminent writer who enjoys the potential to stand the test of time. The judges emphasize that "the novel tells a story of regaining the world. . . . [This] individual tale of a return from the brink of death is positioned both unobtrusively and with great skill in the echo chamber of the historical-political era of change."[1] While politics are much less important than in Kathrin Schmidt's earlier novels, *Du stirbst nicht* seems significant because it is much more than a tale of illness and recovery. It is a woman's quest for agency and positionality, which has been altered due to her ailment and changed by a love affair outside the heteronormative realm even before she fell ill. Born in Gotha (GDR) in 1958 and trained as a psychologist, Schmidt was engaged in the Berlin Round Table talks for the opposition movement during the so-called *Wende* (1989/90). She debuted in the GDR as a poet, and published her first novel, *Die Gunnar-Lennefsen-Expedition* (The Gunnar-Lennefsen expedition) in 1998. Her first three novels investigate family and world history, essentially focusing on incidents from the former GDR that cast their clouds over the present of individuals in unified Germany. Set in the GDR, *Die Gunnar-Lennefsen-Expedition* rewrites German and European history, contradicting hegemonic historiography with a radical feminist point of view. Like her subsequent novels, *Koenigs Kinder* (Koenig's children, 2002) and *Seebachs schwarze Katzen* (Seebach's black cats, 2005), it sports a distinctive writing style that evokes magic realism in the South American tradition, Günter Grass, and particularly the late East German author Irmtraud Morgner.

By comparison, *Du stirbst nicht* is stylistically much less challenging, something Schmidt suggests might explain the wider public reception of the novel.[2] I would even argue that the less problematic access to the novel might have aided the decision to award Kathrin Schmidt the German Book

Prize. After all, *Du stirbst nicht* promises to sell well and serves to establish Schmidt as an emerging writer for a larger audience. Nonetheless, complex fictional characters whose lives are impacted by earlier emotional injuries and who reveal the author's training in psychology — as well as frequently ribald language — mark Schmidt's writing. Whereas the previous three novels depict the erotic, here the physicality of the language positions the protagonist's illness, her damaged body, and the slow healing process at the center of the narrative. *Du stirbst nicht* demonstrates that the body receives and (continually) changes its identity as the protagonist acquires knowledge about her own past and her illness. But while central characters of Schmidt's earlier works, for example, Josepha in *Die Gunnar-Lennefsen-Expedition*, possess a body into which cultural and historical knowledge is inscribed, Helene Wesendahl's body in *Du stirbst nicht* stands apart from wider social and cultural discourses.

Du stirbst nicht conveys the main character's experience of waking up from a coma after an aneurysm had ruptured in her brain and caused a stroke. Helene's recovery is a slow and painful process in which she learns to come to terms with her illness, and struggles to regain her language, speech, physical abilities, and memory. This also includes her life in the disintegrating GDR, the *Wende*, and the years between unification and the beginning of the twenty-first century, but these few political events are not linked with the protagonist's body. While history and politics are not entirely absent from the account of her return from the brink of death, her *Körpergedächtnis* (bodily memory) pertains exclusively to her individual memory, highlighting the ways in which her physical body and her personal history are related.[3]

Du stirbst nicht

In *Du stirbst nicht*, Schmidt entwines her own experience of a torn aneurysm in her brain, two weeks in a coma, various operations, and a lengthy recuperation with a fictional story. The resultant tale incorporates three intermingling narrative strands: Helene's gradual healing process; the trials and final restoration of her marriage with her husband Matthes; and her reconstruction of a complicated, unplanned love affair with the late Viola, formerly Viktor, a transsexual with whom she had fallen in love before she became ill.[4] When Helene Wesendahl wakes up from an artificially induced coma, she only gradually grasps the realities of the hospital. She escapes her nightmares and delusions of the hospital staff aiming to take her life, and begins to rediscover herself. Step by step, Helene remembers her name, initiates the taxing quest for her identity, and recalls her husband and children. Still, she has entirely lost control over her body, including the ability to speak. For a professional writer who realizes that she speaks inwardly but remains mute toward the outward world, this loss of language is particularly grave.

Helene reflects on her lack of language and the discourses cultivated in the hospital and discovers fresh sentences for the speechlessness and alienation that previously characterized her marriage and now pertain to her relationship with the sick body. She gradually understands that her marriage was already about to fall apart before she collapsed, and was also jeopardized by her love affair with Viola. Most excruciating, though, are her attempts to regain agency and her quest for positionality, understood by Leslie Adelson as a set of specific social and discursive relations constituting her agency at a particular point in time.[5] This enduring procedure forces the protagonist to pay attention to personality traits that she had chosen to ignore in the past. In fact, she realizes during the course of this tedious process that she has changed — both due to the specifics of her disease and the reflections about who she is, which resulted from her ailment.

Narrative Structure

The title "You are not going to die" corresponds with the last sentence of the novel, uttered by Helene's husband immediately after her aneurysm has burst (348); it serves as a frame for this tale of recovery. The ending of the novel pertains to the beginning of the patient's calamity, while the text actually commences with Helene awakening in an intensive care unit. Her quest for her positionality is at the center of the novel. It depends both on Helene's current position as a patient, and on the life she led and the personal relationships she cultivated before she fell ill. Yearning for stability, she aspires to create coherence both on the biographical and on the social level by recovering her past. As a consequence, her positionality changes as she successfully engages in the exhausting yet indispensable memory work, accepts the illness as part of who she is, understands her present situation in the medical institution, and deals with her language deficiencies.

The narrative supports Helene's desire for stability by increasingly frequent and extensive flashbacks. These force the protagonist to realize that, preceding her illness, her positionality has already been under considerable strain due to her love affair with Viola. This relationship challenged the heteronormative model governing her previous life, and posed a threat to her marriage with Matthes. The patient's illness and resulting memory loss can therefore be understood to *initiate* the mental journey during which she gradually regains agency. This process depends on Helene's ability to overcome her lack of memory and her language deficiencies, both of which initially contest her desire for the discovery of her positionality. The fragile, often fragmentary memories resist full reconstruction and the text thus problematizes the process of remembering.

The two levels underlying the protagonist's struggle for her new positionality — the present in the hospital and the layers of her past — are replicated on the level of the narrative. *Du stirbst nicht* does not merely begin with a portrayal of the protagonist in her hospital bed, but immediately relates her perception of the surroundings: "There is a clattering noise all around her."[6] The initial sentence, in the German version in all-capital letters, highlights the narrator's familiarity with the patient's auditory sensations. It establishes the narrative voice's proximity to the protagonist despite the third-person narration and the impersonal phrasing, which places the protagonist as object rather than subject.

The heterodiegetic narrative voice, incongruent with the experiencing persona, jumps to Helene's memories in the second sentence, which is motivated by the clattering sound: "When her sister married, their mother put the silver cutlery in a metal dish, bedded on aluminum foil, and then covered it with hot salty water" (6). This is then followed by the protagonist's reported thoughts, "So who's getting married? She tries to open her eyes. No chance. . . . But she can clearly hear her mother's voice" (6). *Du stirbst nicht*'s initial paragraph thus establishes the narrative situation for the entire novel: it comprises an intimate heterodiegetic narrative voice familiar with the protagonist's feelings, thoughts, and physical state, and of two interacting and alternating narrative levels. Particularly poignant when describing the inner world of the ailing woman, the malfunctioning of the sick body, and, later, the experience of slowly regaining the world, the narrative voice ranges between compassionate, uncannily laconic, and mocking. Moreover, the first few sentences highlight the ways that memory and the level of narration impact each other: the sound prompting the patient's memory is caused in the hospital, on the diegetic level of the basic narration; it prompts a memory of the family wedding, an insertion on the intradiegetic level, which leads to the patient's unsuccessful attempt to open her eyes on the diegetic level. This pattern is repeated throughout the entire narrative, and highlights the relation between memory, the body, and language.

Accepting Illness as Part of a New Positionality

Due to her lack of memory, Helene's struggle for her positionality commences predominantly on the diegetic level. She has difficulties recognizing her family members and does not understand her illness. Misinterpreting the intravenous drip as a means to connect her to a network that allows her to be remote-controlled (9, 12), and believing that she is at the mercy of a "bunch of murderers" (11) that wants to kill her as well as everybody else in the hospital, Helene displays her inability to separate her imaginary inner world from the realities of the hospital.

More agonizing still is her lack of self-image. The narrator relates her terror: "What *does* she look like? She doesn't know any more, she hasn't got a picture of herself. These people have stolen it from her!" (13). Already relieved when she recognizes herself in a photograph a few days later (20), the protagonist is keen to catch a glimpse of her own reflection in the bathroom mirror. Following Lacan's concept of subject configuration in the mirror stage, Helene attempts to repeat a child's belief in recognizing herself as an integral entity while ignoring her factual dependency and powerlessness. Unlike a child, however, the protagonist is torn when confronted with her own reflection. While she acknowledges that the image in the mirror belongs to her, she also emphasizes that it has become estranged. The hair on her left has been replaced by little red points, which were caused by the metal clips that were inserted after the brain operations (30–31). Helene's image is thus already fragmented. Her helplessness supports Foucault's notion that any intervention with the body entails the deprivation of the individual's liberty.[7] In fact, the protagonist senses this deficit of autonomy most severely when the combination of her pacemaker and the metal inserts in her head force her to accept that she is alive only thanks to the medical technology inside her body.

While she evokes the cyborg described by Donna Haraway as hybrid of machine and organism,[8] the fact that she does so unwillingly does not allow for reading the protagonist as disrupting traditional categories as a subversive act. Helene experiences the increasing amounts of "metal parts in head and breast" and the resulting dissolution of the human/machine as well as the gendered nature/culture binaries as part of a questionable fate that "pleaded for her kicking the bucket early," yet also "wanted her to live in the age of medical high technology," and thus "effectively averaged itself out by allowing for a compensation" (238, my trans.). Like the characters in Kathrin Schmidt's previous novels, Helene is, at least to some degree, subject to fate. In *Die Gunnar-Lennefsen-Expedition*, characters are at the mercy of various gods and goddesses who manipulate everyone's destiny, while characters in *Koenigs Kinder* and in *Seebachs schwarze Katzen* cannot escape the influence of "love, that whore," and "the old woman, that hag called time."[9]

Helene can neither escape her family and her complicated love relationships, nor the effects of her illness or modern medical technology. Still, the patient fights for her life, and thus to some extent against fate, while she learns to endure the limitations of human agency. She starts to identify with her estranged image, and as a result begins to understand her illness (30–31). Like a child imagining her body as integrated and contained, in opposition to her actual motor incapacity and the sense of the body as fragmented, Helene demonstrates what Lacan calls the shift from "insufficiency to anticipation."[10] The protagonist's mirror image, strange and alienated yet recognizable, thus aids her in the process of the formation of an integrated sense of self. When she praises the sound of the word "aneurysm" and claims it as her imaginary name, *Aneurysma Wesendahl* (34), she demonstrates that she accepts the illness as part of her positionality. Helene indicates the positive outcome of her healing process on a more fundamental level: toward the end of the novel, she appreciates the self-confidence she has gained despite her still-defective body, which others perceive as violating "healthy" norms (319–20).

Reviving Language and Memory

In fact, the process of gradually accepting the illness cannot be overestimated. It marks the first step in the process that leads the patient to eventually accept the artificial metal components as elements of her new body and positionality, as well as in her progression of regaining memory, language, and (limited) control. When she first awakens from the coma, Helene experiences a paralysis that afflicts the entire right side of her body. Her incapacity to control her excretion organs, her constant drooling, her lack of language and memory, and the inability to move are a source of humiliation and shame. The protagonist's body forces her to behave in ways unimaginable under "normal," i.e., "healthy" conditions.[11]

Since the patient's lack of language renders her unable to relate details of her medical history, the medical personnel treats her incorrectly. In combination with her otherwise deficient body, this accentuates her initial inability to actively participate in a discursive space where the construction of a meaningful sense of self would be viable. For example, when the patient hears the doctors use the word *Aphasie* (aphasia), she hears it as an abbreviation for "Anfang sieben" (beginning seven; 16, my trans.).[12] Later, she understands that she is suffering from Broca's aphasia, which explains why, despite the speech disorder, her command of language remains fairly intact inside. Once she has received a certain amount of correct input, she begins to recall words and discovers that her main problem is in the translation from thought to spoken word.

Helene's inability to convey this discrepancy between her inner thoughts and the words she is able to utter frustrates her. Despite being unable to express herself, and particularly to articulate certain sounds, the writer increasingly attempts to communicate — initially only with single words. When she later manages to construct simple sentences, she still struggles to comprehend even slightly complex thoughts (55). Months later, shortly before she leaves the rehab center, the patient reflects on her former extraordinary ability to play with words spontaneously and concludes: "Nothing works any more" (307, my trans.).

Helene also gradually starts to regain her memory. Quickly aware that the weeks before the aneurysm burst are practically erased, she attempts to work with an imaginary memory thread, her "Erinnerungsfaden," along which she can move back and forth to support the recuperation of her memory.[13] Her desire to discover her positionality relies on the reconstruction of her past: "Never before had she spent that much time practicing remembering" (111, my trans.). Each additional detail the protagonist recovers from her past, her relationships, and the roles she played supports her in regaining her voice, and vice versa. Significantly, the text reflects the correlation between this successful memory work and the patient's achievements in improving her language in the narrative's sentence structure: as her language improves, the sentences in the novel also lengthen.

This process of recollecting the past reveals a complicated link between the diegetic and the intradiegetic level. Frequently, an event, smell, food, sound, or image to which the protagonist is exposed in a medical institution on the diegetic level triggers a recollection, sometimes involuntarily. In turn, the outcome of these flashbacks affects the patient's present life, notably through physical reactions reported on the diegetic level. The flashbacks are generally structured chronologically and thus serve to reconstruct past experiences from the patient's life.

Marriage with Matthes

The moment Matthes informs his wife on the diegetic level about her intention to visit her friend Carla right before the aneurysm burst may serve as an example. Helene then visualizes the train ticket on the bulletin board in her kitchen, and this mental picture triggers her recollection of everything she put on the board, including a list of things she meant to take when leaving Matthes. This recollection of the past, and the shock the patient endures when she grasps the state of her marriage, become manifest physically in the present and on the level of the basic narration: "She laughed no more. She intended to move out. Now that she remembers, the left side of her body is lying fixed and stiff, too. . . . She starts to sweat on the spot. . . . She feels queasy" (46, my trans.).

The narrative structure is further complicated by the fact that sixteen years prior to Helene's hospitalization, when Matthes left her temporarily, she reacted physically, too. In those days, the protagonist felt an "infernal pain" and started to vomit whenever she smelled something edible (95). While the patient recounts both Matthes's behavior and its inscription on her body on the intradiegetic level, the memory of both causes a corporeal response in the present, underlining the function of the protagonist's body as a "symptom-body"[14] that repeats the pain she felt sixteen years before. Helene's body is thus exposed as a locus of memory, a *Körpergedächtnis*.

Both the concept of the protagonist's symptom body as a locus of memory and these two key episodes from Helene and Matthes Wesendahl's marriage turn out to be essential for understanding a disturbing sexual scene. When the protagonist is allowed to leave the hospital for an afternoon for the first time, her husband drags the debilitated woman out of her wheelchair and into bed. The sexual assault exhibits every component of marital rape and leaves the protagonist, who does not possess the physical capability to effectively challenge her husband physically, "unable to utter a word" and feeling "*invalid*" (56, my trans.). The italicized word "invalid" reflects the fact that her validity as a subject is questioned through this rape. However, her body (re-)acts when she slowly senses "defense" crawling up "on her left, the intact half of her body" (56, my trans.). This indicates that her body continues to articulate her feelings when language fails — although its performance remains invisible. The narrative calls further attention to the physical limitations when Helene, sitting in the kitchen with her family shortly after the sexual assault, thinks she feels an impulse to move her right hand to pick up a berry that fell off her spoon. This momentary hope is, however, immediately crushed when her youngest daughter treads on the berry. While the paralysis of Helene's body precludes resistance, the text demonstrates the correspondence between recollecting the past and the physical reactions.[15]

The protagonist depends on her memory to reliably discharge the recollections from her past to gain agency and discover her present positionality. Thus, the patient's symptom-body supports her desire to integrate her memories in her life story and simultaneously to link them with her present in the hospital and rehab center. The rape scene turns out to be central in understanding this approach, as Helene Wesendahl's reflections toward the end of the novel demonstrate. After the patient regains her memory, including her marital problems as well as the relationship with Viola, she "sees what happened back then entirely differently. Not the attack, the assault" (337, my trans.). Helene explains the assault as Matthes's attempt to restore confidence in their marriage, and excuses the violence with his desire "to show her how he felt, and not with words, of which he probably did not even know if they would actually reach her" (339, my trans.). The reader might doubt the protagonist's reinterpretation of her husband's behavior. Still, it both underlines the patient's enduring efforts to understand her surroundings and regain her past, and it surfaces as part of her attempts to redeem her husband, an aspect to which I will return.

Relationship with Viola

Next to the reconstruction of her marriage with Matthes, the love affair with Viola emerges at the center of the patient's memory work. Flashbacks are mostly triggered by e-mails exchanged by Helene and her lover, which the protagonist rediscovers on a disk. Helene gradually summons up various stages of the relationship, and her recollections of the past tally with her body's reactions. Her initial memory of Viola, for example, causes her to lose her language for the remainder of the day (128). Her situation improves significantly when she finally recollects her love affair in flashbacks, which are predominantly ordered anachronically and relate to the present events on the diegetic level. The sequence of events allows Helene to understand this relationship in retrospect — her initial irritation with Viola's appearance, the short and clandestine love affair, its distressing ending, and the news of Viola's death — and enables the reader to understand its meaning for the protagonist's situation in the narrative present.

The initial flashback on Viola focuses on the confusion and embarrassment the protagonist felt during their first meeting. When she — at the time writing an article on divorced couples — meets Viola in Sanssouci Park, the writer is merely interested in the story about a forced divorce "from my wife" (133, my trans.), which a mysterious V. previously offered to impart in a letter. (Mis)guided by her heteronormative expectation of meeting an ex-husband, Helene anticipates being confronted by a man — until Viola introduces herself. The protagonist recalls a body that could be identified as male from afar and a male voice (129). Only much later, Helene starts to reflect on her limited point of view that understood Viola as a "special case, an exceptional singularity! But that was not true, she just did not have any eyes for it until she met one of them" (186, my trans.).

The surprising exposure reveals both the unreliability of visual appearances and the protagonist's heteronormative thought and practice. Helene feels guilt and shame when she realizes that she upholds the culturally dominant expectations of gender and sex. Viola challenges these norms, according to which her biological sex has to correlate with an identical gender. Before the sex change, trapped in a male body, she felt she was a woman forced to perform as a man. After the sex change, her gender performance is apparently ambiguous. And in one of her e-mails, Viola comments on the fact that she has exclusively loved women all her life — before and after the operation. Since she does not identify as a lesbian and rather concentrates on her participation in specific sexual practices, she refuses to accept hegemonic categories. In her conscious challenge to the heteronormative demand to desire the opposite sex, Viola reveals her "queerness": she defies the gender/sex binary, as well as heteronormative sexual practices.[16]

Living in a society that does not allow for a life outside the male/female binary, s/he feels the compulsion to change both sex and civil status. This decision, also based on a lack of information regarding the consequences, forces Viola into divorce since she cannot be married to a woman, and leads her to lose custody over her sons. Helene finally reflects about the imposition implied in the "sex-adapting" operation and the legal situation and concludes that it is "aimed at cementing the binary concept of sex. . . . There was no way that one could *demand* such a profound intervention, like the law did!" (187, my trans.). Modern hormone therapy and a sex operation allow Viktor/Viola to alter his/her sex — at least to a certain extent; she cannot escape her male body entirely, even after the operation. Still, medicine offers the opportunity to modify oneself, yet these possibilities also imply a force to comply with the demand to fall into the gender and sex binary. Viola's anxious and often pathetic attempts to perform femininity are repeatedly defied and speak of an "orgy of violence" to which she subjects her body. Attempting to perform femininity with a body that resists this desire, Viola draws attention to the phantasmatic aspect of identity and the "comedic failures" of her performative attempts.[17]

Despite the harsh reality that confronts her, Viola envisions a realm for a third sex inhabiting a liberating space outside the male/female binary. Yet, her self-image as a specific hybrid, a "Vatermutter" (fathermother; 321, my trans.), could only have subversive potential if it were legally acceptable.[18] Eventually, Viola's passing away surfaces as a consistent corollary to the obstacles she constantly faced in her life as a transsexual, and the dubious circumstances of her death replicate the ambiguity of her sexual and gender identity. The narrative hints at suspicious incidents, suggesting that the autopsy had difficulty establishing the cause of death, that Viola "appeared to have *passed away peacefully,* as one says," and "one agreed on coronary failure and decided on June 23 as the obit" (235, my trans.). In addition to the uncertainties regarding the cause of death and Viola's last day alive, she seems to have anticipated her end, which indicates the possibility that she committed suicide (301).

Helene's severe physical reaction to the news of Viola's death — she loses her language again, and experiences a shock that is misinterpreted by the doctors as an epileptic seizure — is reminiscent of other situations in which the protagonist reflects on her body potentially mirroring anxieties on the corporeal level. For example, she wonders whether the cause for her torn aneurysm can be found in her feeling torn between her husband and her lover. After the news of Viola's death, she again engages in the intellectual work of deciphering the signs emitted by her body, which needs to be understood as "communication organ . . . that assumes quasi linguistic functions: The body as language."[19] Reflecting on her body's language, Helene remembers that she "dumped" Viola after a "fierce dispute" before the aneurysm tore (303, my trans.). The violent physical reactions and the insinuated potential guilt she feels about her ex-lover's end (240) can then be read as the patient's suspicion that Viola took her life after Helene's decision to stay in her marriage with Matthes.

Power and the Body in the Medical Institutions

Subjected to various medical institutions and their power structure for several months, Helene Wesendahl gradually realizes that her involvement in a traditional, heterosexual marriage, which allows her husband to represent her interests, has been vital for her healing process: in an early attempt to regain agency, Helene Wesendahl tears out the metal clips in her head (17), and later the stomach tube through which she is fed, which forces the nurses to feed her yoghurt (21). Instead of having liberating effects, though, her actions lead to increased restrictions, which literally surface in the form of the nurse's punishment: "*As a punishment I'm going to immobilise you and take your bed cover away*" (18). Helene, posing a danger to the medical institution by challenging its power structures, is repeatedly punished within the hierarchical structure in the hospital and the rehab center. Ultimately, her weakened body emerges as unable to resist the existing practices of subjectification to the norms of the institution and becomes dependent on her husband as a corrective force in the face of the medical institutions.

In fact, the narrative portrays a climax in the fight between orthodox medicine, which relegates the protagonist to little more than an object of medical interest, and the husband, who forcefully challenges the hegemony of the clinical staff. Thus, Matthes presses for his wife's relocation to the stroke unit and the appropriate treatment after her supposedly epileptic seizure. He brings in an alternative practitioner who diagnoses imminent kidney failure due to the patient's allergic reaction to prescribed medication. Helene and Matthes Wesendahl team up against the medical personnel when they decide to secretly discontinue the dangerous pharmaceutical in favor of homeopathic pellets.

When Helene, happy with the success of the alternative treatment, finally discloses her independent decision, the violence from the authorities infringes on the protagonist's most basic rights (309). Denying her entitlement to take responsibility for her own body, the medical profession claims authority over the patient's disease. The narrative criticizes orthodox medicine for its presumably "objective" epistemic approach. It is exactly this supposedly "universal" approach to science that Luce Irigaray in "Is the Subject of Science Sexed?" identified as "equivalent of a male idiolect, a masculine Imaginary."[20] *Du stirbst nicht* highlights medicine's domination by the male discourse, and moreover points to the resulting violence by associating the — at the hospital, exclusively male — doctors with the military.[21]

In fact, the execution of power exceeds the medical territory in the threat of incapacitation, and its means of exercising power is linked to law enforcement — replicating the legal restrictions Viola/Viktor faces. Similar to her transsexual ex-lover, the patient becomes an object to the institutions of the multidimensional network of knowledge and power.[22] Instead of healing, the emphasis shifts to disciplining the body, a strategy that the nurses also abide by when they leave Helene in a painful trance for hours when she reacts physically to the imminent incapacitation by developing a bilious colic. Following Foucault's understanding of the "patient as a criminal," who is tortured and consequently suffers "indescribable pain,"[23] Helene's body becomes a target of corporal punishment. At the same time, the nurses' "punishment" aims at her correction — they are still hoping for Matthes's approval for the incapacitation process.

Without her husband's interference, the patient would have been at the doctor's disposal — including the threat of imminent death and unwarranted incapacitation. Thus, Helene entirely depends on a man who is forced into the role of a legal guardian by the state institutions and their conduct, which supports the underlying idea that particularly women suffering from disease are not able to participate in finding a reasonably "correct" remedy. The narrative thus appears strangely ambiguous: it depicts medical institutions as participating in the reproduction of the existing hierarchical order between the sexes, and simultaneously redeems Matthes because of his refusal to take advantage of the situation: Praising her husband, Helene is glad to hear that "Matthes protested against that, had said that *his wife* was contractually capable, of sound mind, and on no account a case for a procedure to incapacitate her" (313–14, my trans.). Helene is lucky that her husband, unwilling to exercise gender-specific violence, pleads for her. On the textual level, the importance of the heteronormative relationship for Matthes's influence is stressed with the italicization of "his wife." Since Helene and Matthes's relationship is legalized by a state institution, the husband's judgment receives credibility. Viola/Viktor, on the other hand, was denied the protection implied in a legalized relationship and instead faces death. Supporting his wife, Matthes comes to represent a rather complex point of reference for the patient in the quest for her positionality. Receiving the power to socially control his wife who depends on his judgment, he protects her against the violence emanating from the state institutions. While the narrative criticizes these societal arrangements, Helene clearly appreciates her husband.

Conclusion

Du stirbst nicht introduces us to the complexities underlying a patient's path to recovery. Helene illustrates the link between the body, memory, and language in the protagonist's attempt to regain agency and positionality. While her quest for positionality remains on the individual level and historical events play a subordinate role, her story is political in that it accentuates the extent to which contemporary society is caught in heteronormative thought and practice, particularly with the exaggerated reiteration and affirmation of the heterosexual marriage at the end of the novel. The protagonist, a strong woman who repeatedly challenges dominant power structures in the institutions, is ultimately forced to depend on the support of her husband to regain her health. While constructing a coherent narrative consisting of the people and events that have shaped her life turns out to be essential for discovering her positionality, Helene emerges as unable to defy the power structures governing the medical institutions, a process that surfaces as equally important for her healing process. Still, with the support of her husband Helene stabilizes in the course of the narrative process. Persistent in following her threads of memory and working on regaining her language — a process that is replicated textually in the complicated play between the different levels of narration — the protagonist eventually succeeds in discovering her new positionality.

Notes

1 See www.deutscher-buchpreis.de/de/296797?meldungs_id=342442 (accessed 22 April 2010).

2 Ulrike Hempel, "Interview with Kathrin Schmidt," *Berliner Ärzte* (*Kammerblatt der Ärztekammer Berlin*) 3 (2010): 33, available on www.berliner-aerzte.net/pdf/bae1003 032.pdf (accessed 26 April 2010).

3 On the notion of the *Körpergedächtnis*, see Sigrid Weigel, *Bilder des kulturellen Gedächtnisses. Beiträge zur Gegenwartsliteratur* (Dülmen-Hiddingsel: tende, 1994), 11, and Claudia Öhlschläger and Birgit Wiens, eds. *Körper-Gedächtnis-Schrift. Der Körper als Medium kultureller Erinnerung* (Berlin: Erich Schmidt Verlag, 1997).

4 For another example of a character with a sexually ambiguous body, see Lyn Marven's chapter on Ulrike Draesner.

5 Adelson explains positionality as "a set of specific social and discursive relations in a given historical moment. These relations concern and also produce gender, race, sexuality, ethnicity, and other practices through which power is constructed, exercised, and resisted or challenged." Leslie A. Adelson, *Making Bodies, Making History* (Lincoln: U of Nebraska P, 1993), 64.

6 Kathrin Schmidt, *Du stirbst nicht* (Cologne: Kiepenheuer & Witsch, 2009), 6. Subsequent page references to this edition appear in parentheses in the main body of the text; however, unless marked as my own, translations are taken from the English sample excerpt of *You Are Not Going to Die*, trans. John Reddick, on www.signandsight.com/features/1927.html (accessed 30 July 2010). This initial scene is reminiscent of Gregor Samsa's experience of waking up in Kafka's *Die Verwandlung*.

[7] Michel Foucault, "Body/Power" (1975), in *Power/Knowledge: Selected Interviews and Other Writings 1972–1977*, ed. Colin Gordon (New York: Pantheon Books, 1980), 55–62.

[8] Donna J. Haraway, *Simians, Cyborgs, and Women. The Reinventions of Nature* (New York, Routledge 1991), 149.

[9] Kathrin Schmidt, *Koenigs Kinder* (Cologne: Kiepenheuer & Witsch, 2002), 8 and passim; Kathrin Schmidt, *Seebachs schwarze Katzen* (Cologne: Kiepenheuer & Witsch, 2005), 6 and passim. My translations.

[10] Jacques Lacan, "The Mirror Stage as Formative for the Function of the I," *Écrits: A Selection* (London: Routledge Classics, 2001), 5.

[11] Lyn Marven's chapter similarly emphasizes the extent to which language relates to the body in Ulrike Draesner's *Mitgift*.

[12] John Reddick translates this as "'A phase here': she'd like to say it out loud. That *could* be what it means. The phase when night begins." www.signandsight. com/features/1927.html (accessed 30 July 2010).

[13] Schmidt's "*Erinnerungsfaden*" (memory thread, 39) is reminiscent of Aleida Assmann's *Gedächtnisspur* (memory track). Aleida Assmann, *Generationsidentitäten und Vorurteilsstrukturen in der neuen deutschen Erinnerungsliteratur* (Vienna: Picus Verlag, 2006), 47.

[14] Weigel defines the "weiblichen Körper . . . als Symptomkörper, d.h. als Matrix für die Erinnerungssymbole des Verdrängten." Weigel, *Bilder des kulturellen Gedächtnisses*, 16.

[15] Similarly, Lyn Marven in her chapter refers to an act that one protagonist in Ulrike Draesner's *Mitgift* likens to rape.

[16] On the definition of queer, see Michael Warner, "Introduction," in *Fear of a Queer Planet. Queer Politics and Social Theory* (Minneapolis: U of Minnesota P, 1993), xxvi, and Michael Warner, *The Trouble with Normal. Sex, Politics, and the Ethics of Queer Life* (Cambridge, MA: Harvard UP, 2000).

[17] Judith Butler, *Gender Trouble. Feminism and the Subversion of Identity* (New York: Routledge, 1999), 59. Also see Lyn Marven's chapter for another example of the ways that bodies that fail to fit into sexual norms become subject to violence.

[18] The figure of the "Vatermutter" is a recurring issue in Kathrin Schmidt's work. For an explicit analysis of a transsexual in *Die Gunnar-Lennefsen-Expedition*, see Sonja Klocke, "Die frohe Botschaft der Kathrin Schmidt? — Transsexuality, Racism, and Feminist Historiography in *Die Gunnar-Lennefsen-Expedition* (1998)," *Germanistik in Ireland. Jahrbuch der/Yearbook of the Association of Third-Level Teachers of German in Ireland*. Vol. 5. 2010. Special Issue: *Sexual-Textual Border-Crossings: Lesbian Identity in German-Language Literature, Film, and Culture*. 143–58.

[19] Sigrid Weigel talks about the body as "Mitteilungsorgan . . . das quasi sprachliche Funktionen übernimmt: Der Körper *als* Sprache." Weigel, *Bilder des kulturellen Gedächtnisses*, 59.

[20] Luce Irigaray, "Is the Subject of Science Sexed?" in *Feminism and Science*, ed. Nancy Tuana (Bloomington: Indiana UP, 1989), 61.

[21] The "troop" of men (16, 25) turns out to be responsible for having inserted the metal clips the protagonist notably chooses to call "Panzersperren" (antitank obstacles; 17, 30), and the protagonist depends on the approval of an entire "Ärztemannschaft" (squad of doctors; 136) to be transferred to a rehab center. The protagonist generally associates groups of men with the military. When she is placed at a table in the rehab institution with men only, she labels them a "Besatzung" (occupying force; 241). All my translations.

[22] Foucault "Body/Power," 55–62.

[23] Foucault "Body/Power," 4.

Appendices: Samples of Contemporary German-Language Novels in Translation

Appendix A:

Excerpt from Vladimir Vertlib,
Das besondere Gedächtnis der Rosa Masur

Translated by Jamie Lee Searle

Chapter 16

Dear Mascha,

You may be surprised that I'm writing to you, rather than simply talking to you as I have done throughout the fifty-eight years that have gone by since you died. But you have no reason to fear that this will bring about a change in our relationship. It's nothing but the whim of an old woman. You always gave my life a sense of security and — as you well know — your keen power of judgment saved me from a fair few misjudgments. Back in 1963, after the unexpected death of my husband, it was you who showed me how to find my way from despair to mourning. I found my way back to life. Death can often be a new beginning, after all. Despite that, I was the only one who ever spoke at Naum's grave, while he listened silently. He has never answered me.

I'm suffering from insomnia and mood swings, perhaps as a consequence of the conversations that I have to hold with Dmitrij, the interviewer. Nonetheless, they have become a kind of elixir for me. I'm hoping that the mechanical act of writing will help me to get back to the kind of imbalance one would expect of a ninety-two year old.

The fate of this letter is uncertain. One of the fantasy figures of my sleepless nights is a German post office clerk who conscientiously searches our local branch for the sack labeled "The Other Side." Then, after consulting with his superior, he postmarks and stamps the letter as *undeliverable*, thereby returning it to me, the sender. In reality, though, the German post system hasn't been nearly as conscientious as one imagines it to be in

From: Vladimir Vertlib, *Das besondere Gedächtnis der Rosa Masur* © Deuticke im Paul Zsolnay Verlag Wien 2001.

a very long while. Despite the fact that the Germans number their buildings according to a clear and strictly logical system, they sometimes neglect — perhaps as an act of caprice, or even malice — to number the apartments inside. As a result, delivering the mail demands considerable powers of observation from the postman in order to connect the individual mailboxes and apartment doors (on which there aren't always name plates) to the surnames on the envelopes and packages. In our case, with three people bearing a different surname in the same household, this is no easy task. Some days ago a letter was delivered to us instead of to Fräulein Friederike Schwarz. The old lady lives a floor above us. The letter came from Tittmoning in Upper Bavaria. I took it up to her right away. A letter to Kostik from Isidor, a friend from his student days who has been living in Bat-Jam in Israel for some years now, had in turn been mixed in with the mail of the aforementioned lady. She knocked on our door and handed the letter over to us with a smile. It had already been opened. This annoyed me a great deal, even though Fräulein Schwarz wouldn't have been able to read the Russian script. Kostik accepted the torn-open envelope, muttering something. He leaves the more disagreeable aspects of daily life to his old mother. There are certain things that I've always felt responsible for — whether it be handling his routine bureaucratic dealings with the authorities or just having conversations with the neighbors — because I've never considered my son to be diplomatic enough. Why should he change now, at over sixty years of age?

And so I stand before Fräulein Schwarz, most likely with a rather sour expression on my face, which I always have at times like these, and thank her, trying not to sound either too polite or too curt. Peering over my shoulder, she tries to catch a glimpse of the inside of our apartment. This aggravates me. How can she be so blatant with her nosiness? Are we not worth even the pretence of some display of tact? Perhaps I should invite her in for a cup of tea so that she can look at everything in her own time. She won't find anything out of the ordinary. No mysterious Masonic symbols or Christian children sacrificed for matzoh at Passover. For a moment, I hesitate as to whether I should challenge her about the opened letter, but decide against it. What point would there be? She'd only rip up the next letter to us that ends up in her post box.

"You have relatives in Israel?" the old woman asked.

"M-hmm."

"Then you're Jews!" she pronounces, as if she's revealing that I'd just won half a million Marks in the lottery. I can hear neither resentment nor malice in her voice, just curiosity.

"No!" I say. "We're Udmurts."

"Who?"

"Well, what I mean to say is, my son and I are Udmurts, but my daughter-in-law is Tchuvass, and my late husband was Mordwine."

"Mo . . .?"

"Mordwine."

"So, how does Israel . . .?"

"Well, didn't you know that the Israelis and the Udmurts are great friends? That's why so many Udmurts live in Israel. . . . Good day, Fräulein Schwarz."

You'll probably ask me at this point, dearest Mascha, whether life in this strange land is hard on me. Every day, the same question — I hear your voice in my head — every day, the same answer: I lack for nothing; God knows, things have been much worse for me in the past. Sometimes I feel as though I'm taking flight, up and up, that I'm next to you. We hold each other's hands and look down, watching the bustle of the people on earth — you could write whole studies on their behavior, sometimes it's entertaining, but mostly it's just boring. I feel that it has little more to do with me personally. Then I think of Kostik and fall. The impact is painful. That's how it felt a few days ago, when my grandson Sascha told us that he's leaving Gigricht. His company have offered him a three-year contract in Hamburg, a position that will bring with it a higher wage and more responsibility. You can imagine how Kostik and Frieda took the news. Relocation, especially from one Bundesland to another, is fraught with difficulty for a quota refugee living on welfare. Besides that, Sascha isn't planning to take us along with him, because he has no idea where his company could send him when the three years are up.

Now, you shouldn't take this to mean that I will miss Sascha too terribly. I've never had a close relationship with my grandson. Sometimes I wonder what it would have been like if Schelja had had children. But I don't want to write about Schelja. Every thought of her burns my heart. Every mention of her name shatters the peace at home for days. Kostik is tactful enough to act as though he never had a sister.

In recent months Sascha was calling us regularly.

"What's new, father?"

"What would be new with me?"

"How's the heart?"

"No complaints at the moment. And you?"

"Lots of work, the same as always. I'm content. Soon, when I've got a bit of time, I'll get my driver's license and buy myself a car."

"Sounds good."

That's how most of their telephone conversations ended.

Even on the few occasions when Sascha came to visit us, he revealed very little about his life.

Do you have a girlfriend?" Frieda would ask every time, searching his face for clues, as if he hadn't learned long ago to change his expressions as easily as his clothes.

You're thirty-four years old," said Kostik. "Think of the future. A life with no family or children is worth nothing."

Sascha would eat the leek soup that his mother always made for him, and, without looking up at his parents, would always give the same answer: "First money, then pleasure."

"As long as you have enough time left for pleasure," I sometimes added.

"I've got a lot of staying power."

Even as a child, my grandson was always one of the best at everything he did. The best in his class, the most exemplary young Pioneer, the most active Komsomol member, the hardest-working student. If he ever brought girls home with him, they were always careworn creatures. One glance was enough to know that he would leave them before very long. Frieda was the only one who didn't understand this, treating each one as if she could turn out to be her future daughter-in-law.

At the time of perestroika, he gave lectures about the reformation of socialism, but after the failed coup of 1991 he was the first to leave the Komsomol. He founded his own electronics company with a couple of rather shady guys, went bankrupt, then emigrated to Germany, where he started to build a career within one of the very companies he had once publicly denounced as "capitalist sharks" or "exploiters of the people" when he was a Komsomol activist. What? You want to know where I'm going with this? Of course I can see that he's being sensible. He's not a religious man, and they have it easier in life, for they have no doubts.

"What did we come here for?" Frieda asks me now. "I wanted to be near my son. That was the only reason I came to this land of sausage eaters. Do you think I enjoy spending my old age in this wretched place? What are we supposed to do now?"

As you can probably imagine, dear Mascha, I can't give her a satisfactory answer to this question. What would you have said in my place?

Kostik's reaction was more laid-back. "Hamburg, why not?" he asked. "We hardly see him anyway, our own son. It doesn't really bother me much. The only thing I'm still hoping for is to go — just once in my life — to Aix-en-Provence. Then I might be happy for a little while."

Once, sometimes twice a week, I go to the Institute for Historical Research and tell Dmitrij stories about my life. To start with, he tried to steer my narrative flow and show off his own historical knowledge. Whenever he did that, I just smiled. Was this lad, young enough to be my great-grandson, really trying to impress me? In any case, he quickly realized he couldn't take that tack with me. When it came to details that he was really keen to hear about, I acted as though I could no longer remember, and on others that seemed very important to me I spoke at length, even when I could sense his impatience. He quickly realized: it was my way, or nothing. Before long, his main tasks were to switch on the recorder, give me a keyword, jog my memory, and to bridge the gap between pauses. Yet I don't mean to imply that his role was a merely passive one. He translated everything that I told him into excellent German. He omitted repetitions, tidied up time- and content-related jumps, and brought individual episodes together into proper chapters. I've read the German version. The young man has been rather loose with the translation in places. But I've decided to go easy on him.

Dmitrij knows of course that the most difficult part of his work still lies ahead. He has to find the appropriate linguistic form for the key event in my life. The document I put forward as proof of my story was a decisive factor in my selection to participate in the whole anniversary publication project. But Dmitrij, the cheeky man, said to me one day with his characteristic bluntness that he believed my "so-called proof" was forged.

"That document would never make it past a thorough expert analysis," he explained to me, "they'd only need to test the combination of the tint and the text, and your scam would be busted."

"So why don't you do it?" I asked, challenging him. "If you believe your experts more than an old woman."

"Maybe I would if it was my decision to make, but Frau Wepse is so taken with your story, and so is Dr. Sambs, our boss, and especially the town council . . . and even the mayor — he's really fallen for it! You know how these politicians dash from one appointment to the next and only ever want to be told the most important details in the briefest of words — just in passing, really — but of course, we didn't want to keep this story from them."

"So? What does that mean now?" I asked.

He laughed, winking at me and putting a cigarette in his mouth, but without lighting it, for I had strictly forbidden him from smoking in my presence.

"Should we really disappoint the important people at the Institute by setting something as profane as an expert analysis in motion?"

After that, I didn't say anything more. It's all the same to me as long as I can tell my stories. And besides that, I'm too old to still be of the opinion that the border between moral and immoral is the same as that between truth and lies. But I'm digressing, and there are more important things to talk about.

A few days ago, Frieda received a letter from her aunt Esther, who lives in a old-age home in Beersheba. She emigrated to Israel with her son in the mid-1970s.

In the envelope, there was just a scrap of paper, perhaps ten by ten centimeters in size. The few lines written on it began with the word *Frieda!* Not *Dear Frieda,* not *Hello Frieda,* just *Frieda!*

It disappoints me a great deal, wrote the aunt, *that you, Frieda, have not come out to join us in Israel, our Jewish homeland. Instead of this, you choose to live amongst the children and grandchildren of those who murdered your own people. Have you no pride? For a few dirty Marks of social welfare you sell yourself to those who annihilated us as if we were insects. May misfortune fall upon you and your family there! All kinds of sickness, misery, poverty, and death!*

"She was never quite right in the head," explained Kostik. "Surely you remember how Sascha always called her the *devil's grandmother* when he was a child."

"She's senile!" I added. "These are clear symptoms of senility. But this tendency for pathos, she already had that back then."

"Such things can happen easily in Israel," said Kostik.

"Communism. Capitalism. Zionism. Pacifism. Altruism. My whole life, people have been drumming into me what's right and what's wrong. For a while it's this way, then another way entirely. I won't let anyone force their criteria for moral behavior on me anymore," I declared.

It was another two days before Frieda calmed down. "My whole life I've tried to do the right thing," she lamented. "I looked after my parents until they passed away, and when my aunt was ill, it was me who looked in on her and made sure she was okay. She had no daughters, just a son, and of course he didn't lift a finger to help. And now, in my old age, they spit in my face. So, in my next life I'll be coming back as an earthworm."

At the synagogue club, the content of letters from Israel is a much-loved topic of conversation. Many of these letters are similar to the one Frieda received from her aunt. Someone once even told me that he'd received a small flag emblazoned with a swastika.

"The Israelis always think they are speaking for all Jewish people," explained one man — I think he was originally from Kaunas — during one of the many discussions. "But, I ask you, where would Israel be without the support of the diaspora? Our children will make a good living here in Germany and then support Israel's cause or send donations, because they are Jews. The Israelis should be thankful to us for that. Without us, the Jewish diaspora, those camel drivers out there would have made them into shish kebabs long ago."

"If it were still possible to emigrate to the USA we would have been there long ago," said another. "But they stopped letting Russian Jews in ten years back."

"Well, I for one wouldn't want to go to America. Have you heard how bad the welfare system is there? Not to mention the high crime levels and constant insecurity."

"Yes, but it's America! Just imagine. America! If someone offers you America on a plate, you don't turn it down. In spite of everything, it's still America!"

"Germany isn't even really Germany anymore," pronounced one woman. "It's part of the European Union, and that will soon form one united state. My children will be citizens of Europe. Not Germans, but Europeans."

"Well, either way, they'll still be Jews."

"I think the Jewish community in Germany should be strengthened," said Herr Rotschwants, by way of justifying his immigration there. "It's not just a belated revenge on Hitler, but a step toward humanizing Central Europe." Frau Rotschwants sighed and turned away, but her husband kept on talking. "Everywhere there are Jews, there will be excellence in the arts, culture, and the sciences. It's a well-known fact that the Jews are the salt of the earth . . ."

"Herr Rotschwants," I interrupted him. "Give it a rest! You immigrated to Germany because you wanted to eat beefsteak every day, go for walks in a nice park, and have a modern fitted bathroom. Don't make up stories. Do you know who you're reminding me of? The fifteen-year-old girl who's pregnant but still insists she's a virgin. She claims she bathed in the same water that her brother had just bathed and masturbated in. And a doctor says to her: My dear, if you've already sinned, at least own up to it."

"Well, even virgins can be tramps," muttered Rotschwants.

In the end, though, dear Mascha, it's actually immaterial where I spend the last months or years of my life. Once I'm dead, it will be of no importance whether the corpses alongside me are of Jews, antisemites, Germans, or Russian nationalists. They'll all taste the same to the worms.

Sometimes I wake up in the night and can't get back to sleep. When the first pale light of morning breaks through the curtains into the room and begins to spread out across the parquet floor like a sundial, I count the seconds and wait for the sirens in the lightbulb factory to call its workers to their early shift. The signal fails to materialize, and I get up, confused, dress myself, and go down to the street. By the entrance to the house, I bump into an old acquaintance. "Good morning, Chaim Berkowitsch," I say by way of greeting to my neighbor Rabinowitsch, but he stares at me in surprise and turns away with a shrug of his shoulders. As I walk on, I try to figure out his strange behavior. Was he imprisoned in 1938 or did he only become a victim in the repression of 1948? Or was it 1953? Again and again I keep coming across long-lost acquaintances.

At the park I speak with some of the older people. "The younger ones can't imagine how we suffered," one woman explains to me. "I can still remember clearly that New Year's Eve of 1944, when the Anglo-American terror bombers left everything in ruins. Even the trees in the park were burnt down."

"During the blockade I once feared that my daughter had been killed and eaten," I say.

"The food rationing!" she remembers. "We had so little! In 1945 the homeless Jews were trading on the black market. I had my purse stolen once. For a whole week I only had bread and water to live off. I used to smoke the cigarette butts that the Yanks threw away, to help stave off the hunger."

"Two hundred and fifty grams of bread a day for workers, a hundred and twenty-five for women and children. The men were dropping dead in the street. I had to step over the bodies. I still have nightmares about it now."

"Back in 1952 I was thirty kilos overweight. But the men still liked a big bosom and big ass back then. Nowadays they prefer broomsticks in fancy clothes."

"I weighed thirty kilos during the blockade," I say.

"My husband died in the war. I was a young widow. The men were after me — I tell you — like dogs chasing a bitch in heat."

"After my husband died, there was no one else for me. He was my first and my only."

"Yes, yes," she said, "we had to do some terrible things."

I carry on, veering off from Ulitsa Mayakovskogo into the Nevsky Prospekt and find myself on Gigricht's main square. Things slowly fall back into place but, despite that, I'm still not sure whether I'd just have to turn down one of the side alleys to get to Dvortsovaya Ploshchad and then the Neva.

But, dear Mascha, what I really wanted to do was tell you about what happened yesterday. I was on one of my usual walks through the town. I paused at the bus stop for a break and watched the people getting on and off, talking to one another or smoking cigarettes. The number 9 bus was going to the cemetery. I got on.

Gigricht Cemetery gives the impression that even the dead have to adhere to house rules. I entered the grounds through a white painted door, above which two round-bellied angels sat in splendor. It occurred to me that they were displaying their faces to the visitors, but their sweet little behinds to the dead. The graveled pathways were immaculately neat. There were no footprints to be seen, almost as if someone was following behind all the visitors with a rake, erasing all traces of their presence. All the graves looked as if they had just been put in the day before. Death is a very well-groomed gentleman in Gigricht.

In front of a large black marble gravestone stood a beautifully dressed woman, who I could initially only see from behind. Otherwise the cemetery was empty of visitors, perhaps because it was still early and the weather was bad. The woman, in a close-fitting, ankle-length dress, looked like a marble statue or a Chekhov character, accidentally misplaced from the nineteenth century to the turn of the millennium. The scene reminded me of a painting by an English painter — I can't recall his name — that I had often admired in the Hermitage.

At first I just intended to pause for a moment. Out of the corner of my eye I had already seen a path I wanted to go down. But then I changed my mind, went up to stand next to the woman, and read the inscription on the gravestone. *Dr. Ferdinand von Pfaffenhofen 29.1.1910–13.12.1989. You may be gone from us, but you will always be in our hearts.* The postscript seemed a little superfluous to me. On Naum's gravestone only his name and dates of birth and death were engraved. What I liked here was the style of the writing — elegant, simple letters. I looked to my side. The woman's face was just as beautiful as her slim figure and long neck, which could be described as aristocratic. She was wearing high heels, which must have made navigating the gravel rather laborious, and a gold wristwatch that had probably cost more than all the watches I had ever possessed in my whole life. In her hand was a bouquet of flowers — white and red roses. She was no longer young, perhaps seventy or so.

I must have been staring at the woman quite brazenly, for she turned towards me, visibly irritated. She looked at me for a moment in silence, then turned away again and laid the flowers down on the grave.

"My husband has been dead for over thirty-five years," I said. "In the first few years after his death, I visited his grave every week."

"This isn't my husband," she declared, without looking over at me. Her voice made her sound as though she could have been a hundred years old.

"Your brother? Another relative?" I asked. "Or a friend?"

"Why do you want to know?"

"No particular reason," I answered.

She bent her head forwards so that her chin almost touched her chest, and fell silent. I waited a little, looked at my watch, and then decided to go back. It occurred to me that I hadn't found out how often the number 9 bus went back to the town center. But I hadn't gone more than a few steps before I heard the woman's voice behind me. "I don't even know the man whose grave this is. Today is the first time I've been here. Did you know him?" It seemed to me that she was suddenly anxious at the prospect that I would leave. So I turned back. The woman stared fixedly at my worn-out Soviet-style loafers.

"This is the first time I've ever been to this cemetery," I said. "My husband is buried in Leningrad. I'll probably never see his grave again."

"I'll never see my husband's grave again either," the woman replied, her mouth became long and narrow, with a hint of a smile that made her face look a lot less beautiful all of a sudden. "He's buried here, in this cemetery, row thirty-seven. There are three plane trees there. He certainly didn't earn them, those beautiful trees."

"No plane trees grow in Leningrad," I said, thinking of the alleyways overgrown with weeds and the toppled-over gravestones in the Jewish cemetery.

"I won't do him the honor. No, I won't do him the honor of standing at his grave. Forty years together were enough. And now he's dead. But

I'm still alive. Yes! He would never have thought it. That I would still be alive, and him dead. In the spring, when all the flowers bloom, that's the most beautiful time. That's when I feel it most, how beautiful everything is. And he's buried down there and can't move anymore. Not anymore!"

I've experienced a lot of things in my life, but this concentrated barrage of hatred amazed me so much that my walking stick fell from my grasp. The woman bent over and picked it up.

"But then why the flowers?" I murmured, while she handed me my stick. "Flowers for a complete stranger?"

"I have to go somewhere!" she shouted out. "I don't have anyone else here. Only him. But he won't get my roses. Oh no, not my roses, he won't get them." Her voice cracked.

At first I backed off, and then began to take flight, but after a few steps I stopped once more and turned around, reluctantly but compelled by a strong desire to look into her hate-filled face one more time.

It was, dear Mascha, in this very moment that I felt calm and happy again after so long, and made my peace with the world. I thought of you, and of Naum and all the others that I had lost over the years, but who still touch me often, and the warmth of whose hands I can still feel.

With love,
Rosa

Appendix B:
Excerpt from Clemens Meyer, *Als wir träumten*

Translated by Katy Derbyshire

Little Racer

Round One

We were right nearby when it happened. We were out drinking in the Pilz, Rico, Mark, and I. I don't know why we were drinking in the Pilz that night; we didn't drink there often, even though the beer was cheap. We usually went to the Grüne Aue or to see Goldie at the Traktorist, but maybe we had some kind of sense that something was up that night, and we'd been drinking in Pitbull's cellar beforehand, and sometimes when you've had a few you see the whole truth before you and sometimes even a tiny piece of the future, but if we'd seen what was going to happen we'd have gone looking for Walter, all around our part of town, all around the whole city, and if we'd found him we'd have locked him in Pitbull's cellar, even if Pitbull hadn't wanted us to — he lived down there, after all — or we'd have taken him to Leipzig-Southeast police station and asked the cops to cuff him to the radiator, he knew that well enough, he'd have leaned his head against the wall and maybe slept a bit.

But we didn't sense anything, and we didn't see anything, Rico, Mark, and I; we were out drinking in the Pilz. Paul was supposed to come but he didn't, he must have had another row with his mother. Pitbull had had a row with his mother too, she'd gone at him with a bottle because we'd made so much noise drinking, and now Pitbull was lying in his cellar having a rest.

"I don't get it," said Rico. "Paul's old lady's a control freak, she has to plan everything. When he's allowed out, when he comes back. She should just leave him alone. She should get herself a proper man instead."

From: Clemens Meyer, *Als wir träumten* © S. Fischer Verlag GmbH, Frankfurt am Main, 2006. Translation © Katy Derbyshire.

"Would you do her?" asked Mark. "I mean, just for a shag . . ."

"Leave it out," I said, "It's his mother, for God's sake!"

"She's not bad, Danny, she's not even forty. Maybe a bit dried up, she needs a young lad to get her juices flowing, know what I mean, she's hot for it, you should see how she looks at me . . ."

"Jesus, Mark, stop talking about his mother like that!"

And he really did stop and he was quiet and he looked over at the door, which flew open and Paul was there. We raised our glasses to him, and it was only then that we saw something wasn't right. He was swaying and holding onto the doorframe, and his face was as white as a brand new soccer ball.

"Walter," he said, "Walter . . ."

And maybe we did sense something right then, because we all put our glasses down at the same time, as if in slow motion, and then we got up and walked over to him, to the door, not saying anything.

"Hey!" yelled the landlord behind the bar, "Where are you off to?" We didn't drink in the Pilz that often and he didn't trust us. Rico crumpled up a twenty and threw it on one of the empty tables. There weren't many customers in the Pilz.

"Walter," said Paul and staggered from one side of the doorway to the other, and I grabbed hold of him.

"What's up with Walter?" He pulled me outside, took me by the shoulders so hard it hurt and shook me. "What's up with Walter?"

"Gone. Dead, Danny."

Rico pushed me aside and grabbed Paul by the collar and lifted him up a bit until their faces were touching. "Don't talk shit, you hear, don't mess around kid, don't mess around."

"I'm not messing around," whispered Paul and raised his arm, it was trembling, and pointed over to Prager Platz, which we used to call the meat market because all the lonely girls from our part of town met up on the patch of grass next to the crossroads and walked up and down and stared after every guy because they didn't want to be lonely any more, even though most of them were too fat or too thin or had something else wrong with them. And then we saw the light from the fire next to the crossroads, three or four hundred yards ahead of us. I broke into a run.

"Danny," Rico yelled behind me, "Danny, wait!"

But I didn't wait, I ran ahead to Prager Platz, to the meat market, where there weren't any girls sitting on the benches swinging their too thin or too fat legs for us, there was a car on fire against a tree. I ran faster and I was almost there and I saw the people standing on the pavement and in the middle of the road. Far away, I heard the din of the sirens. Cops, ambulances, fire engines.

"Walter," I screamed, "Walter, get out!"

But Little Walter was already out of the car, lying four or five yards away from it, and the flames couldn't harm him any more. I ran over to him, it was so hot where he was lying, and I pulled him a bit further away from the burning wreck. I knelt down beside him, and then I screamed and tipped my head right back and looked at the sky, no stars in sight, because his face was all black and covered in blood, he had no hair left. His clothes were ripped to shreds, the blood, I couldn't take the sight of the damn blood, but then I leaned over to him and pushed my hand under the back of his head. Then Little Walter moved, he moved his head just a tiny bit on my hand. I looked for his eyes, where were his eyes? Now one was open, blue, in his black face. "Walter," I said, "Jesus, Walter . . ." He moved his lips, and I pressed my ear very carefully to his mouth.

Round Two

We were right nearby when it happened. We were out drinking in the Pilz, Rico, Mark, and I. We were playing thirty-one because Mark was useless at skat, but he won almost every round of thirty-one. "It's just bloody luck," said Rico.

"It's skill," said Mark, putting thirty and a half down on the table and winning the round. We were waiting for Paul, whose mother had probably locked him in again. She'd heard that Pitbull had been locked up in Zeithain for a couple of weeks for some crap, and since then Paul had been under a kind of youth arrest as well, but it probably didn't bother him because he had all his women in all his mags and films at home.

"Run out of matches," said Rico and put his cards down. "I'm broke."

"I'll lend you some," I said.

"Nah, don't bother Danny, I've lost enough. Don't want to get into debt."

"I thought you were a gambler," Mark counted his matches, "I thought you were the world champion inside, in the coffin."

"Keep your mouth shut!" Rico put his hand over Mark's pile of matches and clenched his fist, the matches cracking inside it.

"Hey, what's that all about? That was two beers!"

"You can have your two beers if you don't talk crap."

But Mark never got two beers out of Rico, he'd won all his matches for nothing, because the door flew open, Paul staggered towards us, and we knew right away that something wasn't right.

"What's up, hey, what's up? Did you make a break for it? You in trouble?"

"Walter," he whispered, and now we saw he was trembling, "down the meat market, a tree, a car . . ."

We leapt up and ran past Paul to the door. "Hey, your tab!" shouted the landlord behind the bar. There was often trouble in the Pilz, sometimes the customers didn't pay their tabs, or they started beating each other up until the cops showed up. We ran silent to the crossroads, to Prager Platz, which we used to call the meat market because the most gorgeous girls in our part of town met there, and most of them were hot for us. I ran the fastest, but not because of the girls, there weren't any there that night, there was a car on fire. Dense black smoke, so thick you could hardly see the flames. A security man was leaping around the car, then he went down on his knees and crawled away from the wreck, something leaking out of his mouth.

"Walter," I screamed, "Walter!"

Maybe Paul was wrong, maybe some other guy was burning in the wreck, there were plenty of joyriders in our part of town, almost every young lad in Reudnitz, Anger-Crottendorf, and the other parts of town in Leipzig-Southeast was into it, we did it too, but when I looked into the flames and the smoke I knew, I just knew it, it was suddenly in my head that it was *him* burning in there.

"Walter," I screamed, "Walter!"

It was a pale red VW Jetta; that was his favorite model because the girl from the newsagent's he'd once been in love with had driven one. I walked towards the flames, I felt the heat and reached out a hand, the smoke burned in my eyes.

"Danny," yelled Rico behind me and grabbed hold of me, "Danny, stay here!" He had me by the shoulders, and I pulled and struggled and wanted to go to Little Walter, but Rico wouldn't let me go. Far away, I heard the din of the sirens. Cops, ambulances, fire engines. Then I saw Mark as well, he was squatting on the ground next to me, puking. And it was only then that I saw the people standing around on the road and the pavement, and gawking over at the burning wreck.

"Piss off," I screamed, "piss off, you bastards!" I tore myself out of Rico's grip and ran towards the gawkers and raised my fist, but Rico was fast, he grabbed me from behind again by the shoulders, put his arms round me and held me tight.

"Danny," he whispered, "Danny, it's too late." The sirens were very close now. Rico let go of me, and I dropped to the ground and crawled on my knees to the pavement and leaned against a wall. Flashing blue lights. The fire brigade was there. "He won't have been on his own," said Rico next to me.

"No," I said, "he won't," and then I leapt up again and ran yelling at the burning wreck, the firemen standing around it now, but Rico was behind me and he grabbed at my legs, and I fell to the ground. I stayed where I was and pressed my face against the road.

Round Three

We were out drinking in the Pilz, Rico, Mark, and I. We didn't drink in the Pilz often but it wasn't a bad bar, it had style, even the toilets were clean, and a lot of the drinkers in our part of town started their rounds there, and now we were out drinking in the Pilz because Walter had burned right nearby. We'd read about it in the paper, because on the night when it happened we'd been drinking in Pitbull's cellar. He'd driven his car into a tree, over at the crossroads next to Prager Platz, which he used to call the meat market because the girls from our part of town met there on the weekend before they went out for the night, and sometimes Walter had driven up and down there in a stolen car, but I don't think he ever picked one of them up. There'd been three other guys in the car, joyriders from the Mühlenviertel, and they'd burned with Walter too. The security man who got to the burning wreck first said in the paper they'd been alive for a bit and he'd wanted to get them out, but he hadn't had a chance with all the flames.

"I don't believe that," said Rico. "Nah, I don't believe it. They were doing seventy, eighty, they must have been gone straight away. I bet they weren't even wearing seatbelts."

"Rico," I said, "Rico, just leave it."

"Alright, Danny, alright."

He knocked back his double schnapps, and then another one, we'd lined them up in advance. Walter had been dead for three days, and we'd been drinking for three days. We'd started at lunchtime, and I was glad they'd thrown me out of school a few months before, because now that Walter had gone and left us, I wouldn't have gone back anyway.

"I'm not ever joyriding again," slurred Mark, "I'm never getting in a car again. It's over, you hear me, it's over."

"Yeah," I said, "it's over." I gestured at the landlord. "Another round!"

The landlord behind the bar looked over at us for a while before he nodded and got to work behind the tap. Maybe he sensed that Pitbull was one of us, and Pitbull couldn't go to the Pilz any more, there'd been some kind of incident there, which Pitbull had paid for with a month's youth arrest over in Zeithain, where I'd been not too long ago as well. But Pitbull couldn't have come to the Pilz anyway, he'd been drinking and smoking joints and puking and he was lying in his cellar.

Mark laid his head on the tabletop. "He . . . you know, he . . . God and all that, Walter . . . You remember back then, he used to go to church with his mother."

"Didn't do him any good," I said.

"No, it didn't. You remember . . . remember how we laughed at him, him and his church?"

"Yeah," I said, "I remember."

The landlord brought our round over, and then we fell silent again and drank. The landlord turned the radio on, and we were silent for three songs and drank and looked at the table.

"So are you coming?" asked Rico, lighting up.

"Mühlenviertel?" Mark lifted his head off the table.

Rico nodded.

"We gotta," I said, "we gotta do something."

"Right," said Rico.

"Right," said Mark.

"What about Paul?" I said.

"He's not coming, I bet."

I nodded. His mother probably hardly let him out of the house any more, now that Little Walter had killed himself in that car.

"She's a control freak," said Rico, his torso swaying to and fro, but he still managed to knock back a schnapps, "his old lady, his mother I mean. Control freak. Worse than in the pen." He banged a fist on the table and laughed. I'd never heard him say the word "prison," he always said "coffin" or "jail" or "inside," and back in the day he'd never said "children's home" either.

"He copped out, the chicken," Rico reached for his beer, almost knocking it over, and I wanted to help him but I missed the glass as well, "he chickened out of jail, that little chicken, that's where he'd have ended up, one of these days. Just copped out, and now he's in the coffin for good." He laughed again and banged on the table and his torso swayed.

"Rico," I said, "come on . . ."

"The bill!" shouted Rico and waved at the landlord at work behind the tap, "we want to pay the bill, for God's sake!"

And then we walked over to the Mühlenviertel. We swayed, and our legs caved in, and we held each other up. We were pretty far gone, but we still got our hands on a couple of the joyriders Walter used to hang out with at the end. We beat the shit out of them until we gradually started sobering up. Then we got loads of flowers out of the front gardens outside the new blocks, and then we swayed over to Prager Platz.

Estrellita was lying on one of the benches, right next to Walter's tree. She looked at us and shoved one arm under her head and was perfectly silent. We tucked her up with our jackets.

We leant the flowers against the half-burnt tree and stayed until morning came.

Contributors

HEIKE BARTEL is associate professor of German at the University of Nottingham. She has worked and published on Hölderlin, Goethe, and Celan as well as contemporary German women writers. She was coeditor (with Elizabeth Boa) of *Pushing at Boundaries: Approaches to Contemporary Women Writers from Karen Duve to Jenny Erpenbeck, German Monitor* 64 (2006) and *Anne Duden: A Revolution of Words. Approaches to Her Fiction, Poetry and Essays,* German Monitor 56 (2003). Her research interests include myth and myth reception, she has published books on *Mythos in der Literatur* (2004) and *"Centaurengesänge": Friedrich Hölderlins Pindarfragmente* (2000), numerous articles on the reception of the Medea myth and was coeditor (with Anne Simon) of *Unbinding Medea: Interdisciplinary Approaches to a Classical Myth from Antiquity to the 21st Century* (2010).

ANKE S. BIENDARRA is an assistant professor of German and a core faculty member in European Studies at the University of California, Irvine. Her research and teaching interests concern the literature and culture of the twentieth and twenty-first century, with an emphasis on post-GDR/unification literature, globalization, transnationalism, and popular culture. She has published widely on aspects of identity, gender, and commitment in the works of Kafka, Kracht, Hermann, Röggla, and others; on effects of globalization in literature and film; and on pop literature. Her most recent publications include "Ghostly Business: Place, Space, and Gender in Christian Kracht's *Yella,*" *Seminar* 47:3, 1–15 and "Prekäre neue Arbeitswelt: Narrative der New Economy," in *Das erste Jahrzehnt. Narrative und Poetiken des 21. Jahrhunderts,* edited by Johanna Bohley and Julia Schoell (Würzburg: Königshausen & Neumann, forthcoming). She is currently completing a book, *Germans Going Global: Contemporary Literature and Globalization.*

REBECCA BRAUN is lecturer in German studies at the University of Lancaster, UK. She has published widely on post-1945 German literature and culture, and is currently researching how changing public conceptions of authorship have affected stylistic developments in German literature from 1960 to the present. Recent book-length publications include *Cultural Impact in the German Context: Studies in Transmission, Reception, and Influence,* coedited with Lyn Marven (Camden House, 2010), *Changing the Nation: Günter Grass in International Perspective,* coedited with Frank Brunssen (2008), and the monograph *Constructing Authorship in the Work of Günter Grass* (2008).

Stephen Brockmann is professor of German at Carnegie Mellon University and president of the German Studies Association. He is the author of *Literature and German Reunification* (1999), *German Literary Culture at the Zero Hour* (Camden House, 2004), *Nuremberg: The Imaginary Capital* (Camden House, 2006) and, most recently, *A Critical History of German Film* (Camden House, 2010). From 2002 to 2007 he was managing editor of the Brecht Yearbook, and in 2007 he received the DAAD Prize for Distinguished Scholarship in German and European Studies.

Katy Derbyshire is a London-born translator based in Berlin. She has translated many contemporary German writers including Clemens Meyer, Selim Özdogan, Helene Hegemann, and Inka Parei. She also comments on German-language literature and translation issues on her popular blog *love german books*, lovegermanbooks.blogspot.com/.

Brigid Haines is reader in German at Swansea University. Her publications include *Dialogue and Narrative Design in the Works of Adalbert Stifter* (1991); *Herta Müller* (1998); *Contemporary Women's Writing in German: Changing the Subject* (with Margaret Littler, 2004); and *Libuše Moníková: In Memoriam* (coedited with Lyn Marven, 2005). She is currently researching German writing from former Eastern Bloc countries, in particular Herta Müller.

Valerie Heffernan is a lecturer in German at the National University of Ireland Maynooth. In her teaching and research, she focuses on contemporary Swiss literature and contemporary writing by women. She is the author of *Provocation from the Periphery: Robert Walser Re-examined* (2007) and coeditor (with Jürgen Barkhoff) of *Schweiz schreiben. Zu Konstruktion und Dekonstruktion des Mythos Schweiz in der Gegenwartsliteratur* (2010). She is currently working on an edited volume on women writers of the twenty-first century.

Emily Jeremiah is a lecturer in German at Royal Holloway, University of London. She is the author of *Troubling Maternity: Mothering, Agency, and Ethics in Women's Writing in German of the 1970s and 1980s* (2003). She is currently working on a book about nomadic ethics in contemporary women's writing in German.

Sonja Klocke is assistant professor of German at Knox College (USA). Her research interests focus on literature and culture in the twentieth and twenty-first century, discourses on illness and the body, contemporary writing on modern exile and migration, and aspects of globalization. Recently, she has published on transnational literature, globalization, and literature of the *Wende*.

LYN MARVEN is lecturer in German at the University of Liverpool. Her research focuses on contemporary German-language literature, particularly by authors of non-German origins and from the former Eastern Bloc, and women writers. She is the author of *Body and Narrative in Contemporary Literatures in German: Herta Müller, Libuše Moníková, Kerstin Hensel* (2005); and the coeditor, with Brigid Haines, of *Libuse Monikova: In Memoriam* (2005) and, with Rebecca Braun, of *Cultural Impact in the German Context: Studies in Transmission, Reception, and Influence* (Camden House, 2010). She is also the translator of *Long Days*, by Maike Wetzel (2008), and the short-story anthology *Berlin Tales* (2009).

FRAUKE MATTHES is lecturer in German at the University of Edinburgh. Her doctoral thesis was published as *Writing and Muslim Identity: Representations of Islam in German and English Transcultural Literature, 1990–2006* in 2011. She has also published on German Turkish literature and migration and travel writing. Her current research, which was funded by the Leverhulme Trust with an Early Career Fellowship, focuses on constructions and discourses of masculinity in contemporary German literature, the outcome of which will be a monograph with the provisional title *New Masculinities in Contemporary German Literature and Culture*.

Associate Professor BARBARA MENNEL holds a joint appointment in German studies and English at the University of Florida where she also serves as the director for the Center for Film and Media Studies. Her research interests include transnational cinematic practices, feminist and queer theory, minority cultural production in Germany, and the intersection of urban studies and cinema studies. She is author of *The Representation of Masochism and Queer Desire in Film and Literature* (2007) and *Cities and Cinema* (2008). With Jaimey Fisher she has coedited *Spatial Turns: Space, Place, and Mobility in German Literature and Visual Culture* (2010). Her book *Queer Cinema: Schoolgirls, Vampires, and Gay Cowboys* is forthcoming in 2011.

ANDREW PLOWMAN is senior lecturer in German at the University of Liverpool. He is the author of *The Radical Subject* (1998), a study of German autobiography, and of numerous articles on contemporary German literature. His current research focuses on the cultural representation of the Bundeswehr. He is the coeditor of *Divided, but Not Disconnected: German Experiences of the Cold War* (2010).

JULIAN PREECE has been Professor of German Studies at Swansea University since 2007. He is the author (with Waldemar Lotnik) of *Nine Lives: Ethnic Conflict in the Polish-Ukrainian Borderlands* (1999); *The Life and Work of Günter Grass: Literature, History, Politics* (2001/2004); and *The Rediscovered Writings of Veza Canetti: Out of the Shadows of a Husband* (Camden House, 2007). He has edited numerous books, including *The Cambridge Companion to Kafka* (2002) and, since 1996, the proceedings of the Bradford, now Leeds-Swansea Series on Contemporary German Literature.

KATE ROY researches contemporary literature by culturally Muslim writers in German, and by Algerian-French writer Leïla Sebbar, from a Deleuzian perspective. Her most recent publication is the article "In der Mitte fließt es immer schneller: Grenzen und ein 'politisierter Ortsbegriff' in den Werken Emine Sevgi Özdamars und Leïla Sebbars" (*Zeitschrift für deutsche Philologie*, Sonderheft zum Band 129 [2010]: "Grenzen im Raum — Grenzen in der Literatur," edited by Eva Geulen and Stephan Kraft). She has received research grants from the DAAD, the IGRS (University of London), the Berlin State Library, and the International Research Program on Gender in Tübingen for postdoctoral projects on trends in Turkish-German popular literature by women writers, and on engagements with Ruete's memoirs.

JAMIE LEE SEARLE is a translator from German into English and one of the cofounders of the publishing venture *And Other Stories* that focuses on international literature in translation. Her Anglo-German Cultural Relations MA thesis on Timothy Garton Ash and the GDR was awarded with the 2009 Jethro Bithell Award. She teaches German language and translation at Queen Mary University, London, and also undertakes freelance copyediting and research.

STUART TABERNER is professor of contemporary German literature, culture, and society at the University of Leeds. He has written widely on postwar literature, society, and culture. His most recent monograph, *German Literature of the 1990s and Beyond* (Camden House), appeared in 2005. He is editor of a number of collections, including *Recasting German Identity* (Camden House, 2002, with Frank Finlay); *German Literature in the Age of Globalisation* (2004); *German Culture, Politics, and Literature into the Twenty-First Century: Beyond Normalization* (Camden House, 2006, with Paul Cooke); *Contemporary German Fiction: Writing in the Berlin Republic* (2007); and *Germans as Victims in the Literary Fiction of the Berlin Republic* (Camden House, 2009, with Karina Berger). He is currently working on a monograph on transnationalism and contemporary German-language literature.

Index

CPSIA information can be obtained at www.ICGtesting.com
Printed in the USA
BVOW03*1056250713

326756BV00002B/8/P

9 781571 134219